Rowing

THROUGH THE BARBED WIRE FENCE

Zalgiris eight in 1960

Victory of „Žalgiris" eight in Kiev 1961

Eugenius, Romas, Povilas, Celestinas, Gerdas 1963

USSR Championship 1962, Trakai

Philadelphia 1962

Zalgiris eight in Trakai 1963

Toda channel, Tokyo 1964

OLIMPIADA

Povilas, Eugenius, Jonas and Celestinas
in Tokyo Olympic village

Grand Challenge Cup
Henley Royal Regatta 1964

Tokyo Olympic village, 1964

RIMA KARALIENE

Rowing

THROUGH THE BARBED WIRE FENCE

Copyright © Rima Karaliene, 2017
ISBN 978-1548092573

Second edition
First published in 2017 in Lithuania by Versus Aureus.
Rima Karaliene „Irklais pro spygliuotą tvorą". ISBN 978-9955-34-668-5
First paperback English edition 2017. ISBN 978-9955-651-14-7

Translated from the Lithuanian by Dovilas Bukauskas.

Edited by Annamarie Phelps

Design by Saulius Bajorinas
Layout by Saulius Stirblys

Pictures on and inside the cover are from the personal archive of
the author and the Rowing Museum, Trakai, Lithuania.

Acknowledgement

My greatest gratitude to Annamarie Phelps
for sincere support and generous contribution to my book.

Dedicated to my beloved Father

1

As cold snowflakes swirled outside the frosted windows, they started to twirl, grow red, and slowly drip through the black wall. An explosion rumbled through the darkness and a wave of dusty air whooshed into the corner. The wooden cross on the altar, disturbed by the blast, toppled onto someone's shoulder before falling to the floor and cracking in half. A creaking fuel lamp slowly fell from the ceiling, lighting up their dark silhouettes. He tried to grab the lamp, but it slipped out of his weakened hands, falling to the ground. He grabbed at it again but it slipped, smashing into pieces. As the glass shattered, the lamp and everything around it was engulfed in flames. The fire clawed at the walls before escaping into the frigid night through the windows.

Povilas jumped up, as if awakened by a silent scream, and grabbed his face in his palms to defend himself from the flames. Suddenly, everything went silent. The silent peace of dawn fell on his and the others' beds and rays of blinding autumn morning light streaked low along the ground. "Thank God, it was just a dream..." The frosty windows bore signs of the cold night. The eight men continued to dream their dreams, with only the occasional cough from Antanas. White shirts with the word "LIETUVA" emblazoned in green across their chests hung to dry on ropes strung along the ceiling, and green tracksuits with grey collars and "LIETUVA" in the same grey shade hung from the metal headboards. The men's identical brown suitcases lay underneath their spring-mattress beds.

Povilas sighed as he slowly recovered from his nightmare. He eventually got up and slowly tiptoed barefoot to the window. As he rested his arms on the windowsill and watched the rippling water, he nodded to himself, rubbed his dreary eyes, and returned to bed. He laid his head, tormented by nightmares, onto his pillow, pulled the blanket up to his chin, and let the sounds of morning engulf him. Someone on the other side of the wall was speaking quietly, a sparrow chirped outside the window, and the room was filled with the calm, quiet breath of the other sleeping men.

It was the morning of 23 September 1961, and all of Matveyev Bay[1] was slowly waking up. Povilas could glimpse the silhouettes of rowers who had woken up early for their training session. "It's probably CSK[2]," he thought as he surveyed his teammates' deeply slumbering faces. A sharp and uncontrollable shiver of excitement flashed through his body, the sort that only happens the morning of a race. There were still almost six hours until the start and there was no need to hurry, but there was no way he would fall back asleep. As he gradually returned from his nightmare and chased away his horrible thoughts, he thought to himself, "Everything will be alright..."

All of the country's best crews had come to the USSR Rowing Championships in Kiev. Since Wednesday morning, more than 300 rowers in light and dark blue wool athletic clothes had been zipping back and forth along the sandy road that stretched along the bay. Newcomers were immediately impressed by the size of the camps. The entire coast of Matveyev bay was covered in them. Rowing camps belonging to ten different athletic associations all stood alongside one another. Each had its own structures, boathouses or gazebos to store boats, and some even had their own docks or pontoons. Others simply had sandy shores, with the athletes wading out to their boats.

The teams' coaches worked tirelessly on their shining walnut, cedar and mahogany boats. Any scratch or distortion could cost the crew precious seconds. Athletes who had arrived from other republics lifted the boats off of the special trucks used to transport them, placed them on their slings[3], put on their riggers, and cleaned the slides. The coaches used angles to check whether their carefully aligned gates – or rowlocks – were still correctly adjusted.

The boating area was alive with the voices of men and women coming

---

1   A bay on Truchanov island in the Dnieper river in Kiev, Ukraine.
2   Rus. Центральный спортивный клуб Военно-морского флота (ЦСК ВМФ) – Central Sport Club of the Military-Maritime Fleet (CSK VMF) under the USSR Ministry of Defence.
3   Wooden or metal frames to place boats on.

and going for their training sessions. Shouts from all directions warning crews that had drawn too close to one another mixed with the commands of the coxes themselves.

The rowing course stretched along the shore, and at each camp a team of athletes and coaches watched their opponents' crews as they trained. Some discreetly discussed what they saw with their arms across their chests, while others made no attempt to hide their disdain, laughing out loud and gesticulating at the crews. Others couldn't seem to hide the concern on their faces. Though this was the final race of the season and each team gathered knew their worth, the rumours circulating of crew changes made many uneasy before the start. The forecasts that weekend were for beautiful, sunny and warm weather.

Most of the teams that had come to the championships were housed in rowing camps right on Matveyev Bay. As always, the 30-plus Lithuanian rowers and coaches lived at the Energetik sports centre, which was located at about the one kilometre mark on the course. They slept in large dormitory-like rooms with five to ten people in each room. The manager of the sports centre was a bright, energetic and colourful woman named Jelena Vasiljevna who always met the Lithuanian rowers with joy, called them her favourites, and took great care of them.

Alfonsas Mikšys, who was sleeping nearby, probably had the creakiest bed. After he turned over onto his other side, the rest of the Žalgiris team of eight started opening their eyes, one after the other.

"Alfa, be quiet!" someone, probably Petras, grumbled from the other side of the room.

Ričardas' fingers groped for his watch on his chair. Quarter past six. He put on his shorts and hurried to the window. After looking at the source, he smiled, cocked his head and turned back to the sleeping men. "I could let them keep sleeping, but the pair needs to have breakfast by eight. They race at 10:45," he thought.

Though coach Ričardas Vaitkevičius loved discipline and order, he also took care of his men. This eight was his greatest dream and was a new creation that he wanted to see succeed. At just 28 years of age, he was almost the same age as the men in his team. Despite this, he managed them perfectly well. The oldest among them, Alfa, was less than a year younger than him, and the youngest, Vytautas Briedis, had turned 20 just last month. Zigmas Jukna was 26, Antanas Bagdonavičius, Petras Karla and Povilas Liutkaitis were all 24, and Celestinas Jucys was 22.

Outside the window, they could hear the sound of a motor starting up and churning water. This was followed by the shrieks of women on the shoreline, who must have been splashed.

The eight men began stretching on their creaking beds. One after the other, they got up and passed by the window. Their fatigue from the previous day appeared to have left them, but their muscles still seemed to be sleeping.

After arriving in Kiev late in the evening on Wednesday, the Lithuanian rowers all eagerly fell into their beds. They hadn't even visited the cafeteria, instead snacking on bacon they had brought from home and drinking tea brewed by Jelena Vasiljevna. The difficult trip by train in a regular coach had shaken their bodies and heads clear of any thoughts but of sleep.

Thursday and Friday were just like any other days before a race – unload the boat trailer, rig the boats, try them out, wash them down. Start, sprint, start again. Lunch, a couple of hours of rest, and again – start, sprint. Ričardas fine-tuned his crew to perfection. Organising the men while rowing himself was no easy task. They began to suspect that he might have eyes in the back of his head. "Briedis, use your body mass… Petras, you need to grip faster… Zigmas, don't overexert yourself..." – he could correct the tiniest mistakes without even turning around. In truth, however, Gerdas, the young coxswain, was like a second set of eyes for him. After teaching the cox to report each rower's mistake directly to him, Ričardas knew exactly what his men were doing in the boat even with his back turned to them. If the men failed to improve, Ričardas would stop the crew, stand up in the boat, and climb over the men's heads to wherever his advice was needed most. Sometimes, he would sit on Antanas' shoulders and command the crew from his perch atop the seven man. "Come on, boys, we'll row faster if we row together like clockwork. And if we have long strokes. Long at the catch and long at the finish. Get ready, go!" At the same time, he also had to keep his eyes on the team's four as it passed by and shout out instructions to them as well. The final training runs before the race were exhausting; much of their strength had also been swallowed up by their pre-race anxiety. An anxiety that would not leave the men in peace until after the starting flare was fired, when their anxiety would be replaced by exhaustion…

"Get up, guys!" Ričardas woke his crew.

The first out of bed was the coxswain, Gerdas Morkus, sporting red socks that Zigmas and Antanas had brought for him from Rome as a gift. He was a young boy of only 14, but hard-working and fast. He did whatever he could to help the men. He had a happy face and was a well-mannered schoolboy who was always at hand whenever he was needed. The men loved him like a younger brother.

Gradually, the grown men began to get up out of their creaking spring beds, crowding by the window to check how the water looked. Then, in a hurry to leave the cramped and airless room, they grabbed their tracksuits and shirts from their headboards and put on their shoes – some tied them while others hurried off with flapping laces towards the washrooms in the yard.

"Why wait in line? The water's from the same river anyway," said Povilas as he headed towards the dock. He was joined by Alfa and Celestinas, with white towels wrapped around their necks like scarves.

The men kneeled, dipped their hands into the cold water of the Dnieper, and quietly surveyed the rowing course from start to finish. The calm water reflected the yellowing birch trees on the shore and a flock of ducks that hadn't yet flown south splashed about further down the riverbank.

"What do you think, Jucys, will we show them who we Lithuanians really are?" said Povilas, more to encourage himself than as a question. Celestinas' friends often addressed him by his last name, since it was shorter.

"In thirty hours, everything will be clear," Alfa interjected. He was a mathematician, and his thoughts were often guided by numbers and formulas.

"If Antanas and Zigmas don't overexert themselves in the pair, we should place," Celestinas reasoned as he dried off his face.

It was the first time that the heads of the country's rowing federation had allowed athletes to double-up at the Soviet Union championships. Ričardas used the new rule to strengthen the eight with the European champions and Rome Olympic silver medalists Zigmas Jukna and Antanas Bagdonavičius. Initially, the men weren't too happy about the idea and felt that they had been placed in a crew that was below their level. But after a few training sessions together, and showers of praise claiming that the European champions were capable of anything, they settled down. "After all, we have nothing to lose, the season is over. We can have a go at the pair and then race. These slow doubles have gotten boring, I'd like to feel what real speed is like," Zigmas reasoned. "Sure, two gold medals are better than one," Antanas added. "It'll be interesting."

They were soon joined by James, who had grown tired of waiting in the line at the washroom. Vytautas had been nicknamed James a long time ago and some people didn't even know his real name.

"Fresh water runs so cool, your face will look like new!" rhymed Povilas as he splashed some cold water onto his friend's head and took off.

"Hold on, Povilas! You're lucky you're sitting so far away. If you were any closer I'd whack you with this oar," said James as he tried to grab Povilas' sleeve. James sat in the 5 seat and Povilas in 3.

And so the two giggling men gave chase. Povilas tried to hide behind Alfa, but his foot slipped, he lost his balance, and fell into the water up to his knees.

Ričardas watched the young men play from a distance. "Good, let them play, it'll take their mind off the race," he thought to himself.

"Everybody by the doors at seven-thirty!" Gerdas said, passing on the coach's orders.

The sandy path leading to the cafeteria snaked past a score of rowing camps. The men couldn't help but notice the other athletes preparing for the race. The Burevestnik camp had a team from Moscow under the same association, while the Dynamo athletes were busy exercising at their camp. At the CSK camp, the Moscow-based naval fleet rowers were lined up and listening to their crew leaders: they were last year's USSR champions and the Lithuanians' main opponents. The men shared a few uneasy glances and quickened their pace. As they walked up that sandy path, each of them was lost in their thoughts about the start of the race. The Olympic champions in the pair[4] from the Leningrad-based sports association Trud – Valentin Boreiko and Oleg Golovanov – caught up to them on the path.

"Hey, Zigmas. Are you in the eight now?" they asked.

Zigmas and Antanas smiled back at them and, pretending not to have heard the question, changed the conversation, sharing their memories from Rome. They had always got on well with these men. Despite

---

4   In sweep boats, the rowers row with a single oar on the left or right side of the boat. Sweep boats can be pairs, fours or eights.

their accomplishments, they had always had a good relationship with the Lithuanians. They were physically unremarkable but mentality tough and determined rowers, who were well-known as "technicians" because, unlike the conventional wisdom of "with strength, you don't need intellect," they had perfected their technique - especially after they were insulted by older men on their team, who said they would never be champions.

The nine-lane swimming pool, roped off in the water at the 500 metre mark, was still empty but as the day progressed, it would soon fill with athletes who had finished their races.

As they walked past the busy finish line, they could see the umpires gathering and the race workers bringing them buckets of fuel for their motorboats. A rather round woman was doing her best to pin the starting schedules up on the board. Young children, probably from children's sport schools, were hanging up signs to congratulate the participants on their race.

A few hundred metres from the finish line, through a grove of pine trees and in the middle of a field full of flowers, stood a restaurant that had been built only four years ago. The round building had windows from the floor to the ceiling and a wide, flat, ornamented roof. White bulbous lights hung down from the eaves, making the building look like a colourful carousel. Wide steps led up both sides of the "carousel" and into the restaurant's hall. A bow-shaped sign hung over the door that read "Ресторан Відпочинок", or "Relax Restaurant." The promising name did not quite match the restaurant's standards and the rowers referred to it as the cafeteria.

The Daugava women sitting on the steps greeted the men in Lithuanian – "Good day." Janina, a Lithuanian member of the crew, had taught them some Lithuanian words – or rather, Lithuanian suffixes to translate their Latvian; as the Lithuanian and Latvian languages share so much in common. The rowers, all of whom knew each other very well from their summer camps, felt like brothers and sisters here.

As they entered the 'cafeteria', they were surprised to find a line stretching nearly all the way to the door. The Leningrad rowers spotted some of their teammates in the middle of the line and went to join them with the hopes that nobody would notice. A wave of discontent rolled down the line behind them, as everyone would now have to stand about in line even longer. Some of the rowers already eating at the tables looked up and watched the Lithuanians with curiosity. The Trud four and the jolly Yuri Suslin, sitting by the window, waved to their teammates. Thanks to his bold poetry, Suslin had had to sit out the Olympics in Rome. For some reason, the soviet KGB[5] believed that his poetry had threatened the establishment. His comrades in the Komsomol threw him out and his university's administration withdrew his student registration. Of course, any chance of travelling abroad was closed to him as well. By "banging his head" on every wall and door he could find, Yury proved to the government that he had not had any malicious intent and he was rehabilitated. However, his crew had already left for Rome.

Thanks to the athletic uniforms everyone wore it was easy to spot your own teammates; the woman smiling from the other table was a member of the eight. They had woken up earlier and were already getting up to go.

The men's anxiety continued to grow. Though they usually had proper appetites, the men had difficulty finishing their breakfast, washing down what they did eat with pale but well-sweetened coffee.

"Eat well, the start is still a way off, you won't even be able to paddle," Ričardas encouraged them. "Zigmas, Antanas, put more sugar in your tea."

Antanas and Zigmas seemed calm. Things were easier for them – this was not their first race against the opponents they now faced. They had won the European Championships earlier this year and could therefore rest easy here in Kiev as well – there are no miracles in rowing. Antanas was always calm. It sometimes seemed that he was indifferent to everything and that nothing interested him, and it was probably this attitude of his that helped him avoid burning out.

"You two go home and stretch out your legs, we'll catch up to you soon," said Ričardas, waving to Antanas, "just make sure you wake up. You are in lane 4, furthest from the current, so you should have fewer waves. Gerdas, go with them. You can grease their oars and check the nuts, make sure nobody messed with anything during the night."

At that moment, the coxswain of the Trud eight and three crew members entered the cafeteria. They stood in the doorway, extending their hands in greeting:

---

5 The KGB, an initialism for Komitet Gosudarstvennoy Bezopasnosti (Russian: Комитéт Госудáрственной Безопáсности (КГБ); (English: Committee for State Security), was the main security agency for the Soviet Union.

"Hello, Zigmas, Antanas! How are things?" their friends from Leningrad asked in Russian.

"We're alright, we're heading to the start. How about you guys?"

"We're good. They say we'll be heading to America. We're preparing the documents."

"Well then, good luck," Zigmas responded with a wry grin.

There were rumours among the rowers that there were plans to hold a new eights rowing match between the USSR and the USA like the one that had been organized in 1958 in Moscow, and that the winners at Kiev would be heading to America. There was not a single rower who didn't want to go to America, so everyone who was even remotely capable of competing with the strongest rowers started training in eights. Coaches experimented, looking for the best crew combinations. This was a big step forward for USSR sport and a breath of refreshing freedom for the athletes. The USSR champions – those who would achieve victory the next day – would be going to America.

By the tie they got back to their camp, the men found Gerdas on the shore, polishing his pair. It was a brand new Swiss Stampfli, made that year and that was the only one of its kind in the Soviet Union. The position of the coxswain in the bow of the boat rather than the stern inspired envy in many. It had been brought in just for the Lithuanian crew before the European Championships and they had won their gold medals in Prague with this boat.

A can of Solidol with a wooden stick – a necessity for any coxswain – stood next to the slings. All that was left was to smear grease on the collars of the oars that were covered with leather and check the metal button that held the blade in the gate.

"Good work, Gerdas, very good," Ričardas commended his young teammate, "make sure they don't go nuts out there. Make sure they save their energy. Clean start and then stay cool. There is nothing here to do for them today, they just need to row from start to finish. Now run over and tell them that we're leaving in half an hour; they should start getting ready. Guys, lets go: turn over the boat," he said, turning to the eight, "I'll work on it a bit while you guys rest."

"James, come back, let's turn the boat." Povilas shouted, catching James right at the door.

The six young men lifted and flipped the boat over before carefully returning it to the slings. They checked their foot stretchers and once again used a 10-millimetre spanner to tighten each rigger.

The competition was to begin in 20 minutes. The women's distance, at one kilometre, was half the distance. You could almost see the entire 1,000 metres from the starting line. The far riverbank sparkled with the sunlit colours of autumn. Across the bay, the boat holders, wrapped in warm pea coats, waited for the approaching crews in the six anchored stakeboats. A rope stretched taught over their heads held markers with lane numbers written on rectangular plywood boards. The women's fours were already gently bobbing about on the water, ready to start. The umpires, riding in motorboats, hurried to the starting line with little concern for the waves they were making. The quad sculls[6] rowed along the riverbank. All of the teams' camps had come alive – people were carrying boats, coxes were yelling, and athletes were stretching and warming up. Their coaches were giving their final orders.

"Let's wait until Antanas and Zigmas leave." Celestinas suggested.

The men sat down on the riverbank, tucked their knees up to their chests, and watched everyone hurrying back and forth, preparing for their races. The women's first semi-final crews were moving up to the starting line. The boatholders struggled to catch the sterns of the boats while their coxes shouted out commands: "bow – one stroke", "four – back it", "everyone – back it", "easy oars", "get ready". The women glanced around nervously.

The starting flare shot into the air and the five fours shot out over the water. The coxes' orders drowned out the hum of the motorboats. The USSR championships had begun.

The men heard Antanas' calm voice behind them:

"Well, then. Time for some exercise."

With their seats in their hands, Antanas and Zigmas took their oars and moved towards the water. At that moment, the fours sped past them on the water.

"Look, the Latvians are overtaking Spartak!" Zigmas pointed.

Athletes from various athletic clubs could be seen running behind the camp. Ričardas, however, did not allow his men to run before their races. "Warm up on the water. Running's not for us," he would say.

Ričardas pinned the number four to Gerdas' back. Zigmas and Antanas

---

6   In sculling boats, rowers use two oars. There can be single, double and quadruple sculls.

calmly lifted their glistening shell onto their shoulders and carried it to the pontoon. Only champions assured of their own victory could be as calm as they were.

"Good luck, boys!" shouted their teammates as the pair kicked off of the dock.

Gerdas turned around and waved to the older men standing on the shore:

"See you later!"

The coach followed the pair as it paddled off into the distance. Though everything would be go smoothly for them, Ričardas still paced around on the shore, distracted. He was already thinking about the eight's race. There were still forty-five minutes until the pair would start, so there was time for the men to rest and relax.

When they returned to their room, they pulled their brown suitcases out from under their beds, covering the table in newspapers and loading it with food they had brought from home. The cafeteria food was never enough. They had Lithuanian bread, bacon, cookies, apples, jam and honey. After a quick snack, the men lay down on their beds – some took out books while others wrestled with their thoughts in an effort to conquer their anxiety and excitement. Through the windows, they could see the gently swaying tops of the yellow maples and the clear blue Kiev sky. The wooden wall had a poster depicting Gagarin[7] which had been left over from the spring. He was holding something in his hand that looked like a crystal star, a flying rocket with the words "A FAIRYTALE THAT CAME TRUE – 12 APRIL" on it.

"This race is nothing like space, but everybody does have their own fairytale," thought Povilas, "and we'll certainly have a fairytale if we medal here." One month ago, here in Matveyev Bay at the USSR trade union championships, they had finished third rowing with Petras Karla in the stroke seat while Zigmas, Antanas, Gerdas and Ričardas had raced in Prague, bringing home the gold. Of course, Trud hadn't been there either, as they were also in Prague. However, Trud hadn't done well for themselves there – during the qualification race, their 5-man had fallen off of his seat and the eight didn't even make it into the final. However, the

---

7   Yuri Gagarin (Rus. Юрий Алексеевич Гагарин; 9 March 1934 – 27 March 1968) - a Russian astronaut who flew around the world on a Russian spacecraft, the Vostok, on 12 April, 1961, becoming the first man to enter space.

fact that they had participated in the European Championships at all was cause for concern.

The first race was like a training session for Antanas and Zigmas. With long and powerful strokes, it seemed as though they were simply enjoying the beautiful nature of Matveyev bay and the powerlessness of their competitors to pursue them. They rowed the two kilometres back to camp. There was still an hour until the eights would have to start.

"Everything's alright, but the start is a mess because it's choppy out there," Zigmas reported as he walked into the room. "Good thing we had a middle lane. Vodnik over in lane one almost flipped after catching a crab[8]!"

"So we've had our warm up," said Antanas as he stepped into the room behind Zigmas. "Now we can race. Is there anything to drink?"

"Here's some cold tea," said Alfa, offering a glass as he looked up from his chessboard. "Alright, that's it Celestinas, let's call it a draw."

Ričardas walked into the room behind the pair:

"Alright, boys, it's time to start thinking about the race," he said, as if they could have been thinking about anything else. "We got lane one. It's the worst lane: the choppiest. Hold your oars firmly so they don't get knocked out of your hands. The bay starts 250 metres in and the water will get calmer, but we're going to need to put some work in at the start so we don't fall behind, because if we do, catching up will be hard. In the third 500, as always, we'll pick up the pace. If we win today, we can think about winning medals tomorrow. Trud and the second CSK crew will be in our race. Get dressed and let's go to the boat."

He then took Gerdas aside:

"The first 250 will be hardest for you. There are eddies there that can throw your stern out, so make sure that our oars don't clash. You'll have to keep me updated on the situation constantly. We're in lane one, so everybody will be on your right. At the kilometre mark, as always, I'll take the stroke rate up. It's important that they all maintain it. As always, shout 'For Lithuania,'" the coach smiled, patting his coxswain on the shoulder. 'For Lithuania' was the crew's agreed signal to speed up at the middle of the race.

As the day progressed at Matveyev Bay, more and more participants

---

8   A rower's error in which the blade of the oar changes its direction and gets stuck in the water. Stuck in the water, it acts like a brake and can even flip the boat on its side.

completed their qualification races. The entire shoreline was covered in busy athletes running to and fro – some rowing out to the starting line and others returning after their finishes. Among them were the men's eights heading towards the start. After each of the rowers took up their oars, they lined up next to Gerdas, who was scraping Solidol out of a can and carefully spreading it onto the leather oar sleeves. He carried them onto the pontoon and laid them down with the blades hanging out over the water.

"To shoulders!" ordered Gerdas. The eight men in white shirts lightly threw the boat onto their shoulders and marched off towards the pontoon. "Over heads! Let it down!"

At that moment, the Moscow military naval crew – their main opponents – rowed past. They were to compete in the first heat while the Lithuanians would be in the second one.

The men were quick to place their seats into the boat and lock in their oars.

"Get ready, hut!" at Gerdas' command, the men kicked off of the dock in unison and sat down into the boat. "Bow and two, one stroke! Stop! Let's get in order!"

The young men stuck their wool-sock-clad feet into their foot stretchers – wooden panels that were attached to the boat and had metal heel rests and leather straps tightened by shoelaces. They tied the laces and tightened the gate nuts to make sure their oars wouldn't pop out.

While they were warming up, the double sculls reached the halfway mark in their race. Tyukalov and Berkutov, the soviet team's leaders, were in the lead. "They'll win for sure, but their greatest fight will be tomorrow when they meet Ivanov," the men thought. Lumps of anxiety formed in their throats as they realised that their own race was only half an hour away.

"Let's get ready, arms only, all eight!" ordered Gerdas, and the eight oars began slicing the water of Matveyev Bay with sharp, precise oar strikes.

"In half an hour it'll be over," thought Povilas as he looked at Petras' back. From his position at three, he could see almost the entire crew. The crew of eight men was working precisely, like clockwork. Ričardas' strict discipline and long training sessions had borne fruit.

As they had feared, lanes one and two were the most affected by bouncy water. The southern wind rippled the surface of the water, and the wakes of boats travelling the Dnieper crashed against one another, petering out only towards the more distant lanes closer to the shore. The water hitting the peninsula threw foam high into the air, but not far away, in the bay, the water was calm. There would be exactly 250 metres of intense focus, anxiety and pressure, after which they would simply have to do what they have been trained to do so well – to row.

"Tap down on your handles!" Gerdas reminded them again when the men's blades began to catch on the surface of the water and knock them out of rhythm.

The waves were practically breaking against the boat and the wet oar handles were slipping in the men's hands. Žalgiris' slim and soft boat was especially unsuited to waves. When on smooth water, it flew like a bird, but in these heavy waves, the riggers attached to the saxboard of the shell caught the waves and scooped water into the hull.

"Relax, guys," said Ričardas as he turned back to his crew. "We'll be fine. Just keep focused eyes straight ahead and listen to the coxswain."

The flare launched and the six eights in the first semi-final shot out from the starting line. The athletes could barely be seen through the spray and foam, with only the coxswains' commands carrying through.

"The second eight race may now approach the starting line. Lane one – Žalgiris. Lane two – Trud Leningrad. Lane three..."

"Get ready! Bow four! Stop! Bow and three – forward, paddle, stroke – back it – stop! All together back it down! Stop! One and three, two strokes, two more..."

The side wind kept turning the boat's bow off course. All six of the eights were trying to straighten their boats. There were only a few minutes left until the start, and the umpires couldn't keep the crews straight. The boat holders, with blue-tinged lips, bobbed up and down in their fishing rowboats, wiping splashes of water from their eyes and blowing on their hands in an effort to keep warm.

"Žalgiris ready? Trud ready? Dynamo ready?" the roll call went down the line. It would be the last call-over before the start. Nothing would come after – just the race.

The men took a deep breath and their gazes froze. Their oars were in the water, blades buried, and their legs were ready for a powerful push onto their foot stretchers. Alfa, who was sitting in the bow seat, kept tapping the catch with his oar to keep the boat on course.

The start umpire slowly raised his pistol and fired his flare into the sky. With a shout from the coxswains, forty-eight oars hit the waters of the Dnieper River in unison and shoved six long and graceful boats out towards the finish line. Though the first few strokes had been practised to perfection, the choppy river turned them into a chaotic spray. The blades caught on waves and on the rowers' knees. The men tried as hard as they could to hit the rhythm and catch the water neatly, but one oar or another always flashed into the air.

"Power ten!" counted Gerdas. "Don't jump ahead!" When they could see their opponents getting ahead, some of the men had started to race up the slide.

In fifteen more strokes, the water would calm down. The most important thing was not to let Trud escape.

At the 250-metre mark, their opponents were ahead by a length. Then when the water calmed, their strokes became harmonious and precise, but they could also feel the first signs of fatigue. A coxswain nearby could be heard yelling in Russian: "Come on, ten more!"

"Don't worry, we're not done yet," Ričardas told Gerdas, maintaining the same rate.

The men were now working in unison. With long and powerful strokes, they slowly began catching up to Trud, which was in the lead by more than a length, and CSK, which was half a length ahead.

"There are five more strokes," Gerdas said quietly so only the coach could hear. "We'll get one length ahead."

"Let's go," said Ričardas through clenched teeth.

"Už Lietuvą!"[9] shouted Gerdas commandingly. Nothing more needed to be said. At that moment, the boat crossed the 1,000-metre mark. The men understood that the hardest part of the race had just begun. When fatigue began gripping their bodies and pain began tearing through their arms and legs, the others would begin saving their strength for the final sprint, but Žalgiris was beginning their sprint now. "Twenty!"

With every stroke, the boat gained another half metre. Their bodies were burning with pain and they started to hear a deafening silence in their ears.

"Don't let go! Twenty more!" said Gerdas, passing on the coach's commands.

Echoes of the gathered audience's cries could be heard from the

---

9   For Lithuania!

shoreline – Go! The finish line! Hold on! Some fans were shouting in unison – Sasha, Sasha – or – Le-nin-grad – but they were drowned out by the group of Lithuanian girls who had come to shout – "Keep going! Keep going!" They had finished their races for the day and had come to support the men's crew.

"Let's finish this!" With that, the men knew that they were on their last 500 metres, or last fifty strokes. Their need to scream out in pain would be overcome only by the lack of breath. They couldn't see what was happening around them because their vision was darkening and they felt like their souls were leaving their bodies, which were wound up like clockwork machines no longer capable of thoughts like "what am I doing here and why am I here?" The only thought in their heads was the number of strokes to the finish line – "twenty eight, twenty nine, thirty..." When the gong finally rang, with a second and third soon after, and when the men looked up and saw their opponents' backs through their blurred vision, they understood that the first gong had rung for them. While looking straight ahead, they could see all of their opponents' boats at safe distances behind them.

"Hold it up!" shouted Gerdas: the boat was in danger of running aground on the sandy bank at the end of the course.

The men leaned on their oar handles and pushed them away from themselves – they were panting heavily but they were satisfied. They had barely hoped for such a start to the competition.

"Great job, Rychka!" somebody shouted from the shoreline near the grandstand. Everybody – from athletes to other coaches – called Ričardas "Rychka."

Ričardas looked over his shoulder at his crew:

"Alright, men, the race is done," he said. He was afraid to start celebrating too early, but inside, he was already thinking – "my greatest dream is coming true."

With that, the action at Matveyev Bay calmed down until the next morning. The motorboat engines died down, the spectators left, and the water grew as calm as a mirror. The afternoon sun shone brightly in the faces of the Lithuanian rowers as they brought their boat back to the shore, like a bright omen of great victories to come.

*

A shot rang out in the dark, and then a second and a third, followed by a shout and a moan. Then, another shot... Povilas jumped up in bed, drenched in sweat, and grabbed his head. Antanas had been coughing... He had been suffering from a cold for several days now. "Thank God, it was just a dream...," thought Povilas, sighing heavily before laying his tortured head back down onto his pillow. Nightmares again... It was dark, but the sky outside the window was slowly growing red. "It must be about five," he thought – he couldn't see the hands of his watch in the dark. He closed his eyes and tried to fall asleep, but his heart was still thumping from his nightmare. Antanas coughed again. "God forbid he can't race today. It would be hard without him," he thought, afraid for his teammate's health.

Povilas rolled from side to side, unable to fall asleep because of his dark thoughts. "When will all of this end?" he kept asking himself over and over. The silhouettes of people and objects in the room began to grow clearer, and he could see the crowns of the nearby maple trees' growing brighter outside through the misted up window. "This place reminds me a bit of home. I wonder what the weather's like in Lithuania," he thought. His mind wandered through Vilnius to Čiurlionis Street, which lead straight to Vingis Park, and then to the university courtyards, where the same yellow maples grew, and where a bend in the Neris River and the Žvėrynas neighbourhood could be seen. In that neighbourhood, in a small room in a small apartment in the Faculty of Nature Studies half-cellar, slept his young, beloved wife. On the other side of the wall, her mother was probably making breakfast for their big family. His father-in-law was probably sweeping the sidewalk outside the window, while the many pets of the naturalist Ričardas Kazlauskas' chirped in the next-door apartment. "Thank God for home," thought Povilas as his heart calmed down, fatigue overtook him, and he settled into a light morning slumber. A radio in one of the girls' rooms played the USSR anthem. It was exactly six. Povilas got up from bed, put on his sneakers, and turned towards the window. "It's all calm for now. Calmer than it was yesterday," he thought to himself.

This was the morning of Sunday, 24 September, 1961 in Matveyev Bay. The dawn's bright rays grew brighter and brighter outside the window, catching the white shirts with the word "LIETUVA" on their chests that had been hung up to dry on the ceiling. Gagarin smiled from the wall of the stuffy room. The nine men continued resting after their tough race. Though the Lithuanians were happy with their solid semi-final victory at the USSR championships, they celebrated with reservation – but the victory had given them a great dose of confidence and a greater desire to win. They could begin to believe in the possibility of victory.

"We had the best time. The Muscovites were second, and we were ahead of them by four seconds. However, tomorrow will decide everything. Our tactic worked. Everybody breaks in the third quarter, which is where we can overtake them. We have to give it everything we've got – there's nothing to save ourselves for. It's win or lose. We'll be in the lane three, so we might not get as many waves as we did today," Ričardas said to encourage the men. "The finals begin at three and our start is at 5:30. I don't want you walking around much. Rest up. We'll have lunch at one. The pairs final will be at 4:00."

Their long and torturous training sessions had proven their worth. The Žalgiris crew finally had some real belief that they would break out into the world and feel like equals – though it might only be as rowers, and though they might be competing under a blood-red flag, they still had Lithuania's name on their chests. Though people might refer to them as Russians, they could tell them in their own words who they really were. "If we could've raced for Lithuania, we would have reached the world much more quickly" Ričardas thought to himself remembering how he had started to restore the Vilnius facilities after the war and how he had started building a rowing tank on the other side of the river. During his service in the CSK military, he had tried to learn as many secrets of rowing as he could. Over the years many men and women had been under his tutelage before he had finally refined a truly strong, technical, and amicable crew. They were powerful, dependable and unified – like a fist. Today, this crew would do everything it could – for themselves, for one another, for the people they loved, and for Lithuania.

*

Crowds of people came to Truchanov Island[10] on that sunny and warm September morning. It seemed that, in accordance with communist standards, the city government and the KGB had masterfully pushed the Kureniovka tragedy, which had happened only six months ago, to the backs of people's minds. Gagarin's space flight had also provided a distraction and Kiev's residents once again started to believe in the propaganda of a

---

10   An island on the Dnieper River in front of Kiev's historical centre.

happy Soviet lifestyle and were coming out to enjoy the weekend. Some came by steamboats and motorboats from the river station while others crowded across the Park Bridge leading from the centre of Kiev to the island. The new pedestrian bridge, which was almost half a kilometre long and 7 metres wide, looked like a colourful celebratory parade float. The grandstands at the course were full of local residents enjoying the last rays of sunlight: hundreds came to Matveyev Bay to see the rowing championships.

However, the events of Kureniovka were still on many people's lips. Those who had been near Babi Yar[11] on the morning of 13 March quietly told their loved ones about how a giant avalanche of wet gravel and human bones had swept away everything in its path along Frunze Street. The residents silently cursed the government for its act of sacrilege – they had allowed a brick factory to built and its manufacturing waste to be poured into Babi Yar, the final resting place of hundreds of thousands of peaceful city residents who had been shot by the Nazis in 1941. "The old lady had her revenge," Kievans who had lived further away from the tragedy told one another. Within a few minutes a deluge, of up to three metres of dirt buried the homes of 353 families and many city buses and trams full of people hurrying to work. Covering up the event was impossible, so it was officially announced that about 150 people had died. However, those who were brought in to deal with the clean up of the incident reported casualties in the thousands…

If you were to have made your way to the island and walk about a kilometre, you would have found yourself on a sandy beach near the finish line, from which you would be able to see the entire race course. Behind it, in the distance, was the new Metro Bridge, still under construction. The loudspeakers at the finish line belted out marches, distracted journalists and photographers ran about, caught up in the importance of the event. Several stern-faced umpires prepared for the next race in the wooden finish-line hut. Members of the audience scrambled for the best spots on the benches along the shore, on the slings, or right on the sandy beach. Everyone wanted to see the stars, like Viacheslav Ivanov, Yuriy Tyukalov, and the famous Trud eight, up close.

---

11   Rus. Бабий Яр – "Old Woman's Gully" - a ravine to the north-west of Kiev. Babi Yar achieved international infamy as the site of mass civilian executions – most of them Jews, Roma, and Karaites – in 1941.

The people who had gathered waited impatiently for the men's single scull race, where Ivanov, Tyurin and Berkutov would face off in the final. All of these were strong, they had already won titles, were well-established members of the USSR team, and had become stars in the world of rowing.

The Žalgiris eight, in the meantime, was an obscure newcomer, much like the rest of the Lithuanian team – with the exception of Jukna and Bagdonavičius, of course. The Žalgiris eight were not present at the USSR championships in Moscow two years ago – the team from Kaunas that had won the Lithuanian championships attended instead. Antanas still felt guilty about the "crab" he caught, that day which meant they lost the race right at the finish, and lost the Vilnius Žalgiris eight's right to represent Lithuania. Despite the misfortune, Antanas went to Moscow after all. The next day, he won the pairs race with Zigmas instead of his usual partner, who couldn't come to Moscow. His coaches saw Zigmas Jukna as his most suitable partner. The friends of the Lithuanian team couldn't believe their eyes and jumped for joy when the Lithuanians took third place in Moscow. Everyone was greatly surprised at the pair's unorthodox rowing technique, which was unlike anything seen before. The old-timers of the USSR team laughed at them and called them "grasshoppers": the tall and straight Antanas and much shorter Zigmas had to work to adapt to one another. In an effort to take his stroke as far as possible, Zigmas would have to bend as far forward as possible, seeming to ball up completely from the side. "Bend that aristocratic back!" the Soviet team coaches would shout to Antanas in Russian from their motorboats. Soon, the "grasshopper" epithet became one of respect as the Lithuanians claimed one victory after another bringing silver medals home from Rome. The USSR team coaches began to study and copy Vaitkevičius' techniques. Zigmas and Antanas may have had an easier time of forgetting their defeat in the eight, but it was still a raw nerve and injustice for their teammates. They had felt better prepared and stronger than the rowers from Kaunas, and until the unfortunate crab occurred, they had been leading by more than an entire length. Povilas had recently begun dating Gita, bow of the Žalgiris women's eight, and had dreamt of going to Moscow with her, but he was destined to spend the summer with his aunt in her village. It was the last victory for the Kaunas eight. In 1960, Vilnius' Žalgiris became Lithuania's champions and represented Lithuania throughout the USSR.

"Our last two kilometres will show them what we're worth," said the friends, sharing their hopes and dreams as they stepped out of their room into the sunlight and gazed at the water. "The weather is fantastic and the water looks like glass." Indeed, Matveyev Bay looked calmer than it had ever been, only the air was filled with the celebratory mood of an important race.

"Look how many people there are at the finish line!" Gerdas observed in awe.

"They probably came to see us," joked Povilas.

"Certainly, we're the main attraction," James laughed.

"Well then, we can't disappoint them, can we?" Antanas slowly enunciated, encouraging the crew. "OK, I'm going to get moving in a bit. I want to take a nap before the start. Wake me up if you don't see me for too long."

"If you would be so kind as to show up, that would be great. You don't want me rowing for you again, do you, Antanas?" teased Povilas, reminding Antanas of the incident three weeks ago when he had arrived late for his race at the Baltic championships in Trakai. The chief umpire would not postpone the race – all were equal before the rules, even European champions. Ričardas hurried to find a solution and put Povilas in the pair with Zigmas. When Antanas finally arrived, he had to race in the eight in Povilas' place. Both of the crews won the right to race here in Kiev at the USSR championships.

Antanas waved his hand dismissively as he walked away:

"Don't remind me, Povilas. It's embarrassing."

"So what, Antanas? It's only talk. Surely it's no big deal!" Povilas laughed.

"Everything will be clear in six hours," noted Alfa, seeming not to have heard his teammates teasing each other.

Shivers were still running down the young men's spines, but they also understood that their previous day's anxiety had been mixed up with something else as well – an impatience and a desire to begin their race as soon as possible, to make their boat fly, and to show everything that they were capable of, that they had been working on all year as they practised their strokes on Trakai lake. There had been many moments when some of them simply wanted to get out of the boat, to hang up their oars and leave without ever turning back. When their torn, bloody hands burned from each stroke, when it seemed like their hearts would burst out of their chests, and when they had to train twice a day for hour upon hour on Galvė and Žydiškės lakes despite an entire week of torrential rain that left them soaked to the core. Even then, the men would put on their sweat suits, which were impossible to dry in their tents, and line up by the boathouse.

The day dragged on unbearably slowly. The men paced back and forth as they counted the hours until the race. The women's eight – some with books in their hands and others with knitting – sat on some rocks in the shade of the trees by the shore and chattered away. "They used to have Gita with them as well. It's too bad she's not here now," sighed Povilas. "It was nice when we went everywhere together." They had even been here in Kiev a few times as well, racing in Matveyev Bay and walking in Khreshchatyk with their teammates. This year, Gita completed her university studies and had once again became Lithuania's champion before bidding farewell to rowing and starting work.

They met each other in Vilnius in 1957 at the rowing camp. Gita was an old-timer there, she had started rowing four years earlier while she was still in ninth grade at the school. She was small but strong and very tough, and she was the soul of the "Bunny" four. The girls won one race after another. Later, when she and her sister Vanda were both students, they were invited to row in the eight coached by Eugenijus Vaitkevičius. They won numerous Lithuanian and Baltic championships, and had become Masters of Sport[12] two years ago as well.

Povilas did not initially have the courage to approach her, though he saw her at the camp rather often: Gita was always surrounded by her friends, and he, a rural child, was shy and timid. One day, he realised that the best way to begin a relationship would be by using his photo camera. He had been taught to take photos in his freshman year by his roommate. He bought his first camera, a FED, after working in the harvest in Kazakhstan with a student group, and he was never without it, taking it to all of his camps and competitions. He took many photos, developing them in a specially prepared corner in one of the rooms in his dorm. "Sportas" began publishing his photos from various competitions, and his friends were always happy to receive Povilas' photos from his competitions and trips. One day, he placed all of his photos of the girls' team in an envelope and waited for Gita on Čiurlionis Street, where she lived with her parents. He lived nearby in the university's dormitories. They met,

---

12   An award granted for merit in sports in the USSR.

as if by accident, and he gave her the photos. Then, they talked together all the way to the rowing camp. With that, they began to see each other. From that day on, they were inseparable, unless they failed to both make it into the same competition – like that unfortunate time when the men lost to the team from Kaunas and stayed at home while the girls left with the whole team for Moscow. He had spent that summer with his aunt, and it seemed like an eternity. However, when Gita returned from Moscow, they were reunited – and this time for good. He took her to Palanga Restaurant and to the famous Picolli di Podrecca Italian puppet show at the national philharmonic. He began visiting her at home and got to know her family.

From that day when they first met, most of the photos in each roll of film he shot were dedicated to her – sitting on a dock, looking at Trakai castle, standing solemnly by a tree, enjoying the fountains of Peterhof, bathing in a sea of meadow flowers, collecting amber, drawing in sand at the beach, or laughing and dreaming. From then on, more and more of Gita's friends sought out her company too, eager to make it into one of Povilas' photos and receive it as a gift.

On 30 July, after Gita had received her diploma in physics and they had just returned from the USSR team championships in Kavgolovo, they got married – without much fanfare or ceremony. The wedding had been planned for autumn, but the soviet young specialists' assignment system had its own plans – if she wanted to stay in Vilnius, to work, she had to have a serious reason why. The fact that her husband was a student studying in Vilnius was what "saved" her. However, when their friends found out about a new family of rowers, they started badgering them for a party. "Ok, ok, we'll celebrate once the season ends," Povilas promised his friends.

"Ok, it'll end soon. We'll dance our wedding dances and relax a bit. And visit my aunt and uncle," Povilas thought to himself as he sifted the white sand on the beach. "It's a lot like the Nemunas," he noted, and his thoughts carried him off to his childhood, when he and his brothers ran along the shores of the Nemunas River. They loved to watch the rafts float by down the river. One beautiful Sunday, when the adults had left for church, they went to swim in the Nemunas. Before getting into the water, they crossed themselves and anointed themselves with river water. Once, to prove himself a man, he waded out towards the deep part, where there were underwater clay pits. He took one step further and dipped under water, the pretty bubbles turning his vision white before everything disappeared... Good thing his older brother Kazys had been nearby to jump in and drag him out. After that, he could barely bring himself to approach the water again. He and his twin brother had once set out to visit Kazys at the pasture. It was a good thing that their parents were on their way home by wagon from Prienai and found the two "travellers" on the road and took them home, scolding them that the gypsies that often passed by their home might have grabbed them had they gone any further. They often ran around Bagrėnas hill together with their neighbour, Tamošiūnas, gathering wild nuts and pears. Povilas sighed deeply, understanding that he could never return to those times, and that neither he nor anyone else could change a thing... He grabbed a handful of sun-warmed sand and squeezed it tightly in his fist until the warmth spread through his entire body before slowly releasing it and letting it pour from his fist in a narrow stream as he looked off into the distance. The stream of sand faded into the sandy shore, like the countless moments from the past that had passed him by.

*

A screech from the out-of-tune speakers wrenched the rowers from their thoughts and back into their competitive mindsets for their final race. The girls were already radiating that peculiar pre-race anxiety that only they had, uncontrollably chattering about nonsense, stretching side to side and jumping in place as they lined up by the outdoor shed.

Janina would be the first girl to race. She was no longer to be found at the Žalgiris camp – she had run off to the Daugava camp, convinced by the Latvians, she would be racing in their four, which was allowed in the individual USSR championships. Janina Lukošiūnaitė, the small single sculler, had become Lithuania's champion this year, and at the USSR team championships in Kavgolovo in Lake Hepoyarvi, she finished second. She surprised both her teammates and her coach, with the finish – she had achieved the greatest result in the history of Lithuanian scullers meeting the Master of Sport standard. After the race, the entire Lithuanian team greeted her at the boathouse to congratulate her. The red headlines on the 18 July issue of "Sportas" shouted out "You must fight the way Janina fought!"

The coaches were giving their last bits of advice on the shore. The quadruple scull and the eight would soon push off from the pontoon and row out to their last race of the year. The clock showed half past two.

In the men's room, everyone had their own way of coping with the tension. Alfa and Celestinas were playing chess, as always. Petras was napping with an open issue of "Science and Life" magazine in his hands. Zigmas and Gerdas were sitting off to the side next to a table with a physics textbook in their hands. Zigmas was teaching Gerdas – perhaps to keep his mind off of things, or perhaps to distract himself. Because of his travels with the men's team, Gerdas would only make it back to school towards the end of September, so the majority of his suitcase was filled with textbooks. He would have to once again explain to his teachers why he had missed his classes, and they no doubt be surprised yet again to find that he had not fallen behind his peers at all. Under the tutelage of future teacher Jukna, he often returned from the camps ahead of his peers. He enjoyed seeing his classmates' looks of surprise when he was the first to raise his hand to answer questions. Of course, forcing one's self to sit down with a textbook at the camps was also an act of willpower, but he didn't want the older men in the team to know that.

"Ok, that's enough for now. We'll finish in the evening after the race," said Zigmas, closing the textbook and setting it down on the table.

"Thanks. I'll be right back, I'll just check on the fours," said Gerdas as he ran outside, overjoyed. He wanted to see all of the races. He ran up and down the sandy shore from start to finish, accompanying nearly every race.

Out of breath, Gerdas ran after the Daugava four's race with Janina in. They had kept up with the Moscow-based Spartak until the very end, but lost by a second coming in second place. He ran after Sofija's quad, which had finished sixth but the boy was mostly hurrying to congratulate Baranova, the Spartak single sculler who he considered his friend and who was always kind to him. Just then, however, he heard Ričardas' strict voice:

"Stop! Where are you going? Gerdas, she has been married three times over already!" Ričardas joked. He had noticed the boy's affection for the team's much older friend. "It's time for you to head to the start! You can't keep running around."

Gerdas shrugged, terrified not so much about being late for the race, but that his coach seemed to have discovered his secret. Without looking back, he hurried off to his pair.

"Don't forget to coat the oars!" he heard Ričardas yell after him.

*

The low September sun was dropping behind the horizon by the time the Žalgiris men's eight pushed off from the pontoon for that fateful final race. Zigmas, Antanas and Gerdas, who had just won gold medals in the coxed pair, were beaming. The race had been an uneven one and they had not had to try too hard. They had saved their energy and raring to go for the final race. Though Antanas had kept saying that they were just "passengers" in the eight, their desire to win the prestigious eights race and go to America grew by the minute. The remaining six men understood perfectly well, however, that victory was now their responsibility. Zigmas and Antanas were already champions and would be happy with any medal.

Eight pairs of hard, masculine hands grabbed the wooden oar handles, polished to a shine by their own hands, and rowed out into the "battle" that they had waited so long for. It seemed to them that this race was the most important event of their lives, a boundary between what was and what was to be, the breaking point between "until" and "after." With the blinding sun directly in front of them, each of them could only see the dark silhouette of their teammate's backs – the people whom they valued as much as themselves, for whom they would do anything, and with whom they would never give up, even in their darkest hours. The dropping of the eight oars into the water sounded more harmonious than it had ever been – like clockwork. It was so precise and rhythmic, it was almost mesmerizing, lulling their eyes closed. The men were gripped by that rare feeling when it seems like you could row for an eternity, when you feel your crew rather than see it – its every tiny movement, its breathing, its trusting smile. Their strength, like a warm and powerful spring, flooded their bodies, leaving room for nothing in their minds but blissful joy.

With each stroke, the boat left behind eight trembling puddles, like a beautiful and orderly picture of man and nature, whirlpools gradually melting and flowing into the shimmering surface of the bay. The racers could see the distant crowd of onlookers at the end of the course through a haze as they waited for the victory gong. On the other side of the Dnieper, the bulbous spires of Orthodox churches shimmered in the sunlight, and the entire shoreline seemed like a gilded painting.

"For Lithuania, men!" shouted Ričardas as he turned back to encourage his team.

"For Lithuania!" the seven men responded, dipping their blades into the water to prepare for the start.

The six competing teams glance at each other for the last time before freezing in place, ready for the flare to fire. The minute that was left until the start seemed like an eternity, during which their thoughts raced like a wild carousel. During that final minute, many begin wishing that it was all just a dream. As they hear the umpires begin calling out one team name after another, their bodies suddenly realize that they don't want to suffer – but there's no escape. Some of them wet their oar handles and their lips, which had grown dry from the anxiety, before yawning against their will.

The umpire slowly raised his right hand and the starting flare hissed off into the sky. The silence was interrupted by the six coxswains' shouts. The long and narrow blades of the oars tore into the dark water and forty-eight muscular bodies went taught like springs, connecting the long wooden oars with the water. The men struck the water forty-five times per minute, pushing the long and graceful wooden boats away from the starting line.

"Nine, ten…," Gerdas counted the first strokes of the race.

After twenty strokes, the last remnants of their anxiety dissipated and their legs began to feel the first hints of fatigue. Their disordered breathing evened out but they start to need more air. The five hundred metre mark flashed by them. "Three times that distance left...," though it felt like all of their energy had been spent. The distance seemed endless and their bodies were already begging to stop.

Inch by inch, the prow of Žalgiris' boat forged ahead. The coach's encouragement – "For Lithuania!" – echoed in the men's ears.

"One," Gerdas reported quietly to Ričardas, counting the number of seats they had overtaken.

"Hold..."

"Two."

A cable flew over their heads with the lane numbers. "One kilometre... there's just as much ahead of us..." Their bodies felt like they were being ripped apart, their chests felt like they had been torn open, and they heard a deafening silence in their ears. "I'm about to pass out..."

The men, their eyes focused squarely on their friends' backs, were rowing as one. However, out of the corners of their eyes, they could see that the situation out on the course was changing. There were more and more backs that they could not see at the starting line, and more and more of their competitors' backs were falling behind them.

"Three."

Ričardas nodded.

"Let's go!" Gerdas shouted. "For Lithuania!"

Povilas raised his eyes to the sky – "for you, mom and dad" – and felt as though his fatigue had melted away. It was replaced by a seething hatred for the soldiers rowing next to him that doubled the power of every cell in his body.

Stroke after stroke, Ričardas slowly raised the rate as the seven men behind him grit their teeth and wrung their last ounces of energy for a strong finish. Many hours of training were sacrificed to ensure that they could find the energy and strength to accelerate during the hardest part of the race and keep their speed up until the end.

Without even having to look to the side, the men of Žalgiris could now see that some of their opponents were behind them by a boat's length. They felt the return of the wonderful feeling they had felt before the start of the race. They felt that their bodies were singing, that they could row gracefully because their opponents had fallen hopelessly behind, and that, for more than half of the distance that they had yet to cover, they could feel like winners.

They could hear the rest of their team joyfully chanting their country's name from the finish line.

"Those are the grandstands. Twenty more and that's it..."

"Let's go, Rychka!" someone yelled from the shore to support the team.

Their final strokes were no longer as harmonious, but it no longer mattered. The gong rang, and it had never sounded as loud and as grand. The crowd of spectators roared with yells and applause – they were the witnesses of Lithuania's victory.

"The Žalgiris eight finish first. What a surprise!" said the commentator, unable to contain his emotions. "What do you know? The Lithuanians beat Leningrad's Trud! Leningrad failed to place! The second place was taken by the first military naval crew and third place was taken by the second military naval crew. We congratulate the USSR's new champions!"

When they heard these words, the men still couldn't believe that what they had secretly been dreaming about had come true. They were the champions of the USSR and they were the strongest team in the entire country.

The friends of the team who had gathered to support them couldn't stop chanting the country's name. The other race spectators were giving the Lithuanians a standing ovation. Ričardas' eyes were glistening with tears of joy – "what a crew, my crew!"

Their opponents hid the grief of their crushing victory under polite smiles as they shook the new champions' hands – "congratulations, great work, guys..." – but their hopes to visit America, the country of their dreams, had just been shattered.

When they received their medals at the closing event of the championships, the men celebrated like children. Because of the lateness of the event, there hadn't been time to engrave their names on the medals, but they were still the most precious medals in the world at that moment.

By the next morning, Sovietski Sport would write: "The Lithuanian athletes were a real surprise. They proved to be the best rowers at one competition in two rowing events. First, Z. Jukna and A. Bagdonavičius – European champions – demonstrated their strength in the pair together with their cox, G. Morkus. After that, this pair joined their friends in the eights and once again won gold medals. What's more, the coach of the pair and eight, R. Vaitkevičius, personally rowed in the eight as well. The Lithuanian eight's competitors included famous teams like the 1960 USSR champions from the military naval team and the national champions, Trud (Moscow)."

On 26 September, the Lithuanian "Sportas" newspaper was published with a red headline on the front page reading "The Soviet Lithuanians rowers' 'GOLDEN' SUNDAY. Z. Jukna, A. Bagdonavičius and the men's eight are the USSR Champions!"

The 1961 season had ended. All that was left was the journey home and a brief vacation before everything started all over again…

*

A green military cap with a star flashed past the dark window. Povilas ran to the other window, where he saw another soldier. The third window held yet another. The windows were spinning like a carousel, and more and more soldiers were appearing. They all had red stars on their foreheads and all of them were trying to grab him with their icy, stinking hands. He darted from corner to corner of the dark room, but each one had a soldier with a star on his cap. Their angry black eyes pierced his soul. "Ruki v verch![13]" – A terrible, red-faced NKVD soldier jammed his dagger into Povilas' chest... He jumped up from the pain – "No!" – He nearly cried out loud but caught himself just in time when he saw the smiling Gagarin on the wall and his teammates sleeping nearby. It was his USSR championship medal pricking him in the chest. He had held it in his hand until he fell asleep, as if he feared that victory could still elude him... "Thank God, just another dream..." He wiped the cold sweat from his forehead and fingered the golden medal with its red ribbon. He read the words "Чемпион СССР[14]" with a sigh of relief. The red slogan beneath Gagarin on his poster read "A fairytale that came true". His heart was overcome by a wave of joy as he remembered the events of the previous day. They were the champions! From now on, they would be members of the USSR team and would go to international competitions, to America, and perhaps even to the Olympics! "What would things be like if Lithuania was free?" Povilas thought to himself. "Perhaps we already would have seen the world as representatives of a free Lithuania. After all, we've been Lithuanian champions so many times now. But we'll have to race in a red uniform and everyone will refer to us as Russians... Zigmas said that when they go abroad, everyone calls them Russians because if you've got 'CCCP' on your uniform, you're a Russian..." Povilas squeezed the medal in his palm – "I wonder what things would be like if Lithuania hadn't experienced the war... and where I'd be... maybe here, or maybe somewhere else..."

As his chest swelled with pride in the memories of the previous day, he felt like he could hear the congratulations that were shared by the team's friends and the USSR rowing staff with whom they had celebrated their victory at the restaurant in the centre of Kiev. One of the coaches made sure that the heads of the country's rowing federation sat at the table with the Lithuanian men – the umpires, the team coaches, and Sergei Borisovich Sheremetyev, the secretary of the USSR rowing federation. Some said he was the descendant of a famous dynasty of earls and that, during the war he had almost died of starvation because his family, as enemies of the nation, did not receive food cards. The medals they had just won shone from their lapels. They didn't want to

---

13   Rus. Hands up!
14   Rus. USSR Champion

RIMA KARALIENE

put them in their travel suitcases yet – they wanted to keep reliving the moment of glory and triumph when their boat crossed the finish line. Povilas remembered his friends' surprise when, one starry midnight on their way back to Truchanov Island, he stopped his friends at the middle of the bridge and invited them to his wedding. "Bravo, Povilas!", "What, did Gita say she'd only marry you if you won?", "Now we're going to have a party! Our first rowers' wedding!" "You can make your wedding rings out of your medal". Overwhelmed by congratulations and remarks, Povilas didn't know what he should do – thank them or explain himself. "Gita and I had been planning on a party for a while, but I didn't want any distractions before the championships. Rychka promised to give me the hall at our camp. Gita's already sewing her clothes."

The sun rose on a calm and care-free Monday. Gone was the excitement of the previous few days' races, gone was the tension. All that remained was the indescribable joy of victory. Povilas looked forward to a joyful journey home to his beloved wife, to their wedding celebration, and to their vacation.

*

The 30 September issue of "Sportas" gave the men of Žalgiris almost an entire page: "It was a sensation. The Lithuanian Žalgiris eight became the champions of the Soviet Union. This has never happened yet during our long journey in rowing. Usually, crews from Moscow and Leningrad in this class tend to win the championships. But not this time, not in Kiev: our men overtook their competitors with ease and calm (as if it were an everyday race!)… Who are they, the Soviet Union's new champions? You have probably met them more than once in the streets of Vilnius, tired but happy, on their way home from training. What can we tell you about a crew of eight men? After all, every one of them leads a separate life. Each has a separate fate. Here, however, we have eight men – and a coxswain!" one journalist wrote in his colourful description of the team's members.

In the world of LSSR athletics, there were very few USSR champions. Now, however, nine had appeared all at once, three of whom were champions twice over. Reporters were overjoyed – they would have material for months to come!

*

The autumn of 1961 was exceptionally warm and beautiful. People were still getting used to the new rubles, which replaced the old ones on 1 January and reduced both prices and wages everywhere by a factor of ten. There were whispers about Berlin, about a wall that separated East from West, about how Khrushchev, at the XXII CPSU congress, promised that there would be no taxes for the people by 1965, that communism will be implemented in the USSR by 1980 and that when the congress ended, Stalin was "raised" from his mausoleum. The LSSR sport union council's V plenary decided that there "should be 440,000 athletes in the LSSR by 1962." The image of a worker holding the CPSU's programme in his hand was placed everywhere, even on matchboxes.

A planetarium opened in Vilnius, and Youth Street was renamed to Yuri Gagarin Street.

The displays of stores along Lenin Avenue were soon "decorated" by posters with the happy faces of soviet people and phrases from the "Moral Code of the Builder of Communism," which was ratified by the XXII CPSU congress. They included phrases like "we are all friends and brothers," "all for one and one for all," "those who do not work do not eat," etc. The faithful joked that the communists had written a poor translation of the Ten Commandments in their own language. However, the communist youth quickly introduced the pretty phrases into their own vocabulary. Posters hung on churches and in the streets with children's drawings of an astronaut dressed in red – ostensibly Gagarin – flying over churches and mosques shouting "БОГА НЕТ"[15].

A boat named after Lithuania – Litva – began a route between Odessa and Venice.

Somewhere in another world, screens saw "West Side Story" for the first time, and Walt Disney Presents became Walt Disney's Wonderful World of Color. However, residents of the USSR would not learn of these things anytime soon.

The rowers of Žalgiris gradually returned to their everyday lives and regular training rhythms, but this time with more motivation and even greater dreams. When they returned to their lecture halls, they were beleaguered by curious classmates and professors who wanted to hear all about their victory in Kiev. Nobody wanted to speak out loud, but everyone felt great pride in Lithuania's victory, as small and symbolic as it may have been.

---

15   Rus. "There is no God."

On 7 November, when the soviet people celebrated Revolution Day, the Vilnius Žalgiris winter rowing camp on the other side of the Neris was decorated with balloons and ribbons, with two crossed oars hung above the door. The festively decorated hall and tables decked out in white linens awaited their first rowers' wedding. With help from her sisters and friends, Gita brought all of the tableware and pre-prepared dishes the night before. The 200-ruble prize Povilas received for winning the USSR championships was enough for the food and for a new suit, and his friends helped with everything else: the Žalgiris administrators agreed to lend the hall free of charge and one team mate brought his accordion. Gita's wedding dress was sewn by her aunt Ona, her mother's sister, who lived right next door and had her own sewing machine. A whole crowd of Vilnius rowers and coaches gathered at the wedding – and, of course, Gita's entire family. Povilas' Uncle Gustavas came with his sister Onutė, but Aunt Konstancija remained in Prienai to look after their home and their livestock.

Though the newlyweds had already sported their golden rings all summer, the guests still awaited them with joy and excitement – they were the first of their rower friends to have started a family. At exactly four in the afternoon, they finally saw the bride's white dress as she passed under the crossed oars. Gita was hidden under a veil that stretched halfway down her back. Povilas was dressed in a new black suit with a white bow tie, which matched the white bandage on his chin that hid a cut he suffered after pacing about anxiously in the morning.

The small hall was filled by a long table packed with Gita and Povilas' best friends, their "brothers and sisters of the oar"- the men's and women's eights, their friends from other teams, and their coaches with their wives.

Through the windows, one could make out the columns of the boathouse and the race-weary boats housed within on the other side of the Neris with Gediminas Hill in the background. The noise from the first two-day rowers' wedding celebration nearby didn't seem to bother them.

*

2

In 1961, Christmas Eve fell on a Sunday, so, though quietly and behind their closed window shades, people could celebrate the holiday without thinking of work. It had snowed a few days previously, which brought joy not just to the children, but to the skiers who hurried to Vingis Park to race as well.

The aroma of home-baked goods began to waft through homes throughout Vilnius. Hostesses reached into secret shelves to pull out products they had been saving ahead of time, like herring, cranberries and oil. They laid out their finest linens, sewn by their mothers or grandmothers, and their most precious tableware.

On Sunday night, city residents flooded those churches in Vilnius that the communists had not yet managed to turn into warehouses or, in the best-case scenario, museums. The oldest women were the only ones who went without fear. Many averted their eyes beneath their caps or behind their collars from the "snitches". Any communist youth or communist seen stepping into a church risked finding himself or herself "under a magnifying glass."

For some reason, colleges and universities always held their exams on Christmas day, while intermediary schools held tests as well. However, students had no qualms about bringing in "šližikai"[16] and other pastries on those days, even offering some to their teachers and boasting about the things they had found under their Christmas trees. Soviet ideologues tried, in any way they could, to blow the celebration of the New Year out of proportion in an effort to suppress Christmas Eve and Christmas Day celebrations.

One early Christmas morning, when everyone in his family had hurried off to work, Povilas left for the city centre without telling anyone. He took Čiurlionis Street and then headed down the hill towards the old town to St. Michael's church. He entered the churchyard through the arched

---

16 A traditional Lithuanian holiday snack of baked dough balls often served with poppies or poppy-seed milk.

gate and crossed himself before St. Michael. The saint's statue, seeming to have stepped right out of the Vilnius city coat of arms that had been banned by the Soviet government, stood proudly under the bare trees in the churchyard. With that, Povilas pushed open the church's heavy doors and stepped inside. The incense from the midnight mass still hung heavy in the air. Only a handful of older women were left kneeling below the star-shaped Gothic arches. A woman and her son stood in front of a nativity scene, and she rested her hand on his shoulder as she whispered in his ear, explaining something and pointing to the candle-lit crib. Povilas let out a sob before kneeling in the second row, resting his head on his clenched fist, and froze. It was only the tolling of the bells that stirred life back into him. He raised his head, stood up, wiped his eyes with a kerchief, crossed himself, and turned towards the door. The old town's seniors were gathering for their Christmas mass. Povilas took a look at his watch, pulled ten coins out of his pocket, and bought two candles from the old woman stamping her feet by the door to keep warm. It was raining outside, and there were groups of two or three students walking by, chattering under shared umbrellas. He took a deep breath of the damp December air and headed towards the bus station. "There's half a day left until training, and three hours will be enough to head to Prienai and back."

*

On New Year's Eve, the thin coat of snow that had covered the ground melted away, "painting" the hills and streets black. Only the colourful decorations hanging from the fir trees found on almost every block helped preserve some semblance of a holiday spirit for the upcoming celebration. On the afternoon of 31 December, Alfa hurried over to his friend Povilas on Čiurlionis Street:

"Povilas, did you see this?" he asked, extending the latest 31 December issue of "Sportas".

"I don't read rubbish like that...," retorted Povilas as he opened the newspaper. "What kind of idiot writes this stuff, anyway?"

"Not that part, Povilas," Alfa tried to reassure him. "Look at the last page."

"Give me that, I want to read some poetry," said Gita's brother Bronius, snatching the paper from Alfa and reading in a grand and pompous voice:

"'THE RACE HAS STARTED!'"

"You arsehole! Give it back!" Povilas shouted.

However, Bronius dashed behind the sofa, raising the paper high so that Povilas couldn't reach it. He continued:

"The year is over...

The year has begun,

We bear the future in our hearts

With pride, we guide the entire nation forward

For a closer look at the Sun."

"Why is 'Sun' capitalized?" Bronius interrupted himself before continuing:

"'Once again, we stand at the starting line,

With a long distance ahead of us

It will be hard, as it always is,

But oh, what a finish awaits us at the end!'"

"That's enough, Bronius, give me that," said Povilas, grabbing for the "Sportas" paper. But Bronius jumped back and, emboldened by his success, continued with an even greater theatrical flourish:

"None have yet had such a goal – the finish line –

Before them as we do now.

None have ever achieved

Such a great speed at the finish line.

The shot was fired.

The twenty-second.'"

"Is this about the communist congress?" Bronius asked with surprise and glancing up at the headline. Having confirmed that he was indeed reading the "Sportas" newspaper, he shook his head and laughed mockingly.

"The race has started. The pace increases.

The communist cosmos grows closer.

We are the Prometheuses of a new age

We bear the future in our hearts."[17]

Bronius read the last line dramatically, puffing out his chest, as if he was standing at a podium, before collapsing onto the sofa. He raised his hands in defeat and surrendered the newspaper to Povilas.

"Some great poets we've got these days... pinkos, the lot of them. They'd be better off competing in a sport as well instead of kissing the communists' arses.

---

17   By Petras Keidošius

"Shhh, be quiet," Povilas hushed him.

"These walls are thick and everyone around us is cool. Isn't that right, Alfa?"

"You know me, I'm not one of them," Alfa assured him. "Turn to the last page, Povilas. They don't have our photo, but they wrote that our eight was the Team of the Year, and that Zigmas and Antanas were the greatest athletes."

"Seriously? That was obvious for the pair, but I'm surprised that we got first place. Who drew that caricature of them?" Povilas asked with surprise.

For some reason, the page had Zigmas and Antanas' heads cut out of a photograph and placed next to a drawing in which Zigmas was stirring a boiling pot over a campfire with a canoe paddle.

"They finally noticed us too. All that work was worth it. It's nice to remember the win," Alfa smiled.

"It definitely is. Everybody stopping us, asking us things and taking our pictures. I'm not used to so much attention," Povilas admitted modestly.

"Yeah, it's been strange for me as well. I was at the Polytechnicum about a week ago with James. They had organized a meeting with athletes for the schoolchildren. I didn't feel like myself on the stage at the "presidium." Though I am used to speaking in front of students, I still got sweaty palms when they invited me to speak on the stage."

"You're good at speaking, it couldn't have been hard."

"Sure, but when I finally opened my mouth, all I managed to say was a joke about how a rower can quickly become a swimmer if they're not careful."

"So what? That was entirely appropriate. What should they be hearing, how 'delightful' our training is?"

"Alright, it's time for me to go. Give Gita my regards, I'm out of here," said Alfa as he turned towards the door. "Have a nice celebration!"

"Thanks for the "Sportas" issue, Alfa. By the way, happy birthday! We probably won't see each other tomorrow," said Povilas.

"Thanks, guys!" Alfa smiled as he put in his cap and left. He waved to Gita through the window from the sidewalk as she entered the room.

The early evening twilight flooded the dull, grey Čiurlionis Street. A boy struggled with a sledge he was pulling along the dirty sidewalk. In the sledge, wrapped in furs, sat a red-cheeked girl – probably his sister.

The sledge screeched on the snowless sidewalk. "They probably found an snow-covered hill somewhere in Vingis Park," thought Povilas as he brushed his hair aside and hugged Gita. He hadn't told anyone yet, but there was a third heart beating in their young family.

All the women of the household were hard at work in the small plywood-walled apartment. They had been toiling in the kitchen since the early morning, cleaning the home, and doing the washing and drying. The small, cozy apartment was filled with the love, warmth and respect that Povilas had yearned for for so long. This would be his first New Year spent in his new home together with Gita's family – which was now his family as well.

*

True winter took its time coming to Vilnius that year. The snow that had fallen at the end of November offered only brief delight. There was occasional snow at the beginning of January, but it all immediately melted again.

Both the athletes and regular Vilnius residents couldn't wait for some serious snow and cold. Children looked with longing at squares that should have become skating rinks by then. Their winter break had been ruined. Sports events organisers had found themselves in a terrible fix. They'd begin organising skiing or skating competitions the moment it snowed, only to find puddles of mud the next day.

The mercury thermometers often rose above zero, soaking the streets with water. Not just skiers, but rowers were also disappointed by the warm winter. Skis were irreplaceable tools for rowers in the winter. Coaches often said "good skiers make good rowers."

If it wasn't for skis, Lithuania could not have produced excellent rowers like Eugenijus and Romualdas Levickas. When they were still children, they would watch with envy as their Polish neighbour's sons pulled out their skis whenever it snowed. They wished, one day, to learn to ski the way their neighbours did. When they lived on Konarskis Street near Vingis Park, they gazed enviously at passers-by heading to the park with their skis. In 1955, when Romualdas – or Romka, as his friends called him – turned fifteen, and Eugenijus turned fourteen, they heard from their friends that Pavilionis, the Žalgiris rowing team coach, was handing out skis. They immediately hurried off to see him. The brothers quickly learned the "art" of skiing and began participating in – and winning – ski competitions. At the time, all they wanted to do was enjoy their skis. They didn't dream that, in the spring, they would have to take their places in a boat and would go on to become the first Masters of Sport of Lithuanian rowing.Throughout the cold and snowy winter competitions were held almost every weekend, either in Vingis Park or Sapieginė and the rowers raced neck-and-neck alongside the best skiers – and even won sometimes. Gita won the LSSR junior skiers' championships when she was still a schoolgirl, and Eugenijus and Romas took victories in the youth relay race. As a student, Romas participated in the winter biathlon competition, skiing and performing jumps. In 1960, he became the LSSR champion. But when spring came, they would all return to their boats.

The rowers often gathered for training at Vingis Park. This was a convenient location for the university students living in dormitories near the park, as they didn't have to travel across the city by bus or change their clothes. They'd simply walk out the door and get on their skis. The hills of Vingis Park were perfect for training not just their endurance but their power as well. A few 5-kilometre laps up and down the park's hills were just like a good water session.

✻

3

After rocking the Union team to its core, the rowers of Lithuania's Žalgiris eight were written onto the team's candidate list and invited to the USSR team camp in January. It was to be held near Moscow, in a city called Podolsk, where people were still discussing the people's uprising of 1957[18].

Ričardas, who had previously taken just Zigmas and Antanas, now attended with an entire team of his men – his fifteen best rowers. Skiing courses and sports halls were used to ensure the athletes' general physical fitness. In the qualifying competition, the new members from Lithuania produced excellent results during their skiing races, and won competitions in the weightlifting hall. The young men from Trud and CSK shot unfriendly glances at the Lithuanians. This wasn't just because they were doing better at their skiing – but also because they had snatched the USSR champions' title and the chance to visit America.

In March, when Lithuania's lakes were still covered in ice, the members of the Žalgiris team packed their bags for a long season and left for the USSR team's camp in Poti[19]. This sub-tropical Georgian city awoke from its winter slumber much earlier, allowing the rowers to start rowing in early spring. The river Rioni flowed through the city, and if you weren't careful, you could row out to sea and get grabbed by the border guard. The much narrower Kaparcha River flowed into the Rioni, and this river provided access to the rather large Lake Paliastomi. The distance between this lake's shorelines was 5-6 km. The rowers often trained on the Rioni – though it flowed quicker than the Kaparcha, it was also much wider. Though the city was a dirty one, it looked exotic, with green palm trees, strangely shaped buildings painted in unusual colours, and indecipherable

---

18   An ordinary uprising of the Soviet people against the anti-national CPSU occurred 10-11 June 1957 in Podolsk. The cause of the uprising was the death of a driver who was beaten by militia. About seven thousand people (other sources claim three thousand) participated in the uprising. The uprising was suppressed with 15 casualties and 9 convictions.

19   Poti - a Georgian port town 312 km from Tbilisi

signs. The funniest thing, however, was a monument of Lenin and Stalin talking to one another which was painted in silver.

"Can you imagine? Lithuania's still covered in snow and ice, but they can row all year round here!" the men exclaimed, overjoyed at the early spring and the training they had begun on the water. They were full of enthusiasm and ambition;dreaming of new victories. Because of this, their coaches' seemingly impossible tasks seemed perfectly normal. They all wanted to prove that the victory in Kiev in September hadn't been a fluke.

The Russians had begun arranging a new composite eight with rowers from Moscow and Leningrad and planned to defeat the Lithuanians and travel to Philadelphia. Because they no longer felt like the masters of their domain, they initially gave the Lithuanians a wide berth. Eventually, however, they began forming new relationships.

The first days passed by in the blink of an eye – exercise, breakfast, training, lunch, rest, training, dinner, sleep. And then all over again.

Before every training session, they'd all gather with their coach to listen to his instructions and to hear his advice after their training. Ričardas always asked how everybody felt and what they were feeling, what the team needed and what the team needed to fix.

∗

"Is everyone here?" asked Ričardas as he looked around before the morning training session.

"Raise your hand if you're not here!" shouted Povilas, and his teammates laughed.

"That looks like everyone," said Zigmas as he scanned his friends' heads.

"We have a new team member," said Ričardas as he turned to the tall blonde man awkwardly shifting about next to him. "Meet Dima Semionov, from Moscow. He will be rowing in the five seat, in Liutkaitis' place. Povilas, you'll be in the four."

The men looked at one another – "Why?" Povilas' eyebrows shot up with surprise and he looked at his coach with a questioning glance – "Me?" Ričardas turned away from him and continued.

"In the morning, you'll be rowing in the eight, and rowing in pairs and fours after lunch. I'll tell you who's with whom later."

The men had heard about the USSR coaches' efforts to shoehorn as many Russians as they could into each crew. However, nobody could understand how they chose whom to exclude. As newcomers they had not yet managed to understand the Soviet team's rules. All they knew was that they, the Lithuanians, would have to stay one or two rungs ahead of the Russians if they were to keep their spots in the team.

With the hope that the transfer was a temporary one, Povilas rowed even harder in his four that day. Thoughts were racing through his head and he didn't want to believe that he was too weak to row in the eight. On the way to the USSR championships in Kiev, there had been no question that he would be in the crew. Even when Antanas was late to his race, it was Povilas who was put into the pair with Zigmas rather than anybody else. His coaches praised him for his endurance, for his fighting spirit, and his good technique. When it came to the fitness tests near Moscow, he had been one of the strongest.

"Why me?" Povilas asked Ričardas when he caught up to him after his session.

"Samsonov's orders," Ričardas replied curtly before looking away.

His teammates shrugged. However powerful Dima from Moscow might be, he would have a difficult time adjusting to the Lithuanians' rowing style.

Povilas, who was ordinarily happy and sociable, became withdrawn. His good-natured blue eyes glazed over as if they were looking off into space.

"Povilas, they're just testing something," his teammates reassured him. "They'll put you back. Dima is having a hard time adjusting to us."

However, day after day, Povilas was switched back and forth between the four and the pair. Whenever he wasn't rowing, Povilas read books or wrote letters home to avoid discussing the situation with his friends. He sent out a letter or postcard every day and looked forward to his letters from home. He walked to the post box each day in the hope of receiving a letter, something friendly and close to his heart that could reassure and strengthen him. He often took his book and went outside to read, sitting off to the side on a bench – even though the spring weather wasn't very warm yet. Other times, he'd take pictures – of the awakening springtime nature, blossoming flowers, or birds.

As the camp reached its halfway mark, the athletes' homesickness grew in intensity. One Sunday afternoon, when they looked forward to their free half-day after a strenuous thirty-kilometre training run, Povilas took his notebook and an envelope and left for his bench. He opened the notebook and pulled out two postcards he had bought the day before with pictures of Poti on them. On the first one, he wrote, in Russian, "Lithuanian SSR, Prienai, Panemunė 11, Česėkaitė Konstancija" – for his aunt and uncle. Povilas enjoyed writing and wrote much and often. He could describe seemingly everyday forgettable occurrences and sights in excruciating detail. He used his exceptionally flowing handwriting, mastered at primary school, to write both letters and essays for his studies. He chose a postcard showing the Rioni River flowing into the sea for Gita.

"What are you writing, Povilas?" said James as he sat down next to him.

"A letter for home," said Povilas as he raised his head and flipped over the postcard.

"I won't peek, I won't peek, you can keep writing," smiled James.

"Oh, it can wait..."

"Povilas, you seem down."

"What have I got to be happy about?" Povilas shrugged.

James could see that something was weighing heavily on his friend's mind. This was not the same Povilas with whom he had spent so many months in a boat with. That Povilas was tireless and never seemed to be discouraged. He'd always raised everyone's spirits and could find a way out of any situation.

"Yevgeniy Borisovich, this is my team and I know what I'm doing," they heard Ričardas talking in Russian somewhere nearby.

Yevgeniy Borisovich Samsonov had been the USSR team's head coach since 1959.

"Rychka, that's impossible right now. Semionov is strong, he won't let you down.

"Why Liutkaitis? He's strong and dependable."

"Not everybody thinks that he's dependable. His documents didn't pass. He can't be allowed to leave the country."

Samsonov's words in Russian cut the young men like a knife – "nevyezdnoj[20]." "Nevyezdnoj" meant that all paths towards participation in international competitions were closed to him and that all of his training and dreams would amount to nothing.

---

20   Rus. A person who has been forbidden from traveling abroad.

"Perhaps it was a mistake... What for?" Ričardas asked, surprised.

"There was some sort of issue with his family. You know they don't discuss these things openly."

Their voices grew more distant, leaving the men sitting together. They dared not look at each other.

"Did you hear that?" James turned to Povilas, unsure of what to say.

Povilas nodded and managed a sad, crooked smile:

"Well, I guess everything's clear, then..."

"And I had no idea why they had switched you out..."

Povilas froze, covered in cold sweat, as he gripped his postcard and tried to understand what he had just heard. It felt like a cold wind had picked him up and blown him back in time sixteen years to his childhood, to a village on the shores of the Nemunas River, to his family's last Christmas in Rūdupis. He could see before his eyes the burning homes, his mother lying in the snow in a puddle of her own blood, his father's last glance as he looked at his children and receded into the dark, hands tied and led on both sides by NKVD agents, his sister Elzbieta sobbing before she too was led off into the darkness after her father... and the terrible faces of the drunk *stribai*[21]. He remembered that cold night in the Prienai *stribai* office where he and his brother Juozas lay on the ground hugging their sister Ona and unable to sleep all night. A cold shiver ran down Povilas' spine as he remembered the events of December 1945. Every time he remembered that fateful Christmas evening, his heart was gripped with pain and terrible longing. His eyes could never forget the sight of his mother as she fell from the ladder and his ears still rang with her moans of pain and his father's cries. He would never see nor hear them ever again. For many years, Povilas had tried to forget the memories of that terrible Christmas, but they kept returning to him and suffocating him, and he felt a sense of vicarious guilt that crushed him like an iceberg. He had only been eight years old at the time, but he

---

21   Destruction battalions, colloquially istrebitels (истребители, "destroyers", "ex-terminators"), abbreviated – *stribai* (in Lithuanian), were paramilitary units under the control of NKVD in the newly annexed territories of USSR. They consisted of local people collaborating with the Soviet occupiers, and were often alcoholic and depraved Soviet labourers. In 1945, members of these battalions were officially named Defenders of the People. *Stribai* participated in NKVD operations against Lithuanian partisans and often guided the NKVD's agents. They were especially active in helping the occupiers arrest people and deport them to Siberia.

always felt that, perhaps there was something he could had done, some small step or childish touch or just a word, and everything might have ended up differently...

*

In the pitch-black of night, he could hear voices, like a prayer in a church or a mournful cry. A silhouette began to emerge from an unseen crowd, growing lighter and lighter... The prayer grew distant, the moaning grew quiet, he was approached by his mother, who was light and happy and dressed in white. Her eyes radiated love and joy. She extended a pale hand and stroked Povilas' head. "Mother, you're alive!" exclaimed Povilas as he embraced her before she faded away...

Povilas opened his eyes with a jolt, drenched in warm sweat: "a dream..." He closed his eyes, wanting to return to his mother; he could still feel her hand where it had caressed his hair. However, his beating heart wouldn't let him sleep. He buried his face in his hands and sighed deeply, getting up from bed and placing his feet on the cold floor. He rested his elbows on his knees, lowered his head into his trembling hands, and sighed again. A springtime seaside day was slowly dawning outside the window.

Povilas put on his green tracksuit, put on his shoes and went outside, taking care not to awaken his teammates. The horizon was slowly growing red and he could hear the morning's first bird songs. Povilas' thoughts wandered over from his beautiful dream to the previous day's events. How he wished that all of that had simply been a dream! "Why the hell would I want to fight for a country like this? Do I really want to put on a uniform with the letters 'CCCP' on it?" His head was filled with doubts, and Povilas couldn't separate his desire to be a simple rower dreaming of new victories and his hatred for the people who had murdered his parents.

The outside doors creaked and out came Alfa, rubbing his eyes.

"Can't sleep, Alfa?"

"Yeah, I'm used to waking up early for my classes. As soon as it's light out – bam, I'm up. After that, I'm too lazy to lie back down," he laughed.

"The sky is beautiful," said Povilas as he looked off into the distance.

"Povilas, what's wrong? What's the problem? We don't recognize you anymore. Everybody's worried. Are you angry with us because they took you out of the eight? We don't understand why they did that, either. Rychka's quiet, he won't tell us anything."

Povilas stood quiet, his lips sealed. The wrinkle he had had on his forehead since early childhood grew even deeper, and his half-closed eyes looked off towards the horizon.

"Please be a mate and tell me what happened. Did we say something wrong?" Alfa wouldn't let up.

"Alfa, please stop..." said Povilas, choking on his words as his emotions boiled over. This had begun in his childhood, when he was eight years old.

"Tell me, don't keep it quiet, there's something weighing you down."

Povilas remained quiet.

"I give you my word, nobody will find out about anything from me," said Alfa, placing his hand over his heart.

"Yesterday, I found out that I'm 'nevyezdnoj,'" Povilas admitted with a trembling voice as he swallowed the lump that had been gathering in his throat.

"There it is... but why?" Alfa asked.

"Because of my family. But I don't want to talk about that, Alfa," Povilas said as his eyes began to glisten.

"Ok, of course, if you don't want to talk about it, don't. I think they'll get me as well. It's strange that they haven't moved me out yet. My turn will come as well, I imagine."

The men sat together quietly on the backrest of the bench and watched the slowly rising sun.

Povilas was the first to speak:

"The waves are glittering so beautifully... When I was little, during the war, it was so wonderful to watch the flares take off from the trees in the woods towards the sky. There were some barracks near us. You couldn't see them from any homes beyond the bend in the Nemunas and the corner of Žvėrinčius forest, but the soldiers apparently had nighttime training so they launched lots of flares – white ones, green ones, red ones. At first I was afraid of watching them and would put my feet up on our bench, but I later grew a bit bolder and thought they were beautiful."

"Yeah, that's a very colourful sunrise..."

"Once, when I was still a child, I found four rocket charges from the Germans nearby. I put them into our stove when my sister was making dinner. I had no idea they'd burn so well. The fire went up to the ceiling! It's a good thing that we had a good stove and that my sister was quick to cover the hole with her pot..."

"Seems like you were a crazy kid!" Alfa laughed.

"Yeah, but my parents never beat me. Somehow, they managed to discipline us without beating us. Maybe that's why we grew up so good," Povilas finally smiled.

"Where are you from, Povilas?"

"From Rūdupis, but I later lived in Prienai."

"How many children were there in your family?"

"I have two sisters and two brothers. There are five of us. Elzbieta is the oldest – she was born in '27. Kazys was born in '30. Juozas and I are twins, and we were born in '37, and Onutė's the youngest – she was born during the war in '43."

In an effort to get Povilas to talk and to let him speak, Alfa chose his questions carefully:

"What did your parents do?"

"Why?" asked Povilas, looking at Alfa suspiciously.

"No reason, just curious. You know, we're all from different regions and different families. The only thing that brought us together was rowing," Alfa smiled.

"My father was a forester. In 1918, he and his two brothers volunteered for the army. In return, they received land in Rūdupis village, and the volunteers also received forest materials and grains for sowing to start their lives with. My uncle Juozas was a border policeman and my uncle Pranas worked for the foresters. Because my uncle Pranas was friends with a forester, they made my father the forester for Rūdupis forest."

"Is your mother from Rūdupis, too?"

"No, Strielčiai."

"Really? There's a girl from Strielčiai in the technical school. What was your mother's last name?"

"Česėkaitė, Ona. She had three brothers and a sister."

"Had? Where are they now?"

"My parents are up there," said Povilas, pointing to the sky. "We've been orphans since '46."

"They died?"

"Yeah...," sighed Povilas.

"Do you have any relatives? Anyone close to you?"

"Yeah, there are still a few left..."

"They died too?"

"Pretty much..."

Povilas quieted down, as he didn't want to explain his relatives' fates. He once again remembered the day when his uncle Pranas was exiled to Siberia. His father had barely managed to make it to the railroad station in Mauručiai on horseback to bring them some food. They exiled Povilas' aunt, uncle, and his cousins Vytautas and Algirdas to the Altai region. His uncle was immediately separated and nobody ever heard from him again. Povilas' parents received a single letter from his aunt in Altai, written in purple ink on the page of a book. All they could read was "Dear Stasys and Ona," – everything else was illegibly washed out. Those who remained were constantly beset by *stribai*. One late autumn, a wagon full of drunk *stribai* drove by and stopped by their neighbour's home. After some time, a grenade went off on a ditch near the river Nemunas by their home, and Kazys yelled "the Kurilavičius house is burning!" The *stribai* had burned their barn for no reason and took them away in the summer. His son Petras had left for the woods and had died during a shootout on the riverbank of the Verknė... He was a good man. When visiting one summer, he had seen that Povilas had tied a rectangular box to some string and was pulling it about the yard like a wagon. He had been four or five at the time. The next day, he brought four roofing tiles cut into identical round pieces. He mounted them onto a square dowel to turn them into wheels and nailed them to the bottom of the box, giving little Povilas a real toy wagon...

"Whatever, Alfa. That's all history and we can't change a thing. We can't bring back our loved ones," said Povilas as he noticed Alfa's curious glance and returned from his thoughts to their conversation.

"Oh, I know what you mean... The worst part comes right after the war. I was eleven at the time, so I definitely remember what it was like," Alfa shuddered. "Who raised you, Povilas?"

"My aunt Konstancija, my mother's sister. She didn't have any children of her own," said Povilas before growing quiet again and looking off into the distance. He probably wouldn't be able to explain how his uncle Gustavas was exiled to a concentration camp somewhere near Kalinin – probably simply because he was Prussian. Nor that he returned after they had moved in with his aunt, and that he lived with them, half in hiding, so they wouldn't take him away again, he walked about in the dark because he had heard that his name had been put on a list... Povilas kept this story to himself and continued:

"At first, we lived in a small apartment in an attic in Prienai. It was my aunt and uncle and us three kids – me, Kazys and Onutė. My twin brother grew up with another aunt in Strielčiai. After that, my aunt won five thousand rubles through bonds, so she and my uncle built themselves a home on the other side of the Nemunas in 1950 right on the riverbank."

"Who did your oldest sister grow up with?"

"Elzbieta? She didn't grow up in Lithuania...," Povilas blinked slowly "I very much look forward to her return. All of us were scattered around the world..."

"Forgive me, Povilas, I didn't want to hurt you," said Alfa as he understood what Povilas meant and shuddered.

"There's nothing you can do. Thank God that at least she stayed alive...," said Povilas as his eyes glazed over again. He turned away.

"So when you keep going to Prienai, it's your aunt you're visiting, right?" Alfa asked in an effort to change the subject.

"Yeah. They have a large garden, so I have to help them work it. And a homestead, too. Pears, apples... When Lithuania was independent, the head of the Prienai Žiburys high school was a priest named Martišius, and he had a large orchard. When the Russians came, he gave his students' parents fruit tree saplings for free. Kazys and I brought a number of them home and planted them to make our own garden. Until they began bearing fruit, I'd go to Strielčiai and bring home bags of apples from my uncle Povilas, my mother's brother. I'd carry them on my shoulder to the Nemunas and then cross the river in a rowboat so I wouldn't have to take the long way across the bridge."

"So that's where you learned to row!"

"Sure," laughed Povilas. "Apples weren't the only thing I transported across the river. I once rowed about twelve kilometres against the current to get a few bags of pine needles for bedding. We didn't have any straw so we gathered sticks and needles from the woods. Collecting them was hard work. I brought firewood by boat. I'd occasionally catch pieces of logs or fallen trees in the Nemunas. Kazys was taken into the army in 1952, so my uncle and I were the only two men in the household. I had work from morning until evening.

"How did you end up in Vilnius?" Alfa continued, curious.

"I wanted to escape my aunt's house," Povilas confessed. "I didn't have my own space there. I never heard a positive word either, though I took care of the entire homestead – the home, the cow, the gardens; I was never able to leave - for anything."Povilas was again overtaken by memories of how he begged his aunt to be let out with his friends or classmates. When his class prepared a play, they gave him a role, but his aunt forbade him from participating. When there was an excursion to Kaunas on a steamboat along the Nemunas, he couldn't go then, either. When his class had a trip to the "Goat's Stove" near Verknė – he couldn't go. There were three pairs of skates at home but she wouldn't let him skate on the Nemunas. She taught him to say that his wrists hurt so he wouldn't have to go to his physical education classes. At the time, Prienai had a football team and every class at the school had its own football team. One of the class' former counselors, Lakickas, had played basketball for the high school during the Smetona period... The school's administration bathed its schoolchildren in the public sauna, and his aunt wouldn't let him into the sauna, either. It was nice during the warm season, when the Nemunas melted and he could bathe and swim as much as he wanted.

"My aunt protected me from other women like I was a house pet," Povilas smiled. "The first time I went to a dance, I went in secret. And every time after that, too. All of my friends in middle school went to dances and I didn't want to be left out. It was a good thing that my classmate Aldona asked me to the dance first. After that I grew bolder…"

"Your aunt must have loved you very much to protect you like this," Alfa laughed.

"Sure she did… When I finished school, I found out one day that there was a car headed to Vilnius, a truck, with the school principal Napoleonas Jacunskas and a classmate named Antanas. That was my opportunity to submit some documents. I didn't know anything about higher education so I chose math at the Institute of Education," Povilas fell silent as he remembered how the director of the Institute, a former revolutionary named Mickevičius, stood by the window and saw the Vytis[22] watermarks on Povilas' application. Leaving this unspoken, he continued: "I passed my exams and that's how I wound up in Vilnius. I could finally play football and sports and have my own bed and closet. I remember the first time we went to Vilnius, Jacunskas and I. We went to the Cathedral. They wouldn't

---

22   The Vytis – a white rider on a red background – was a national symbols of the independent Lithuanian state during the inter-war period. Under the Soviet occupation, it had become a forbidden symbol.

let anyone in, but the principal gave the guard some cigarettes so he let us in to look around. I had never seen such a large church."

"Povilas, don't give up. The times are changing, things will get better," Alfa consoled him. "Look, they pulled Stalin out of his mausoleum. Maybe they'll stop persecuting people."

"I'm poorly suited for this government. And it's poorly suited for me," Povilas blurted out, remembering how everyone in school had been encouraged to join the Komsomol. The principal would lock everyone into a room and wouldn't let anyone out until they had written a request to join the Komsomol. The class teacher took one look at Povilas and said "There's no point in writing one for you, they won't take you anyway." He knew Povilas' family and what had happened to them. He had been a lieutenant in the Lithuanian army himself. That was how he had avoided the Komsomol as well.

"Who is it suitable for? Some people remain true to themselves, but others will sell out for a penny…"

"I wonder why they aren't putting our own guys into the eight. They could use Romas and Eugenijus, they're Masters of Sport."

"I think I heard that their documents aren't in order, either…"

They heard the creak of the doors as the rowers filed out one by one for their morning lineup.

"Alfa, not a word…" whispered Povilas as he put his finger to his lips as he suddenly realised that he had allowed himself to say too much.

"My lips are sealed," responded Alfa, placing his finger to his lips as well.

Ričardas, as if sensing that Povilas had some sort of suspicions, approached him after the morning lineup.

"Listen, your documents have been held up, they won't let you go to America. We don't know who'll go yet – us or Trud, or even CSK. There will be a selection race, but they're preparing the documents now. Yours have been rejected. Don't give up, we'll try to do something else for next time."

Povilas quietly listened to his coach, squinting as he looked off into the distance past his shoulder. Not a single muscle on his face betrayed what was happening inside of him. He nodded and turned towards his new team. Ričardas grabbed his arm:

"Yours aren't the only ones that have been held up. They're messing with everyone. We're a huge headache for the KGB people. It's the first time they've had to take Lithuanians abroad, and to America of all places, and there are few of us that don't have 'histories.'"

The tension was growing in the team. In an effort to prove that the Lithuanians' victory had been down to luck, the Union's coaches held one qualifying race after another. Ričardas caught on quickly and put his men in smaller boats so that the Lithuanians won easily when the qualifying races for fours and pairs came.

Povilas found an inner strength; he began writing letters home and reading all of the books that he had brought and the books his friends had brought. He closely observed "his" team, which no longer had room for him, licking his wounds and beginning to practise hard pushing aside thoughts of his own day-to-day well-being. He truly believed that he could surpass the others and return to the eight.

The training was long and arduous, the sort that was only done in the spring, and the many qualifying races took their toll on the strong and patient men of the Žalgiris team. When one or another of them began shuffling, barely able to handle the strain, Ričardas nearly lost his temper:

"What, have you guys gone soft already? Don't forget that a pair once rowed to the Black Sea! That I could understand complaining about! But you guys can't even row thirty kilometres?"

Nobody tried to argue with Ričardas. There was no point. "He always brings that story up to inspire us. There's no comparing a tourist's trip with the fight for a place on the team. Apples and oranges," the rowers thought to themselves. Of course, when they began rowing three years ago, in 1958, that journey had seemed like an absolute feat of endurance.

In 1958, P. Normantas and V. Ditkevičius decided to set out from the Kaunas Athletic Institute in a fine sculling boat– from the Baltic to the Black Sea. They converted the boat into a coxed double scull and departed from Kaunas on a rainy 8 July, rowing along the historic Oginski canal and arriving in Kherson in Ukraine 47 days later. They covered 2,200 kilometres over 36 days, including a few days for rest and repairing their boat. During one especially spirited day in Ukraine, they rowed 130 kilometres along the Dnieper.

Many coaches were fond of reminding the men of this story. And the rowers, though they couldn't understand why nobody had yet prohibited it, secretly rejoiced that they were still able to commemorate the historic Grand Duchy of Lithuania in this way.

*

The days rolled into one. Only the nature changed around them – the trees grew green, birds began to sing, and the grass began to sprout. All they had time for between training sessions was sleep and writing letters home. And walking to the post office.

"Janytė, wait!" shouted Povilas when he saw single sculler Janina Lukošiūnaitė walking ahead of him. Friends often called her Janytė. She had been invited to the USSR team's camp after taking second place in the USSR championships last year. "Hold on!" Povilas said, only catching up to her by running. "What's the matter?"

"Nothing's wrong," she said, looking down and forcing a smile.

"How can nothing be wrong if you're crying?"

Janina looked up at the sky, trying to stop the tears that were coming. Povilas took her arm:

"I'm not crying…"

"What's wrong?"

"Oh…"

"You won't tell me?"

"They told me my documents won't pass…"

"Nevyezdnaja? You too? I've been thrown overboard as well, "vrag naroda[23]." Why'd you get it?"

"A Siberian exile… It's no secret…"

"Really? I hadn't heard… What did you do wrong?"

Janina shrugged and sighed. Her lips began to tremble. What could she do? Explain how her parents had been farmers and had owned land? That their neighbours, out of envy, had labelled them kulaks[24] and fascists working against the Soviet system? She didn't want to remember 22 May, 1948, when she heard that her parents and younger sister and brother had been exiled without the right to return… She only discovered from her loved ones that they had looked for her and her brother as well, questioning people and issuing a warning: "we'll let them go for now d

---

23   Rus. Enemy of the nation.
24   A derogatory Russian term used to refer to peasants and farmers who were better-off than their neighbours.

take them for free this time – next time, they'll have to pay for it." Her mother didn't believe that she would survive so she didn't say a word to her older children – "perhaps at least they'll survive..." Janina and her brother aged eleven and twelve, had been studying at the high school in Pakruojis and living with their uncle at the time. Several long, anxious and fearful months passed before they received a letter from their parents. However, the knowledge that they were still alive comforted and soothed them. Three years passed until her parents finally established a home in Siberia and were able to stand on their own feet. They found a way to invite Janina and her brother so that the whole family could be together. The long journey through Moscow to Krasnoyarsk seemed like it would never end... Her heart still pounded when she remembered seeing the platform of the railroad station in Magansk growing closer through the train window. The platform was full of Lithuanian villagers who had come to meet them, as well as their parents, whose cheeks were covered in tears of joy when they saw how much their children had grown... Nobody called them fascists or bandits there. Over three years, the locals got to know the Lithuanians and learned much from them...

"Where are you from?" asked Povilas, changing the subject when he understood that Janina didn't want to discuss her troubles.

"Zimbiškės, near Linkuva."

"Is it a big village?"

"It was just our farmstead, eighty hectares..."

"How did you return to Lithuania?"

- I returned alone. I decided to enter the athletics institute in Kaunas."

- You were interested in sports?"

- Yeah... I had completed my studies at the athletics technicum[25] in Krasnoyarsk, though I had initially wanted to study geology."

"Did they accept you easily in Kaunas? Did they give you any trouble?"

"No, there weren't any issues. All I had had to do was write a Lithuanian essay and score a three or better."

"And did you?" Povilas smiled.

"I did," Janina smiled back.

"Did your parents stay behind?"

"Why do you ask?"

"Oh, no reason, I was just curious." Seeing that this was a topic Janina

---

25   A technical school .

did not want to discuss, he tried to reassure her: "Don't worry, they might sort everything out yet. I think we'll dig our way out of this. Somehow."

"I don't know…"

"What do you think you'll do next?"

"I don't know… Maybe I'll continue rowing for a bit in Lithuania. After that – we'll see."

"You see, even if you're not an enemy of the nation, they make you do as many qualifications as it takes until they can take the Russians instead of the Lithuanians."

*

When there was only one week left until the end of the camp, Alfa was sidelined as well. Juozas took his place in the bow seat.

"What did I tell you, Povilas? I knew they'd mess with me as well."

"Welcome to the Enemies of the Nation club!" smiled Povilas as he patted his friend on the back. "We could row an 'Enemies of the Nation' pair if we weren't both bowside[26]," he tried to joke.

"I think they'll find us some friends. If not an eight, then at least enough for a four," said Alfa, also trying to keep from slipping into depression.

"It'll be interesting to see who they are," laughed Povilas. "It would be so nice to have a clear-cut crew, to simply practise and know that you're getting your medal because of your accomplishments rather than your politics. I wish my former friends wouldn't stare at me coldly like I was some sort of criminal. I've suffered enough but they keep on punishing me…"

"Nonsense, nobody thinks any less of you. Everyone's afraid for himself or herself. Any one of us might be thrown overboard."

"You know, Alfa, I feel like I'm surrounded by a barbed wire fence…"

"We all are, all of Lithuania is…"

*

---

26   Bowsides row on the starboard (right-hand) side of the boat.

4

There was barely any snow left by the beginning of April, but there were still ice floes floating down the Neris.

There were whispers among more intelligent folk that the Catholics had lost another church – the church of St. Michael the Archangel in Kaunas. The soldiers had taken it on 16 March tearing out its treasures and altar throwing it all into the street.

Soviet television began to play the Mosfilm comedy "The Girls." Communist poet Eduardas Mieželaitis was the first in Lithuania to receive the Lenin prize for his book of poetry. The Vladimir Lenin All-Union Pioneer Organisation celebrated its 40th anniversary.

The world of sports had its own separate life as well. Lithuania's swimmers received their first Master of Sports and the first motor racing car – the Estonia-3 – arrived in the Republic.

When the rowers returned from their camp, they found everyone else practising in the winter rowing tank. There was still more than a month left until the next competition. They were hurrying to catch up with their classmates, so they spent their days in the libraries and auditoriums and their evenings at the boathouse.

*

When he returned home, Povilas found Gita wearing a much wider dress. There were less than four months left until the baby was due to arrive. In two to three weeks, they expected to hear the cooing of her sister Vanda's child as well.

Their home, full of love and life, felt as safe as a fortress protected by her strong, wise mother. No matter where they were, everybody wanted to return home for another visit.

It had been fifteen years since Gita's family had moved here – since fleeing Tauragnai after the war, selling their previous home for a ham and packing only what would fit in their wagon. There were many people from Tauragnai living in Vilnius who had fled the terror of the post-war years – when one force would come from the city by day and another would come from the forests by night. Back then many homes on Čiurlionis Street had been destroyed by shelling, and the university had been converted into a military hospital.

If you turned off of Čiurlionis Street, which old-timers still called Pogulianka, onto Sierakausko Street alongside the university building, you approached a gate that opened into a large yard. Right behind the gate, there was a low door leading to a long, wide corridor with several apartments on each side. The windowsills of the apartments were level with the pavement outside, so all that could be seen through the windows were tree trunks and the shoes of passers-by. The apartments were restored by German military prisoners, deployed to rebuild the destroyed buildings on Čiurlionis Street and the university building. These hungry prisoners would beg Gita's mother for potato peels, and she felt so bad for them that she often gave them soup as well. The men told her, as much as they could without knowing the language, about their families and their homes, showing her photos as they wiped tears from their eyes.

Her mother had a cow at the time that the children herded in Vingis Park. Gita's father had also brought a horse from Tauragnai and left it out to pasture in the park; but it was gone by the following morning. It was lucky they didn't need it in the city. After the war, things got even harder. Food was issued with ration cards, and everyone got a slice of bread a day. Their shoes and clothing had to be altered as they outgrew them. Her father got a plot of land on the outskirts of the city and used it to grow potatoes, cabbages and beets. Her mother, like all their neighbours, maintained a small garden near their home on a slope from which she could see Žvėrynas and the Neris, growing carrots, herbs and flowers.

The older children – Genutė and Bronius – had left their parents' home and were living independently, but they still visited at least once a week.

"Hey, Povilas! Long time no see!" said Bronius, glad to see that Povilas had returned. "When did you get back? Are you back for good this time?"

"I got back on Friday. I'm going to stay home for a while now."

"You're so tanned! How was Georgia?"

"I didn't see much of it, to be honest. I rowed and rowed. It's so warm and sunny there, and the trees are already budding."

"How's your eight?"

"It's not mine anymore. I'm going to be in the pair or four. We'll see."

"Why? What happened?"

"I'd rather not, Bronius…"

"Oh come on, what's the matter? Are you going to keep secrets from me?"

From the day they first met, he and Gita's brother Bronius felt like brothers. Bronius was four years older than him, but they still found things to talk about and got along well.

Povilas looked around to see whether anyone would overhear him. When he saw that Povilas wanted to speak in private, Bronius threw a coat over his shoulders, grabbed his own coat, and nodded towards the door: "Let's go outside," he said, shouting to the women in the house: "We're going out for a breath of air!"

The two men left and turned towards the slope. They could see the Neris River bend, the bridge, and the wooden houses of Žvėrynas through the trees. Small patches of snow still dotted the slope.

Bronius looked around to make sure nobody could hear them.

"Well?"

"My past came back to haunt me…," Povilas said in a hushed tone, before had even decided whether he actually wanted to tell Bronius everything.

"What do you mean?"

"I'm apparently nevyezdnoj. The eight is preparing to go to America but they won't let me go. I'm politically untrustworthy, vrag naroda. They've thrown me overboard…"

"What did you do? Tell me!" Bronius asked anxiously.

"I didn't do anything wrong. It's all because of my parents…"

"But they're dead, aren't they? You told Gita they died during the war…"

"That's basically true…," said Povilas, trailing off as a lump rose in his throat.

"Povilas, who can you speak to about this if not us? Sit down, let's talk."

They were surrounded by silence. Povilas wrestled with his emotions. He choked on his words. Bronius waited patiently until Povilas calmed down.

"It's a long story, Bronius…"

"I have time. Tell me."

"The partisans[27] and *stribai* crossed paths at our home on Christmas…"

"In Prienai?"

"Near Prienai. We lived in Rūdupis with our parents. Juozas, Elzbieta, Kazys, Onutė and I. Elzbieta and Kazimieras were in high school. When the Russians came, in '45, Elzbieta's teacher left for the woods. Elzbieta became a partisan liaison. Initially, nobody in our home knew about this. When they did find out, they weren't very supportive of it… after that, she began frequently inviting them into our home. The most frequent visitors were Kazys Bartulis and Pranas Kazlauskas. Elzbieta was probably too friendly with some people, both in conversations and letters. There were difficult times ahead."

"I know, I know, it was the same with us in Tauragnai. During the night, one side would come from the woods with guns. They took everything – shoes, sausages. They knew we had them. Our neighbour probably told them. During the day, the other side came, stood our father up against the wall, and threatened to shoot him. That's why they decided to leave the village as quickly as possible."

"We didn't make it in time… or maybe my parents didn't think we'd need to run, though our relatives from my mother's side had already moved to the West. I remember that when the Germans retreated, the entire village of Tartokas moved towards us – the Germans were preparing for a fight. Our family moved towards Rūdupis forest as well and spent the night in a large gulch with high banks that the Rūdupis creek flowed through. I couldn't hear anything, but they later told me how much shooting there had been and how the mines started exploding when the Russians came. We left with our wagon, with the cows tied to it, through Bagrėnas and Strielčiai to Čiudiškiai, to my mother's homeland. We barely found anyone home. My mother's cousins – Bronius, a former pilot, and Alfonsas – were ready to leave for the West. They taught us how to dig a bunker so that no bullets or shrapnel would get through, and to make the entrance in the side. A few days later, there was a battle at night. In the morning, we saw Russian tanks with machine gunners on them thundering through the fields. Then, we returned home. We saw the chimneys of burnt homes and fields of grain trampled by tank treads. Luckily for us, all of the homesteads in our village were

---

27   The Lithuanian partisans, also known as "Forest Brothers," were freedom fighters who resisted the Soviet occupation of Lithuania from 1944 until 1953, with some remaining active until the 1960s.

fine. At night, they bombed the brewery, the sawmill and two mills… Uncle Bliokas worked at the brewery. He lived there with my aunt. They were left homeless and came to live with us. They slept in the barn. Every morning, my aunt left to work in Prienai, but my uncle no longer had a job… Later, in autumn, they moved to Prienai. My uncle began to work for a carpenter who made various types of furniture. He kept working until, one day, they took him away to a concentration camp somewhere near Kalinin… Ah, I seem to have gone off track, Bronius," said Povilas, recomposing himself after having gotten lost in his memories.

"Keep talking, I'm curious about all of it," Bronius encouraged him.

"Alright. Eventually, the Christmas of '45 came. The partisans decided who would be celebrating where. Kazys, Pranas and a few other guys came to us. Nobody could ambush us so the partisans felt safe. Christmas Eve passed quietly and the adults left for the church in Prienai in the morning, returning for lunch. My aunt Konstancija came over from Prienai, too. After lunch, a woman named Sofija Radžiukaitė paid us a visit. She didn't stay long, but my aunt became very agitated and wanted to go home at once, so my father took her home in the wagon. People said that Sofija had reported her husband to the *stribai* because of his ties with the partisans, and they jailed him. Many suspected the Radžiukai family, so everybody avoided them."

"So they were snitches?"

"Yeah – you could be sure trouble would follow wherever they went. But God punished them…"

"What happened next?"

"We – the kids – skated around on frozen spring water at the bottom of the hill until it grew dark. When it grew dark, Povilas Tamošiūnas, my father's sister's husband from Tartokas, came. They celebrated Christmas under the light of a gas lamp. Nobody noticed that the home had been surrounded by *stribai*. Suddenly, somebody shouted 'Russians!' The partisans ran to the attic, and some hid behind the house. The *stribai* might not have noticed anything when they entered, but they saw a few slices of bread on the table and began shouting in Russian. I didn't understand Russian at the time. Then, they instructed my mother to climb the ladder to the attic. I heard her say 'I probably won't be climbing down this ladder again…' Then, I heard an automatic weapon go off. My mother swayed and Tamošiūnas grabbed her and took her outside. A flame ignited and a firefight began…"

"Bastards!" Bronius cried.

"After that, the Russians ordered my father to burn his own barn. I can still see now how his hands trembled, when he took a bundle of straw and had to burn what he had built and cared for with his own hands…"

Povilas grew quiet. He could see the young partisans' faces right before his eyes. His brother Kazys' classmates had gone into the woods[28] as well. As a child, they seemed like grown men. But they were only about sixteen years old… Twenty years after those terrible events, Kazys' classmate Justinas[29] brought this to light in his poetry: "Sixteen-year-olds, sixteen-year-olds, born in 1930, young and beautiful, slim as trees, took guns into their child-like hands."

"Our entire home was ablaze. My sister Onutė, two years old, was in Tamošiūnas' arms, swaddled in our mother's cotton clothing. When he had placed her on the ground, she said, 'uncle, my feet are cold.' That's when he noticed that she was barefoot." Povilas' voice trembled as he buried his face in his palms and began to sob.

Bronius pressed held his hand to his mouth and waited. He didn't want to pressure Povilas.

Eventually, Povilas brushed the tears from his eyes and continued:

"There had been a lot of uncle Kazys' uniforms and medals at home – he had been a colonel. The *stribai* thought they had destroyed a big partisans' hideout. They took the bodies away in three wagons. After that, they stood us in a line, tied us up and took us to the *stribai* office in Prienai. That's where we spent the night. We, the little ones, spent the night in the room next to the *stribai* on the floor, and I don't know where the others went. In the morning, they called Aunt Konstancija and gave the three of us to her and she took us home. We buried my mother three days later. Only our burnt home and well were left, and plenty of wild pears. Because of that day, Christmas became the saddest day of the year…"

"How about your father?"

"My father and Elzbieta were convicted and exiled to the concentration camp in Ukhta for ten years, and they added five years of deportation as well. That was where my father died – he didn't survive in the camp for long. My sister was moved from the Ukhta camp to Voyvozh and then to Balkhash. She was released from there and married a Lithuanian. She had

---

28   A Lithuanian euphemism for joining the partisan ranks.
29   Justinas Marcinkevičius, a famous Lithuanian poet.

two sons – Gediminas and Algirdas. Kazys and Juozas settled down in Balkhash as well when their service in the Soviet army ended."

"Forgive me, Povilas, I didn't know that it had all been so bad. Good thing you told me. Why should you carry that burden alone?"

"There it is. That was the end of my happy days, when we herded cows in my parents' fields, played with our neighbours' kids, and went outside."

"Where did your aunt live? She wasn't in the same village?"

"No, my aunt lived in Prienai, in an attic apartment with a room and a kitchen. She locked it when she left for work. My brother Kazys went to high school, and she'd only let me out into the street when he returned."

"Why did she lock you up?"

"I think she was afraid that we might see the partisans' bodies laid out in the market square for the bolsheviks to mock... or maybe so the children of *stribai* wouldn't beat us... If only you'd seen what the Russians did with the dead – you'd never forget it... We still once managed to see dead men whom we had known... they were disheveled, naked, their eyes were poked out, and still the *stribai* walked by them and kicked them... Juozas and I always made plans to get revenge for our mother, always crying quietly... Until they took him..."

"Who took him?"

"Our other aunt... after a few weeks, she came and asked whether either of us would like to live in Strielčiai. Juozas offered to go because our aunt bred rabbits there. Then, only Onutė and I were left, with our memories of stoking the fire, herding cows, and popping bullets in the fire. Our little cottage life continued like this until I brought home a cow from the Tamošiūnai in the spring. I had to take it to pasture outside of the city in the hills, walk it through the woods, and herd it. I met many new friends whilst I was out with the cow."

"How did the story end with the partisans?"

"The story goes that, whilst our house burned, Pranas crawled along the field towards the Nemunas. After making it to the Rūdupis forest, he lay by the road. On the second day of Christmas, a woman on the way to church found him and took him to somebody's house. He had been shot fourteen times, he died two weeks later."

"Did somebody finish off the snitches afterward?" Bronius asked angrily.

"I heard that they killed Klemensas Radžiukas with a five-kilo weight to the temple in their barn. The wife and the son were shot with a pistol. After some time, they shot Sofija Radžiukas and their middle son, Justinas. Only the youngest son was left, Levas. They didn't just snitch on us. They had betrayed many partisans."

"I don't know what to say, Povilas…"

"I haven't told Gita everything. At first, I was afraid that she'd leave me. Now, I don't want to worry her."

"Nonsense! There's nothing to be afraid or ashamed of! You know what? We're your family and we'll always be with you. You're like a brother to me. If you need anything – to talk or whatever – just ask."

"Ok, Bronius. What I'd want is to forget everything, but I can't escape it. I have to visit my aunt and uncle in Prienai, and that's where the memories always return. I visit my mother's grave, cry for her, visit the old pear tree in Rūdupis, visit my old neighbours…"

"What will happen now with your rowing?"

"I'll keep rowing. Perhaps this will be temporary. We just got married, so maybe they'll let me go more easily if my family is here."

"Sure. You think they're afraid you'll escape?"

"Who knows what they're afraid of… I'd like to continue competing. I'd hate to just drop everything, I've worked too hard for it. After all, my body needs it, I'm used to hard work. You know what's the worst, though? How you're forced to fight your way through that barbed-wire fence to defend the occupier's honour. That's the worst thing…"

The men grew quiet as they watched the Neris flow around the bend. Povilas' hands and shoulders grew tense, as if he was rowing on the water. He had rowed along the Neris so often that it seemed like he knew every ripple, every bend in the riverbank. He could feel the eddies pushing the boat's stern and hear the wind whistling in his ears as he rowed downstream… He rarely rowed to these reaches. Normally he would row upstream towards the city's northern suburbs, and return downstream.

However, he could distinctly remember one incident as he looked at this, the penultimate bend in the Neris. He had recently begun rowing and the educational institute had bought a new plywood eight made in Riga. There were few skiffs back then, so they primarily rowed with wide and heavy training boats. The new, elegant boat, smelling of lacquer, became the crew's pride and joy, and they cared for it like a child. After the university Spartakiad[30], they left the eight in Trakai because, at almost 20 metres in length, there weren't any vehicles available to take the boat back. Coach Zinkevičius, however, was insistent it got back to Vilnius. They say the young are too foolish to know when something's impossible, but the young rowers decided to row the boat back to Vilnius. There had been many previous springs when athletes transported boats from Vilnius to Trakai, but they had never made the trip back against the current. They took a map, studied it, and decided that they could row from Trakai to the Neris by water, there would only be a short distance they would need to carry it. And so, one Sunday morning in September, they departed on a journey that had never been travelled before. After leaving the camp, they turned off to the east between a peninsula and a small island a few hundred metres away, entering Skaistis lake. The rowers knew this lake very well – every curve and island. It was less than 5 kilometres to the end of the lake. After crossing Skaistis Lake, they walked along the bank and pushed their boat through the narrow Tiškevičius Canal towards Didžiulis Lake. There, they could continue rowing, though not for long – about a kilometre. With that, they had covered 12 kilometres by water and carried the boat for two kilometres through Grigiškės on their shoulders with their oars in their free hands. Upon reaching the Neris River, they once again crewed their boat and rowed to Vilnius – against the current. Initially they rowed six at a time so two could take turns resting. The fast-flowing Neris was a real challenge, even for men as strong as they were. Stopping was not an option, as this would immediately carry them back. After rowing about sixteen kilometres along the Neris, they reached Vingis Park. On that particular Sunday, there was a festival taking place in the park. After enjoying some kefir and bread at the festival, they rowed back to the camp. They had travelled 20 kilometres to this bend in the Neris. Beyond, they could see Žvėrynas Bridge and the spires of Vilnius. The last three and a half kilometres seemed like they would never end, but the thought of quitting never crossed their minds. The journey was as unforgettable as it was difficult.

*

---

30   The Spartakiad was an international Soviet athletic competition that was later held nationally in Eastern block countries as well. It was considered the Soviet Union's response to the Olympics.

5

On 22 May, all of the best rowers from Vilnius and Kaunas gathered at these cities' competition in Trakai. The traditional competition between Lithuania's largest cities ended with a victory for Vilnius. The two cities' specialisations became readily apparent – the Vilnius rowers won all of the sweep oar races and the Kaunas rowers won all of the sculling races, except for the women's pair.

The next morning, the men of the Žalgiris eight left for Leningrad – without Povilas and Alfa. The Moscow-Leningrad race would be held that weekend in Kavgolovo, and this race would also serve as a qualifying race. The winners would leave for Philadelphia, in America, the land of dreams. The second-place team would travel to the Henley Royal Regatta in England. In addition to the Žalgiris eight, single sculler Janina also left for the competition.

That same Saturday, 26 May, was also the first "Amber Oars" competition for fours, where crews would race for the "Komsomol Truth[31]" prize.

The rowers had been very keen to support and promote the "Amber Oar" regatta, and without setting out to do so, they became the godfathers of a new international regatta. In late autumn, before all the commotion surrounding the Žalgiris eight's victory in Kiev had died down, the entire team was invited to an interview at the Editorial Office of the "Komsomol Truth" newspaper. The editor, Joana Civilkaitė, could barely fit the men into her small office. They had a full discussion: everything from their victory, their team, their dreams and their plans. It was all new and interesting to the journalist. During the interview, Zigmas set out his dream of an international regatta in Trakai in Lithuania. The editor was immediately interested: "What sort of help do you need?" Of course, the most important issue was that of prizes, because the rowers had everything else – a lake, boats, umpires and the energy to make it

---

31   Lit. Komjaunimo Tiesa – A Lithuanian Communist Youth (Komsomol) newspaper.

happen. Each member of the editorial staff promised to help the men in any way they could to found a new rowing competition in Lithuania.

Only half a year later, crews from Lithuania, Latvia, Moldavia, Belarus and Georgia gathered in Lithuania for the first "Amber Oars" regatta. The event was only for coxed fours at first, but they believed anything was possible – perhaps every class of boat would compete in the regatta in the future. What's more, the teams' scullers felt short-changed as they would have to row sweep boats or watch the race from the shoreline. Or they could race as coxes, which is what sculler Sofija did when she joined a four crew that had been made by splitting the Žalgiris women's eight into two fours. "Komsomol Truth", as promised, provided the prizes. The trophies were odd black wooden rectangles with stylized boats made of real amber and four metal oars with amber paddles and amber waves, commissioned exclusively for the competition. Each had the "Komsomol Truth"'s name stamped on it, just like on the upper right-hand corner of the newspaper's front page.

Nine women's teams and eight men's teams fought for the right to compete in the final.

Having stayed behind in Lithuania, Povilas and Alfa competed in a four with Romas and Vitalijus – a canoe Master of Sports. Vitalijus wasn't the only athlete to have traded in his paddle and canoe for an oar and boat. James, who had paddled a canoe during his time at the Polytechnicum, had also made the jump from canoeing to rowing.

On the first day of the competition, the rain that had been drenching the rowers in training cleared up and the final races were greeted with a sunny sky. Galvė Lake was as smooth as glass.

The Vilnius men's four won by a huge margin – 9 seconds – against the Kaunas team, receiving the first "Amber Oars." They, as first winners of the Amber Oars, would go down as a part of the regatta's history – as long as that history was to extend beyond this first regatta.

The following day, Vilnius was hit by a hail storm. Boats left out of the boathouses were barraged by huge balls of ice, up to 3-5 centimetre. Flowers and newly-sprouting tree leaves were mercilessly ripped apart by the rain of ice. The local children, however, enjoyed the occasion – when the storm ended, they could enjoy some of the winter fun they had missed, albeit briefly.

In the mean time, the Žalgiris eight in Kavgolovo had a serious battle with the Moscow and Leningrad teams, but managed to secure a victory – and the journey to America that they had been dreaming of. But not all of them... Before they had even managed to make it home, their team was presented with another new member.

*

"Hello, Celestinas. What are you doing here?" Povilas asked, surprised to see his teammate at the Trakai camp, flipping through Švyturys, a monthly magazine. "What are they saying?"

"There's an article here about the eight. Didn't you read it?" he answered, turning the page to an article entitled "Eight Strong-Willed Men."

Povilas saw the photo first.

"They've already got Dima smiling there in my place," he noticed. "Did they praise us?"

"Yeah. There's a lot about our victory in Kiev, and all of the last names have been mentioned. They've written something about everyone, including you. Listen: 'accounting specialist in training P. Liutkaitis is also interested in photography,'" Celestinas read out loud. "Here's another bit, 'D. Semionov sometimes takes Liutkaitis' place when he can't race.'"

"I see, whenever I can't race... Whenever they don't let me race! That is, they don't let me at all... But wait, why are you here?"

"They left me here to keep you company, Povilas," Celestinas sighed.

"They took you out, too?"

"Yup."

"Why?"

"The same as you..."

"Nevyezdnoj?"

"That's it."

"When did you guys return?"

"Yesterday," said Celestinas, who didn't seem very talkative.

"Who took your place?"

"Tchiorstwij from Trud. Remember him? He had thick hair, about my height, a bit older."

"Son of a bitch," Povilas swore. "But you raced, didn't you?"

"I did. After the win, they came and said I was free to go, that they wouldn't take me because my documents didn't make the cut."

"So, what now?"

"They said I'd be in the coxed pair with you for now, and maybe in the four with Alfa and Romas," Celestinas responded shyly.

"Wonderful! We'll show them what we can do, Celestinas, don't let them get you down!" Povilas reassured him. "Why didn't you pass?"

"My grandpa's in America. My mother's father."

"I see… They're afraid that you'll run away, too," Povilas reasoned. "I thought perhaps your parents were in Siberia."

"They almost were," Celestinas offered shyly. "Why didn't they let you go?"

"That's a long story, Celestinas. It'll bore you. When are we going to try the boat out?" asked Povilas, changing the subject.

"We could try it today. I'm ready," Celestinas responded, his face brightening up.

"When are the others coming back?"

"They're still seeing all the different party committees about their papers."

"Nobody else from our team got pulled out?"

"I don't know. I heard that they hassled James, but I guess he got everything in order if he stayed in the boat."

The months that followed were an ordinary summer for the rowers at the Žalgiris camp in Trakai. From the very beginning of spring, the area off to the side of Trakai Castle was full of rowers from throughout Lithuania. It wasn't clear when one camp was ending and another was beginning. Rowers came and went. The shore began to grow crowded, as did the lake itself. Rowboats, kayaks, canoes and yachts plied the water from morning until evening.

The shore of the lake was littered with sculling boats, pairs, fours and eights. The peninsula that belonged to the rowers was surrounded by Galvė Lake on two sides, and the third side was the beginning of Bernardinai Lake. The base was a large wooden building with rooms installed in all three of its floors and the attic. As athletes moved in, the building gained a busy, youthful atmosphere. The windowsills and railings were covered in drying kit. The outdoor stairs had four large columns that gave the building a look of stability and importance. Upon entering, there were doors to the main hall that held about twenty beds. Between the wars, when the building had been a yacht club, this hall had been used to dry sails.

On the side of the peninsula where Galvė Lake met Bernardinai Lake, there was a square to the rear end of the building which was the main location for opening and closing competitions, for the role calls, and to hold celebrations. Sometimes, in the spring, the water would rise so high that the entire square would find itself underwater together with the stairs along both sides of the south face of the building and leading to the hall-turned-bedroom.

There was a wooden finish tower built right next to the building – a small windowed hut on wooden columns with wooden stairs for judges and photo-journalists.

It was less than 100 metres from the peninsula to the town's shoreline, but reaching the other shore was only possible by rowing across in a fisherman's boat rowed by the athletes themselves. There was plenty of incentive to not be late returning from their "shore leave," as they would have to sleep on the opposite shore, swim across with their clothing tied on their heads, or walk 5 kilometres along the shore.

The athletes also had to ferry themselves across to the other side to eat – three times a day – at the cafeteria near the church. Whether they wanted to or not, the rowers were always rowing. The starting bridge, a long pontoon with six "tongues" protruding from the side, would be stored in the cafeteria during the autumn, and it was only in early spring, when the bridge was still on the course, that the rowers could cross to the other side by foot.

They used lake water to bathe and do their laundry, drying their clothing on railings, headboards and ropes stretched across the ceiling on their rooms.

On the northern shore of the peninsula, two large wooden boathouses stood next to one another at ninety-degree angles. Their doors formed a small shared square, down the centre of which was a pair of tracks for lowering motorboats and sailboats into the lake.

Two long pontoons stretched from the shore towards the castle that were connected into a large H by a third. The boats often arrived and left from these pontoons. They were always busy with men and women hurrying to and fro with long wooden oars in their hands, exchanging shy glances and witty jokes as they passed one another. Another smaller pontoon for smaller boats was extended into the cove. The other shore of the cove had pontoons with sailboats moored to them.

Hammering could often be heard off beyond the boathouses. There, shelters were being built for boats that didn't fit into the boathouses in preparation for the USSR Championships, which was to be held here in early September.

The boathouses were almost always open. Coaches would spend any free moment they had there to repair, polish and adjust the boats and their oars. The wooden house didn't have enough room for all of the athletes who came, so some had to stay in tents that they put up towards Nerespinka Lake.

There was a basketball basket mounted on the rear wall of the boathouse facing the main building. In the evenings, the men would gather there to play basketball.

The spectators' grandstands lined up on the shoreline were where many of the athletes would spend their evenings watching the sun set behind the castle, sharing gossip, jokes, and striking up relationships that sometimes blossomed into love.

Once a month, and sometimes more often, the location hosted various competitions. The two-kilometre race course on the lake fit perfectly in between the shorelines and islands.

The spectators' "home stretch" of 250 metres could be reached by hand. During races, the shorelines and grandstands were filled with spectators. The shade under the large trees on the peninsula would fill up with various structures as the competitors tried to place their slings as close to the water as possible.

The members of the Lithuanian team wore their green track suits with the word "Lietuva" on them with pride. Others had to make do with blue wool track suits with zippers and white stripes on the collars from the store.

*

6

The men's eight left for Jelgava almost as soon as they returned from Leningrad. There, they could look forward to intense preparations for the competition between the USSR and United States of America in Philadelphia. On 4 July – USA's Independence Day – there would be a regatta featuring America's greatest teams and the USSR's rowers – the eight, the single scull and the double scull.

The two Russians who had replaced the Lithuanians tried to adapt to the team. The Russian rowing style was very different to that Ričardas had been teaching, so they had to spend all of June changing their technique to fine-tune the crew's precision and preserve the crew spirit.

The sports officials, and politicians also prepared intensively for the departure of the first Soviet athletic delegation to the USA. All of the rowers' biographies had been analysed under a microscope – recommendations were gathered and Komsomol and Party approval was secured. Meetings were held to teach them what to say, when to say it, and how certain questions had to be answered. Some athletes had to fill out their forms all over again, explaining certain circumstances, naming relatives who lived overseas and family members who had been deported, signing oaths, and joining the Komsomol. KGB officials scoured the men's home towns to root out any links with the partisan or anti-Communist movements. They interrogated local residents, neighbours and even passers-by about the men's histories, about their worldviews, and about their loyalty to the Soviet Union. Even Antanas, who had been on numerous excursions to the West – Germany, Italy, and Czechoslovakia – wasn't safe. KGB officials visited his hometown of Bobėnai and spent almost a month there.

With only a few days left before their departure, the team's coxswain, Gerdas, was replaced by a Russian from Leningrad's Trud team named Yuri Lorentsson. Nobody could say, or nobody wanted to say, why Gerdas had been replaced. All that Ričardas, who was powerless before the Russian "selection" system, could do was apologize to Gerdas. The young boy, who had never yet experienced such an injustice, found it difficult to understand why he, someone who had led the team to victory on more than one occasion, was being replaced by a Russian. Was it because he was older? More experienced? Was it because he was a Russian? He took the injustice to heart and it stayed with him for the rest of his life.

*

The Lithuanian SSR Championships took place in Trakai on 26 June, while the Žalgiris team was still waiting for the issue of their visas in Moscow with their bags packed.

Povilas and Celestinas' coxed pair received no serious challenges at the event. The Kaunas rowers who took second place finished 31 seconds behind them.

"Our work paid off, Celestinas."

"So what?" retorted Celestinas, letting his resentment show.

"What do you mean 'so what?' We worked all winter, so now we can finally see the results!" said Povilas, surprised by his friend's apathy.

"I left my university because of our winter… No scholarship and nothing to show for all of this work… I should've stayed in school. Now I've been cast overboard on both fronts… I don't know how I'll survive."

"It sucks, Celestinas, but we'll survive. This is all temporary. Our turn will come. In my second year, I worked nights at the bread store loading bread. When I went to training, I'd only slept an hour. Then I went to my classes and then back to training. Of course, I wouldn't want to repeat all of that now, but we can do that if we have to – it won't kill us."

"You're incredible, Povilas. The worse things get, the happier you seem to be," Celestinas smiled.

"Good work, boys!" said Povilas, extending his hand to Eugenijus as he passed them by. "That was a great run, you won by almost 250 metres."

Eugenijus had raced in a coxless pair with Romas Šarmaitis, who had been his crewmate since they had gone to school together.

"Thank you, thank you, congratulations to you guys, too, you did no less," Eugenijus smiled. "We're all doing pretty well. Medals for everyone."

"I heard they changed the rules, that they won't hand out medals to people who lag behind by too much when placing," Celestinas added.

"That's right," Eugenijus agreed. "Did you see the women's race? The

Kaunas eight barely made it to the finish line. Third out of three. Why should they get a medal?"

"The quality of the competition has fallen. And they're not even here..."

"Why aren't you with them, Celestinas?" Eugenijus asked, surprised.

"Povilas and I are nevyezdnoj."

"I heard," Eugenijus answered angrily. "My brother and I are, too."

"You guys too?" Povilas jumped up. "I couldn't understand why Ričardas wouldn't take you into the eight. Why?"

"Forget it," Eugenijus waved the question off. Regardless of how much he trusted his friends, he couldn't tell them that his uncle, his father's brother, had been a Lithuanian military pilot and that nobody knew where he currently was. Nobody could find his grave. They were afraid that he was alive somewhere in the USA or Canada. Nor could he tell them that his father had been avoiding being shot by living in the forests in his homeland. He had been sentenced to death by a Russian military tribunal because his friend was discovered with a pistol when a Russian officer had been shot in Vėpriai where they lived. They were only children at the time, who hadn't seen their father in two years, but the NKVD agents still kept asking them – "Where is your father?" His family had escaped to Vilnius in the hope of hiding from their persecutors and their constant fear...

"Why'd they take you out?"

"Because I'm an orphan," Povilas smiled sadly.

"I'm sorry, Povilas," Eugenijus asked, embarrassed.

"That was a long time ago, Eugenijus. I'm just angry that I can't go anywhere."

"What will you guys do?"

"We're training in a four for the Union. With Alfa and Romas. We're waiting until Romas defends his diploma to start training."

"How's Gita?" asked Eugenijus.

"She might give birth soon. I'm afraid of being away somewhere when she'll need to go to the hospital. I go home every day. After the award ceremony, I'm heading off straight to Vilnius."

"I see," Eugenijus smiled. He shook the men's hands and turned to leave. "Give her my regards!"

"Of course! Right away!" said Povilas. "Well, Celestinas? We rest tomorrow and then get back in that boat again? Do you have the schedule?"

"No, I don't. Ričardas told it to you."

"Me? I wrote it down, but I thought I gave it to you. It was a green notebook. Maybe I gave it to Alfa... Have you seen him?"

"I saw him next to the boathouse about half an hour ago. Let's go, we'll ask him about the camp."

There was about half an hour left until the competition ended, so the men were in no hurry to find their teammate. Alfa was the eldest and had was doubling up as coach until Ričardas returned from America with the eight.

"Alfa, what are you doing?" the men asked, surprised to find Alfa next to the four with a tape measure in his hand.

"I'm rigging it now so we won't have to later," said Alfa. He was hard-working and precise, and could spend hours measuring, calculating and adjusting a boat.

"Do you have the schedule?"

"I do. Do you need it?"

"Not necessarily, but now we know where it is. You won't forget to bring it to the camp, will you?"

"I won't... There's a problem with the camp. We'll have a room but there won't be any food."

"What do you mean no food?"

"Ričardas didn't have time to organise it," Alfa responded with a look of guilt.

Celestinas and Povilas looked at one another. They couldn't believe what they were hearing.

"They couldn't give a damn about us!" said Celestinas, unable to hide his disappointment.

"That's right, Celestinas. They've left for America and we're left with nothing. I thought we were a team," Povilas agreed. "I'm an enemy of the state, you see."

"So how are we supposed to prepare for competitions now?"

"Relax, guys, we'll think of something. Or we'll bring some home cooking," Alfa reassured them as if he was guilty of the misunderstanding himself.

"Are you serious?" laughed Povilas. "What do you think... did they do this on purpose?"

"Of course not, Povilas, it just happened this way," said Alfa, trying to reassure him. "I'll try to talk to the Žalgiris administrators tomorrow."

The young men focused on overcoming their anger and sense of hurt.

"Let's go, Celestinas, we won't give up like this. We've seen worse, haven't we?" Povilas patted Celestinas on the back as they turned to leave.

"Let's meet on Tuesday, Alfa," Celestinas said before they turned off towards the ending ceremony.

During the parade, the two men couldn't hide the dejection in their faces. When their names were announced, the rowers next to them had to nudge them with their elbows to snap them out of their melancholia. Medals were the last things on their minds. They didn't want to believe that they had both been written off like that.

While the athletic directors delivered their speeches, Povilas had an idea:

"Listen, Celestinas. Let's go to the tourist camp and ask the wonderful ladies to boil some extra porridge for their tourists."

"Are you serious?"

"Yeah, they usually have too much food as it is. We'll bring them some candy as a gift."

"I don't know, Povilas…"

"Nobody's going to offer us anything if we don't ask for it!"

"You want to go now?" Celestinas asked doubtfully

"Now's the best time. Why delay? It'll be a load off of our minds if we know that we'll be able to train properly. Otherwise, we'll just have two more days of stress."

The tourist camp was a stone's throw away. After crossing the dock and the several-metre-wide strait between the Bernardinai and Nerespinka lakes, they reached a beautiful field. On the hill in the centre of the field stood the tourist camp, a wooden building that had seen more than a few winters. A row of white tents that had been erected for visitors stood behind it. The men had known the staff in the kitchen for ages – from before their famous victory, when they trained and skied along the lakes. The women loved the tall, beautiful rowers. They were happy to see the kitchen manager because they didn't think they'd find her at work on a Sunday. They didn't have to be too persuasive. The woman was proud to know USSR champions personally, so she listened and didn't take long to make a decision: "Come by when the visitors' hours are over. You'll be able to take what's left. Just don't tell anyone. How many of you will there be? Four?"

"It's not a good feeling, Povilas. It's like begging," said Celestinas when they left. He felt uncomfortable.

"I know, it's terrible, but sometimes you've got to fight for yourself. I never got anything easily in my life," Povilas agreed.

*

On 4 July, the Žalgiris men's team won the eight race by a large margin in Philadelphia in front of a crowd of several thousand people including US senators. This was a country where rowing was focussed on almost entirely on the eights and in the city where American independence was declared in 1776. The stunned spectators were witnesses to a crushing "Russian" victory. The Soviet press had a field day with the symbolic significance of the victory. This was more than just a sporting victory – it was a victory in the battle between two opposing nations. For a country that had nothing to show the world but military force and Gagarin's space flight, the simple Lithuanian rowers raised the USSR's prestige in Americans' eyes to new heights. Of course, nobody knew that they were Lithuanians, and nobody knows if anyone was interested that they were. However, the men did all they could in their broken English to convince everyone that they weren't Russian.

During their visit, all doors were open to the men of Žalgiris and to John B. Kelly, who was responsible for escorting them. Wherever they showed up, they'd hear whispers – "It's Kelly and his Russian boys" – and the crowd would part.

The USSR's Ambassador to the US, Anatoly Dobrynin, couldn't contain his elation: "In one race, you men have done more than our embassy did in ten years." He sent a telegram from America to Vilnius to CPSU[32] Central Committee secretary, Antanas Sniečkus, to thank the Lithuanian rowers and to express the value of their victory.

Upon their return to Lithuania, the men were met by their loved ones alone, but after the Ambassador's telegram, the country's sports officials sprang into action. The men of Žalgiris were showered with praise and awards. Every one of them received their own apartment. The men had never received that many ovations, commendations, awe and praise in their lives, so it was no wonder that some of them felt like they stood a head taller than their teammates who had stayed behind in Lithuania.

---

32   Communist Party of the Soviet Union

Back in Trakai, Povilas, Celestinas, Romas and Alfa were rowing their four, hurrying off in between training sessions along the pontoon to the tourist camp to recoup their energy with leftover food. Thanks to the gracious chefs, they had plenty, but they still had the sinking feeling that they had been thrown overboard. They had to make due with scraps like common beggars.

Though the men hadn't spent long training in the four, the boat moved quickly and easily. It raised their spirits and their confidence. Alongside came the hope that they might one day return to the eight.

It was a cool summer that year. Some sunny days got up to 20 degrees, but they weren't treated to warm days very often. The lake was rarely empty, but this didn't bother the rowers. When the waves on Galvė Lake were too big, the men went to Skaistis Lake, which usually had calmer water along one shore or another. Alfa, who rowed at bow, tried to control the four's work as much as he could – he felt a responsibility for the team that he had been left with. Though he was smaller than the others, he had an excellent sense of rhythm and supported the stroke well. When the weather was nicer, they also often raced alongside the pair.

*

After the victory in Philadelphia, not all of the men from the eight returned to Lithuania. Celestinas was put back in place of Tchiorstwij and Gerdas returned as the cox. The four was once again in a difficult situation, as Celestinas once again had to be replaced by Vitalijus.

The USSR Championships in Leningrad was quickly approaching. The country's strongest crews would be racing at the end of July in Kavgolovo. Despite Žalgiris' victory in America, they would have to undergo another selection race because the men's crew that won the USSR Championships would be sent to the World Championship in Lucerne, while the winning women's crew would go to the European Women's Rowing Championships in Grünau. There was only a month left until Lucerne, and instead of preparing for the race, Ričardas was once again tasked with reviewing and adjusting his preparatory plans. The men were openly upset. They felt that they were the strongest and most worthy to race for the USSR team, but these new rules were the rules, that had been brought in over the winter.

When everyone finally gathered in Trakai, Ričardas was given responsibility not just for the training sessions, but also for the yet-to-be-resolved organisational problems. Ričardas tasked Povilas with rewriting their training schedule. Though nobody said it out loud, everybody knew that Ričardas had difficulty writing correctly because he hadn't completed any higher education. Povilas, whose handwriting was especially elegant, always helped him. He had received a perfect grade for his Lithuanian grammar.

Though they had difficulty discussing things with their teammates who had returned from America, the men from the four still felt better. At least they were now once again equal members of the Lithuanian team. They no longer had to walk to the tourist centre like beggars to feed on leftovers.

Povilas had, at least temporarily, come to terms with his status as an enemy of the nation and he no longer wondered about any sort of "what ifs." His heart raced at every thought of the child that would soon arrive. He awaited the day with joy and anxiety, and dreamed about how he'd hug and rock his child, press it close to his chest, stroke its head, watch its every move, take it to Vingis Park in a buggy, teach it to draw and read and write, go skiing with it, take photos of it and hang them all over their home, and bring it to Trakai and show it the castle and the boats. He felt and believed that this young child wouldn't have the same fate as his, that it would grow up with loving parents, that it wouldn't experience poverty, fear or war, and that perhaps, with God's will, it might live to see Lithuania free again. He knew he'd never give up hope for a better life for his child, not even in his darkest hour, and that his own parents, Ona and Stasys, would protect their grandchild from up above. "Look at all of these races… I hope they don't hurry too much so I'd manage to return..." Povilas thought to himself. "But Gita has so many strange superstitions..."

*

7

On Saturday, 21 July, the Lithuanian team left for Leningrad. The selection races at the USSR Championships would start on Tuesday. The Lithuanian teams loaded their boats – both eights, the men's coxed four, Janina's single, and the men's coxless pair.

The national championships were like the gateway to next year's national team. They were also the final selection competition for the year's World and European championships. But this wasn't the case for everyone – only for those whose documents were in order for travelling abroad. There was only a month left until the championships, and during that time, there was no way that the KGB's bureaucratic apparatus would manage to ensure that the team's new members' papers were in order, even if they did win by a wide margin. They managed to waste more than a month on just confirming biographical facts, let alone securing meetings and discussions with the Komsomol, the Communist Party and other committees.

It was harder in the four without Celestinas, but the men were happy to hear that he had been returned to the eight. If Celestinas' name had been cleared, that meant that the barbed-wire fence wasn't as insurmountable as they had thought. With any luck, their turn would come as well.

The rowers encountered beautiful, sunny weather in Kavgolovo. The small village, with only two hundred residents and just fifteen kilometres from Leningrad, was the primary training camp for the military naval rowers.

Boats darted across the surface of Lake Hepoyarvi's blue water, and in the golden sunset, the lake looked positively otherworldly. The name of the lake meant "horse lake" in Finnish. It was thought the name came from its horse-head shape, but even local residents couldn't say where and when the name had come from; Finland had five different lakes with the same name. This calm lake was located amidst low hills and forests and was about two and a half kilometres long, occupying an area of four square kilometres.

The finish line was located right by the camp. A long pontoon stretched out from the boat house on the shore for departing and returning crews. There was another pontoon to the left with a 25-metre-long "walled off" pool at the end and a diving tower. During the races, the finish line judges would sit at the top of the tower. There were no regular grandstands, but local spectators fitted perfectly on the log-reinforced shoreline and the nearby steep hill covered in fir trees.

The cosy stadium nearby where the opening parade was held also served as a meeting point for the competitors.

The slope that rose up behind the boathouse had military tents lined up one after the other, with another fifty in a large square field. This was where the rowers' lived; eight people to a tent.

There were 400 participants from nine republics, and Moscow and Leningrad, present at the competition. Most calmly prepared for the next day's races, but the two champion eights from that summer – the CSK and Žalgiris crews – shot murderous glances at one another. Barely three weeks ago, Žalgiris had won a historic victory in the USA, while CSK won the main prize at the Henley Royal Regatta. Both of the teams felt like they were the season's heroes and that they had earned the right to race in the inaugural World Rowing Championships.

Reporters looked forward to Zigmas and Antanas' race with impatience, hoping that the Lithuanian champions would once again row as a pair. Other competitors cursed at the sight of the Žalgiris team rowing on the lake with a new coxed pair boat. Their opponents watched the Lithuanian stars uneasily. The Žalgiris men's eight felt the same way, however, as they suddenly began to realise that their path to the World Rowing Championships could be slipping away from them. They understood that, because Zigmas and Antanas had decided to race in two boat classes, the team may have to "sacrifice" one of the races by rowing with restraint – and this was with only a couple of days left until the selection was to be made. The two stars, who had missed their pair, believed that they could win not just here, but in Lucerne as well.

The final decision, however, came down to the champions themselves. After a practice with the pair, they realised that they were in danger of biting off more than they could chew. The Žalgiris eight would need to race at full power.

*

"Good job, Celestinas," Povilas said after they completed their preliminary heat.

"It's not over, we'll see tomorrow. You're in the repechage?"

"Yeah. We had a poor start and got left behind, and we had Leningrad's Trud. With you, we could've tried to catch up to them, but who knows what would've been left of us," Povilas laughed. "We'll catch up tomorrow. We'll make it to the final one way or another."

"We also had a hard time of it. Trud was so fast that we spent the whole race catching up to them. I thought we wouldn't make it."

"You'll win tomorrow, Celestinas. And you'll go to Lucerne, too," Povilas encouraged him. "My turn will come some day."

"Don't be angry, Povilas," Celestinas said, feeling guilty for the teammates who had been left behind.

"Nonsense! I'm happy for you that you'll be able to leave!"

"You know, I have a hard time talking to them…" Celestinas quietly admitted, barely hiding his hurt.

"Don't worry about it. Their vanity will disappear one day. In sports, stars rise and fall quickly."

"It's no fun racing on a team that considers you to be a failure."

"Only time will tell where everyone stands, Celestinas."

Celestinas waved dismissively and gave a tight-lipped smile,

"It just gets more and more nerve-wracking. Are they jealous or what?"

"I don't see why they've got to strut about like that in front of their friends," Povilas noted.

"Remember when we still rowed the pair? Back then, there were people who'd come by whenever we won…"

"There were also people who'd try to stop us from finishing."

"Yeah, they'd stick their motorboats right in our faces to tow out their favourite pets…"

In 1960, Povilas and Celestinas had primarily rowed in the coxed pair. While Zigmas and Antanas were preparing for the Olympics, Povilas and Celestinas were the Republic's strongest pair, winning the championships in May. In July, they won at the 75th anniversary of the Lithuanian Rowing Championships.

"Yeah, yeah… But life has a way of putting everything into its place."

"Are you going to take some photos?" Celestinas had only now noticed that Povilas was hiding his FED camera under his tracksuit.

"I wanted to take a photo or two – "Sportas" asked me to – but it's raining."

The drizzle that had begun overnight was growing worse.

"It's a good thing somebody's taking photos of us. Any chance you'll give me one?"

"Of course I will. Have I ever failed you?"

"You didn't give me one from Odessa!" Celestinas retorted.

"Oh come on, how could I have known that the roll had already been exposed? I took photos of every moment, hoping to give everyone some photos. That asshole sold me some cheap cinematic film, so I thought I'd have some to spare. You should've heard me swear when I developed the shots! You can't imagine!"

"I can," Celestinas laughed.

Laughing, the two men descended from the wet slope and turned towards the boathouse, whose wall was already plastered with results from the qualifying races. The paper, soaked by the rain, was on the verge of tearing apart, so coaches were hurrying to write the results into their notebooks, while the athletes watched over their shoulders, trying to find their names.

"Look how badly you beat Trud! By almost six seconds!" Povilas exclaimed.

"I can't see, what's our time?" asked Celestinas as he tried to get closer.

"6:04.4, and Trud's was 6:10. CSK aren't even in the running – they got 6:15.2 in the other heat. You guys won't have anybody to really race tomorrow."

"When will this rain end?" they heard Alfa ask next to them. "I don't have any dry clothes left to change into."

"Look, it's Alfa! What are you waiting for here, the ladies?" Povilas laughed. "The ladies won't go for a guy that's soaked to the bone like you!"

"I have nowhere to go. The guys by our tent snore so loud that you can't sleep or relax there at all."

"How much time until the race?"

"It's another three hours. I wish it was all over already…"

"It shouldn't be too hard to get some rest," Povilas encouraged him.

"Nobody's going to row it for us, we'll have to suffer through it ourselves," replied Alfa.

"Come with us, we'll have some tea," Celestinas invited his former crewmates.

"No thanks, Celestinas, we'll take a nap in our own tent – we still have a race today."

The men turned towards the tent area – towards the orderly military tent square with spring mattresses, damp bed sheets, luggage, and the treats they had brought from home. The kit they had hung out to dry on the tents' supports were being "washed" by the summer rain. You could tell where each team could be found by the shirts they had hung up. The horizon was growing lighter in the distance, and it seemed like the rain might die down in the evening.

*

25 July, the final day of the competition, began with a warm and sunlit morning. All of the Lithuanian crews had made the finals. Only the men's coxless pair missed their final – they had had to with draw due to illness.

The morning wind finally dried the kit. One after another, the tents opened up as the rowers poured out into the sunlight. Some went to warm up and exercise, others went to the lake to bathe, or to the cafeteria for breakfast. It was a typical finals day, when one's body had already suffered through the initial race and had had its first good run. When one could feel every muscle aching and the fatigue building up in it. When all of the rowers were looking forward to their final race, which would determine everything. They looked forward to finishing and hurrying to pack up so they could wait, care-free, for the journey home.

After the last race – the eights – and the award ceremony, everything would suddenly empty out. The flags are lowered, the storage trailers covered in boats will roll out, and the athletes will hop into buses or hurry off towards the train station with their luggage. The only thing that will be left will be a sort of yearning emptiness among the locals and those who, at one point or another, had been the last to leave the competition. Leaving is always easier than staying.

"Hey, Povilas. What are you so focussed on?" joked James as he caught up to Povilas.

"I'm having a hard time forgetting my dreams. I'm wondering whether everything's alright at home. I had a strange dream."

"A nightmare?"

"No, but I saw Gita leading a little girl by the hand. I'm afraid that she won't be able to wait until I return and that she'll give birth."

"So perhaps you'll have a daughter," James smiled.

"I really want to be at home when the time comes," said Povilas with a hint of sadness in his voice.

"But how can you help her, Povilas? She won't be alone. Somebody will take her to the hospital..."

"Of course they will. There's always somebody home, so there'll be somebody to call the ambulance. It's not far to the telephone. But I won't be there, and I'd so much like to hold her hand on the way to the hospital... I'm barely ever home as it is. I'm always on the road."

"Well, what can you do? Don't worry about it. We'll be home tomorrow."

"I hope she waits a bit longer. I have no way of finding out, either. I can't call her or ask her... I wrote a letter when I got here, but it probably hasn't reached her yet."

The summer sun bathed the blue waters of Hepoyarvi Lake and the rowers resting on the dock in warmth. The rays of sunlight reflected off of the mirror-like lacquered wooden boats.

The athletes, dressed in white shirts with the word "LIETUVA" on them in green, encouraged one another before the last race of the day. The country's strongest rowing crews were about to face off for the champion's title – for the right to, at least briefly, break out into the free world.

*

"Gerdas, come here," Ričardas said as he took the cox for his eight aside. "Once you leave the start, go hard. We have to get ahead by three or four seats[33]. Then, begin really pushing them. We've got to leave them some dirty water. The most important thing is that we make it out ahead as quickly as possible. Got it?"

---

33   By three or four rowers. This is the distance that the corresponding number of rowers take up in a boat. In an eight-seater boat, this would be about 5-8 metres. In rowing, leads can also be measured by hull lengths or fractions of hull lengths.

"Yeah, got it," Gerdas nodded.

"I'll give you the sign."

"Got it."

"We've got forty minutes left, so let's get the boat," he said, patting Gerdas on the shoulder.

"Everybody hands on!" shouted Gerdas and the team lined up by the eight.

"Get ready, hut! To shoulders."

A merciless battle for the journey to the World Rowing Championships was approaching. Though Žalgiris' victory in the semi-final had been more than comfortable, that didn't mean much – that had been a different race with different opponents, and the wind could have been different.

Gerdas' hands were trembling. He rarely got such instructions – ones that were on the verge of dishonesty. God forbid something happened… God forbid he fails at steering… winning here was of the utmost importance!

"Vnimanie, marsh![34]" the green starting flare shot up into the sky and the finish-line umpires pressed down on their timers. The six eights shot out into the race course.

"One! Two! Three!" Gerdas cheered the team on. "And, hup, that's it!"

The Žalgiris boat shot ahead, but CSK had clawed itself away from the pack as well.

"Ten more! One! Two!"

Stroke by stroke, the Lithuanians caught up until the boats were nose-to-nose.

"Don't let go! Ten strong ones! One! Two! Three!"

After 500 metres, the Lithuanians were in the lead, but the difference was too small.

"Ten more!" said Gerdas, driving the team on.

Their lead grew to almost half a hull's length.

"Push them," Ričardas spit out through his gritted teeth.

Gerdas pulled the rudder with his right hand and the boat's direction changed slightly. The men's bow-side oars began overlapping their opponents' lane.

"Žalgiris, adjust your steering!" they heard the umpire's voice through a megaphone on the motorboat.

"Don't listen, push them," Ričardas calmed Gerdas.

---

34   Attention - go!

The bow-side oars were nearly close enough to hit CSK's stroke-side oars and the men began looking uneasily off to their left. One careless stroke and you might catch a crab or, even worse, break your blade. The naval crew cursed as they began to feel their oars grabbing at nothing but the whirlpools and dirty water left behind by Žalgiris' puddles.

"Žalgiris, return to your lane!"

"Let's go, don't listen. Threee…"

The thousand-metre mark flew past over their heads.

"For Lithuania! Ten strong ones! One! Two!… Ten more!"

Žalgiris was ahead by a length. Their boat was flying along CSK's lane.

"Lithuania, correct your course!" the umpire continued to shout.

"Fix your course," said Ričardas once he could see that CSK could no longer do anything with only 200 metres to the finish line.

The Žalgiris eight crossed the finish line first, with CSK's gong going off three seconds later. Gerdas looked at Ričardas with a questioning glance as if to ask "is everything OK?" Ričardas gave him a thumbs-up and smiled.

The umpires' motorboat crossed the finish line together with the last boat and the umpire raised a red flag up high, veering off towards the finish tower. The men's joyful faces turned to stone. Gerdas, frightened, looked to his coach. He understood that his actions could have disqualified the entire team.

"Relax," Ričardas said quietly, though it was clear that he had not expected this turn of events. "Relax."

"What will happen now?" Gerdas asked uneasily.

"Let's go in."

The quietly rowed back to the pontoon and were completely silent when they got out of the boat. The red flag could only mean trouble. They could be disqualified, maybe forced to row again if they could prove that their boat had malfunctioned, or something else… It could be that they might lose the right to race at the World Championships…

None of them, however, dared blame the cox for what happened. They knew their coach well and trusted him completely. They understood that only he could have come up with such a risky plan. Gerdas had coxed the eight many times and couldn't have mis-steered it by accident. Nobody would have dared to complain to their coach, either. All they had left was to wait for the umpires' decision.

Ričardas hurried off to the office, where he expected to receive an answer or possibly even use his own methods to solve the problem at hand.

After about half an hour, or perhaps less, though it felt like an eternity for the rowers, they heard a squeal from the announcer's megaphone:

"The Žalgiris team has won the men's eight race…"

This made things easier. They couldn't call it a triumph, since they knew that part of their victory had to be attributed to a riskier game than the one they had played. Their joy was accompanied by a deep sigh, but it was still a weight off of their shoulders.

*

That Saturday, "Sportas" would write: "Compared to athletes from other fields, rowers are at a disadvantage: there are no records or record-holders in rowing. This is unfortunate, because (as Komsomolskaya Pravda noted), the Žalgiris men's eight would not just be the USSR champions, they would also be its record-holders. No boat in the country had ever rowed two kilometres faster than they did – in 5:55.2. The Vilnius rowers themselves had never rowed such a quick race. In rowing, it is said that if a boat finishes in less than 6 minutes, it can be considered in another class."

It would also publish Povilas' photo along with the article, which showed the happy men of the eight crew with their white shirts and the words "LIETUVA" on them with medals on their chests, flowers in their hands, and the lake in the background.

The men had the journey home to look forward to, a few more sessions in Trakai, and the last camp in Jelgava before their journey to Lucerne – to the inaugural World Rowing Championships.

*

8

The journey on the night-train from Leningrad in a shared train car dragged on and on, and the last kilometres to Vilnius seemed like they would never end.

Povilas, who was the first to jump out onto the platform, quickly waved goodbye to his friends and raced off to the bus station. The newspaper stand window shone brightly with the headline "Žalgiris' eight is headed to the World Championships!" Povilas fished three coins out of his pocket, gave them to the lady behind the counter, grabbed an issue of "Sportas", and ran off to the bus that had just arrived. Eugenijus and Romas jumped in after him just before the doors closed. They were headed in the same directions. Povilas, with one hand on the railing and his bags between his legs on the floor, waved to his friends with the magazine in his hand.

"Where are you off to in such a hurry, Povilas? We barely caught up," the two brothers, out of breath, wondered.

"Home, of course! I've missed Gita and I haven't had any news since we left on Saturday. I might not even find her at home," Povilas said anxiously.

"Ah, I see, you're expecting a son?"

"It doesn't matter if it's a son or daughter, as long as it is born healthy and strong. I want nothing more."

"That's right. What did "Sportas" write?"

"Mostly about the eight."

"How about us?"

"Hold on…" he said, scanning the text. "Here, 'the coxless pair, Levickas-Šarmaitis, faced good odds before the race but the latter fell ill. After a repechage, the men's coxed four made it in as well,'" – with his left hand on the railing to keep from falling as the bus rumbled through Vilnius' potholed streets, Povilas opened up the magazine and continued: "Yes, yes, here," – he had found the surnames – "'The Vilnius women's eight also did well, coming in fourth. The women achieved the Master of

Sports standard. The first among the women was Moscow's Trud crew. Janina Lukošiūnaitė came in fifth. The Vilnius men's coxed four achieved the same place, with A. Mikšys, V. Šalyginas, P. Liutkaitis, R. Levickas and cox I. Pavlovas. As such, Lithuania's rowers put up an honourable fight.'"

"What photo did they use?"

"The eight. I think it was taken by Šeinius. The same one they had with the article in Švyturys in June. I don't remember the title, "Eight Men" or something."

"Yeah, that was the one where they wrote that, during training, you could hop out of the eight, take a photo from the dock, and hop back in without missing a stroke…"

The men laughed out loud, drawing the attention of other passengers in the bus.

"Journalists have wild imaginations," Povilas waved them off dismissively. "I'll have to manage to develop the new photos from the competition. "Sportas" asked me to. They want them for the Saturday issue."

"If it weren't for you, Povilas, there wouldn't be any photos at all, unless somebody in Lithuania took our photos."

The trip home was a little over two kilometres, or five stops on the bus. Povilas had to walk a few hundred metres more by foot. That morning, Čiurlionis Street smelled of linden blossoms and dew-laden grass. Everyone had already hurried off to work. Students were on vacation, so there wasn't the usual hurried shuffle of students late to their classes. An elderly grandmother leading two girls by their hands – probably her granddaughters – was walking down the street, and a young mother was pushing a sky-blue baby stroller towards Vingis Park. Povilas' glance couldn't help but wander towards the infant sleeping in the stroller. His heart thrilled and he ran off towards home with his luggage in his hands. His feet seemed to be running of their own accord. His heart felt like it would burst and his mouth grew dry. Here was the clock under which Gita used to wait in the evenings and here was the corner of his house, the gate…

Povilas burst through the door:

"Good morning! Is anybody home?"

"Povilas! You're home! Congratulations, your wife just gave birth to a daughter!" Gita's mother was the first to greet him.

"A daughter!" Povilas exclaimed as tears began to stream down his face. He began laughing with joy and gave Gita's mother a strong hug, "a daughter!"

Irena ran into the room as well once she'd heard that Povilas had returned. She had been the first to find out!

"I spent all night running to the phone booth. Congratulations, Dad!" she said, kissing Povilas on the cheek.

"When was she born?" Povilas asked, unable to contain his joy.

"At six in the morning. What will you name her?" asked Gita's sister.

"Whatever Gita wants. We haven't thought about it yet."

"Today's Ona's name day," Gita's mother pointed out.

"Ona... How's Gita doing? It's too bad I couldn't return in time..."

- It's ok, Povilas, don't worry about it. Irena went to the phone booth, called the ambulance and they took her to the clinic in Antakalnis."

"I'm just going to shave and head over there," said Povilas, dropping his luggage. "When will they let her go home?"

"They'll keep her for about a week. I don't think you'll get to speak to her when you go there, you can just give her a package or some letters through the window."

"Then I've got a week to prepare everything. We need a crib, a stroller, nappies... what else will we need?"

"Congratulations, Povilas!" said his father-in-law as he walked in the door. "Daughters are great. I've got four and I love them! They're hard-working and beautiful. Sit down, let's celebrate!"

"Maybe later, not right now," Povilas declined. "I'm off to the hospital."

After quickly bathing, shaving and putting on his Sunday best, he grabbed his camera and hurried off into that refreshing 26 July. "A daughter! On Ona's name day... My mother made sure her granddaughter would be born on her name day... She'd be so happy now to hear the news... Maybe she's happy up there, too. Of course she is..." he thought to himself as he raised his eyes to the sky and instinctively crossed himself. "I wonder who she looks like. I've got to think of a name," his thoughts were racing. "Good thing we're with the parents-in-law, they'll help us. How am I supposed to hold such a little child? Swaddle her and put her to sleep? Sing lullabies?" His anxiety and joy became one, along with other new emotions that he had never felt before. "I'll buy some berries and flowers at the market. There's a post office nearby so I'll buy a postcard, too. But what am I going to do with my camera? Nobody's going to let me see them, unless I spot them through the window… Trolley bus number 9 will take me right to the hospital… I'll have to buy her a layette, too… but where will I get the money? Perhaps Bronius will have some to lend me… Oh my, I'll have to develop the photos and take them to the editorial staff tomorrow as well..." The thoughts came faster and faster in his head as his feet carried him to the place where, that morning, a new, happier and more beautiful stage of his family's life had begun.

*

9

On Friday, everybody gathered at Trakai again. The athletes, who had suitcases full of kit in their hands, had missed Trakai Lake and the rowing camp. They were excited by their recent victories and the wide open world of international rowing that lay before them. In the building's central hall, which was full as always, faces old and new congratulated the champions and wished them the best of luck in Lucerne. Povilas' friends congratulated him as well, asking about his daughter's name. The girls wanted to know who she looked like and when she'd return home so they could come and visit her.

Though the cool, rainy and windy weather prevailed, the rowing season was still at its zenith. Athletes from Vilnius, Kaunas and Klaipėda hurried to and fro at the camp.

Workers were also hurrying around the camp to prepare it for the USSR team championships, which would begin in a month. The sheds behind the boathouses were still being constructed, the starting pontoon was being repaired, and they were erecting columns near the finish line that looked like they'd be the supports for a new tower.

The men gathered by the grandstands and shared the news while they waited for their coach – about new USSR champions Tamulis and Pozniakas[35], about the recent film "The Queen of the Gas Station," about the new 44-seater TU-124 Soviet passenger plane, about the new fragrance in Paris that smelled of money (that none of them would ever experience), and about the fact that one could watch a black-and-white TV in colour by placing a cleared x-ray sheet over it that had been coloured with stripes of different colours. Most of them laughed at this bit of advice from Science and Life[36] because none of them even had a TV yet.

Ričardas appeared at twelve on the dot. He was pedantically precise and expected the same from others, so the men tried to arrive early whenever they could. Ričardas was even an authority figure for old and accomplished team veterans. Nobody dared oppose him. If you didn't

---

35   Lithuanian boxers
36   Lit. Mokslas ir Gyvenimas, a Lithuanian magazine

want to be kicked out of the camp, don't complain and don't whine, no matter how hard and painful things got. You'd be replaced quickly – Ričardas had raised himself plenty of big, strong and tough athletes.

"Alright, guys. Here's the situation. The eight will be the same as in America: Jukna, Bagdonavičius, Briedis, Karla, Jagelavičius, Vaitkevičius, Semionov and Tchiorstwij. Dima and Slava will join us next week in Jelgava. We'll be rowing in pairs and fours here."

Everyone's eyes suddenly turned to Celestinas, who grew red-hot with surprise. He looked down and began nervously kicking at the gravel on the shore. A murmur of discontent spread among the men. Even the newspapers had written that Celestinas would replace Tchiorstwij, so why had everything suddenly changed? Ričardas continued, understanding that his news had shocked his listeners:

"Yes, Tchiorstwij is weaker, but there's nobody to replace Celestinas. His documents aren't in order and we've got no time to lose. Celestinas, Liutkaitis, Romas Levickas, and Mikšys will prepare for the Union team championships in a coxed four. Eugenijus and Šarmaitis will be in a coxless pair. Šalyginas will join the Kaunas eight. The competition is on the third and fourth of September. We won't be here but you'll have the home-turf advantage. It's twelve now. Our trailer should arrive at three, and we'll all help unload it. We won't unload the eight because that's going straight to Jelgava. We'll hit the water at four. That's all. You're free until three."

The men from the eight, deep in conversation, walked off towards their rooms with their luggage in hand. The friends from the four, weighed down by a sense of guilt, shifted from side to side, unsure of what to say.

"Don't let it bring you down, Celestinas, we'll think of something," said Povilas, trying to reassure his friend.

"What is this nonsense? When they need to win, I'm fine, but when they need to go abroad, I'm not?" said Celestinas, clearly hurt.

"They want to stick in some Russians," Romas said angrily.

"They might not have won without you. At least, not that easily," Alfa said. He could see that his friend was on the verge of giving up and wanted to help him.

"I don't want any of this anymore… I worked like a dog all summer without a cent to my name and ate tourists' leftovers. All I did was help others make it through and earn their stipends. Now my studies are as good as gone…"

The men stood together with their heads hung low. It was hard to find the right words. Celestinas was right – nothing could be done. It had been a hard summer for all of them. After such a sensational victory in Kiev, it had seemed like their efforts should have been at least somewhat appreciated. They had, but not to their benefit. Their former teammates were living in private apartments and had received stipends and awards from the sports committee. They, on the other hand, were left exactly where they had been a year ago, only now they had been insulted and rejected as well. That was what hurt the most. Not the money, not the awards, not the fame, but the Lithuanian – and human – dignity that the communists occupying their homeland wanted to take away.

"Nu shto[37], vragi naroda," said Povilas, trying to raise their spirits. "There's nothing left for us to do but show them that we can be strong without the eight as well. Let's go back up to our rooms. I have some bacon from home we can eat."

"Yeah, let's go, Celestinas. Sooner or later, everything will sort itself out," said Romas, patting him on the back.

"Povilas, Ričardas wants you!" said Gerdas as he ran out the door.

"He probably wants to rewrite his schedules again. I'll go, but you guys grab a bed for me. Here's the package of bacon. Slice it up by the time I get back," said Povilas, handing off a package wrapped in newspaper and hurrying off to the coach's room to write down the coach's dictated schedule in his elegant handwriting as he always did.

The men gathered up their things and followed Povilas up the stairs past the large columns that held up the roof and balcony. Alfa, suddenly becoming aware of the cold that had seeped into his bones, shuddered:

"What a July. It feels like autumn."

"It looks like it'll rain in the afternoon," Romas noted.

They turned around to look at the choppy lake water before ducking through the large wooden doors. Heavy rain clouds were gathering in the west, beyond the castle. A single ray of sunshine briefly pierced the sky and ignited the red rooftops of the castle before disappearing, cut off by the approaching clouds.

---

37   Rus. "Ну что" – "Well, then"

"Ričardas, I need Monday off," said Povilas as he looked up from his notebook after writing down what Ričardas had said.

"What happened?"

"I have to take Gita and my daughter home from the hospital."

"Ah, that's right, congratulations! Atta boy, Povilas! Alright, of course, you can stay in Vilnius. Give Gita my regards."

"Of course, thank you."

"What's her name?"

"We don't have one yet, we'll think of one when they get back. I haven't seen her yet so I can't even say who she looks like – like an Ona or like a Marytė," he laughed.

"We'll have another rower! You've got good genes!"

"We'll see," Povilas smiled.

Povilas had difficulty imagining what lay in store for his daughter. The most important thing now was to see her and hold her close. On Monday morning, he would hurry off to the hospital in his wedding clothes with flowers and all of the nappies he had bought with borrowed rubles. There, he would see his first-born daughter for the first time, hold that small, warm bundle in his hands, and hug his dear Gita, glowing with pride and joy. They'd sit in the taxi and come home to Čiurlionis Street, where their entire family would be awaiting them. They'd all gasp with joy and admire the child's black hair and dark blue eyes. They'd pick names for her and joke while he took pictures of the first days of her life.

But all of that was to be on Monday. Now, however, the next stage of preparations for the championships was just beginning. Some would face the World, others would face the Union, and yet others would face the Republic. For each person there, the championships was their most important task. Each of them had their own dreams and goals.

At 3:05, the boat trailer slowly rolled into the camp along the road. It was loaded with boats, dusty from the long journey. The lacquered wood, which was usually polished to a mirror sheen, was barely shining at all, though it had passed through rain numerous times during its journey from Leningrad.

The first task after unloading a boat was to wash it. The men brought buckets from the boathouse and rags that had once been well-used towels and bedsheets. They untied the tightly lashed ropes and carefully removed the fragile boats. They cradled the boats carefully but took them down in random order. Each boat had tens of hands holding it over their heads and carefully making sure it wouldn't hit any trees on its way to the prepared slings, which stood at different distances for each boat. The rowers untangled the riggers and carried them to the boats. Then, they untied the oars and laid them down on the grass one by one, carefully so they wouldn't crack. The coxes gathered their seats, rudders, tools, and cans of Solidol.

The constant reassembly of the boats was an unavoidable element of competitions and camps. It was a common rowers' ritual that occasionally bored them but also gave them a sense of pride, as it was a ritual unique to rowing. Even the girls had no problem with having grease-stained hands and carrying clinking 10mm or 14mm wrenches in their purses.

After long journeys, the boats were frequently left with "scars" – scratches or, even worse, holes. However, the worst holes or even breaks occurred when boats collided on the water. Lacquer and some sanding and polishing were usually enough to fix a scratch, but holes were a craftsman's job that was often done by the coaches or the athletes themselves. If it was a crack lengthwise along the wood, some quality glue and lacquer would suffice. If the wood was penetrated, however, they would have to cut a patch out of a similar piece of wood and masterfully glue it into the hole. Every irregularity, no matter how small, could lose them seconds along the course of a race, meaning that they had to scrub and polish their boats to perfection. This was why, every spring, all of the boats, even the clean ones without any scratches, were scrubbed, lacquered, polished, lacquered again, sanded and polished until the hull of the boat shone like glass – before even lowering them into the water. To ensure that the new litre or two of lacquer wouldn't weigh the boat down, the old layers had to be removed by scrubbing with sandpaper until they almost reached the un-lacquered wood. Lacquering the boats was another ritual that they performed all together, as a team. It would take them several days in a row, layer by layer. They often worked with their bare hands to ensure that the lacquer remained free of streaks.

Their oars – the primary tools of their work – also required love and care. Here, lacquer was just for beauty and for protection from the water, so polishing was not necessary. There were more issues with the thin wooden blades, which could easily break– and God forbid that two teams ever caught on each others' oars during a race. In those cases, you could even lose half of your blade. Every rower protected and valued their oar, as that was what their hands and entire bodies would grow accustomed to.

After inspecting the cleaned and assembled boats, the coaches could breathe a sigh of relief. With all of the boats in good shape, training could begin in earnest. They'd then push the motorboats from the boathouses on their rails, fill them with fuel, and start them up. The coxes on the pontoons would begin instructing their teams…

*

10

For the entire month up until the competition, Povilas took the bus from Vilnius to Trakai during the mornings and evenings. He didn't want to miss a single day of little Rasa's life, so the kilometres he walked to and from the station and the many sleepless hours meant nothing to him. At home, the little girl's nappies were hung out to dry on a rope alongside developed photos. At night, a small red lamp would light up in the small bathroom and Povilas' portraits of his baby girl would begin to develop in their enamel bathtub.

However, he still came to training on time and gave it everything he had in the boat.

The eight soon left for Jelgava. It would be their final camp, where every kilometre they rowed along the water of Lielupe River would be another kilometre closer to the World Championships.

Everyone else at Trakai continued their preparations for the USSR Championships.

August was no different from July, with only momentary pauses in the wind and the rain. The temperature during the day rarely rose higher than 18 degrees.

The Soviets' propaganda machine was rumbling ahead at full steam. Lenin's country held the first group spacecraft flight – Vostok-3 and Vostok-4 took off into the skies within a day of each other, on 11-12 August. The communist press and TV gleefully dissected the details of "rotten capitalist" actress Marilyn Monroe's death, but remained silent about the AN-10A aircraft that crashed into a mountain on 28 July with 74 passengers and 7 crew members while flying from Lviv to Sochi. The USSR was performing nuclear trials in Novaya Zemlya, and Eastern German border guards shot an eighteen-year-old who was trying to escape to Western Germany and left him to bleed to death in sight of reporters and journalists. There was good news from abroad as well, but the press was even less willing to discuss it because it didn't match communist ideology and would do harm to the Soviet youth. These included things like the sweeping tide of mini-skirts that had conquered the west, that John Lennon had secretly married in Liverpool, that the Beatles had a new drummer named Ringo Starr, that London had had its first Rolling Stones concert, and that Robert Zimmerman had changed his name to Bob Dylan.

At the end of the month, more and more trailers began to appear at the Trakai camp – teams were beginning to gather for the Championships. The prizes were brought from Moscow – two impressive trophies with the USSR coat of arms on one side and a rower on the other, with one for the winning men's team and another for the women. The grand prize, a relief of a single scull rower, would go to the association that won the final tally overall. Leningrad usually won the team championship prize, followed by Moscow and the RFSFR[38]. Last year, the Lithuanian men's team had come in fifth while the women's was fourth. It was difficult to expect anything better this year, as Lithuania lacked its strongest rowers – they were in Lucerne. However, Moscow and Leningrad's Trud and CSK had also sent their best rowers to Lucerne as well, which would help level the playing field.

The leaders of the USSR Rowing Federation frowned when they arrived from Moscow. The finish tower wasn't complete yet, and a tent stood in its place; the umpires' seats were located on the steps; white stakes were sticking out of the water; none of the motorboats worked; the connection to Trakai was difficult; the participants were poorly fed; and the tents were dishevelled and uncomfortable... And the worst part was that the competition's senior umpire and his deputy hadn't arrived yet. A federation official named Slanksnys helped sort the situation out by quickly gathering a brigade of umpires and resolving to defend the "honour" of the Lithuanian Rowing Federation. The cherry on top was the windy and rainy autumn weather, even though the calendar insisted that it was summer. Perhaps the weather was why everyone was so upset. Though they say that "there's no such thing as bad weather," about eighty percent of the success of a rowing competition depended on the weather. If the sky had provided them with sunlight, warmth, and still waters, they wouldn't need any tents and there wouldn't be any issues with waves on the race course or the rocking of the start pontoon.

Though they burrowed their heads into their shoulders, rubbed their cold hands together, and stamped about in place, the rowers were still anxious about the start. The unrest in their stomachs and the weakness that came

---

38   The Russian Soviet Federative Socialist Republic.

over them in waves helped remind them of the upcoming races. The girls were especially uneasy, because the championships had brought together the strongest rowers of the USSR, and the Lithuanian women's rowing team still found them to be untouchable. The men's team was already on their way to the World Rowing Championships, so the Lithuanian team had two large absences – a coxed pair and, of course, the eight. Everyone on the shoreline was watching the tall rowers from the Moscow Trud women's eight. They had won the European Championships in Germany and had hurried home to "pick up" their USSR Championships medals as well.

The opening parade at the peninsula's traditional square took only a few minutes – that was all the time that the teams needed to march out, raise their flags and march back in, though their return seemed more like a hasty retreat given the rain. After the Baltic Championships last year, the Trakai rowing camp and its dismal opening and closing ceremonies were roundly criticized. This year, the building had speakers, and the sounds they played helped somewhat to preserve a festive atmosphere.

The women would be starting the programme, so the boating area was soon full of women. The shivering coxes were apparently dressed in all of the clothes that they had brought, because they looked less like coxes and more like short rowers. The men still hoped that the rainstorm would let up until their races were to begin and tried to keep warm however they could – in their tents, in their rooms, in the boathouse, in the main hall, or on the steps.

Things were tense with the brigade of umpires. The umpires that Slanksnys had gathered in haste rushed back and forth in an effort to cover everything at once. Though they were sharing their duties, certain uncompleted tasks began sprouting up like poisonous mushrooms: the typewriter got stuck so the racing schedules were late, somebody got the rowers' names confused, the numbers weren't handed out in time, the water hadn't been removed from the motorboats, the motors hadn't been brought, etc...

Finally, the umpires gathered their suits, flags, timers, megaphones and freshly-printed schedules and headed out into the rain. They surveyed the scene, hunched over – there was no end in sight. They waved to one another and left for different directions – some went to the boats while others went to the finish-line tent. There was an hour left until the first race. The last race of the day was scheduled to end in eight hours.

*

On 1 September, when the streets of cities and towns throughout Lithuania are filled with school children in uniform carrying colourful bouquets of flowers, the final races of the USSR Rowing Championships were just beginning. Despite the Lithuanian team's "losses," six boats made it into the final – four women's crews and two men's. Reporters with photo and film cameras began gathering at the camp in the early morning. A USSR Championships was a rare thing in the world of Lithuanian sports, and people were currently more interested in rowing than usual. They were afraid that they'd be late to the races on account of the line by the ferry, so they showed up on the shoreline long before 8:00. Journalists from throughout the country, with their cameras covered in raincoats and bags, were waiting for the races. From time to time, they'd secretively drink from flasks of something to keep themselves warm and save themselves from the merciless weather.

*

The men from the four and pair crews, all of whom lived in a room with eight beds on the second floor of the rowing building, could barely see each other through all of the athletic clothing that had been hung up to dry on ropes in their room. They were so used to their wet clothing that, when it came time to training, they were no longer disgusted by the smell of wet wool or the cold dampness that stuck to their skin. One after the other, they'd get up from their beds and press their faces to the glass, looking off to the right at the choppy lake with the hope that perhaps the wind will die down, or at least change direction. The rain wasn't as much of a problem and there was nothing to be done about it. The water here on the last half-kilometre to the finish line, which was sheltered between islands and the peninsula, was manageable. The most difficult area was the first kilometre, where the waves could pick up speed across the lake and make it seem more like an ocean.

"Well, shit. It's bad out there. Should we raise the riggers a bit[39]?" Povilas suggested, turning to his friends. "We're in lane six, right?"

"Yeah," one of the guys replied – probably Celestinas.

"We'll have the largest waves," Romas nodded.

"We have to survive the first kilometre and things will get better. The important thing is not to let Trud break away. Which lane are they in?" asked Povilas, tying his shoe as he continued to gaze out the window.

"I think they're in the first one," their cox said from the bed in the back of the room.

"We have to hope that they're unaccustomed to weather like this and that they'll wind up splashing too much," Alfa said, reassuring himself.

"How can they be unaccustomed if they train in Khimki? It's like a proper sea up there!" Romas complained. "Remember '59? When Jukna and Bagdonavičius came in third because of the terrible waves? Ah, right, you weren't there... They were in second, but at the finish line, there were long waves that launched them right up into the sky! They were in the first lane, so the waves would bounce of the shore and hit them again! That's why they took third. It was on that reservoir they have there. There were boats going back and forth, and little motor boats, too. It was a mess!"

"Yeah, they have nice grand stands there but the course is terrible," Eugenijus agreed. "And they always give their own people the best lanes, farther away from the grandstands where there are less waves."

"It's no better in Leningrad. If it's windy, they'll get waves just like ours," Celestinas added. "I think they'll probably have a better time in the waves than we will."

"Who's that shouting?" asked the other Romas, who had just woken up. He stretched in bed and sat up. There were two men named Romas in the room. When one called them, either both or neither would respond.

Outside their window, a crowd of athletes were chanting "bu-re, bu-re."

"Hey, come quick, look!" Povilas shouted out loud. "Burevestnik is really going to town on Trud!"

The men crowded around the window and pushed past one another to watch that day's greatest sensation. Trud's women's eight was approaching

---

39   Riggers are adjusted for each rower's size. When raised higher, the oars' handles move along a higher trajectory during the stroke and the blade's recovery phase.

the finish line in third place. There were only 50 metres left and there was no more hope for a win.

"Would you look at that! They've been flogged. European champions, huh?" the men commented to one another, stunned by the sensational victory.

"Well, what do you expect? It's barely been a week since the European Championships. No matter how much of a champion you are, racing that much will take its toll," said Alfa, taking pity on the crew of champions.

"Who was second? Spartak?" Celestinas asked, trying to read the team's name.

"Where did Kuybyshev's crew come from?" Eugenijus asked with surprise.

"How did our girls do?"

"Looks like they're sixth... but look, they weren't that far behind – maybe two lengths from first place. They all seemed to finish fairly close to one another," Povilas noted.

"It's time for us to get ready because the ladies are done. We've got an hour and change," said Romas, looking at his watch.

"So what are we doing? Will we raise our riggers or not?" Povilas remembered.

"Maybe we should... What do you think, Alfa?" Romas asked, turning to Alfa.

"We can try it. It can't hurt," Alfa agreed.

"I've got to raise it by at least one so it won't hit my legs," said Povilas, turning to Celestinas and smiling mischievously. "Celestinas will have to raise it by two so he doesn't catch any octopuses."

The men laughed, and Celestinas also cracked a half-hearted smile. They were always reminding him of the old but painful misfortune from his first competition in Klaipėda. While rowing in the Vilnius eight, he caught a powerful crab. They lost the race to the Klaipėda crew, and one of his teammates said that what Celestinas had caught was an octopus, not a crab. He had been brought to tears – because of the lost competition and because of his team...

"We have to leave in fifteen minutes if we want to do anything," Celestinas shivered as he checked his watch.

"Be sure to take your jackets so you don't get cold before the race starts," Alfa warned them.

"We should wear long sleeves," Romas suggested.

"We can't race in shirts like these," Celestinas grabbed a balled-up sleeveless shirt with the word Lietuva on it in his fist. "We'll freeze."

"Yeah, we definitely will," Romas agreed. "We should put something on under them. What do we have with long sleeves that are the same colour? Anything blue?"

"My blue shirt is totally soaked," Povilas said, frowning as he touched his hanging shirt.

"You don't have anything else?"

"I have a blue button-up shirt. The colour's almost the same," said Povilas, holding it up to his soaked shirt to compare the colours. "It's dry."

"That will do," Romas agreed.

"I'm off, then. I'll try to raise my rigger," said Alfa. As always, he was in a hurry to adjust their boat. "Romas, should I raise it for you?"

"Yes, please, just by one."

"One will be enough for me, too!" Celestinas shouted to Alfa as he closed the door.

The men suddenly grew anxious. They quickly changed their shirts, put on their sneakers, and put on their wool rowing jackets with lengthened and waterproof backs before heading for the door. The team ran down the creaking wooden steps and out towards the lake. A chorus of shouts could be heard from above:

"Hey, good luck in your race, guys!" the girls gathered on the balcony waved to them.

The men looked around before looking up and waving to their "fans." As they hurried off towards the boathouse, their pre-race anxiety started making all of their movements more sudden and sharp, and their dry mouths kept them silent. The rain stopped and the sky began to clear up, though the wind and the waves showed no signs of stopping. In the distance, they could see a motorboat towing the starting pontoon to the end of the lake towards the two-kilometre start in the bay by the pioneers' camp. During the competition, that camp was full of rowers as well. The pioneers' camp often hosted teams from Ukraine and other republics, who brought their own trailers and boats.

The shoreline was full of women celebrating and congratulating or consoling one another. Their races were all finished, so they were hurrying off in various directions like ants with their boats and oars on their shoulders. Some were disassembling boats or loading them onto their trailers, others were tying them down or loading the riggers and seats, and yet others were carrying baskets and luggage. They were hurrying to put everything in order before the men's races.

At the boathouse, Alfa was unscrewing the riggers on the boats, which were still on their racks, and sliding in spacers.

"Hold on, we'll take them down, set up the slings," Povilas shouted to his cox.

The men raised their arms and carefully lifted their four onto the slings. While Alfa worked on the riggers, they tightened their stretchers, checked their pins, and polished their slides with rags.

"Where's your number?" Celestinas said, suddenly remembering his cox.

"On my shirt, under my coat. I'll take it off before the race," Pavlovas reported.

"Alright. Don't forget to grease the oars."

"Ok, I won't."

"Do you have a watch? How much time do we have?"

"About fifty minutes."

"We have to hit the water in fifteen minutes. We need a good warm-up in weather like this."

"I'll be done in a moment," said Alfa, overhearing the conversation. "Give me another thin spacer."

The cox searched through the nuts and bolts until he found a few spacers. The men took down their oars, waited for Alfa, and then marched down to the dock all together. Trud and Spartak's oars were already there. When they turned around to return to the boathouse, they nearly collided with the Leningrad team, which was carrying its boat. They exchanged polite nods and turned away from one another, their bodies once again overcome by anxiety.

There was a bit more than half an hour until the race. The umpires' motor boats started up noisily and left the shoreline for the starting positions. The fours and their coxes gathered by the dock. Traditionally, they kick off both the men's and women's programmes. More and more rowers were gathering by the boat houses and on the shoreline, and the grandstands were gradually filling with spectators who had warmed up during the break.

Eugenijus and Šarmatis, the coxless pair, hurried over to the boathouse. They would race immediately after the fours race and the pairs' small final.

"You haven't left yet?"

"We're going, we were raising our riggers," Alfa responded.

The men gathered by their boat.

"Alright, let's go the way we always do. The important thing is not to catch any crabs at the start – keep pressure on your oars," said Alfa, who was substituting for Ričardas while he was away. "Celestinas, we have to speed up after a kilometre. If nothing extraordinary happens, I think we'll place. After yesterday, we can see who…"

"Nonsense, Alfa," Romas interrupted him. "Yesterday was yesterday. Today, everything starts anew."

"That's right, there's no reason for guesswork here. Everything will be clear soon enough," Povilas agreed.

"Let's go," Celestinas said, encouraging them.

"Lift!" the cox commanded, and the four men raised the boat over their heads and marched off in single file towards the dock.

The four men had not yet lost the hope to one day stand shoulder to shoulder with the best – despite their short but painful histories, their injustices and injuries, the complete control that the communist government occupying Lithuania had exerted over their lives, and the fact that their parent's and ancestors' loyalty to their homeland had determined these men's futures.

They stopped by the dock and waited for the Moscow team to push off before lowering their boat into the water. The waves beat against the side of the boat and nearly swept over the sides. The cox jumped to the boat, grabbed it by the rigger, and pushed it off slightly so it wouldn't crack against the dock. The men locked in their oars, tested them out, placed their seats and, as a matter of habit, pushed them back and forth along the slides. The well-greased oars spun easily in their brass swivels.

"Get ready guys, hut!" the cox ordered, and the four gave a strong push off of the pontoon. Romas, who had brought his seat as far forward as it would go, struck the water with his oars and used short strokes to row away from the pontoon until he could be joined by his stroke and the two bowsides. Now that Celestinas was back in the four, Romas was rowing in the two seat. After getting far enough from the pontoon not to splash it and not to collide with other boats, the men stopped, tied in their feet, and tightened the screws.

"All four, paddle!" said the cox, beginning their warm-up.

The strong northern wind was like a wall. They stayed close to the shore so they wouldn't take on water and rowed around the island by the Tiškevičius manor. They then turned around and sped up, rowing towards the kilometre mark.

"Goddamnit," Povilas whispered to himself. "With wind like this, I can barely feel the catch." The coxed fours that would be rowing in the small final were gathering at the starting line. "Fifteen minutes until we race," he thought to himself.

"Fifteen minutes left," the cox announced after looking at his watch.

On the patched starting pontoon stood pieces of plywood as tall as a man with the lane numbers written on them. Near them stood the umpires, wrapped in their coats. The one in the middle raised a white flag and yelled into his megaphone: – "Go!" Six boats took off from the pontoon and raced off towards the finish line.

"Our turn," said Alfa.

"Let's wait until they invite us," Celestinas said, clearly in no hurry. As soon as he heard the umpire's invitation, he nodded to the cox.

"All four, half slide, go!"

The four crossed the entire course from the first lane to the sixth and turned its stern towards the handler. He was a curly-haired youth laying on a polyethylene blanket on one of the start pontoon's "tongues." He grabbed the stern of the boat so that he wouldn't interfere with the rudder and pulled it closer. Behind him, a cameraman hurried back and forth across the pontoon.

"Let's take our tops off," Alfa shouted from the front of the boat.

Povilas turned to look back over his right shoulder and ensure that the boat was looking straight at the finish line.

"Romas, give it a couple of strokes, our bow is drifting quite a bit."

Celestinas, with his arms around his knees, tried to overcome his anxiety. Alfa splashed some water on his handles. They were no longer looking at their opponents' boats. There were only a few minutes left until the race began. The most important thing was not to be left at the start and not to catch any crabs. They knew everything else well enough – how to row and how to endure.

The team survey began. This was it – the last few seconds. As soon as their name was called, the race would begin.

"Žalgiris, gatov[40]?"

---

40   Rus. „Ready"

The cox nodded.

"All ready! Square blades!" the cox shouted.

"Attention! Go!"

The stern of the boat slipped out of the handler's hands and took off down the course, carrying the Žalgiris crew towards that day's finish line at 46 strokes per minute. They kept their blades high to avoid any chance of clipping the water. "Good thing we raised the riggers" the men thought to themselves when they saw how the crews alongside them were being splashed. The wind at their back pushed on their oars like sails during their stroke recovery. Though Spartak were the first out of the starting line, they gradually evened out with the Lithuanians and Moscow's Trud.

Eugenijus and Romas, who were warming up alongside the race course, stopped to watch:

"You're making good speed! Keep it up!"

The three boats had been rowing bowball-to-bowball for almost a kilometre. The remaining three crews were so far behind that they no longer presented any challenge – unless something unexpected happened like a broken oar or an overturned boat. Having felt that the medals were within their grasp, the men focused all of their strength and, at the kilometre mark, the halfway point of the race, they began to speed up. Trud was ahead by half of a length, so they could still be caught, but the castle island, which would block the wind, was still a few hundred metres away.

"Let's go!" the cox urged his crew on. "Stroke… stroke…"

The Žalgiris crew was now right on the heels of the Trud crew. Spartak's cox could be heard shouting "Давай, ещё десять![41]"

The cox looked to the left. He knew Russian well.

"Let's go! Ten more! One!"

Out of the corner of his eye, he could see that Trud's boat was getting closer, stroke by stroke.

"Five hundred! Let's finish this!"

Celestinas picked up the pace even more. His ears, deafened by the intense pressure, could barely hear the cheers of the spectators in different languages as they carried across the water. "The grandstands… just a few more strokes..." – it seemed like there wasn't a single cell left in his body that didn't hurt. "Where's that finish line?" His head was ringing, his legs felt like they were made of stone, his eyes grew dark, and he felt as though

---

41   Rus. Come on, ten more!

his arms could no longer be drawn back to his waist. And just when it seemed like his soul would soon depart from his body, he heard a gong – like a church bell somewhere off in the distance. A second later, another gong, and then another. The men fell onto their wooden oar handles and tried to regain their breath.

"Second!" the cox shouted joyfully. The men moved back and forth in the boat with their hands on the oars. They could barely feel their legs – the only sensation was the mad beating in their chests. When they raised their eyes, they saw the last three teams catching up to them and understood that they had just won the silver medal in the USSR Championships.

"That was close," said Alfa, who was the first to catch his breath. Since he was rowing in the bow seat, he had the best view of the action.

"How much did we lose by?" said Povilas as he turned around. He was still having trouble with his breath.

"A third of a length."

"When did they get ahead?" Celestinas raised his head.

"At about two hundred," the cox commented.

"I had no idea we could possibly place…"

"Let's spin!" the cox shouted, "Bowside forward, strokeside back."

With their arms still trembling with fatigue, the men picked up their wooden oar handles and turned the boat around – the bowside drawing the oars towards themselves and the strokeside pushing them away. "It's over… it's over… the difference was so small… I could have taken just a few stronger strokes… no, I couldn't… silver is fine… but we were just a hair away from gold… too bad… it's over…".

They could hear thunderous applause and congratulations from the grandstands. The men looked back and shy smiles spread across their faces. With long and beautiful strokes, as if to thank the spectators for their support, they rowed past their fans and lined up at the dock. At the kilometre, they could see the pairs approaching.

"It's the small final. Eugenijus races afterward. Let's hurry up and get out," Povilas noted.

"You're right, let's make sure we can watch," Romas agreed. Out of all of them, he was the most concerned about watching his younger brother compete. "Hurry up."

At the pontoon, they were met by a throng of friends who had come to congratulate them.

"Good work, guys! That was a great race! Congratulations!" their friends said, shaking their hands and kissing them. "You guys are great! Our first medals!"

Though their fatigued legs felt like rags, they clambered out of the boat, shook each others' hands, put on the thoroughly damp tracksuit bottoms they had left in the boat, and finally understood that it was all behind them – all of the anxiety, tension, pain and fear of failure was behind them. They had accomplished more than anyone had expected of them, more than they had openly expected of themselves – though who's to say whether they hadn't occasionally dreamed of victory.

"Get ready! Hut!" they raised the boat over their heads on their trembling arms. With every step, their fatigue faded and they began to feel their extremities. They even began to want to share in the joy of winning silver.

After placing the boat on the slings, they quickly dried it off and carried it into the boathouse.

"We'll bring the oars back later. Who's going to go watch?" Romas urged them on.

"Let's all go," said Povilas, hurrying off behind him.

"Do you see anything? Alfa asked, staring off towards the horizon. "Which lane are they in?"

"Second. Doesn't look like they've started yet," said Romas. He was more anxious than he had been for his own race. "What time is it?"

"It's half past."

"Then they should be starting."

"I think they're moving now."

The men, who had crowded onto the dock to get as close to the race course as possible, squinted to see the distant start line better.

"Looks like the wind's dying down," Alfa noted.

"It just looks calmer here. It's a real ocean over by the starting line. See them splashing?" Romas disagreed.

"It's neck and neck," said Povilas, rubbing his hands.

"I hope they don't catch any crabs," Romas said uneasily.

"They're making good time," Celestinas agreed. "It looks like they're overtaking them."

"They're at the kilometre."

"Look, they're first!"

"It just looks that way because they're dressed in white," said Romas, who didn't want to celebrate too soon.

"No, they're way ahead!" Povilas said gladly.

"They've still got a way to go."

"Let's go! Let's go! Let's go!" the grand stands began to chant in Lithuanian, though the finish line was still more than five hundred metres away. "I doubt they'll hear us."

"Go, Romas!" the men couldn't contain their joy.

The pair easily widened the distance between themselves and their opponents. Their progress seemed effortless.

"No way!" Romas shouted happily.

"Thirty-four at the finish, just like in training!" Alfa exclaimed with surprise.

The men's pair rowed past them, more than two lengths ahead of their opponents.

"Go!" yelled Povilas.

The spectators were on their feet and clapping furiously. The second gong went off a full seven seconds after the first. Up until then, the eight and the Jukna-Bagdonavičius pair had been the only ones to win the USSR Championships.

Povilas clapped his hand on Romas' shoulder:

"You see? You had nothing to worry about!"

The four waited on the pontoon at the head of the line – they wanted to be the first to congratulate the champions. The men's coaches and friends were there shaking their hands, kissing them and celebrating before they had even gotten out of their boat.

"You guys are great!" Povilas joyfully shook the new champions' hands. "Congratulations!"

"Thank you, thank you! How did you place?"

"We were in second place. We lost by a second."

"Good work!"

While celebrating their victories, the men of Žalgiris weren't thinking about their futures. They weren't thinking about what these victories would lead to or where their USSR titles would take them. They simply wanted to enjoy their moment of good fortune, which was so brief and would quickly recede into the past. The following day would be a new day, and there would be new champions – or perhaps the old ones would step aside and hand over their places to them. This was the only day when they could wear their medals shamelessly and enjoy their friends' congratulations.

*

"What are you going to do next week?" Povilas asked a worried-looking Celestinas as he packed his things.

"I'm going to visit my parents. I'll be back on Wednesday."

"So are we meeting on Wednesday or Thursday?"

"It would be nice to do some rowing again on Wednesday. What do you think?"

"Alright, let's meet on Wednesday around lunchtime," Romas joined their conversation. "How about you, Alfa?"

"Yeah, yeah, I'll be there. According to our schedule, we should be doing race pieces by Thursday. Let's leave the boat like this for now, don't take it back down. We'll see what the weather's like."

"Alright, guys, I'm off, I've got a long road ahead of me," said Celestinas, who was headed for the door after quickly packing his clothes.

"Hold on, Celestinas," Povilas waved. "Isn't this yours?" he asked, picking up a brown envelope from the dresser.

"That's mine, give it here," Celestinas grabbed the envelope.

Povilas only had time to see the first line of the address – "MOCKBA[42]" – before the envelope slipped out of his hand. Without a word, Celestinas went out the door. After putting the envelope into an inner pocket of his coat, he descended the stairs and hurried off towards the fisherman's boat. The long letter that he had crafted, word by word, sentence by sentence, after starting and tearing it up many times before, finally had to be sent out. Nobody could know about or "intercept" the letter, so he couldn't send the letter from Vilnius. On the way to his parents' homeland, Celestinas was to hop out of an unknown train station, take the brown envelope to a mailbox, and return to his seat with a deep sigh of relief. "Now, whatever will happen will happen, there's nowhere to run." The familiar sights of his journey home would soon flit past him in the window. The cottages might be a bit more crooked, the trees might be a bit bigger, and the bushes might be a bit greener, but it was all there. The closer he got to Kretinga, the clearer his inescapable recollection became of that sunny May morning in 1949 in Klausgalvų Medsėdžiai. The starlings' cries still echoed in his

---

42   Rus. Moscow

RIMA KARALIENE

ears, and he could still see the *stribai* lined up outside of the window. He was only ten when the *stribai* surrounded his home, drove them all into one room, and read a letter out loud indicating that they were being removed from Lithuania. His father tried to open the window and run, but one of the *stribai* grabbed him by the shoulder and stopped him: "Don't be stupid, Jucys. Pack your things." "Run wherever you can, children. They'll shoot you dead!" his father had said, still hoping to save his children from death. Celestinas took off through the cellar that led to the yard, through the nearby ditches and into the forest. From far away, he watched a loaded wagon take his family away to their fates. He walked along the forest for a long time, unsure of where to go. However, the *stribai* that were looting the cottage noticed him from afar. "Take this one, too!" one shouted, but he was so absorbed by looting the farmer's cottage that he forgot about the child, and Celestinas escaped. He was hungry, cold and afraid, and he didn't know what to do and where to hide. Suddenly, his neighbour appeared. "Come with me, Celestinas," he said, taking the child's hand. Celestinas remained in a dream-like daze until he came to his neighbour's cottage and saw his thirteen-year-old older brother waiting there. He had managed to escape the *stribai* as well. They both remained with their neighbour – though he was poor, he wouldn't leave the two boys to fend for themselves. Though they had to sleep in one room with a goat and its kids, they had a roof over their heads and adults nearby that they could feel safe with. A week later, a rumour spread throughout the village that his family had been released from the train car. Earlier on, his father's brother, Adolfas, had told him: "If anything happens, send me a telegram." He was a scientist and an associate professor at the Physics Faculty of Vilnius University. Four years ago, he had received a USSR PhD in Physics and Mathematics and was appointed an associate professor, and he had been a director at the Vilnius Pedagogical Institute for a year. He was a man with authority, and not just in academic circles. A telegram to his brother Adolfas was the last straw that Celestinas' father had grabbed for on his way to the train station. There was only an hour or two left until the train was supposed to move out when they were unloaded onto the train station and told to go home.

They had avoided exile and the destruction of their family through a miracle, and the family was able to gather once again at their ancestral home.

Not everyone had waited to see whether or not they would be exiled. Celestinas' grandfather – his mother's father – didn't expect anything good from the communist government and had fled to America with his younger children at the beginning of the war. He had no idea that his actions might earn his loved ones a name as "enemies of the people." He did not think and could not have known that his grandson would become a strong rower who would nonetheless have to endure injustices and insults. He would not have known that, while his team was preparing to leave for Lucerne, Celestinas would be marching along a dusty road towards his childhood home with a suitcase in his hand.

✳

The finals of the first World Rowing Championships were held in Lucerne that Sunday. At the suggestion of FISA president Thomas Keller, all of the small finals – for places 7 through 12 – were to be held in the morning. This rule received broad support and would eventually become permanent.

The Soviet propaganda machine once again searched for ways to sully the name of the organisers of the event and the international rowing federation. In an effort to remove politics from the sporting event, the organisers decided to play the FISA anthem during the event rather than participating countries' anthems. They also decided not to tally countries' results into a medal table.

FISA had not yet acknowledged the German Democratic Republic, and the German teams could only participate with one crew in each boat class. Therefore, a qualifying race was held the day before the Championships between the teams of East and West Germany.. The West Germans and their coach, Karl Adam, triumphed in all of the sweep events, and the only sculls available were singles and pairs.

In the eights final, five crews finished in under six minutes. Though everyone was talking about how "easy" the waters of the Rotsee were and how surprised they were at their results during their training sessions, this was still an impressive achievement.

Letters from all over the world flew into Lucerne with special 10-cent postage stamps issued just for the championships. They featured images of a rower bent over in his olive-coloured boat on a sea-green background. The white lettering on the top of the stamp read: "RUDER-WELTMEISTARSCHAFT LUZERN 6-9.9.1962 HELVETIA."

The next World Championships would only be held four years later.

9 September, 1962 was an eventful day not just in Lucerne, but around the world as well.

Kęstutis Orentas set the LSSR record for running 5,000 metres at a competition in Tallinn – 14:13.0. Lithuanian basketball player Jūratė Daktaraitė had an excellent game with the USSR's basketball team as the top scorer in the first women's game between the USSR and Poland.

Russia celebrated Tankman's Day and the government renamed all locations that had been named after Molotov, Kaganovich and Malenkov, since they had tried to eject Khrushchev from government in 1957. Those in Vilnius who had television began seeing Moscow central television programmes.

A train without a crew began to operate in New York. More than three thousand people died in a landslide in Peru. Yves Saint Laurent presented his leggings in Paris. Within a few years, they would spread through Czechoslovakia to reach Soviet women as well, though bearing a Czechoslovakian name – "kolgotki[43]."

＊

---

43   Czech. "kalhoty" – pants

11

"Povilas, can you develop these?" asked James, handing Povilas a roll of film.

"Hey, James! Wow, you're sure dressed up. Where are you going? What is this?" asked Povilas, taking the roll of film and inspecting it.

"You'll see. These are our future victories," James smiled mysteriously.

"I wonder what you've come up with here. Alright, I'll do it. Do you need them quickly?"

"The sooner you get them done, the sooner we'll hand them over to the factory. These are photos of the Germans' oars."

"Where did you get them?"

"When everybody left the course, Rychka and I measured them and took photos."

"Well you guys are proper spies, aren't you?"

"Nobody else in the world rows with blades as long as ours anymore. We look funny next to them. The Germans' oars were totally different. There's no way we'll beat them with our old ones."

"You think somebody here will make them for us?"

"Rychka will take them to Kaunas, Startas should make them. A man named Antanas Baranauskas works there, they say he's a master craftsman and that he makes all of our oars."

"Tell me how things went in Lucerne."

"You probably know all about it by now."

"I know that you were second and that the Germans were first. And that's it. But how did it go?"

"It could've been better. There were two false starts. The Italians did one and they said we did the other. So on the third start, we sat still until everyone had started moving."

"So you had to catch up?"

"We caught up at about five hundred, but then the Germans picked up the pace and left us behind. We tried to catch them at the kilometre mark but then they took off too and we could no longer keep up. We lost by less than a length."

"Silver's good too!" Povilas consoled him.

"It is, but we wanted to win so badly!"

"At least you went, James. There was no chance for us…"

"Don't worry, Povilas, everything will end up alright. By the way, how did we do in the Union championships?"

"Our four was second, we lost by a second. Eugenijus and Šarmaitis won."

"'Atta boys!" James said happily.

"Yup… but what's the point… How was Switzerland?"

"It's incredibly beautiful there. The town was very beautiful, and the Lake Lucerne was so clean and blue. It was surrounded by mountains, and everything was green and covered in flowers. The hotel was nothing like the ones here. It was orderly, beautiful, and the food was good. The championships event was on another lake, Rotsee. It was smaller and narrow so there weren't any waves."

"How was the weather?"

"Nice and sunny. It only rained one day – all day during the opening. After that, the weather was fine. The wind was at our backs a bit during the final, but you know us, we prefer rowing up against the wind. With the wind at their backs, the Germans rowed like nobody's business. We gave it everything we had at the final…"

"Which boat did you race with?"

"A Swiss boat. They gave it to use as soon as we got there, straight from the factory."

"And how was it?"

"Where do I begin? It was a totally new experience! We needed a few sessions to get used to it and regulate it, of course, but it had a much stiffer hull and didn't drift the way ours does."

"Did you take the "German" with you, too?"

"No, we let the Romanians borrow it. At one point, we regretted this because, the day before the final, we found that someone had messed with our new boat. We found it in the morning with a crack. Stämpfli fixed it for us, but it's strange because we weren't the only ones with this misfortune. I think that the coxed four also had something wrong, and Trud's pair as well."

"So who do you think sabotaged the boats? Could it be that you guys just made a mistake somehow?"

"I doubt it. Either our opponents or one of ours, out of envy. Who knows? The night before the final, Samsonov set up guards."

"That's strange… Did the other teams' boats break?"

"We didn't hear of anything."

"You guys went there early. Did you get bored at all? What did you do until the championships?"

"At first, Petras and I went to the movies in the evenings. It was interesting, except that we didn't really understand the language so we stopped going soon enough."

"What will you do now?"

"We're going to Crimea to relax, in Gurzuf. They bought us tickets."

"Well, that's good for you guys."

"I'm not sure how good it is. I've abandoned my studies again and I have to catch up to everyone. But I'll probably go. The season has been a very tiring one and I want to rest without thinking about anything. How are things for you, Povilas? How is your daughter?"

"She's growing up beautifully. Gita's going to have to go back to work soon, so my mother-in-law will take care of her. It's too bad that I don't have much time to be with her. However, I usually return in the evenings. I don't stay in Trakai."

"Give her my regards."

"I sure will. So what are you all dressed up for? Will there be some sort of reception?"

"We're going to Žalgiris stadium this evening. There will be some sort of ceremony. They told us to take our medals."

"Ah, I see. Rychka said that there won't be any training tonight. I couldn't understand why."

"You know what I think, Povilas? I think that we would have beat the Germans with you and Celestinas. With Dima and Slava, it's not the same…"

Povilas managed a smile with one corner of his lips:

"Those are empty words, James."

He juggled the roll of film in his hand, threw it up, caught it, and put it in his pocket.

"I'll do it, James. Come by tomorrow. Or we can meet in Trakai."

*

On the evening of Thursday, 13 September, Vilnius residents gathered in Žalgiris stadium[44] – which had recently been renamed from Spartakas stadium – after work to support their football team, which was battling Leningrad's Zenit for the right to remain in the A class. In the mean time, the rowers from Žalgiris' eight – Vaitkevičius, Jukna, Bagdonavičius, Briedis, Karla and Jagelavičius – were anxiously waiting for the half-time break with their medals on their jackets.

A fresh sign hung between four flagpoles near the western grandstands that read "WE CONGRATULATE OUR ROWERS – THE WORLD VICE-CHAMPIONS!" Where they were seated on the first row, they were close enough to the action to reach out and touch it. They had kicked a ball around many times during their practises and competed amongst themselves, and even watched football games in that same stadium, but they couldn't help but point out the contrasts: "It's all so different from how we do things when we row. When you're tired, you can walk for a bit. When you fall down, your team keeps going. If you're exhausted, there's a bench of players waiting for you. Even if you sat through the entire game, you'll still get a medal if your team wins… You can't do that in a boat… You can't give up for even a single stroke. If you catch a crab, that's three to five seconds lost for your entire team, and sometimes more. If you're exhausted, you'll have to suffer until the finish line. Nobody will replace you in the middle of the race, there's no bench… And you can't even relax for a moment during training, either. And you'll never have as many spectators as there are here in this stadium. Well, not unless you go to a world championships or the Olympics." Despite this, however, they were captivated by the game, watching Beinoravičius and Stankevičius kicking the ball – which would sometimes fly within centimetres of them. After receiving a pass to the left corner, Glodenis made the first goal of the game, and the rowers jumped up together with the rest of the fans, their medals clinking on their chests. The surrounding spectators soon noticed the tall men in suits. "Look, it's the rowers! Yeah, I saw them in the newspaper!" they heard some young men nearby guessing at their identities. "That's right, that big one's Bagdonavičius. He's an Olympic champion!" "No he's not, they were second..."

---

44   Construction on the stadium began immediately after World War 2. It was completed in 1948 by German prisoners. It was called Dinamo at first, and then Spartakas, and was renamed Žalgiris in 1961.

The umpire's whistle marked the end of the first half and the players left for the locker rooms. Two workers quickly rolled a red carpet out onto the grass and brought a table, covering it in a tablecloth. The announcer introduced the world silver medallists who had come to the stadium and the grandstands erupted in applause. With their legs trembling, the six men rose up from their seats, lined up like a wall, and marched together in step along the carpet towards the table, where various city representatives were lined up in front of the microphones. After stopping in front of the crowd of thousands, the men shifted their weight about in an effort to control their anxiety as they listened to the congratulatory speeches.

At first, Ričardas began arranging the words for his response speech in his head, but then he turned to Zigmas and said, "You speak for us." His lips barely moved as he asked Zigmas to speak.

Nearby, a team of reporters busily snapped pictures, and they all had identical cameras. Cameramen were filming every moment of the ceremony.

"We feel a sort of debt for this warm reception. Your applause, attention and welcome have inspired us to reach for more than what we've achieved so far, we are indebted to you. In our team's name, I promise not to spare any of our strength in our fight for new victories," said Zigmas, thanking those who had gathered. With that, all six of them turned away towards the running track.

The lap of honour, which they would complete as the stadium applauded and waved to them, was a rare honour that not every athlete gets to experience, and certainly not every rower.

And the men understood this perfectly well.

*

At the end of September, a long-awaited piece of news reached the rowers – they would soon be joined by yet another rowing family. All of the Žalgiris rowers and coaches were invited to the wedding celebration. Eugenijus Vaitkevičius laughed that his brother Ričardas' rowers had "tempted" another lady out of the women's eight he was coaching.

"Hey, Povilas," said Zigmas as he knocked on Povilas' door on Čiurlionis Street.

"Oh, Zigmas! Hey! What brings you here?"

"I have a request…" said Zigmas, shyly stepping in through the door.

"Let's hear it."

"Could you take photos at our wedding?"

"Do you really need me to?" asked Povilas, testing his teammate's patience.

"Nobody can do it better than you."

"Nonsense!"

"It's true, Povilas. We'd really like for you to take the photos," said Zigmas, now afraid that Povilas might refuse.

"Alright, alright, I was just pulling your leg."

"I really was afraid there for a second," Zigmas sighed.

"I'd promised Irena long ago that I would. Perhaps before you guys were even engaged," Povilas laughed.

Povilas and Irena had been friends and classmates since their first year at the university. Povilas, who was fun and affable, often dragged his classmates out of their boring CPSU history and political economics classes to walk through Vilnius – and he always had his camera with him. His young classmates, who had come from Lithuania's villages to study, enjoyed the walks along Vilnius' streets and alleys. They'd visit the city's parks and climb up Gediminas Hill or enjoy the nature and the changing seasonal sights. Just like anyone else arriving in Vilnius, they felt obliged to take pictures sitting on the rock in Gediminas' square in front of the castle or on the banks of the Neris in front of Raduškevičiai Manor. Povilas, who used his film roll freely, took pictures of his smiling classmates as they admired the panorama from Gediminas Hill, as they walked by Vilnius Cathedral, as they enjoyed the winter's first snow, as they studied in the university's courtyards, as they walked along the banks of the Neris, or lined up in front of Pushkin's bust at the foot of Gediminas Hill. Then, at night, he'd develop the photos and bring them to his classes the next day. His friends nearly got into fights when sharing the photos amongst themselves, so Povilas tried to make sure that there were enough for everyone – as many photos as there were people in them.

"Hold on… when exactly are you guys getting married?" Povilas tried to recall.

"On 29 September, it'll be a Saturday. Gita didn't give you the invitation?"

"Oh right, she had showed it to me. I'm just not sure if Gita will be able to make it. Rasa is still too little to be without her mother."

"Maybe just for a little while?"

- Maybe she'll come by to the civil registry, but I'm not sure about the party."

"But will you be there?" Zigmas once again grew uneasy.

"Of course I will, I promised. Whatever happens, I can't let Irena down," Povilas laughed. "Where and when should I show up?"

"Could you meet me by the registry before one? We have to be there at one."

"Got it."

"We'll pay you for your work and for the materials."

"That will come afterward. I've got to take the pictures first. Successfully. Who knows, maybe they'll get exposed or something," Povilas teased Zigmas again.

"Stop that, I'm already wound up tighter than before a race."

"Why worry? I was totally relaxed during my wedding. It's a celebration, after all!"

"Alright, sure. Who did that to your chin?"

"My razor, of course! I had nothing to do with it," the men laughed.

"Were you really totally relaxed?"

"What is there to worry about? Now women, with them I understand. They need to get organize their oufit, jewellery, and all sorts of gloves and nonsense… There's so much running around between stores when they're all empty!"

"I thought that might be a problem while I was still in America," Zigmas confessed shyly, unsure of whether he should continue. "I bought some white cloth for Irena's dress."

"Really? Were you guys already planning your wedding back then?"

"I was, I had just forgotten to tell her," Zigmas smiled.

"That's great!" Povilas laughed. "Now that's confidence! It's a good thing she agreed, because otherwise, you'd be sewing window curtains!"

"If you only knew how long I stood there before I chose something, Povilas! There were so many fabrics! And they were all so beautiful… we don't have anything like them here…"

"On the other hand, we do have the most beautiful women! And everything suits them, too."

"That's true," Zigmas smiled.

"Have you invited a lot of guests?"

"I invited everybody. Our team, Irena's team, our relatives, Rychka and the other coaches, Dima Semionov from Moscow, and all sorts of acquaintances."

"Who will your witness be?"

"James and Audra."

"I see. It'll be fun. Will you be celebrating at Žalgiris?"

"That's right. I just hope it doesn't rain, I don't want to get wet."

"I heard that the last week will be sunny. It might not be terribly warm, but there shouldn't be any rain."

"Well then… We'll be waiting for you, Povilas. Thank you."

"It was nothing, at least not yet, anyway."

"There is, there is. Alright, I'm leaving. Give Gita my regards!"

"Thanks. In that case, I'll see you next Saturday."

*

12

After the sunny Saturday of Zigmas and Irena's wedding, the Žalgiris eight left for a vacation in Crimea.

Those who hadn't "earned" tickets, on the other hand, continued their lives in Lithuania. They began their studies, visited their parents, or simply relaxed.

Povilas found more free time to walk around Vingis Park with his stroller and to visit his aunt and uncle in Prienai. He helped them with their autumn yard work and garden chores. He found time to develop leftover photo rolls from that summer, to develop the photos from Zigmas' wedding, and to take new photos not of rowing, but of the people he loved. The rowers only gathered at the rowing camp once a day for training. They'd spend some days simply running somewhere closer to home and visited Trakai on the weekends.

There was an Indian summer at the beginning of October. The days were sunny and warm, with the temperature sometimes rising up to 18 degrees, so the rowing season at the Žalgiris boathouse in Vilnius had not yet ended.

Young rowers, schoolchildren and students rushed up and down the rickety wooden steps. Pranciškus the "Boatswain" observed them all watchfully from the corner of the terrace. This mustachioed gentleman was an integral part of the boathouse, a permanent fixture. Everyone who came to their first rowing practice here saw him, always in the same spot, always the same.

Pranciškus had lived here since before the war. When his wife's sister's home burned down on the other side of the Neris in 1942, Pranciškus brought the family to live at the boathouse with their two children – eleven-year-old Eugenijus and nine-year-old Ričardas. The boys grew accustomed to touching the boats and the oars from an early age and watched the big men row along the rapid river Neris. During the German occupation, soldiers would often come knocking on the door of the camp, looking for a place to row. At their request, Eugenijus would steer the pair, and they'd give him a couple of marks for his trouble. He'd spend them on a movie or buy some candy. At the time, nobody thought that these boys would become dedicated rowers. Though Mr. Pranciškus didn't row himself, he had taught them much – about how to identify different types of boats and how to care for and repair them.

Pranciškus was the director, guard and cleaner for the camp – he did everything. That's why they called him the Boatswain. Many didn't even know his name. Nobody who headed out onto the water could escape his watchful eye. The Boatswain had a thick journal that all of the athletes had to sign when leaving and returning with boats. A new journal appeared at the beginning of every year, and the old one, with a worn-out cover and scribbled full of dates, surnames and signatures, would be stored on the shelves in the boathouse. God forbid you'd forget to sign it – you wouldn't be able to return to the water for two days. That was the punishment the Boatswain had decided on.

"Are you guys going to go rowing?" the Boatswain asked with surprise when he saw Povilas and Alfa entering the gate to the camp.

"If we find a boat for ourselves, we will. Ours is left in Trakai," said Povilas, crossing the terrace and leaning on the railing to enjoy the sights he had seen so long ago.

The Neris flowed on underneath him without stopping. The Vilnelė River flowed into it on the left, just a few metres away. The eddies at this rocky confluence had struck fear into the hearts of many beginner rowers. The strong current constantly carried them downriver, and there would be no way to return other than to "dig in" with their oars and row up the river.

Two white steamboats were moored farther downriver. They would soon be taken up the river to spend the winter in a calm backwater. The wake from these boats always upset the rowers, as they'd have to stop and wait for the waves to peter out as they hit the shore. The worst part, however, was finding yourself between two steamboats that were passing one another. At that point, the river became more like the finish line at the Khimki reservoir. Sometimes, it seemed like the fragile boats would snap in half when lifted up on the waves, and that the oars, lifted out of the water by the waves, couldn't save the rowers from an inevitable bath.

A new, white swimming pool shone on the opposite bank of the river. Beyond that stood Žalgiris stadium. The green hills beyond stood further still on the horizon. They rarely rowed with the current towards the centre of the city.

There had been races to Žvėrynas Bridge and back again, as was the case during Povilas' first autumn of rowing when he raced in a gig boat. As he steered, the coach, Zinkevičius, handled the turns perfectly, steering the bow of the boat into the calmer waters behind the bridge's pillars while the current carried the other end. They won with the best time.

The rower spent most of their time to the right of the camp, upriver, past the Sluškos Manor. The manor had been a political prison since the time of tsarist Russia. The agricultural mechanisation school had been transferred there only a few years ago. Older Vilnius residents would recount how they saw German prisoners being ferried from the building to the stadium construction site.

The neighbourhood of Antakalnis started just beyond the towers of the Church of Peter and Paul. The riverbank there was dotted with fishermen, who'd sometimes complain that the rowers were scaring off their fish. The higher right-hand bank across from Antakalnis was covered in bushes. There were talks that the construction of a new neighbourhood would soon begin in the area.

Wherever the river grew shallower and quicker, the boats would nearly come to a stop against the current – no matter how hard they rowed. However, the rowers had fun flying through the shallow areas on their return to the camp. They'd sometimes day-dream about flying along at the same speed during a competition.

After rowing five kilometres, you'd reach a beach with a round pavilion. On hot days, the beach was covered in bathers and teenagers who, ignoring the warning buoys, would grab at the oars and occasionally get an oar blade to the neck. It was a good thing that the summer training was now held in Trakai and that they no longer had to "battle" the beach-goers.

"Have you seen Celestinas?" asked Alfa, turning to the Boatswain.

"I saw him," he replied, waving towards the locker rooms. "Long time no see, gentlemen! How is everything?"

"Good," Alfa answered briefly. "The season's is ending."

"They say it'll be a nice October. Perhaps you'll do a bit more rowing?"

"Maybe… but we've just about had our fill. The season's been longer than ever. I'd like to rest a bit as well."

"Summer and autumn have traded places. We were cold and wet all the way up until October, and now, the summer we've all been waiting for!" Povilas added.

The men leaned against the railings and watched how a young men's eight rowed off from the dock. Throughout the summer, the water level had receded considerably. The wooden posts that had been hammered next to one another into a solid wall near the concrete riverbank stuck out of the water and over the dock by more than half a metre. Climbing up had become difficult. They had to jump down to board, and getting back up with the boat on their shoulders was even more challenging.

"Look how low the water is, even though it's been raining all summer," Povilas noted.

"It's always like this in autumn. It was even lower last year. Remember?"

"Did Romas come by?"

"He said he'd be ten to fifteen minutes late."

"Looks like he misses the slippers," Povilas laughed. The Žalgiris men had come up with their own traditional punishment. Latecomers had to prepare their backsides to receive a "slipper," or a whack on the behind with a sneaker, for every minute that they were late. It was even worse during their training programmes, when late arrivals would either lose their cold snacks or their dessert. Nobody ever challenged this and everyone followed the rules.

They heard the chatter of voices coming up from below. Some new trainee women were leaving the boathouse with their oars. The oars would catch on the columns and on each other, and they'd start giggling after each whack. They probably saw the grown men watching them from above. They passed the oars down one by one to the dock so they wouldn't have to climb back and forth and crowded back into the boathouse. The coach at the door was patiently explaining the rules for carrying out the boat and watched to make sure they wouldn't catch the other boats or the boathouse's wide doors with the riggers.

"Everyone has to go through this. Remember what fools we looked like at first?" said Alfa as he watched the new girls.

"And how we dragged those training boats around... If not for Zinkevičius, I don't know if I would have gotten so interested in rowing," said Povilas, who waved to his first coach when he saw him getting out of his motorboat. "He told us such interesting stories in the beginning and said we'd be champions."

"He wasn't lying," Alfa laughed.

"He was rowing in the eight himself back then..."

"He's only three years older than me. How old is he now? He should be thirty one."

"Hey, guys!" Petras Zinkevičius waved from below. "You guys are finally here!"

Zinkevičius climbed up the stairs to greet them.

"We were just discussing your age. Are you thirty one?"

"Why? Do I seem older?" Petras laughed.

"No, no, we were just saying… we were trained by people no older than us."

"Who better to understand you than people your age?" Petras said happily as he shook the men's hands.

"There are a lot of young people," Alfa noted.

"With results like these, everybody wants to start rowing. There's more than ever this year. They've joined me, Jonis and Eugenijus. Everybody's hoping to travel to America together," he laughed.

"I just hope the winter doesn't scare them off. Good thing they're getting to try it out on the water."

"If they get scared off, they've got no business rowing, right? The best will stay, and that's all we need."

"Right."

"You guys going to go rowing?"

"Probably."

"It'll be dark by six thirty, so hurry up," the coach warned them.

"It's only four now, we'll have plenty of time!" Alfa laughed.

The much shorter October days change the men's training schedules as well. The rowers hurried to the club immediately after their lectures and classes.

The doors to the terrace opened and in walked Eugenijus, the women's coach.

"Hey!" said Povilas, extending his right hand.

"Oh, hello! What are you guys all watching?" the coach responded happily.

"We're enjoying the beauty of Vilnius. We're enjoying the autumn."

"Ah, I see, I see. And what do you see that's so beautiful?"

"We've missed this place, so everything's beautiful to us."

"Everything's changed so much since the war. It used to look different. You see, over there?" Eugenijus said, pointing to the other riverbank.

"Those big boathouses next to the winter base, where the barracks are? That used to be a military club. Oh, what fine boats they had. The military club was a very wealthy one."

"What did they have those boats for? Did they row to war?" Povilas joked.

"What for? Well, to row, of course! After the war, the Russians threw the boats out of the boathouses and turned them into garages. They stacked the boats one on top of another like firewood. The Russian soldiers got into those boats with their combat boots and tried to row them with sticks. The boats were made entirely of redwood! They were German and Danish. They were spectacular boats! Such a shame…"

"It sure is. There's nothing left of them?"

"Rychka and I were just little runts back then, so we'd row to the other bank at night and drag the boats to the river, one by one. We'd fill them with sand, sink them in the Neris, and then drag them to our camp a few days later. We managed to save a few. Now the kids row them."

"I see. If it weren't for you, we'd have nothing to row!"

"After the war, there was just one single eight in all of Lithuania. We even had our competitions while sharing it. One team races, then we switch and another team races. We'd compare times at the end."

"How do you train with one boat?"

"As well as you might expect. We shared it. Everybody fought over space in the boat. There were lines and scandals… Of course, there were fours and pairs as well, but for a long time, we had only one eight."

"I see! What an interesting story. I never would've thought. It seemed like everything had always been this way."

"Oh, and how many more of those boats simply left our country! After the war, they brought a train car from Germany to Vilnius with training fours and pairs. They lay around in the old stadium for about half a year, stored under the grand stands. I don't know whose they were. Later, they exchanged them for boots and football clothing and took them out of Lithuania."

"Who did?"

"Who knows? There was no order after the war. Everybody did as they pleased. We only had whatever we gathered ourselves here. They had to be protected, after all."

"So this club has been here for a while, then?"

"Yeah. They first built it in 1912, I believe, but it burned down, so in

1931, the Polish built a new building on the same cement. The Boatswain said that they opened it in 1933. At home, we have a little board that my mother called a 'cegelka.' It says, in Polish, 'I donate such and such a number of zloty for the construction of the club,' and there's a sketch of the club on there as well... I can show you later. People made donations for its construction. When we moved in here, the list of people who donated and how much still hung on the wall. I don't know where it is now, maybe the Boatswain took it down. They didn't have the other hall at first. It was added on later. There were no walls, either. We kept the boats here under this balcony, behind the columns."

"It's strange... We've been rowing here for so long and never knew any of these stories. Rychka ever told us anything," Povilas said, surprised.

"Well, Povilas, the young people only had a few things on their minds... rowing and dancing with the girls," Alfa laughed.

"Over there, towards the Sluškai manor, right next to the prison fence, there was a Jewish club as well," Eugenijus continued. "It was one of the wealthiest. The Muscovites took it all away after the war. We brought a few boats home with us, quads. The schoolchildren's club was close to their club, about twenty metres away. It was just a wooden boathouse, a bit further from the bank up on the house, so they didn't get wet as often."

"So many clubs! Where are they now?"

"Before the war, there were about eleven clubs here. You know, everything changed. There were firewood shortages during the war, so they dragged away board after board until there was nothing left here but the foundation. They used the other ones to make garages, warehouses and other stuff."

"It's a good thing this one survived. And that one, too," said Povilas, nodding to right, where two rowers were rowing out of the nearby rowing club.

"Of course! The Boatswain wouldn't have allowed them to destroy it. This is his only home. There's nothing convenient about it, but what a location! He had to get water from across the street with a bucket, though he had to bathe in the river."

"Was the water cleaner back then?"

"Maybe it was, but they ferried rafts through here for a long time, so rowing was impossible. There were all sorts of trash in the water, and there would have been a danger of collisions."

"Hey, guys! Sorry I'm late," said Romas as he came in through the gate.

"Hey there, Romas!" said Povilas, extending his hand. "Where were you?"

"Ah, sorry, I was at the cinema. I told Alfa."

"Yeah, he said. What were you watching?"

"A comedy. 'The Dinner Party.' It came out recently. The most interesting thing, however, was the journal clip[45]. We were in it!"

"What?"

"It was during 'Soviet Lithuania.[46]' They showed the Soviet championships in Trakai. It had our four and Eugenijus and Romas. They showed the women's eight, too."

"Really?"

"They showed us at the starting line, how we prepared and how we started."

"That would be interesting to see."

"Then go to Kronika[47], they should be showing it."

"That'd be nice, but I don't know how long I'll have to wait until I see 'Soviet Lithuania.'"

"Make sure you go, they won't show it later."

"Alright. We should move, it'll get dark soon. This was an interesting talk, coach. Thanks."

"Oh alright, go on then. My kids are just rowing back now so I'll go meet them. By the way, how is Gita doing? How's the child?"

"She'd good, she's growing, it's all wonderful. She likes to sing at night sometimes so we wake up in shifts."

"Good on you for helping Gita."

"What else can I do?"

"You've got to send Gita my regards. And Vanda, too," said Eugenijus. He never forgot his trainees.

"For sure, thanks!"

"Where are the others?" Romas looked around.

---

45   Documentary (propaganda) films that were shown before a movie began.

46   A documentary film journal.

47   A movie theater that was opened in 1957 in an Evangelical Reformers' church that had been open until 1953. The theater only showed documentary films. Films were played non-stop, and for a single 10-kopeck ticket, a viewer would receive unlimited viewing time.

"Celestinas might be in the locker room. Alfa was here just a moment ago."

"Finally, some nice weather," Romas noted joyfully.

"Yeah, I hope it stays for another month or two."

The men laughed.

At the bottom of the stairs, they could hear the uneasiness in the voices of the first-year students who were just returning.

"I don't know, but I heard that they pulled out Lina."

"Where did they get them?"

"At the Pelėda."

"Somebody weaseled their way in?"

"Probably. They must have been well hidden. Everybody was talking there, so there's no way to know who ratted them out."

"But why?"

"They said they had foreign records. Ultra-modernist music. Western culture, imperialist influence."

"And that's it?"

"She also told some anti-Russian jokes there, too…"

"How many of them were there?"

"I don't know, exactly. Ten or eleven."

"Were all of them one of us?"

"No, I think he was the only one. There were several from the university and one girl from the Russian middle school."

When they spotted the older men chatting on the terrace, the younger men stopped talking and began to hum loudly and purposefully.

"What happened, guys?" asked Povilas after overhearing their conversation.

"Nothing, just…" the young men shrugged, unsure of what to say.

"If you say so. Weren't you cold on the water in short sleeves?"

"No, it's pretty warm," they said, hurrying off to the hall. They turned back for a moment but, convinced that nobody had heard or "noticed" their conversation, disappeared behind the door.

KGB officials saw danger everywhere – even in foreign music. Wherever youth gathered, they'd be followed by the eyes and ears of the KGB. Communist youth and young people in general could appear on the KGB services' lists for listening to Western music or recordings by emigrants, or simply by dancing together in the evenings. Later, they'd be called one by one for "preventative discussions."

＊

"Hey, Celestinas," said Povilas as he stepped into the locker room. "What's new?"

"Hey…"

"You're quiet. What is it?" said Povilas as he threw his bag down on the bench and began to pull out his clothes. "Hey, Celestinas!"

"What?"

"Why are you so quiet? What happened?"

"I spoke out of place, and I'm afraid I'll never make it out of the blacklists now."

"How'd you manage that?"

"I had no idea they were snitches…"

"Who?"

"I met Vladas and Pranas from our grade on Lenin Avenue. You don't know them. They began asking me about the competition and why I never go anywhere."

"And?"

"I got angry and told them that, capitalism be damned, but if I ever get to leave, I'll stay there out of spite."

"Wonderful, Celestinas!" Povilas chuckled. "What a great topic of discussion! All you had to do was go down to the party committee and tell them all about it."

"Stop it…"

"Alright. But it's funny. Alright, don't be mad. How'd you find out that they snitched on you?"

"A good friend told me. They said, 'did you know that your documents were already on the move? And what kind of nonsense are you sharing with every person you meet?' I had no idea they'd say anything… They were students, after all, we're in the same grade…"

"Celestinas, didn't you know that every grade has an 'Uncle Vasya?'" – That was what they called informers who'd been recruited by KGB officials.

"I did… But that they were the ones?" Celestinas said, surprised.

"What did you tell them?"

"Nothing, really. They began the conversation, asking about the competition. They asked why I hadn't gone to the World Championships…"

"And what did you tell them?"

"I got worked up and told them that they wouldn't let me go, but that now, I'd stay there out of spite if they'd only let me go."

"Good work, really," Povilas laughed. "You seem like a grown man, but you don't know when to keep your mouth shut."

"What will happen now?" Celestinas asked, growing pale with fear.

"Don't worry, you won't be any worse off than you are now. Unless they call you in for re-education."

"I won't be any worse off, but things won't get better, either. And I had hoped to find a way out of this mess."

"Yeah, yeah, I'd like to be sunbathing in Crimea now and living in my own apartment, too."

"That's what I'm talking about. I sacrificed my studies. And what for? No stipend, nothing, just a bed in the dormitories. And even then, I'm afraid they'll throw me out."

Romas and Alfa stepped into the locker room and the conversation stopped. Though the men shared similar fates, they couldn't discuss them out loud. Every one of them carried their stories with them.

*

13

In the middle of October, a wave of unrest rippled through the country, and there were worried rumours of war. Soviet propaganda went wild: "the world has been shaken by news that has inspired a wave of anger: the imperialists of the United States of America have performed an unprecedented act of violence against the young Cuban republic... in violation of all international diplomatic norms, the government of the USA has enforced a naval blockade of the Republic of Cuba. This is an act of piracy unprecedented in the time after World War II and is a great threat to global peace."

On 26 October, all USSR radio stations interrupted their broadcasts to deliver a message on the growing conflict in Cuba. Newspaper headlines screamed "The world in anger over aggressive US actions – the world stands with the island of freedom!" "Get your hands off of Cuba!," "Cuba – we're with you!," and "Stop the aggressor!" In bold letters at the top of its front page, the Russian newspaper Pravda threatened to "Suppress the audacious American aggressors!" and "Stop the aggressive American imperialists' plans!"

In factories and institutions throughout the Union, workers were gathered for protest meetings to unanimously support the USSR government's statements. Though Cuba seemed distant and unreachable to Soviet people, the tensions caused by the propaganda and the fear of a new war hung over every step they took. KGB officers with gas masks visited schools, kolkhozes[48] and factories, instilling people with fear of a new war.

In secret, people listened to Voice of America in an effort to find out what was really happening in the world while KGB agents hounded them.

Those who managed to listen to Voice of America explained that a US spy plane that had been flying over Cuba took photos and found evidence that the Soviets were installing nuclear missiles in Cuba that would be able to destroy the entire American continent. Kennedy ordered a blockade of Cuba in the Caribbean and to forbid the entry of USSR ships with new

---

48   Rus. колхоз – Soviet collective farms.

missiles. Khrushchev was prepared to deal a blow to America, which was allegedly looking to topple the pro-USSR regime of Fidel Castro. Through the static of the radio, they kept hearing a new name – the "Caribbean Crisis."

A war-time mood and fear gripped Lithuania. Its people maintained vigils by their radio receivers day and night, whether at home or at work. Only children and the youth had forgotten the recent horrors of the previous war. Everyone else was prepared for the beginning of a new war at any moment.

At Gita and Povilas' home on Čiurlionis Street, Father would sweep the sidewalk alongside the university every morning and then sit by the radio. He'd only leave briefly to go to the store and bring back bread, which Mother would slice, dry and load in a bag. She also listened to the news and knew everything that was happening, or rather, everything that the Soviet radio told her and everything that her neighbours who listened to the Voice of America told her. She would look after her two little grandchildren – Rasa and Audrius – from sun up until sun down, and all the while, she would prepare food stores for the entire big family – calmly, without scaring anyone, lost in her thoughts and her faith. The bags of dried bread began to pile up by the door, one after another.

During the last days of October, the tension receded a bit and the world breathed a sigh of relief. Radio receivers began to play news praising the USSR – "the Soviet Union has prevented a global war," "The nations strongly support the USSR government's wise actions."

That same October, the USSR celebrated the fifth anniversary of the launching of the first man-made earth satellite into space. A recording of "May the sun always shine!" sung by a choir of children became the most widely-bought record in the USSR, and the year's most popular film was The Amphibian Man – based on Alexander Belyaev's 1927 novel.

The USSR Rowing Federation analyzed what they called the "partial success" in Lucerne. The team's senior coach, Samsonov, was once again called to the Party Committee to explain the results at the World Championships. The one gold medal, three silver medals and two bronze medals they won seemed like a respectable victory, but losing to Germany in the overall number of medals was a significant defeat. Specialists from the Union-wide coaches' council looked for reasons for the loss. Some blamed unlucky draws in the qualifying and repechage races or the poor weather. Others blamed the team's poor or old racing or training equipment. Finally, they blamed the team's poor psychological focus on placing for a medal rather than total victory. The issue of equipment was discussed more fiercely than it had ever been before. As they attended international competitions, the coaches watched what other countries' teams were doing and understood that a leap in technology could soon leave the Soviet rowers in last place. The Germans had changed the shape of their rowing blades. Not only did they adjust the oar inboards differently for each class of boat, they also adjusted them individually for each athlete. Before the race, their coaches would measure the direction and strength of the wind before adjusting the oars' collars.

In an effort to catch up with foreign boat builders, the specialists ordered them to make new boat models.

However, the greatest focus was once again on the athletes' morals and wills, and on the development of their consciousness of the battle for their country's honour.

Lithuania's rowing specialists complained that there was no new replacement generation being developed to replace the current elite, and that junior rowing wasn't receiving the attention it deserved. Junior rowers weren't being allowed to participate in adults' competitions. At the Lithuanian Junior Championships cities were fielding rowers who barely moved their boats' waterlines just to fill their crews. Junior competitions were poorly organized. Athletes went to Union-wide championships with old boats that looked more like historical museum exhibits than racing boats, and they didn't even get matching shirts.

Gita's family, however, was happy – her sister Irena had won the youth Žalgiriada[49] that summer while rowing in the quad, surpassing the Kaunas crew who were everyone's favourites. However, it was the Kaunas crew who went to the Union-wide championships, not them...

The Startas factory in Kaunas began to study the new oars' photos and sketches. The oar blade, painted with the colours of the German flag and white Olympic rings, would be the standard for contemporary oars and they would have to change all of their production technology. By that spring, they would have to make at least twenty sculling oars and at least as many pairs of sweep oars using fir and ash planks.

The eight returned from Crimea more cold than hot. The weather

---

49   The Žalgiris sports association's athletic competition.

during their stay had been nothing like the balmy vacation weather they had been dreaming of. To escape boredom, the men walked along the seashore and went to Saturday volunteer points to help locals pick their grapes. They had missed their training and their friends, and the day after they had returned, everyone was back at the rowing camp.

*

14

Winter came much more quickly than it had last year. That is to say, it came on time. Not only had it been late by more than a month last year, it also hadn't looked much like winter.

It had already started growing cold during the first half of November, and a few weeks later, ice floes could be seen flowing down the Neris. The rowers closed up their boathouse and "moved" to the other bank of the Neris, where they gazed longingly at the boathouse surrounded by bare trees, and the columns as they grew white with snow. They'd wave to the Boatswain as he fussed about the terrace with a broom and stirred the standing water out of the basement area with narrow paddles made from oar fragments. They also waited for the snow – so they could put on their skis and escape from their boring hall.

The members of the Lithuanian team were hurrying to put their studies and other affairs in order, because soon, right after the New Year, the new season's training would begin. After successful races in the USSR team championships, Povilas Liutkaitis, Celestinas Jucys, brothers Levickas and Romas Šarmaitis' names once again appeared on the list of team candidates. They were once again invited to the team's winter camp and the selection races. They didn't have much time to stay home. They wanted to make use of every free minute they had away from their training.

Thrilling news made the rounds in the middle of November. Instead of "hello," people's first words to each other were "have you read Novyj Mir[50]?" The 18 November issue, with grey and unremarkable covers and a blue headline that read "Новый Мир 11 1962," were passed from hand to hand. Only a few of the issues that made it to Lithuania's kiosks were even placed on the racks – they were "shared" among acquaintances and friends, who would read it in a single go and hand it on to someone else. Novyj Mir rocked not just the Soviet Union, but the whole world by publishing Alexander Solzhenitsyn's story, 'One Day in the Life of Ivan Denisovich'. The presidium of the Central Committee of the CPSU gave in to pressure

---

50   "New World," a Russian literary magazine.

from Nikita Krushchev and agreed to the publication of the story. People who had only read the truth about the gulags from letters from their loved ones believed that the time of censorship and Stalin's era of terror had ended. They hoped that the killings and persecution would end with it.

In this unexpected move from the communists, the Lithuanian athletes also felt a glimmer of hope to escape from behind the barbed "wire fence." And not just the rowers. Algimantas Baltušnikas, a discus thrower, was a three-time USSR champion who had never left the USSR because of his uncles' partisan pasts and his own deportation. There were many like him who had never been allowed to leave.

*

The first snow brought a festive mood due to the approaching holidays as well. The winter sports competitions began. Every field, stadium and court became a skating rink. The city's forests and parks were criss-crossed by skiing paths. Though the layer of snow was thin, this was no obstacle for sports enthusiasts.

On 3 December, Pravda[51] published an enormous report an exhibition on alternative art at the Moscow Manege. The report was published under orders from Nikita Krushchev, who grew completely furious upon visiting the exhibition on 1 December. Those who had been at the exhibition heard Krushchev yelling: "What are these faces? Don't you know how to draw? Have you no conscience?," "Do you love the West, is that it? This is pederasty! Why do pederasts get 10 years while these people get awards? Why? Let's look at this – does this inspire any sort of emotion? I want to spit on this – that's how it makes me feel!" and "The Soviet people don't need any of this. I'm talking to you, got it?... Ban this! Ban all of this! End this madness! I order it! I order it! And monitor everything, the radio, the television, the press – destroy all of this art's followers!" Krushchev demanded that the artists who participated in the exhibition be thrown out of the USSR artists' union and the CPSU and be forbidden from engaging in any sort of artistic activities.

In the meantime, the Lithuanian Art Museum was holding a national portrait exhibition. Zigmas and Irena's friend, an artist named Aleksandras Vitulskis, created impressive portraits of Zigmas and Antanas for the occasion. The rowers' penetrating and willful stares drew the exhibition's

---

51   The official newspaper of the Communist Party of the Soviet Union.

visitors, among whom were a number of rowers, schoolchildren from the nearby Salomėja Nėris School, and students from the university and the polytechnic institute.

Just like every year, "Sportas'" journalists held a vote for the best athletes of the year. The rowers were in the lead this year as well. Track and field athlete Antanas Vaupšas was selected the best athlete and the Žalgiris eight was voted the best team of the year. When asked about their dreams for the next year, they all said the same thing – winning wasn't as important as making a comeback against the German eight crew.

The Soviet Union celebrated its 40th anniversary and "Sportas" wrote in grandiose prose: "If, today, our rowers win against the America, if J. Daktaraitė wins the gold medal in the continental championships, if A. Vaupšas is named alongside the world's best jumpers – the foundation for all of these victories is the national friendship that was formed 40 years ago into a brotherly union of Soviet nations."

Only one or two rowers came to training on Christmas Eve. They all found their own reasons – classes, exams, colds – and some came up with more interesting excuses. The coaches understood perfectly well what hid beneath their excuses, but this was the one time during the year when they could forgive their athletes for their lies. They themselves were glad to be able to leave early to sit down at the Christmas Eve table, though they were afraid to discuss this amongst themselves.

A beautiful wintery day with a fresh layer of snow brought the secretive Christmas Eve to their homes in Vilnius. In an effort to suppress Catholics' desire to celebrate Christmas Eve, functionaries from the Central Committee only allowed for Christmas trees to be sold after Christmas. However, one way or another, every home already had Christmas trees illuminated by candles. The city's Christmas tree, with a red star on the top, was erected next to the monument to V. M. Kapsukas across from the Art Museum. The tree would only be illuminated right before the New Year, but this made Catholics only more determined to celebrate Christ's birth, regardless of any threats or condemnations.

The happy and witty 31 December issue of "Sportas" was published with green headlines. The first page was decorated by an artistic photo of Antanas Vaupšas looking off into the distance. Žalgiris' eight received no less attention – an eight boat with flaming oars flew out from between the eight crew members' caricatures over a background with a map of Lithuania. The line under the title read: "The new year's path leads straight to the Spartakiad of Nations," and under that was the first four-line poem for the rowers:

THE MIGHTY EIGHT

There's nothing left to say – bravo, men!

The New Year will soon replace the old.

They started with silver in Lucerne,

Will Tokyo give them the gold?

On the last page, among all of the best athletes, there was a photo of Ričardas holding a camera. The cover on the lens had TOKYO 1964 written on it. The caption read "Ričardas Vaitkevičius, the coach and a member of our mighty Žalgiris eight crew, seems to be looking off to the near future optimistically." At the bottom of the page, the editor "lined up" drawn portraits of all eight of the crew members.

31 December was properly cold and clear for a winter's day. The intermittent snow, that had lasted all week, stopped. On the last day of the year, 120 couples were married in Vilnius. A crowd at Vilnius airport greeted the first TU-124 aircraft in the nation, and the first thermal power plant complex was launched in Elektrėnai. The Soviet people reported exceeded annual norms and awaited the Kremlins's commendations. Stores were completely emptied out. Those who had prepared well in advance – a month or two ago – by buying champagne and food for their tables enjoyed the holidays. Those who already had television sets were glad that, on 31 December, they would be able to watch the holiday Blue Lantern show, which was being broadcast from Moscow to Lithuania for the first time and would run until midnight. The show was to contain more music than political propaganda. Those without TVs prepared to visit them as guests.

*

15

The January of 1963 brought good news for everyone – athletes, sports enthusiasts, and, of course, children. There was plenty of snow and ice and everyone's competitions went off as planned.

The USSR sports committee announced the criteria and deadlines for the summer sports' Olympic qualification competitions. To become a candidate for the USSR Olympic team, rowing representatives had to meet the following requirements from 1 January 1963 until 1 September 1964: "within a single season, take first place or second place twice in Spartakiad of Nations, USSR championships or USSR cup competitions. Achieve the following results twice during the season at Union-wide or national competitions: eight – 5 min. 55 sec., coxed four – 6 min. 40 sec., coxless four – 6 min. 30 sec., coxed pair – 7 min. 35 sec., coxless pair – 7 min. 10 sec., double scull – 6 min. 42 sec., single – 7 min 18 sec." The Lithuanian coxed four had already rowed a race with a similar result at the Amber Oars, coming in at 6 min. 49 sec., while the eight had already cleared the standard at the World Championships. It wasn't going to be difficult to get rid of unnecessary seconds that year, but they would once again have to prove that they were the best and once again clear the set requirements – and, of course, once again finish first.

On 16 February, "Sportas" was published with a blue headline rather than a red one. Though this was to signify the beginning of the national unions' winter-sport Spartakiad, some Lithuanians quietly rejoiced with the hope that the editorial staff had Lithuanian patriots who had done this to commemorate the strictly forbidden holiday of Lithuanian independence. Simply mentioning this holiday's name carried the risk of being called to speak with KGB officials, while celebrating it meant incarceration. However, there were homes where birthdays were celebrated on that day, and during those celebrations, every second toast was given for freedom. At Povilas and Gita's home on Čiurlionis Street, every 16 February was a holiday – Gita's birthday. This was written on her passport, which was always kept handy in the event that militiamen heard them celebrating and came to check up on them. They usually doubled their patrols on that day. On the morning of 16 February, a birthday postcard lay in their mailbox.

From the beginning of February, Lithuania's strongest trained at the USSR team's camp in Podolsk. The continental climate near Moscow was different from Lithuania's, but not by much – the cold, dry and snowy winter was very good for the rowers. They skied in the mornings and lifted weights in their sports hall after lunch, preparing intensively for the upcoming season. Or, more specifically, for the upcoming competition to join the USSR team. This was the hardest race, after which the international competitions, if they were to even make it there, would be a hard-earned prize.

In addition to the six regular rowers from Žalgiris' eight, the four men from the four – Celestinas, Povilas, Romas and Eugenijus – were also invited, despite their "crimes" against the system. They hadn't given up hope. Yevgeniy Borisovich, the team's senior coach, greeted Ričardas with a question: "So, how's it going?" "There's nothing new for now, but they should pass. We're doing everything we can." Ričardas also believed that his men's "issues" would be resolved.

As always, they had to complete six general fitness selection tests at the end of the camp: they lifted weights that weighed seven kilograms more than their body weight, pushed weights, did squats with 80-kilogram weights over 30 seconds, crunches, hung from wall bars for thirty seconds, and participated in skiing races – 5 kilometres, 15 kilometres, and a relay race with three legs of 5 kilometres each. The Lithuanians came first in almost all of the competitions, and the overall winner was Juozas. The four battled the USSR team's veterans as equals. Romas and Eugenijus were among the first in their best event – the ski race.

When they returned home, the Žalgiris men found Lithuania gripped in a deep winter. There was less than a week until the next camp, and they still had to catch up to their classmates, take care of their domestic affairs, and spend as much time as they could with their loved ones. Over the last year, more of the team had gotten married. Their beloved women were understanding, and let their men go off to their camps without any questions or complaints. It seemed as though it couldn't be any other way, as many of their wives had only recently left rowing behind themselves. They exchanged the blisters on their palms from gripping the oars for blisters on their knuckles from washing their babies' nappies. Their backs hurt not from lifting weights, but from standing in long lines. They hurried back and forth to their jobs, leaving their children with their grandmothers or at day care centres and worrying themselves sick about them. When the men returned, however, if only for a week, they'd find their wives there waiting, dressed up and smiling. In the beginning of March, they loaded their husbands' suitcases with freshly cleaned sportswear and bundles of Lithuanian delicacies before seeing them off for two months of training in Georgia.

The rowers were to spend three weeks at the Bakuriani mountain skiing resort, which was located at 1,700 metres above sea level. From there, they'd take a bus the whole 250 kilometres to Poti, where they would finally be able to row. Before leaving, all they had to do was load their boats, which would travel to the coastal city of Poti while they skied in the mountains.

*

The three-hour trip by bus from the Tbilisi airport along winding mountain roads struck fear into the hearts of even the strongest men, so when they reached the town at the foot of Mt. Kohta, they breathed a sigh of relief stepping out of the bus, their trembling legs, and onto the white snow of Bakuriani. The men, who were visiting real mountains for the first time in their lives, could not believe their magnificence. The sunlit peaks, which they had only ever seen in postcards or films, were even more impressive in person. Many of them were left speechless. Some were not just speechless, but breathless.

"What's happening? Why is it so hard to breathe?" the men asked, surprised. They couldn't manage to catch their breath.

"Ah, yes, that's exactly why we're here," Ričardas laughed. "Here, at a higher altitude, the air is much thinner, making it harder to breathe. Don't worry, you'll get used to it soon. When we descend, you'll see how easy things will be. Your bodies will grow used to the lack of oxygen, and that's very important for rowers. You must learn to work when you don't have enough oxygen.

"I can't believe it, my head is spinning."

"In two or three days, you'll get used to it and forget all about it."

"I feel like I'm about to reach the finish line," Petras said, smiling quietly.

"It really seems like my lungs don't have enough room," Juozas agreed.

"Don't worry, stay relaxed and breathe calmly," their coach soothed them.

"But just look at these views!" said Povilas, grabbing his camera.

"You're like a poet, Povilas," said James from behind him. "You see beauty everywhere."

"So? Isn't this beautiful?" Povilas shot back jovially. "Just look around you!"

"Just a moment, Samsonov will show you some beauty as soon as we start crawling up those mountains on all fours," said James, who could remember the incredible strain of the USSR training camps.

"Romas, look, a ramp! You'll be able to do some jumps," said Povilas, waving towards the mountain. Last year, Romas had participated in a ski jumping competition.

"That would be interesting to try. We don't have very good ramps in Lithuania. From here, this one looks great. However, I'd need special skis," Romas said, as if in a daydream.

"Don't you dare. You'll break your bones, and with the whole season ahead of you!" said Ričardas, who had grown fearful after hearing the men's idle chatter.

"I was joking," Romas smiled.

"We'll just go for a walk today. Tomorrow, we're skiing," Ričardas announced. Everyone picked up their luggage and headed for the mountain sports centre, where rowers from Moscow and Leningrad were already gathering.

Though they lacked oxygen, the men's eyes and their souls were delighted by the skiing exercises, surrounded by snow-covered mountains. The streets of the towns in the valley were almost free of snow, but the ski runs stretched through endless kilometres of ancient pine and fir forests along the mountain slopes, each ending at the main ski route. Few of them could remain upright throughout, on their cross-country skis. They had never seen slopes as long and steep as these back in Lithuania. The sunny days were nothing like a typical Lithuanian spring. The fresh, dry mountain air smelled of pine needles. When the sun was out, it was warm enough by midday to ski with their shirts off, even though the snowdrifts were up to their knees. The men, who had missed the sunlight, took brief breaks to enjoy sunbathing, and threw snow at each other like children. On a few occasions, Povilas took his camera with him to the training camp. Though it was additional weight, he couldn't miss the opportunity to shoot the beautiful sights. The downhill and uphill areas required much more effort here than they did in Lithuania, but the magnificent views – and Ričardas' promise that they would enjoy a burst of strength upon descending to the sea – made it all worthwhile.

During the first ski practice, Romas' fine Estonia ski cracked after hitting a footprint in the ski track. Only members of the ski team received skis like his, to the envy of everyone else... However, the ski was quickly fixed by the talented craftsman-artist and Olympic champion, Yuriy Tyukalov, who was now rowing in the double scull. He had been trained as an artist and sculptor, so both wood and stone bent to his will, and he spent much of his time repairing his teammates' boats. By the next morning, Romas was standing on masterfully repaired skis.

The food at the local cafeteria was rather poor, consisting primarily of pasta and Georgian bread, with bacon brought from home for "dessert". However, there were unlimited supplies of mineral water from Borjomi, a town just thirty kilometres away. The men probably drank more of this water there than they had ever drank throughout their entire rowing careers. Their rooms were lined with green bottles of Borjomi. Those who wanted to see the springs, which had been famous for more than a century, could simply take the narrow-gauge train down along its jolly winding track through the mountain pine forests and find themselves in the town of Borjomi in just a few hours. On their days off, some of the men tried the famous Bakuriani-Borjomi narrow-gauge train.

There was a steady stream of postcards from Bakuriani to Lithuania by post, all featuring mountain landscapes and skiers. The men felt like they were on the edge of the world as they awaited news from home.

On 14 March a telegram reached them – Romas' family had had a daughter: another little girl into the family of rowers, whose father would only see her between camps and competitions.

There was still no news regarding positive developments with the men's documents, but their coach didn't let the men doubt for a moment that their situations would change. Povilas, Celestinas, and the brothers Levickas worked harder than the others to secure places on the team and to provide a significant reason to review their files one more time and free them from their unearned imprisonment: a burden and an insult for them. They wanted to be able to express themselves and to tell their friends the tragedies they had experienced, but the fear of being misunderstood and condemned kept their lips tightly sealed. They bottled up the hurt deep in their hearts, like a cairn of heavy stones.

Every evening, once everyone had gone to bed and turned off the lights, Povilas would cross himself in the dark and say his prayers in his head. He'd speak to his parents, just like he did in his childhood when his mother, exhausted from her work, would sit down on the edge of his bed, calm and smiling, and caress his and Juozas' heads. His father would sit by the kerosene lamp on the table and carve something quietly, occasionally humming a folk song under his breath. As sleep overcame Povilas, his thoughts would drift to the banks of the Nemunas, to the fields of Rūdupis, or to his home in Vilnius, where his Gita and his Rasa lay together, the mother caressing her child and quietly humming to herself. "It's been three weeks since I held them close to me," thought Povilas, sighing as he remembered how wonderful it felt to be held in his mother's arms. "God forbid my child ever experiences such a fate..."

At six every morning, they were awoken by a brigade of scientists, who came to check their pulses, take cardiograms and blood samples, and record all of the results for analysis in their dissertations.

The sun would rose from behind the mountains later than they were used to in Lithuania, but it was much brighter and clearer reflecting on the snow-covered peaks. When it rose, Bakuriani once again came to life with the colours of busy skiers, athletes and holiday-makers against the blinding white background. It helped them forget their longing for home, filling them instead with new determination and strength.

At the end of the camp, the Lithuanians were once again among the best in the USSR trials.

*

"Men, I have some news," said Ričardas when the men had gathered in a recreational room on the first floor in preparation for their trip.

Ten pairs of questioning eyes looked at him and awaited his news eagerly.

Ričardas smiled mischievously, prolonging their suffering and enjoying his role as the harbinger of good news.

Zigmas was the most eager to hear. His child due very soon. He couldn't forget his worries for a single moment –how his wife, Irena, was doing back home, who would take care of her, who would take her to the hospital on time, and who would bring her back. The ski centre's caretaker had even selected a name for the newborn: "Zigmas, if she gives birth to a son, name him Otari," the Lithuanians' friend told Zigmas in a thick Georgian accent.

"Well, what is it?" Zigmas blurted out impatiently.

"It's something good," Antanas guessed. "We can wait a bit for good news, it's not like it's going anywhere."

"You can wait if you want, Antanas, but we want to know now!" the others protested.

"Our new oars will be shipped straight to Poti!" the coach announced with a grand flourish.

"Oh, the new ones?" James was the first to react.

"The German ones? With the wide blades? From Kaunas? Has anyone seen them yet? Will we be able to row right away?" the questions came one after the other.

"Yes, the German replicas," said Ričardas, encouraged by the men's joyful reactions. "We'll be able to try them right away. We're taking the old ones as well in case they don't suit us. However, I think everything should be fine. They did their best. I went to check on them after the New Year. If we like them, they'll make more. We'll have to adjust to them and do a good bit of rowing."

"We'll beat everybody with oars like those!"

"What can we do so that the Russians don't copy them?"

"Maybe we shouldn't reveal them until the competition..."

"Cut it out, men, they won't manage it in time. There are two months until the qualifiers, nobody's going to make them new oars," said Ričardas, reassuring the men after seeing them get worried. "We need to row with them, so we won't be able to hide them. Everything will be fine."

"I wonder what they'll look like," James said impatiently. "Rychka and I were so sneaky when we took those photos! We felt like thieves..."

"Where did this happen?" asked Eugenijus, who hadn't heard the story.

"In Lucerne, during the World Championships. When everybody left the course, we sneaked up to the German boats, took photos of the oars from every angle, placed a board next to them to measure all of the bends, and drew them."

"Wow, just like spies!"

"What can you do? As long as everybody's moving ahead, we'll always be dragging behind in second place with our long, narrow blades."

"It'll be interesting to try them."

Encouraged by the news, the men left the white mountains of Bakuriani by bus to travel west towards Poti. They had missed their boats, the water and their oars. They could already see the water sliding by the sides of their boat in their minds, the water churned by the delicate puddles they left behind. They weren't thinking about the exhausting monotony yet, however – all they wanted was to once again feel the rush of water below their boat and their acceleration as they forged ahead. Those first spring oar strokes were always special – it didn't matter if they took them on the Neris or anywhere else. And the sooner they got to put their boats in the water, the better the rowers felt.

*

April came. It was still winter on Čiurlionis Street, which, along with the rest of the city, was covered in piles of frozen snow. Skiers were still going to Vingis Park, but every morning, the mailbox had a new, warm, springtime postcard or letter with the words "ГРУЗ.ССР ПОТИ[52]" stamped on it.

"We've arrived in Poti today. It's springtime proper here and the magnolias are about to bloom. The temperature is 18 degrees. We're about to go assemble our boats. We'll see our new oars, too – they're just like the Germans' and they made them just for us in Kaunas. Nobody in the Union has oars like these yet. My nose is still peeling from the sun in the mountains, but I'm overflowing with energy. I'm sending kisses to you and Rasa. Give my regards to everyone at home. Povilas, 1963 IV 3."

"It rained today, so we didn't go rowing. The river has risen almost to our home and is carrying all sorts of trash and sticks. I guess that's why they call it "Поти на болоте[53]." We might go rowing on the lake. There's a big acacia shrub blooming nearby. It smells like heaven. How is Rasa growing? I wrote to my aunt and uncle, but I'm not sure I'll get a response. Write me a letter or something. The address is on the envelope. I look forward to it. Kisses, Povilas, 1963 IV 3.

"We rowed in the eight today. I've missed the big boat. It's going well,

---

52   Rus. Georgian SSR Poti
53   Rus. Poti in a swamp

but unfortunately, they've replaced Celestinas with a Ukrainian, and he rows differently. We tried the new oars. It was a strange feeling, but I liked it. It looks like the boat is going much faster, but we have to pull harder as well. The days are summer-like but the nights are still cool, so I had to ask for a blanket for the morning. Well, that's enough news for now. How are you guys doing? Is Rasa running around yet? How is everyone at home? Write me a letter, I'm waiting. Povilas, 1963 IV 4."

"We rowed in pairs today, and we're going to row in the eight again after lunch. Rychka likes the crew line-up and wants to leave me in. I want to stay, too. The days are sunny and I'm afraid that we'll be red as crayfish again. We get so tired during the day that I'm usually snoring before my head hits the pillow. Send me a newspaper or something so I don't forget how to read Lithuanian. Kisses for you and little Rasa. Povilas, 1963 IV 5."

"Thank you for the letter. It's nice to hear good news and that everything is well for you. The weather's grown a bit cooler, and it rains a bit occasionally. The peach trees are blooming. They have bright pink petals, and what an aroma! There are all sorts of blossoming flowers and shrubs. I don't even know their names. We mostly row pairs and fours, and row the eight every second day. The boat is absolutely soaring. Those new oars must be helping. I just realised that it will be Palm Sunday tomorrow there. You're probably all in a pleasant Easter mood right now. We'll have to knock white eggs together[54] because we won't have any way to paint them. I want to go home already – I miss everyone, and you and Rasa most of all. Kisses, Povilas, 1963 IV 6."

On 7 June, a Sunday, a telegram arrived in the Lithuanian rowers' "camp," which was located in a large and spacious house not far from the river Rioni. It was for Zigmas: "Congratulations, it's a boy. 1963 IV 6." The homeowner pulled a large bottle of red wine that he had made himself from his cellar and they all said a toast for the new rower. "For Otari!" the men joked. None of them ever told their wives, in written or spoken word, how the celebrations went in that restaurant. The table was completely lined by empty wine bottles, and none of them managed to get up for training the next morning. These things stayed in their memories and as the occasional mischievous jest in casual conversations.

---

54 A traditional Lithuanian Easter game in which boiled eggs are tapped against one another to see whose is the strongest.

Povilas' letters continued to fly to Vilnius every day by post.

"Thank you for the letter, I was very glad to get it today. I congratulate Rasa on growing a new tooth. She'll be able to eat nuts soon. Everything's the same over here. They had the qualifying race for the coxed pairs this morning. I raced with Celestinas against Juozas and Sterlik. They gave us a rower in the cox's place, presumably so we wouldn't win. After lunch, we'll race in the eight. I miss Lithuanian bacon and rye bread. The Georgians don't have anything like it. I'll have to eat my fill when I get back. Give Irena my congratulations if you see her. We all celebrated the birth of Zigmas' son here. Happy Easter to everyone, and I hope the Easter eggs turn out beautifully! With big hugs, Povilas, 1963 IV 10."

"We had a qualifying race again today. We rowed in the fours. We won once and came in second the second time. During training, I row in the eight. All of the gardens here are blooming and the park is full of flowers. It smells beautiful and the birds are singing. There's one more week left before we pack up for home. During my free time, I sit with my books and prepare for my exams. However, I just can't seem to get the scientific communism into my head. I don't know how to learn such nonsense. I'll have to hurry to the university when I return. We'll be at the camp in Trakai, so I'll be home more often and I'll get to play with Rasa. I miss both of you very much. We'll see each other soon. Povilas, 1963 IV 14."

*

Armed with their new oars, the Žalgiris eight impressed not just their opponents, but the senior coach as well.

"Your guys are doing well," said Yevgeniy Borisovich, stopping Ričardas after the session. "How are the new oars?"

"They're great. We've adapted to them already."

"It's a good crew. It's the best composition I've seen yet. How are your men's documents?" He could feel Yevgeniy Borisovich's support and desire for Žalgiris to win again.

"Well, we should find out soon. I think we'll return and that everything will be alright," Ričardas lied, hoping that they wouldn't destroy his team and fill it with rowers from Moscow and Leningrad. Perhaps everything would indeed resolve itself by the first trip. He himself hoped that the documents would move along, but he understood perfectly well that he wouldn't find anything when he returned. Such matters never resolved themselves. One had to visit them, beg them and convince them. This was a huge and difficult undertaking that was often fruitless. He had to find people to vouch for his athletes, people who had ties to the KGB officials and the central committee's executives. This was difficult for him to do: he was a coach, not an organiser. He did what he knew best – row and train the other rowers. He didn't have time for anything else. As it was, he already usually cared for the boats and managed the team's affairs while his men slept. "Maybe I should ask my brother? He always has friends everywhere. He knows how to talk and how to ask, and he's not afraid of asking for favours when he needs to... everyone likes him."

"It's a good crew," Samsonov noted again. "They could win. Do your best, Rychka."

"Yes, yes, of course, Yevgeniy Borisovich."

"We have to submit everything by the end of May."

"Ok."

Ričardas' mind and shoulders were burdened by his worries. "Last year, we tried to get by with two men from Moscow and Leningrad, but it was much better with our own guys. They've harmonised with each other, their techniques are identical. This is no time to 'break in' rowers from different 'schools'. My men have been working all winter without a break and their physical condition has improved considerably. It's a pleasure to row with your own team and they all work as one. Juozas had a hard time initially. He had a different coach with a different technique. Now, he's used to us. CSK's style is different – it's sharp, choppy and aggressive. When someone like that is placed in the boat, everybody feels it. The rowing goes out of sync and the crew can't hit the rhythm. Trud's technique is different again: sudden, but shorter. You'd feel something's off with one of them as well. How can we replace the people who are irreplaceable? Celestinas is nevyezdnoj and so is Povilas. The Levickas brothers are hanging on by a thread. Everything began so beautifully a year ago. I never even imagined that such obstacles could appear in sports."

*

16

Upon returning to Vilnius, the rowers found that the ice had just left the Neris. The flooded river nearly overflowed the Žalgiris centre's boathouse. Lake Galvė in Trakai was still covered in ice. The boats hadn't yet returned from the south, so there was nothing to row with. The men spent a day or two taking care of their academic affairs before meeting at the Žalgiris centre in Vilnius.

"Look how flooded it is! I've never seen it like this," they were all surprised.

"This is nothing," said Eugenijus Vaitkevičius as he approached the men. "They had such dreadful floods back in the old days! When the water rose, you'd see wooden houses floating down the river!"

"Houses?" Antanas repeated incredulously.

"Old Vilnius folk remember when shacks used to float down the river. The water used to tear out the walls of our boathouse!"

"How did it tear them out?" Petras asked with wonder.

"Easily. The water would rise right up to here," said Eugenijus, placing his hand on the floor of the terrace. "There were no more walls for a long time after that. Before floods, we carried the boats up here to the hall or hung them up on the ceiling, where the water almost reached them."

"So you could row right out of the locker rooms!" Povilas laughed.

"We once tried that, but we didn't row from the locker room, we did it from these stairs here. However, the current was too strong and we were afraid to do it. You know, when there's that much water? Oh, and when it carried ice... the embankment was only built in '54, you know. Before that it was just a bare riverbank. Do you see that triangular piece of concrete? It was made to break ice."

"I thought that was why it was there."

"It worked well. It shattered all of the ice when it came down."

"Really? Seems like a good idea," James joined in.

"A couple of times, the water rose so high that we rowed our eight past the Cathedral. At the time, we had the only eight in Lithuania. It was in '51: I still have the photo. Do you remember, Alfa?"

"Yeah, I remember. The people stared in awe because the boat looked like a centipede on the water," Alfa smiled.

"Petras showed me the photo. It would be interesting to row through the streets," Povilas smiled.

"I don't think we will anymore. The Neris doesn't rise like that anymore after they built the power plant in Belarus. Hey girls, let's move!" Eugenijus shouted to his crew. "We'll take the fours because the eights aren't back yet!"

"And what will we do?" Antanas asked, looking around. "Rychka isn't here yet? Is our boat here yet?"

"Doesn't look like it. They're probably taking them straight to Trakai," Zigmas reasoned.

"We'll go skating on the ice, then," Povilas joked.

"I've never seen the ice stay for so long in Trakai," Romas noted with surprise. "It used to melt by 20 April at the latest."

"By the way, Zigmas, how's your son? What's his name?" Povilas remembered.

"Ah thanks, the little guy is fine. He looks just like me. We named him Artūras," Zigmas smiled.

"Just like Otari," James laughed.

"Will he be a rower?" Alfa asked with interest.

"I don't know. If he wants to, he will. We'll see in about fifteen years," Zigmas smiled.

"Oh, Algis, hello there! What are you doing here?" Alfa greeted his former teammate who had just arrived on the terrace.

"I was taking the trolley bus past, saw that the centre was full of people, and decided to pay you a visit," the young doctor said, shaking the men's hands.

"Have you missed rowing?"

"I have, of course, but I don't have time for it anymore. I have to work."

"Algis and I began rowing together in about '52," said Alfa, turning to his friends.

"We were two-time Lithuanian champions in the eight. In fifty-three and fifty-four. We raced here on the Neris at the time."

"That's right. I was sitting at bow."

"I was in the two seat."

"You've been rowing since school?" Povilas asked.

"That's right. I was born in Vilnius, and I'd say that all Vilnius kids probably rowed at school," Algis laughed. "I started attending this centre when I was fourteen. Here, between Dynamo centre and ours, there was a swimming pool as well. This is where I held my RLD[55] tests as well. There was almost no current here, so I had to swim from this corner here to Dynamo and back. I hadn't prepared at all and I passed!"

"I remember that pool, too," Alfa nodded. "There were plenty of kids there in the summer! They loved jumping, splashing and diving about. It was fun."

"There was a LPFA sports club here before the war, right here, where the winter centre is," said Algis, pointing to the other bank of the river.

"What does LPFA stand for?"

"The Lithuanian Physical Fitness Association. Their sign hung on the front wall."

"It's the doctor! What's up!" Antanas turned around. "I was wondering who it was telling these interesting stories."

"Hey, Antanas!"

"He was so good at the RLD test that he then ordered everyone to compete in the race in Trakai!"

"Nonsense! I didn't order anyone, we all decided to do it," Algis laughed. "We raced in the eight in '57. There were incredible waves. We took on so much water that we were rowing underwater by the time we got past the castle. We got out and began pushing the boat. The umpires came to us and helped pull it. We said, 'we're not getting out, we'll finish this!' They said, 'we'll still give you last place in the final.' But last place was second place because there were only two boats!"

"Yeah, that was a wonderful swim, wasn't it? That boat was awfully low. We placed strips of plywood in between the riggers but it didn't help."

"Who did you row with back then?" Alfa tried to recall.

"With Eugenijus. The first coach had been Žebriūnas[56]. I raced with

---

55   Ready for Labour and Defence – a state general physical exercise system created to develop patriotism among Soviet youth. The RLD programme was mandatory in various educational institutions and covered various types of sports. Different RLD standards were set for different age groups.

56   Famous Lithuanian film director.

him in an eight at one competition in Moscow. He was stroke and I was second."

"Žebriūnas was a coach?" James looked surprised.

"Briefly. He trained me in the beginning."

"You see, Eugenijus doesn't train men anymore, just women. He says he got tired of arguing with his brother, so one took the men and the other took the women," Alfa explained.

"When I rowed, Rychka was still in the army. He rowed for CSK. When he returned, I had already quit. I rowed the single sometimes, but I no longer raced anywhere."

The centre had a springtime energy to it. Everyone wanted to escape the boring exercises in the tank in the basement and feel some real rowing along the river. Those who hadn't gone anywhere and had spent all winter training in Vilnius felt especially excited – they would finally dip their oars into the fast-flowing Neris.

The pontoon had risen up high, almost to the door of the boathouse. This made it much easier to carry the boats out, but the river current tore at the boats as they were placed on the water. One moment of carelessness would mean the loss of valuable equipment.

Sofija, Ala and two Aldonas were carrying oars and seats. Coach Eugenijus was putting on a warm sweater, preparing to cox their boat. The women and men, all of whom had missed their home waters, returned from Poti together with handsome tans. The sight of the river Rioni had begun to bore them, and they now wanted to see the beauty of the banks of the Neris, awakening from its winter slumber. The women carried the four out into the dazzling sunlight and gently lowered it into the water, installing the seats and the oars. Rowers with other boats were lining up behind them by the dock. The medal-winning men watched from above as the girls set their right legs into the boat and waited for their coach's signal.

"Hey, tighten your gates!" James shouted from the terrace, but the coach gave his signal at the same moment and the girls kicked off. The gates for their stroke-side oars jumped up and both of the right-hand oars hung in the air, only secured by one of their rowers' hands. Startled, the girls lurched to the side and lost their balance. The boat suddenly tipped over, plunging all four of the girls into the icy waters of the Neris and pulling their coach in with them.

"Soggy hens, the lot of you!" shouted Eugenijus as his head emerged from the water and he grabbed the side of the boat.

The women gasped from the surprise and the cold. Everyone who saw them from the shore was chuckling. The men grabbed the bowside oars and managed to hold it before the swift current carried it away towards the centre of the city. The women tried to hide their shame with loud laughter. After crawling out onto the shore, they squeezed their wool tracksuits between their palms, wrung out their hair, and ran up the steps. Pavilionis' men emptied the boat of its water and carried it into the boathouse.

"Soggy hens, ha ha," the men from the eight laughed. "What did they teach you there down south, anyway?"

"Yeah, yeah, it's your turn now. Show us what you know!" retorted a shivering Aldona before retreating to the locker room.

Nobody had any doubt that the girls were experienced, which was why they could joke so boldly – they knew they wouldn't be insulted. However, falling in was a great embarrassment for a novice – one that they carried with themselves long after everyone else had forgotten it. Many of those who had been on the shore at the time had once felt such a thing, and were secretly happy when someone else fell in reminding them that they weren't the only ones.

"Celestinas come here," Ričardas' stern voice rang out.

Celestinas looked around before marching off towards the coach, who had just appeared. He didn't sound happy, and that made Celestinas nervous. Ričardas looked Celestinas right in the eyes, trying to guess what the athlete's heart was hiding.

"We've been called to the Central Committee[57] together tomorrow at ten," he said, not mincing his words.

"So they snitched on me after all," Celestinas thought, feeling as though he had fallen from a great height. The words "Central Committee" were already frightening enough, and the idea that he would be called there personally to explain himself made his knees quake.

"What?" he asked in a trembling voice, as if he had misunderstood his coach's words or simply wanted them to go away.

"Central Committee. Tomorrow. Ten o'clock. Are we clear? Do you know where it is?"

"Of course."

---

57   The Central Committee of the Communist Party

"You'll find it?"

"Probably. But why?"

"You tell me why! I know nothing! What did you do?"

"Nothing, really..." Celestinas was stunned and didn't know whether or not he should tell Rychka.

"Let's meet at Lenin Avenue by the Central Committee at five to ten," Ričardas interrupted him and ran down the steps to the boathouse.

The news stunned him. His head began to hurt, and his friends' idle chatter and jokes seemed a million miles away. He couldn't form complete sentences when spoken to because his thoughts about the next day dominated both his mind and his emotions. Lost in thought, he turned around to hurry out the gate and into the street.

"Celestinas, what's gotten into you?" said Povilas, seeing his friend hurrying out. "Where are you going?"

Celestinas stopped suddenly and looked around him with terrified eyes.

"What's wrong with him?" James wondered.

"What do I know?" Povilas shrugged.

"I saw him talking with Rychka."

"Really? About what?"

"I didn't hear, I just saw that he went completely white."

"God damn it..." Povilas swore, having remembered the conversation they'd had here in autumn.

"Do you know something?"

"No, nothing..."

Celestinas couldn't remember how he got home after training. Without managing to swallow a single bite of food, he jumped into bed. It was the longest sleepless night of his life. His head was filled with questions, answers, suspicions and excuses. He arranged the words in his mind and crossed them out again. The next day could be a fateful one for him and he didn't know what he had to do for fate to be on his side. "Perhaps Moscow's Central Committee received my letter and read it? They probably checked my documents. They probably found out where my grandfather is. They probably found out that they were supposed to deport them. Why are they calling us in? They probably called Vilnius. What will they tell us? What should I say? Did I do something wrong? I just want to row, study, and be like everybody else. I didn't do anything wrong. I was still a child. What could I have done? They probably checked at the university, probably questioned people. Who told them? I didn't do anything bad to anyone. What comes next?..." Celestinas tossed and turned, but the same thoughts kept running through his head in circles. Once he understood that he wouldn't fall asleep, he got up at six in the morning, bathed, got dressed in his suit, put on a tie, put an apple into his pocket that he had brought from his childhood village, and walked out into the still-sleeping city street. The first buses were filled with workers, and janitors were sweeping the yards and the sidewalks. The springtime head that had arrived just a few days ago had receded, making for a cold morning. After walking the streets and alleys of the Old Town, he walked down Gorky Street towards Lenin Avenue to the Central Committee. The clock read 9:15. There was almost an hour to burn until his meeting. His exhaustion and the cold air calmed his thoughts. "Come what may, I have nothing to hide"- as he looked at the grey doors of that terrible institution, Celestinas took a deep breath, followed by a second, and strode up the steps.

Celestinas' letter had indeed reached Moscow... and Moscow's Central Committee had ordered the Vilnius Central Committee to "resolve" the issue. The next Monday, he would return to his university, where he would be given a stipend. The ban on international travel over his head would be lifted for all time and he would be promised never to encounter any more obstacles from them.

*

17

The second Amber Oars Regatta was approaching. It had been decided to add one more event this year – the double sculls. The scullers were glad not to feel like second-class rowers anymore, but the main "Amber Oars" prize was still reserved only for coxed fours.

By 25 and 26 May the Žalgiris rowing centre in Trakai was crawling with rowers. Lithuania's rowers, who had missed Lake Galvė and the pre-race excitement, looked forward to meeting their friends, opponents, rowers from other republics, and their summer loves with joy and anticipation.

The weather was no better than it had been during last year's regatta – strong headwinds and rain seemed to be a signature element of the Amber Oars Regatta.

With only a few days left before the Moscow-Leningrad-Lithuania match in Moscow, the coaches decided against splitting the men's eight into two fours, instead choosing to row in the four event non-competitively to test their strength.

The only event the Lithuanians didn't win was the women's double scull – near the finish line, Janina Lukošiūnaitė and Sofija Grucaitė veered off course and locked oars with the women from Kaunas, losing to the Latvians by 1.6 seconds. However, Sofija still got her Amber Oars prize – immediately after that race, she raced as a cox in the women's four. They grabbed a surprise victory against the Latvians, who had won the country's championships last year.

Everyone in Trakai carefully inspected the Žalgiris crew's new oars. Nobody in Lithuania or even the entire Soviet Union had oars like them. However, their superiority was clear after the eight's first race. Other associations' coaches gave Ričardas no peace as they tried to find out where and how he had gotten them. Before even drying off from the races, the oars were loaded onto the trailer together with the boats and sent off towards Moscow. The next weekend, teams would gather in Khimki to fight for a place in the USSR team and for a trip to the Duisburg regatta.

*

The rain that fell over the Amber Oars Regatta finally cleared up after two days, once again revealing the clear, sunny May sky. All of Lithuania smelled like a garden or park in bloom. School girls, with the sleeves of their brown woollen uniforms rolled up, hurried through the streets of Vilnius with wings of black chiffon flapping from their aprons, sprigs of lilac and bird cherry in their hair, and mysterious smiles that betrayed the emotions gripping their young hearts.

During the last days of the school year, the schoolchildren ploughing away at their desks waited impatiently for the fitness camp that began at the Trakai rowing centre at the beginning of June. During the camp, an avalanche of tents would come together to form a separate life, unlike any other, for the rowers. There were nighttime apple picking expeditions, new loves, dances, initiations for newcomers, pranks – the training seemed like an afterthought. They were far from home, far from their parents, far from their teachers, and far from the Komsomol secretaries. A few of them, inspired by Žalgiris' victories, would be inspired to become just like them. They'd begin to train intensely, day after day, and follow all of the coach's instructions. Most of them, however, would continue to enjoy their carefree summer adventures, which would stay with them for the rest of their lives as some of the fondest memories of their youth.

For the men of Žalgiris, the beginning of June heralded a new, unpredictable and intriguing rowing season.

*

The Lithuanian team hurried to the Khimki Reservoir as soon as they arrived in Moscow and dropped off their luggage at the hotel.

The Dynamo Water Stadium was a grandiose concrete structure on the left shore of the reservoir. It was built there in 1935. Its two stories of spectator seating could fit more than three thousand spectators and looked like an enormous water sports arena. The highest corners of the grandstands were decorated by metal sailboats affixed to concrete "waves." Decorative columns supported the roofs and canopies, and the ends of the massive railings along the main stairway were decorated by elegant concrete roses. There had once been three swimming pools installed in front of the grandstands for swimming, diving, and water polo. Diving boards extended from both sides of these pools like seagull wings. Inside, there were locker rooms, halls and a boathouse. Outside, there was a track and field facility and areas for games and gymnastics as well. The finish line was right next to the grandstands, but spectators who climbed up higher could see almost the entire two-kilometre racecourse. That summer, there were plans to mark the racecourse with buoys – to install the Albano system. The Women's European Rowing Championships was approaching and the racecourse had to be installed according to the FISA international standards. At last, steering off-course would no longer ruin rowers' results or moods.

The only problem was that the water stadium design didn't take into account the intense waves that would be caused by numerous boats on the reservoir, making it unsuitable for light and narrow racing boats. The concrete shoreline descended from the grandstands straight into the water. The powerful waves that travelled hère all the way from the right-hand bank would pick up even more speed and bounce back into the racecourse, or at least into the first few lanes on the course. Woe to those who were unfortunate enough to race in the first or second lanes – their loss was almost guaranteed. What's more, it wasn't always clear that the lane positions here were a question of chance. Rumour had it that the first lanes were always given to teams that had to be removed from continuing in the tournament or joining the USSR team. Thoroughly un-summerlike Moscow weather – wind, rain, and dark, heavy clouds greeted the participants of the competition. Daytime temperatures never exceeded 14 degrees, and cold rain fell almost every hour of the day. Despite the inclement weather, countless motorboats, yachts, steamboats, and racing motorboats dotted the water from the early hours of Saturday morning, and the rowers took their boats out on the water as well. The Žalgiris rowers proudly removed their new wide-bladed oars from the trailer like secret weapons and lined them up against the wall. Their opponents' nervous glances filled them with sweet satisfaction.

"What do you think, Povilas, by how much will we beat CSK by?" the coach valued his opinion.

"I think by about seven seconds," Povilas answered boldly, watching the CSK team doing practice starts.

"You think so?" Ričardas liked Povilas' answer, but he wanted to believe it himself, too.

"I do! Want to bet on it?" Povilas said, extending his right hand.

"Alright, alright, if you say so, then perhaps that's what'll happen,"

Ričardas said, unwilling to bet. "I just hope nobody gets sick. We have to win."

"If we have to win, we'll win," this phrase had essentially become Žalgiris' motto.

"I just hope we don't get lane one," Ričardas said with concern.

"I hope to God we don't," said Povilas, cocking his head and watching the large waves beat against the concrete shoreline. "Waves like these could break our boat."

"What do you think about Volodia?" the coach said, suddenly changing topics.

"Why?"

"Who do we row better with?"

"I think we're better off with Celestinas, but I don't know what the others think. Why?"

"No reason," said Ričardas, closing the topic as quickly as he had introduced it and losing himself in thought. Finding the best crew composition took lots of time and stress. The big, strong men that Ričardas valued so much weren't always the best bet. His men's precise and harmonious rowing, which made their boat absolutely fly, was the result of long training sessions and hundreds of kilometres rowed together. Achieving such mastery within a single summer would be impossible. And what was he supposed to do with the men that the KGB officials didn't want to release under any circumstances? They had worked so hard; focused so much on their strength and fitness, and put all of their hopes and dreams into the sport. How was he supposed to tell them once again that their documents hadn't gone through? How was he supposed to tell them again that there was no room in the boat for them? How much longer could they exhaust themselves under the belief that something might change? And then there was the constant pressure to replace Lithuanians with Russians, to destroy his team, and to register non-Lithuanians as part of the Lithuanian Žalgiris Association so that they could race for Lithuania. How much longer could they torment him with never-ending selection and qualification competitions, after which the athletes could barely manage to think of continuing to compete?

Boats from Moscow, Leningrad, Latvia, and Lithuania were rowing back and forth, practising their starts and their accelerations. The coxes shouted their commands and raincoat-clad coaches ran to and fro along the dock with tools in their hands, adjusting the boats' gates and stretchers as they floated on the water. Beyond the racecourse, motorboats bobbed up and down among the waves. Meanwhile, Ričardas stood back, leaning on a concrete grandstand column, and tried to untangle the impossible puzzles that he was facing.

The sun gradually began to set somewhere behind the grey clouds and the frantic movement of the motorboats on the reservoir began to calm down – only the racing motorboats continued to howl across the surface of the water like wild beasts. Groups of green people began to gather on the shoreline – the Lithuanian crews were the last to complete their training before the races. The rowers gathered below the roof of the grandstands and shared their experiences and concerns from the day's training. The usual waves of anxiety began to grip them, and they all began to want everything to end as quickly as possible, or even that the race wouldn't take place and that they wouldn't even have to approach the starting line.

The Moscow-Leningrad match was the first competition in the season that had all of the strongest teams in one place. The next day, the core of the USSR team would begin to take shape.

*

The men's races were to begin in two hours. They gathered in the grandstands and watched how the women's doubles, singles and eights rowed out to warm up. The fours were set to race soon, but the Lithuanians had no contenders there.

Crowded into the few rows in the grandstands that didn't get any rain, the rowers waited for their race time. Some rested their heads on their knees in an effort to compensate for their long and sleepless night, while others flipped through pages of local newspapers that had been left behind, chatted one another, or stared into the distance, trying to quell their anxiety. Their breakfast sat in their stomachs, and their legs would begin to tremble every time they thought of the approaching races.

A few spectators began to trickle into the grandstands, having sorely missed the water and athletic events during the winter. The intense wind that had blown all day died down, and only a few racing boats on the water disturbed the peace.

"The women have really developed a wonderful rhythm over the past few days," James noted, pointing at the women's quad approaching the finish line.

With Sofija at stroke, Janina, Rita and Gaila seemed to be in perfect harmony.

"You're right," Povilas agreed. "But it's too bad they got the lane one..."

"Maybe the waves won't hit them too hard," Juozas added.

"There's no telling when the waves will pick up and when they won't. If a barge or a Raketa[58] passes by, then nothing will save you," James nodded.

"Yeah," Juozas agreed, stretching out on his bench.

"Are we in the lane three?" Petras joined the conversation.

"I think so. All I know is we're not in one."

"Look at them go! They're first!"

"First or second. They're fighting Spartak," Povilas guessed.

"Nonsense, they're definitely first! Go, go, go!" James jumped out of his seat.

The women's boat was approaching the 250-metre mark and the grandstands. Their teammates had jumped up out of their seats and couldn't believe what they saw. The never-before-seen Lithuanian quad was leading against the strong and experienced women from Moscow and Leningrad.

"Where's your camera, Povilas? What shots!" James couldn't contain his excitement.

"I left it at the hotel... I didn't want to bring it because of the rain."

"Look at them go!" even Antanas had stood up from the bench.

"I just hope they can keep it up!"

Beyond the rowing course, two Raketa boats, like white swans, passed each other. The passengers waved to the grandstands and to one another, enjoying the beautiful summer day. White bursts of foam shot out from their sterns and rolled towards the shore in two interwoven sets of waves.

"That's all we needed!" the men complained out loud.

"Maybe they'll make it through in time?"

"They won't..."

There was only a bit more than a hundred metres left until the finish line when the waves crossed the course, lifting and lowering the women's

---

58   Raketa – a line of passenger riverboats with hydrofoils manufactured in the USSR starting in 1957.

fragile boats, reaching the grandstands and returning back towards the course. What the women wanted to avoid most was happening at the worst possible time. With its power doubled, the wave rolled right into lane one and right onto the Lithuanian women's bow. The women's bowside oars were submerged up to the collar and the arena echoed with their cry of surprise. The massive crab that all four of them had just caught stopped the boat completely turning it perpendicular to the racecourse. In an instant, the women regained their balance, but putting the boat back on course and accelerating took time. Two Moscow boats and one from Leningrad passed them, leaving the Lithuanians in fourth place.

As they heard the finish gongs ring out, the women bent down over their oars and their backs began to shake. Their strong start had given them a cautious glimmer of hope that they might make it into the USSR team and to the European Championships – and all of that was taken away by a single fateful wave. The women sat in the boat with their hands around their knees, doing their best to control their grief. Only when the pairs passed them after their race did they take their oars into their hands and slowly start turning around. With long, slow strokes, they rowed back past the grandstands, their eyes averted from the spectators, their applauding teammates, and the coaches who wanted so much to console them.

On the course, it seemed like there might be another upset on the way. The Žalgiris women's eight was hanging on doggedly right behind the Moscow Trud crew, which was leading. All six of the opposing teams were Masters of Sport - strong and experienced. All of the Lithuanian women, except for Irena, were first-ranked athletes who had not yet seen a serious victory. Apparently, as they fled the Burevestnik eight, the Lithuanians hadn't even noticed that they were within centimetres of Trud. That was how the race ended, with Trud winning by a hair – 0.2 seconds – and Burevestnik coming in 0.8 seconds later. Eugenijus, who had run along with the girls from the very beginning of the grandstands, couldn't contain his joy, and ran back to them, glancing about in a search for approval and waving to those who were congratulating him.

"Great job, Eugenijus! They almost won!" Ričardas congratulated his brother before turning to his men. "That's it, boys, it's our turn now. Let's go!"

In the distance, they could see the start pontoon being pushed back to the two-kilometre mark. There was an hour until the men were due to start.

Three Lithuanian crews were to race that day and fight for places on the USSR team. Ričardas, Zigmas, Antanas, James, Povilas, Volodia, Petras and Juozas in the eight. Celestinas and Eugenijus were racing the coxless pair.

The men gathered by their boats, checking one final time whether anyone had tampered with their equipment: loosening any screws, poking any holes, removing any bolts, or – worst of all – removing seats. Unfortunately, things like this happened in the world of Soviet rowing. Victory – or your opponent's loss – at any price and with no sense of guilt – was tolerated and even encouraged by some countries' coaches. It was fine if you caught them in time. If not, you might not make it to the start line.

This time, everything was fine. They couldn't find any problems or damage, so all they had left to do was polish their slides and grease their oars. The water was gradually growing calmer, the tourists' water activity centres were closing, and the racing boats were returning to their docks. Barely any cargo shipping took place on Saturdays, so there was little chance of the men facing what had happened to the women's crew. In addition, they had the good fortune of not being in lane one.

The new pair – Celestinas and Eugenijus – had been formed just for this competition, but they seemed strong. At least, that's how they looked from the outside – only the men themselves knew what was going on inside of them. Their primary opponents were title-winning Olympians Boreiko and Golovanov, who had won just about everything up to this point. The only people who could expect some sort of miracle were those who knew nothing about either rower's achievements. When Eugenijus and Romas Šarmaitis won the USSR Championships the previous year, it had seemed that their pair had great victories ahead of them, but at the time, nobody had guessed that Romas would end his active rowing career.

The Žalgiris eight was on its way to the starting line when they were passed by the Lithuanian and Leningrad pairs, heading neck-and-neck towards the finish line. They stopped for a moment so they could hear the announcer's voice, which proclaimed that the Lithuanians and Russians had fought up to the last few metres, where Boreiko and Golovanov pulled off a victory, finishing in 7.30 and only one second quicker than Celestinas and Eugenijus.

"Alright," Ričardas thought to himself. "That means we should do well for ourselves, if that's how well our subs are rowing." He didn't call them that out loud, but anyone who didn't make it into the eight or couldn't travel abroad was considered a sub. He used them to win qualifications and national championships, after which others would take their places – people with clean backgrounds, the "politically trustworthy," or Russian speakers.

Žalgiris' eight was the favourite to win the race and nobody expected any surprises in the event, even though the Moscow military naval eight crew had done a faster time than Lithuania's over 2,000 metres that season. However, the Lithuanians hadn't been there when they had done so. No two races are alike – the weather, the water, and the wind could all help or hinder rowers, which is why records aren't kept in rowing. The first race against Žalgiris filled the military rowers with unrest. The Lithuanians' victories last year had been impressive. And those oars... Winning today was extremely important. The winners would head to the Duisburg regatta – and then to Lucerne.

When the starting flare shot up into the air and the eights' oars struck the water, Povilas' promise of "seven seconds" was still stuck in Ričardas' mind. When, at the quarter mark, Žalgiris found themselves in the lead by an entire length, Ričardas glanced at his oar blade. "Even though it's wider, it's no harder to pull." What he didn't know was that the other men had secretly narrowed his blade and readjusted the collar so that he, the stroke, would have an easier time pulling and would be able to maintain a high rate for the entire race. They decided to do whatever it took to keep up. They didn't tell him so he wouldn't feel embarrassed. They didn't want to hurt the feelings of their stroke and their coach, who was the smallest member of the team by size and weight but had an excellent sense of rhythm.

At the halfway mark, Žalgiris was ahead of the competition by two lengths – and the gap was getting bigger. They could hear the spectators' echoes from the grand stands, though it was impossible to identify any languages or voices in their shouts. This meant that the finish line was fast approaching. It was the sort of finish that every rower dreamed of – a confident lead and a confident victory without the need for tearing themselves apart to the verge of fainting, without the taste of blood in their mouths. When they heard the gong, the men saw that their greatest rivals were in third, and that the Ukrainians were second. "First place – Žalgiris

Vilnius, 6:08.4, second place – Dynamo Kiev, 6:15, third place – KJL, 6:15.8," the announcer reported.

"Seven seconds," Ričardas smiled to himself. "Seven and a half seconds!"

"I almost guessed it," Povilas thought joyfully as his team rowed back towards the dock. "Seven and a half seconds!"

*

"Well then, time to teach Ratzeburg a lesson?" said James, celebrating their victory.

Satisfied with their impressive victory and the approaching journey to Duisburg, the men's eight set about derigging their boat and preparing for the trip.

"That's right, it is," Antanas agreed.

"If it goes as well as it did today, then we'll definitely win," Juozas reasoned.

"With a crew like this, we will definitely win," Zigmas added.

"Why are you so quiet, Povilas? Aren't you happy?" James asked, noticing Povilas, quieter than ever, polishing his slides.

"Yeah, I am, I knew we'd win. Before the race, I told Rychka that we'd win by seven seconds."

"So what's got you down?"

"I don't know... I think they'll probably take me out again."

"Where'd you get that from?"

"I saw Rychka go to talk to Leningrad..."

"Maybe he was just going to chat with them about something."

"Maybe you're right. We'll see... Shhh, he's coming. What did I tell you? He's not alone..."

"How's it going, men? Have you loaded your oars? We have twenty minutes to pack up," Ričardas said, running his palm along the wet edge of the boat. "Don't forget to wipe it down so it doesn't get covered in dust during the trip. Cox, bring me a rag!" he shouted to the cox.

The men looked up and stared at the cox standing next to their coach – Yuri Suslin, the same Suslin from Leningrad's Trud whom KGB officers had once forbidden from going to the Olympics.

"Hey, Yuri," Zigmas greeted him in Russian.

The men, surprised, looked to their coach with questioning glances. Only Povilas continued polishing his slides without looking up.

"Yuri will be headed to Duisburg with us," Ričardas came out and told the men directly and, seeing that the men were looking for an explanation, looked to Povilas: "instead of Povilas."

In an effort to ensure that Yuri wouldn't understand, Zigmas pretended to be telling a joke, and jumped up to the coach. He had a big smile on his face but eyes like daggers:

"We don't want to change the crew. The boat is working well and we don't have time to learn how to row again. Why can't Povilas go?"

"He just can't. His documents aren't in order," Ričardas explained. He had always respected Zigmas' opinion, but there was no escape this time. "I know, I don't like it either. I don't want to change the crew, but what can we do?"

Povilas hung his dirty rag on the edge of the sling and, without a word, squatted down to tie up the riggers. A ball of pain was rising in his throat and his eyes began to shimmer. He turned away to look at the waters of Khimki so his friends couldn't see his face as he tried his best to swallow the pain. It was nothing new, really – he had experienced this pain many times before and had almost gotten used to suppressing it. It was like a well-known exercise. He knew how long it would take to overcome, he knew what would come after, and he knew how it would end. After tying up the port-side riggers, he stood up, brushed the back of his hand across his forehead, smiled with his tightly pressed lips, and turned away towards the trailer.

"Povilas, Celestinas and the Levickas brothers will prepare for the Grand Moscow Regatta in the four," he heard the coach's voice, who had begun to speak in Russian. "Yuri, when will you be able to make it to Trakai?"

"I'll be there on Wednesday."

"We'll meet there on Wednesday, then," said Ričardas, turning to his men. "Clear? Let's take the boat!"

"Clear."

Celestinas caught up to Povilas:

"They threw you out?"

"As you can see."

"It's not the first time. We'll manage. Don't eat yourself up about this."

"I'm not."

"You are, I can see it. I know how it feels."

Povilas remained silent, loading the riggers into the truck and taking a deep sigh.

"Povilas, we'll show them what we can do with the four," Celestinas soothed him.

"I worked so hard all winter, I did so much, and they threw me overboard again," Povilas blurted out. "I don't know if I want to row anymore. Why should I? It won't do anything for me. I've got enough Lithuanian championship medals. No stipend, no apartment, and yet I must live on somehow and support my family. But I keep getting thrown out."

"I understand you. Better than the others. They threw me out of the eight, too, even though they said everything was alright with my documents."

"It's a real mystery why they replaced you. It must've suited someone. They don't want the entire boat to be Lithuanian."

"I think so, too. It's important that they aren't all Lithuanians. Then they can say out loud afterward that a Russian team had won. Just like in America, where nobody even knew that they were Lithuanians. All of the newspapers wrote 'Russians, Russians,' you remember the ones they brought home? This isn't sport, it's politics."

"I don't know, Celestinas, if I still want to be pushed around anymore. I'll start working as soon as I get my diploma. It'll be my last summer like this. If they don't accept me into the team, there's no point."

Celestinas had nothing to say. The two men turned quietly towards their team, which was happily chatting with the new member of their crew.

*

$$18$$

A line of IL-7 and AN-7 aircraft stood in Vnukov airport, waiting for their passengers. They would soon be flying to Vilnius. The TU-124, which had just begun flying between Vilnius and Moscow a few months ago, was still shiny and new; the first jet plane to ever fly in Lithuania. Even its crew seemed tidier and more helpful. Flights to Vilnius, which had been shortened to just an hour and 15 minutes, seemed like something from science fiction.

An elegant women with a light lilac suit and a hat of the same colour, her hands filled with boxes and packages tied with decorative bows, hurried towards the end of the line of aircraft on the tarmac. She immediately drew the other passengers' attention, seeming as if she was from another planet – she was smiling, which was such a rare thing in this country, and unlike everyone else, she seemed happy and cheerful. Her wardrobe, certainly not a Soviet one, looked stunning in the line of grey and black passengers. The entire line couldn't help but turn and stare at her.

"Good day, Missis Mizarienė," said Zigmas, the first to understand who she was as he waved. "Come join us."

"Oh, hello, boys! You guys were in America! I remember you, I do!" she said, recognizing the rowers. "What are you doing here in Moscow?"

"We had a competition. Here, let me help you," said Zigmas, grabbing the packages from her and nodding to his teammates for them to come help.

"And how did it go?"

"We won, thanks for asking."

"Well, bravo! So when will you be visiting us in the US again?"

"Probably not this year. We're headed to the FRG now, and then to Lucerne afterwards. Maybe to Copenhagen, too. Are you headed to Lithuania?"

"Yeah, yeah, Lithuania."

After climbing into the cabin of the airplane, which reeked of cigarettes despite being so new, they stored the colourful packages on the shelves and the rowers went to find their seats.

"Who is she?" Povilas asked James quietly so others wouldn't hear.

"Ieva Mizarienė, wife of Rojus Mizara. He's an American Lithuanian, a writer. When we were in America, we spoke during a meeting."

"What did he write?"

"I'm not sure, I haven't read it," James laughed.

A stewardess passed them in the aisle, offering passengers caramel sweets on a tray. During take-off, this was the best relief for ear pain. The men unwrapped a sweet each – the wrappers read "Aeroflot" – tossed them into their mouths, leaned back on the leather seats, and closed their eyes. The fatigue from the competition seeped into every muscle in their body and drew them into a deep sleep. Outside the windows, Moscow receded into the distance, with all of its bustle, Stalinistic towers, and unending residential neighbourhoods, with its Khimki reservoir and its terrible concrete arena, and its euphoric victories and tearful defeats. It wouldn't stay lonely for long. In exactly a month, the Lithuanian team would return for the Great Moscow Regatta.

*

When the wheels of the airplane touched down on the landing strip in Vilnius' airport, the sunlight glittered on the tarmac that was wet from a recent rain. There was a crowd of people gathered by the airport building to greet the passengers and the shiny black Pobeda[59]. Sometimes, someone would come right up to the tarmac to greet important guests, like Central Committee leaders, artists or athletes, but this time, it seemed that they would be greeted by the highest levels of government.

The TU-124 rolled to the airport building and came to a stop. When the passengers could see the ramp rolling up to the aircraft, they got up and began to gather their belongings, luggage and raincoats. They lined up, impatient to get off of the plane.

"Ms. Mizarienė, please, let us help you," this time Ričardas was the first to offer the lady help with her pile of beautiful packages.

The men distributed the packages and followed each other out down the steps on the ramp after letting Mizarienė out into the front.

The Central Committee lined up in front of the ramp, awaiting the

---

59   A four-seater sedan produced in the Soviet Union by GAZ.

famous American Lithuanian. In the centre of the men, clad in black raincoats, stood the First Secretary of the Lithuanian Communist Party Central Committee, Antanas Sniečkus.

"Welcome to your motherland, Ms. Mizarienė," the First Secretary said, extending his hand.

"It's wonderful to see you," said Mizarienė, greeting the Central Committee leaders who had gathered before turning back to her helpers. "Thank you, boys! These are rowers, they're returning from a competition," she said, introducing them to Sniečkus.

"I know, I know them, they're good men. They were world silver medallists last year! How did it go in Moscow?"

"Thank you, it went well. We defeated our primary rivals, the military naval crew," said Zigmas, who always had the least qualms about speaking to government officials. "They made us new oars in Kaunas, so we had a huge victory."

Seeing that their friends were talking to Sniečkus himself, all of the men gathered to greet him.

"Hello, Secretary!"

"Hello, hello, men! Where are you headed to now?"

"To Duisburg, and then to Lucerne."

"Well then, good luck to you. You need to eat some more bacon," he said, turning to James, "so you'd have some more fat on you."

James smiled, unsure of how to respond.

"Good luck, men! If there are any problems, let me know."

"Thank you, thank you."

The men handed the lady's packages to Sniečkus' entourage and turned off to head for the door.

Suddenly, James realised that this was the first – and probably last – time he would have direct access to the country's First Secretary, the country's highest ruling official.

"Zigmas, listen, let's go! Let's ask him about Povilas! We'll never have a chance like this again!"

"Yeah, let's try it," said Zigmas without hesitation. "Povilas, let's go!"

The men took off back towards Sniečkus, who was leaving with his entire group. "Comrade Secretary!"

Sniečkus turned around inquisitively.

"Now, we do have one question..."

"Yes, I'm listening," Sniečkus said attentively.

"So, we won the competition and we have to go abroad, but we have to bring a weaker rower and leave our stronger rower, Povilas, behind."

"Really? Why is that?"

"They won't let him travel abroad."

"What do you mean they won't let him?"

"His documents won't go through."

"So what did he do?"

"We don't know... he didn't do anything. They won't let him is all."

"Ah, so the KGB won't let him go?"

"That's probably it."

"Do you guys really need him?"

"We do."

"I see. And you, men, can you guarantee his conduct?"

"Yes," Zigmas, Antanas and James responded confidently all together. "The same as for ourselves."

"Yes, there have been very good responses regarding you guys... alright, men, if there aren't any problems there, I'll take responsibility for it. On Tuesday, you and your coach," he said, gesturing towards Povilas, "come to the Central Committee and see Kairelis. He's the head of the Administrative Organs department. I'll call him tomorrow and let him know."

"Thank you, we'll be there," Povilas politely thanked him.

"I think we'll manage to put everything in order," said Sniečkus, shaking the men's hands, waving to the others, and hurrying off towards his guest.

"Thank you, Secretary, thank you very much," the men bowed down lower than usual when saying goodbye. Overjoyed by their unexpected success, they hurried off towards the door.

"You see, Povilas, everything will be alright, he promised to take care of it," said James, proud of his idea and of the conversation, which had gone much better than expected.

"Let's hope he takes care of it..." said Povilas, still unable to process the glimmer of hope that had appeared before him.

"He's a man of his word, and he's helped us more than once," Zigmas encouraged him. "Everything should be alright now."

"That's right, he keeps his promises," Antanas agreed.

"Thanks, guys," said Povilas. He still didn't believe that something might change, but he was thankful to his friends for the support. "Thank you for vouching for me."

"It was nothing. I just hope everything ends up alright."

"Who's Kairelis?" asked Povilas, turning to Ričardas.

"Kairelis? The Central Committee has its own security division. But if you pass through there, then that's it – not even the KGB will stop you. They have the final word. I'll hold your hand," Ričardas laughed. He too was happy that a silver lining had appeared for his trainee.

*

19

The morning of 4 June finally arrived. From the early morning, the city was filled with throngs of schoolchildren who had finished their school year. The summer that had just begun hadn't been an especially warm one, but a pleasant day was expected nonetheless. Forecasts said it would be 18 degrees outside.

Povilas and Ričardas met by the door of the Central Committee at 9:50. The meeting they had been scheduled for made both of them anxious. There were horrible stories about the Administrative Organs department. Nobody ever wanted to face them. However, this meeting could be an exception. The fact that they had been called there by none other than Antanas Sniečkus filled them with trust and hope.

They were stopped by a stern guard as soon as they entered.

"Destination?"

"Kairelis, 10:00."

"Last names?"

"Vaitkevičius, Ričardas."

"Liutkaitis, Povilas."

"Documents!"

"Here you go," they both extended their passports. The guard drew a line under the previous day's list of visitors in his log book and wrote "1963 VI 4" across the middle in block letters before beginning to fill out their names, surnames, and arrival times: "Sign here!"

The men signed and slid their passports into their inner coat pockets.

"Wait by that office," the guard motioned. "They'll call you."

Ričardas squeezed that day's issue of "Sportas" in his hand.

"Want to read it?"

"Is there anything interesting? Anything about our race?"

"Yeah, here, read it."

Povilas took the issue of "Sportas". His hands were shaking. On the first page, he saw the title – "A Pleasant Surprise" – and an article under it about the race they had just won in Moscow. His eyes scanned the lines, but his mind was elsewhere. Povilas began reading again from the beginning when he realised that he couldn't recall a single word he had read. He flipped to the second page, where the article continued, and scanned that as well.

"I'll buy it when I leave," he said, returning the newspaper to Ričardas. "I can't read right now."

"You nervous?"

"Why should I be? It can't get any worse, can it?" Povilas smiled, though it was clear that he was extremely nervous.

Both men realised that, here more than anywhere else, the walls had ears, and so their conversation ended there.

"Liutkaitis? Vaitkevičius? Come in," a chubby secretary poked her head through the open office door.

"Please, sit down," the master of the office said to the two men, gesturing towards chairs on the other side of his desk as he flipped through papers. He looked up at the men once they had sat down: "I'm listening."

Ričardas was the first to speak:

"Comrade Sniečkus told us to come meet with you.

"Yes, I'm listening."

"We're rowers. From Žalgiris."

Kairelis wrote something down.

"USSR champions."

"Yes, I know, the Secretary informed me."

"See, his documents aren't being let through and he can't travel abroad."

"Surname?"

"Liutkaitis," Povilas managed despite his parched tongue.

"Why won't they let you go?"

"I don't know, they wouldn't say."

"Are you in the Komsomol?"

"No."

"Why?"

"It just happened that way...," Povilas didn't want to tell the truth, but he didn't lie, either.

"Married?"

"Yes."

"Any children?"

"I have a little daughter, she's almost a year old."

"What does your wife do?"

"She's a physicist. She's working in her field right now."

"Where are you from?"

"From Prienai. I was born in the village of Rūdupis."

"Do your parents live there?"

"I don't have any parents," Povilas' voice trembled and stuttered, but he continued: "I was orphaned after the war."

"Why is he asking me these things? Everything's there in my papers. They know everything about me. Are they checking to see whether I'm lying?" Povilas thought, but the questions kept coming:

"They died?"

"My mother died in a firefight."

"Your father?"

"He died..."

"Where was he buried?"

"I don't know..."

"Did he die in Lithuania?"

"No, in Ukhta..."

Silence. Kairelis' lips tightened and he stared at the opened case before him.

"Whose case is this? My father's? Elzbieta's? There are so many pages... What's in there?" the thoughts ran through Povilas' mind a mile a minute.

"I see...," he continued, his voice now colder. "Do you have any brothers or sisters?"

"I have two sisters and two brothers."

"Where do they live?"

"One sister lives in Prienai. The other sister and my brothers live in Balkhash."

"So they're all within the territory of the Soviet Union?"

"Yes."

"What are they doing in Balkhash?"

"My brothers stayed there after their service in the army. They work in construction."

"Did you serve in the army?"

"No, they didn't draft me. I began my studies immediately after school."

"Do you have any relatives abroad?"

"I don't think so, at least not that I've heard of."

"Did anyone leave for the West during the war?"

"I don't know, not to my knowledge."

"Where do you live?"

"In Vilnius, on Čiurlionis Street. With my parents-in-law."

"Do you work? Do you study?"

"I'm finishing up my studies. Only the state exam is left."

"What do you plan to do when you finish?"

"I'll work. I'll continue with sports if there aren't any obstacles."

"What sort of obstacles could there be?"

"The biggest one is leaving for international competitions. If I can't go with my team, I won't continue rowing."

"What does your coach think?" he turned to Ričardas, who had remained silent until now.

"I think we'd lose a lot without an athlete like him. He's very strong, responsible, dependable and friendly. It's very difficult for our crew to replace someone. Our times get considerably worse when we have to. Povilas has been in our eight from the very beginning. We've never had any problems with him."

The coach and his trainee made eye contact for a moment, and Povilas managed a quick smile of gratitude.

Kairelis opened the case, squinted, wrote something down, signed it, stamped it, pressed a carved wooden drying pad to the stamp, closed the case and looked up:

"Comrade Liutkaitis, we won't stop you from heading abroad. Good luck in your sport and personal life."

In Povilas' head, which was ringing with anxiety, those words felt like a verdict of innocence. The men couldn't help but rise up out of their seats.

"Thank you, thank you so much," Ričardas thanked Kairelis, grasping the official's right hand in both of his.

"Any more questions?"

"No... Well, actually, we have two brothers, the Levickas brothers, and they're being held up, too. Could we somehow take a look at them as well?"

Ričardas was now determined to fix everything he could, now that he had an opportunity.

Kairelis wrote down the last names on a piece of graph paper and, without saying anything else, shook the men's hands:

"I wish you the best. Bring us home some medals!"

"Thank you," Povilas responded with a trembling voice, feeling as though he must be dreaming. With that, they turned to leave.

Povilas' chest felt like it was going to burst. He held the ball of joy down in his throat so he wouldn't erupt with shouts for joy. He barely felt his feet as he descended the steps onto Lenin Avenue, which was green with linden blossoms. This time, every passer-by seemed like his best friend. The ice cream vendor, with her white sleeves, seemed like a fairy, and the driver of the trolley bus seemed to wave to him in congratulations as he passed.

"You see, Povilas? Everything will be alright!" the coach said joyfully. "Sniečkus wasn't lying."

"We were lucky to see him at the airport! I wonder if they'll take care of my papers quickly now."

"They won't manage it in time for Duisburg, everybody's papers have already been sent to Moscow. But we might yet make it to Lucerne."

"That's too bad. I really wanted to row in the eight..."

"We'll see after the Great Moscow Regatta. Now, you guys need to prepare well for the four."

"Yes, of course, we will. How are things with Celestinas' papers?"

"He straightened them out. He's 'vyjezdnoj.'"

As they happily marched along the avenue, the men stopped by a newspaper kiosk. Povilas extended three kopecks and took an issue of "Sportas".

"Now I can read it, too."

"Are you in a hurry? Let's go sit down," Ričardas waved toward a bench on Chernyakhovsky Square[60].

The men sat down in the shade underneath a linden tree. Ričardas looked intently at his trainee, though they were almost the same age.

"Listen, Povilas. I didn't know anything about your past. I didn't know you grew up without parents."

"Well, we can't go back and change that, can we..."

"I assume you had a difficult childhood."

"Yes, but I grew up. My aunt cared for me when she could. She let me go pursue my studies. Our relatives didn't leave us to our troubles."

"How old were you when you lost your parents?"

---

60 Since 2007, this square has been known as Vincas Kudirka Square.

"Eight..."

"Still a child... and that's why you were 'nevyezdnoj?'"

"Probably. I think it had more to do with the fact that my Father let himself die in Ukhta..."

"What's in Ukhta? A concentration camp?"

"That's right, for political prisoners," said Povilas, tight-lipped.

"That's alright, everything will be taken care of now, you'll catch up, Povilas."

"Yeah. I'm alive and kicking, I've got my arms and my legs, my head's still on my shoulders," he smiled.

"How's Gita? How's your daughter?" Ričardas changed the subject, noticing that Povilas had grown upset.

"They're alright, she's growing. A beautiful, happy girl."

"Does Gita miss rowing?"

"It doesn't look like it. She seems to have forgotten completely that she used to be a rower. She's completely absorbed by her new life – nappies, bottles, the pram. And then there's her job... And I'm never home..."

"That's a rower's life for you, I guess," Ričardas laughed. "She knew who she was getting married to. Now, you'll be gone even more, since you can travel abroad."

They both smiled, remembering the successful end to their Central Committee visit. As they stared at the refreshingly green trees, the receding tension finally brought them back to reality.

"So we'll be meeting at Trakai tomorrow at 10:00."

"Yes, I know. I've got to run to my university today. I have to take a few tests."

"You guys will be training in the four. Gerdas will be your cox. The school year is over, so he can spend all summer in Trakai. See you tomorrow, Povilas."

"I'll see you tomorrow. Thank you, Rychka. Thank you for your help."

Ričardas smiled. They bid each other farewell and went to tackle their own plans for the day.

*

20

Day by day, June grew warmer and warmer. One could say that the summer days and the weather were in perfect alignment. However, by mid-June it has started to rain. The weather wasn't the good for anyone doing outdoor sports, but the rowers were used to rain – as long as there wasn't any lightning. It's all the same water, just that it was now falling from above as well. In fact, the summer rains would have been preferable to the sun, if only they had a place to dry their clothes. When it rained, the wind usually died down and the surface of the lake became smooth. The rain refreshed them, washed away their sweat, and cleaned their tracksuits. It even made it feel like they were doing something heroic.

In the middle of June, the press kiosks were once again "graced" by big, red letters – Russian astronaut Valentina Tereshkova had become the first woman in space. One more victory against America in the crazy space race. Not only did the astronaut receive a slew of awards and medals for her efforts, she was also titled a Master of Sports.

The training and racing season hit full swing in Trakai. After only a couple of weeks of training, the eight left for Moscow, where they awaited their journey to Duisburg. The rowers lost precious pre-race training time in the weeks leading up to their journey to the foreign capitalist country. The majority of their days consisted of waiting – for passports, visas and other documents. The primary race for the eight was on 24 June, but by 16 June, they had to leave their teammates behind and fly to Moscow. They would all only reconvene towards the end of the month, right before the Great Moscow Regatta.

The Great Moscow Regatta, which was first organised in 1956 between the USSR and Czechoslovakian teams, grew into a truly great regatta, though no foreign rowers were to participate that year. In addition, the regatta was the men's primary qualifier before heading to the European Championships in Copenhagen.

All of the teams, of course, dreamed and hoped to make it into the USSR team and leave for Denmark.

The Žalgiris eight brought the victory over Ratzeburg that they had been dreaming of home to Moscow. It was down to a photo finish, and it was only by 0.2 seconds, but a win is a win. Finally, Žalgiris believed that their greatest opponent could be overcome and that they just might be the best in the world.

After hurrying to the Khimki Reservoir, the rowers saw a sight they knew all too well – the usual waves and wind. The boat traffic during the tourist season was even more intense than usual. Lane one was still the worst place to be. All they could hope for was an honest draw when selecting their lane and some help from a higher power.

The day of the qualifying races began with an unpleasant surprise for the Lithuanian team – Zigmas and Antanas were late for their race. Alfa and Šarmaitis came to the rescue to salvage the situation, but they had just raced in their pair. It was no surprise, then, that the Žalgiris crew lost to the CSK eight – their main rivals – by 5 seconds. Upon noticing the crew changes, which hadn't been foreseen in their application, the umpires immediately entered the Žalgiris eight in the individual racing crew list, meaning they were not in the running for the main prize. Losing the prize, of course, was a shame, but it would be an even greater shame to lose the right to attend the European Championships if the pair of Olympians was to repeat their little "practical joke" on the day of the final.

Having felt a whiff of freedom, and with the chance to become members of the USSR team within arm's reach, the four, with Celestinas, Povilas, Romas, Eugenijus and Gerdas, scored a confident victory in the semi-final. Having cast off the chains of "politically untrustworthy" and "enemies of the nation," it seemed that the weight holding their boat back had finally been cast off. The wind and waves of Khimki couldn't stop them and their boat glided along effortlessly, as if sensing its rowers' hopes. "This isn't over, the final is the most important part," their teammates reassured them. "Don't celebrate too early." But they were happy. They were happy to be free, though conditionally. They burned with a desire to win, and they believed in themselves and their victory.

The Lithuanians' oars were no longer a surprise for anyone. The Russian teams hurried to have similar wide-bladed oars made at the Dynamo factory in Leningrad. On the shores of the Khimki Reservoir, however, those with sharp eyes spotted another innovation. Members of Leningrad's Dynamo – student Valentin Sergeyev and engineer Yuri Utyochin, though they weren't racing at the regatta – brought oars designed by Yuri the likes of which had not yet been seen anywhere in the world. The oars, which had been made at the same Dynamo factory, were different from ordinary oars – they had an asymmetrical design with an asymmetrical blade that looked like an axe that had been chopped off on the top and made parallel to the water. The majority of the blade was below the shaft. The enthusiasts excitedly explained, to anyone who'd listen, that scientists had proven that these oars were better than the old ones, and that they were not only more efficient, but that they wouldn't bend during the stroke as well. The coaches' sceptical glances showed that they didn't have time for new experiments, and that they had to win the qualifying races here and now. What's more, the new oars still had the smell of lacquer on them.

*

"The women's quadruple scull was third!" Gerdas announced as he ran over joyfully from the grandstands towards his crew, who were preparing their boat. "Though I thought they'd be second. Spartak was first and Trud second. The eight is about to race."

"Alright, but no more running around," Celestinas scolded him. "We're about to go. Grease the oars."

"I already have!"

"Good work. Take the seats to the pontoon."

"I did."

"Alright, then. Do you have your number?"

"I do," Gerdas replied, turning to show the large six on his back.

"Guys, maintain the pace once you start. Don't let Trud get ahead," Ričardas said, hurrying to his crew. "Pick up the pace in the third quarter and keep it up. We need a confident victory so there aren't any uncertainties. How much time?"

"Fifty minutes," said Gerdas, checking the clock.

"Alright, hit the water in ten minutes. Arms, short strokes, as always. Don't row into that zone so you don't get soaked."

The men suppressed their anxiety by hopping in place, stretching, and chewing on their dry lips. The pre-race anxiety was an inevitable part of any competition that few were able to control – only those whom nature had gifted with nerves of steel. The most important thing was not to grow over-anxious, not to "burn out," and not to allow apathy to settle in and drain their energy. Over so many years, the men had learned to identify that state of mind and made sure they were never consumed by such gripping fear. Eugenijus tried to crack jokes while Povilas sang a monotone verse from one of the countless songs his brain held.

"Get ready, lift!"

The men threw the four onto their shoulders and marched off towards the dock. The fans' cries echoed from the grandstands as the women's eights raced towards the finish line.

"Looks like our girls are fifth," Gerdas noted before dashing onto the dock.

The men, in their green and white Žalgiris shirts, looked down the course at their lane, lane six. As always, the Khimki Reservoir was choppy like a sea. They were happy, at least, that they had a good lane.

*

"Внимание![61]" the starting line umpire shot the starting flare up into the sky, giving the finish judges their cue to start their timers. The six coxed fours shot forth from the start line, fighting for their single chance to get a ticket to the European Rowing Championships.

The men's harmonious and precise start set a good rhythm for the rest of the battle. Sometimes, the first six strokes could put a team so off-balance that they'd only manage to recover at the halfway mark. Not this time, however. In just twenty strokes, the Žalgiris crew had forged ahead. Though the only thing each of them could see was their crewmates' backs and the line separating green from white, their cox's elated voice told them that their opponents were falling behind. At the one-kilometre mark, they didn't even have to look around to see the other crews behind them. The wave from the Raketa boat that had passed by the far shore hit their lane and lifted the boat by half a metre, but the men quickly regained their balance without losing a single stroke. Their bodies shivered with excitement and the wave of adrenaline gave them a renewed burst of energy.

"For Lithuania!" Gerdas shouted out their well-known codeword as they passed halfway.

Celestinas picked up the pace and his three crewmates supported their stroke's pace – like clockwork.

---

61   Rus. Attention!

"Five hundred left! We're first! Keep it up!"

The chance to race in the European championship was within their grasp. The grandstands were chanting in Lithuanian and Russian, but the men's ears were deaf with pressure, and they heard only a steady hum and the announcer's muted cries through the loudspeakers. Trud was trailing by two lengths and the distance was growing. "We're going to win, we're going to win..." – Povilas' head was spinning. "Twenty more strokes, nineteen, eighteen... four, three, two, one, that's it, the last one..." The gong rang out and the joyful athletes leaned back with victorious grins on their faces. The next gong rang six seconds later. Somewhere off in the distance, they heard the announcer's voice:

"First place, Žalgiris, 6 minutes and 46.2 seconds."

*

"Good job, guys," Ričardas said, greeting them as they came in. He already had one foot in the eight and was preparing to head for the starting line. "Shave six seconds off of that and you'll be Olympians!"

After a brief greeting with their former crewmates, the eight pushed off of the pontoon to bring back their own victory.

There had never been such a great achievement in Lithuanian rowing before – two Lithuanian boats were headed to the European Championships. The country's athletic leadership celebrated, while that of the Union grew uneasy. The four that had pushed the Moscow crew out of the team was nothing special and hadn't yet achieved anything great. And their "push" had been more like a "shove" – they won by almost three lengths, and on Moscow's home turf.

Immediately after the competition, the men were sat down to fill out forms and other documents. They entered their heights, sizes and shoe sizes and received the preparation camp schedule.

"I've filled out so many countless forms that I know it all by heart. By God, I hope something will come of it this time," Povilas didn't yet know whether the Central Committee would fulfill its promise and whether the KGB officers would hold up his documents.

"Careful with that 'God,'" Eugenijus quietly warned him. "If they hear you, you'll be thrown out."

"That's how I was raised. What am I supposed to say, 'by the party?'"

"I just hope we're not wasting paper," Celestinas agreed.

"Did you fill it out?" Ričardas collected five piles of documents, checked again to see whether he had missed anyone, straightened them out, and placed them in a cardboard folder.

"Sure, we did, but will they take us?" Povilas said doubtfully.

"We'll see," Ričardas said, afraid to promise him anything. "You guys are going home tomorrow and racing in the Lithuanian Spartakiad. We're staying here and flying straight to Lucerne. They're not taking the four to Lucerne. We'll meet in Trakai. We'll stay at the camp until the Spartakiad of Nations and then go to Jelgava. Federation officials will tell you everything in detail."

Afraid of testing out the good fortune that had so suddenly befallen them, the men kept the joy of their victory locked up inside. They were afraid to even discuss the journeys that awaited them, to distant, unreachable and "forbidden" countries. They had heard "you'll be replaced by..." so many times that they probably wouldn't believe any of it was real until they were getting on the plane to Copenhagen.

*

21

On Monday evening, Belarus Station was busier than usual. The relentless rain herded all of the travellers from the street into the station building. Luggage, bags and suitcases were flying everywhere, children were crying, and fat saleswomen argued behind their storefronts. The hall was filled with cigar smoke and the mugginess of a rainy summer day.

The Moscow-Vilnius train was to bring the team of happy Lithuanian rowers back home. Eugenijus, Romas, Povilas, Celestinas and Gerdas were much happier with their medals than the eight, who had grown used to their victories. The wide new waters they had been dreaming of had finally opened up for them.

Povilas stopped by the newspaper kiosk to buy a few postcards so he could write to his aunt and uncle on the way home, and maybe to Elzbieta, and perhaps to Juozas – he'd have to think about it. He quickly grabbed the coins he needed and threw them on the newspapers in front of him, trying to keep his eyes on his teammates as they walked through the crowd towards the train. It was fortunate that the rowers stood out from the crowd, with their enormous height and their neat suits. They always walked together, too, making it easy to spot them. After gathering his change and putting the postcards into his inner coat pocket, Povilas grabbed his suitcase and hurried down the station towards his friends.

"Liutkaitis, here!" Romas shouted to Povilas as he climbed up into his train car.

Povilas looked up at the station's giant clock. The train was to depart in seventeen minutes. The rain intensified, seemingly out of spite, and he was completely drenched in the few steps it took him to make it to the train. "No problem, I'll dry off, it's only water," Povilas thought to himself. Inside, he could still feel the extraordinary joy of the previous day's victory. Every time he remembered the last few strokes of the race, his body was overcome with uncontrollable joy. He wanted to tell his friends all about it again and again, to remember every detail and every metre of the race.

"Your ticket?" he was stopped at the steps by a uniformed attendant. "Go ahead."

As he stepped into the vestibule, which reeked of cigarette smoke, he pulled a wet handkerchief from his pocket and brushed the drops of rain from his face.

"Liutkaitis?" he heard a nasal voice from the corner of the vestibule.

Povilas turned around and saw a man whose age was difficult to guess. He had an old black coat, but it has been ironed to a shine. He watched Povilas with exhausted, dull eyes as he dragged on his Belomor cigarette with trembling lips.

"Liutkaitis…," Povilas responded with surprise, unsure of what language he should address his fellow passenger with.

"I heard that man call you," the man explained in Lithuanian, waving Povilas in towards the depth of the train car.

"Ah, that was Romas, from my crew. We're rowers on our way back from a competition."

"How did it go?"

"It was great. We won and we're probably going to the European Championships!"

"The Lithuanians won?"

"Yes, and not just us. Zigmas Jukna's eight won, too. You know Jukna?"

"No, I don't…"

Povilas was surprised – everybody in Lithuania knew Zigmas.

"Who are you?"

"I'm… how do I explain…" the man seemed to be delaying his answer, testing Povilas.

"Have we met?" Povilas tried to figure out what the man wanted.

"I knew a Liutkaitis. I thought you might be related."

"Povilas, we're over here!" Eugenijus shouted from the other end of the car.

"I'll be right there!" he shouted, turning back to the stranger. "There aren't that many Liutkaitises out there. Perhaps you know one of my brothers, Juozas or Kazys."

"No, he was older than you. Stasys…"

"Stasys Liutkaitis was my father. I don't know any other Stasys," Povilas said, suddenly overcome by grief and curiosity.

The man dragged on his cigarette and closed his left eye, as if measuring something:

"And where are you from?"

"Rūdupis. I grew up in Prienai and now live in Vilnius."

The man smiled sadly:

"Then yes, he was your father. Stasys was from Rūdupis, too. See how big you've grown! So strong!"

"My father was strong, too."

"I don't know… When I met him…"

"Where did you meet?" Povilas interrupted him.

"In Marijampolė…"

"When? How? My father rarely went to Marijampolė."

The man fell silent, as if considering whether or not he should continue.

"When?" Povilas wouldn't relent.

"Long ago… in '46, in the spring… We shared a cell…"

Stunned by his unexpected words, Povilas grabbed the stranger by his shoulders:

"Wait here, I'll set my suitcase down, don't go anywhere! I'll be right back!"

With his heart racing and his legs shaking, Povilas hurried down the train car's narrow corridor towards his friends, holding his suitcase over his head. As luck would have it, there was a mother ahead of him slowly making her way down the aisle with two babies and some luggage.

"Give me that, I'll carry it for you," Povilas grabbed her luggage and followed her to the end of the train carriage.

When he returned to his friends, he could already smell the fragrant bacon that they had saved throughout the entire competition on the booth table. Alongside it laid a few slices of Lithuanian bread and some cookies they had bought at a store in Khimki.

"Sit down, let's celebrate. They'll be bringing us tea soon."

Povilas threw his suitcase up on the shelf, quickly hung up his damp coat, pulled a notebook out from one of the interior pockets, and brushed the sweat from his brow on his sleeve:

"I'll be right back," he said, disappearing behind the booth door.

"What happened?" Celestinas shouted after him, surprised, but Povilas couldn't hear him. He was pushing past the travellers headed in the opposite direction, past their suitcases and luggage, and strained his neck to search for the stranger. In the distance, however, all he could see was an empty room and a throng of moving heads. "Did he really just leave?" Povilas thought as his heart began to race even more. He ran up to the window, pulled it down with a thud, stuck his head out, and scanned the platform.

"I'm here, son," he heard the now-familiar voice from the door to the first booth. The man had sat down and placed his brown suitcase next to him. He eyed the other passengers, who had begun to settle into their seats by the windows and pull out bottles of vodka, with distrust. It was clear that those dull grey eyes had seen much.

"Are you traveling alone?"

"Alone for now," the man responded quietly. "Care for a smoke?"

"I don't smoke," Povilas responded automatically, but once he understood that the man was hesitant to speak around strangers, he turned towards the end of the car. "Alright, let's go. What should I call you?"

"I'm Vaclovas… Vacys."

Povilas opened up his notebook and pulled out a photograph that he always carried with him. It was a photo of his mother, father and Elzbieta at around six years of age. He extended it to Vacys.

"Yes, that's Stasys… when he was still young and healthy. Is that your mother?"

"Yes. And my sister, Elzbieta."

"How about your father? Did he return?"

"No…"

"They separated us," Vacys continued after sighing. "They took him away earlier, and I went later. I don't know how and when."

"Tell me what you know about him."

"What do you need that for, son? Leave that doomed past behind you. Live your life. You're a young and beautiful man. Do you have a girl?"

"I have a young wife and a daughter named Rasa. She's a year old."

"Love them and cherish them. Just like your father loved you. He talked about you all the time and suffered greatly for you. And for his wife, your mother. He said he couldn't even bury her."

"He couldn't… when they arrested him on Christmas, we never saw him again. My aunt never told me much. Not about Marijampolė, not about his trial, and not about his deportation. Maybe she was protecting us, as children? Or maybe she was angry because of her sister… She doesn't want to talk about it now, either. She's still afraid."

A uniformed attendant closed the train car doors and, with a hiss, the train slowly began to move. The rain was still falling on the platform. The expanse of Moscow faded away outside the foggy windows.

"They said they took him away in August, after his tribunal. I don't know where."

"To Ukhta. That's where he died. He didn't last long. I think about that often and I can't understand how such a strong man could only survive one year after being arrested. No work was too hard for him. He was a forester. He had logged, worked the fields, and never complained about anything."

"Son, when they break you, it's not just your body, it's your soul. It's hard to endure. You can go hungry, go thirsty, endure the blows, but when they trample everything you were raised by, the things you were taught, when they tear you out of your life and your family, it's like they suck the life out of you."

"So my father was in Marijampolė until August?"

"Yes. We shared a cell together until August. After that, I only heard from others that he had been sentenced and deported. They don't let you spend too much time there so you wouldn't make any friends. We told each other so much. However, he had already been tortured extensively. He was thin, nothing like the man in your photo."

"Why didn't I know anything…," Povilas quietly mumbled, lowering his head.

"How were you supposed to know? Nobody knew anything back then, nobody said anything…"

"I would've gone to Marijampolė by foot to see him…"

"Nobody would've let you see him, child."

"Why didn't my aunt tell me anything? Couldn't she see how our hearts were crying without our parents?"

"Don't judge her. Those were different times. She might not have known anything. When they shut you up in that cellar, you can howl like a wolf and nobody will hear you. And the NKVD was just looking for excuses to lock more people up. Maybe your aunt was afraid that they'd lock her up, too. How would you have remained together then?"

"They tortured him?"

Vaclovas grew quiet, turned away towards the window, pressed his lips together, and took a deep sigh.

"What do you win by learning everything? It won't be any easier for you or him."

"So they did..."

"We're Lithuanian, we're strong people. But those dogs, they wanted to take as many of us away as they could, so they did everything to make you confess, no matter if you were innocent... They'd take you for interrogations at night. They'd interrogate you long into the morning, with bright lamps in your face, and they'd make sure you couldn't sleep during the day, either. Once you're on the verge of collapsing, you'll say anything just to get to rest a bit and heal your wounds. It seemed like things couldn't get any worse for it. Many confessed, if only so they wouldn't have to sit on that stool in front of the lamp again. During every interrogation, they'd ask you the same thing to see if you answered the same. And different people would interrogate you each time."

The door to the vestibule flew open and three noisy soldiers in field uniforms marched towards the next car. The men grew quiet, listening to the soldiers' conversation and Russian swearwords. "They're not Lithuanian," the two men nodded to one another and continued in Lithuanian.

"At first, your father was interrogated by a man named Lazarev. I had encountered him as well. He was a hardened NKVD agent. After that, there was Koklin – also a brute."

"Did they beat him?"

Vacys grew silent again, pulling another cigarette from his worn carton and managing to light it with his trembling fingers. The smoke from the Belomor cigarette filled the vestibule.

"They beat some more than others. Depending on their will to resist. Some returned from interrogations with bruises while others returned bloody. Some were thrown into their cells barely able to breathe. The cells were small and smelled terrible. You had to sleep and, excuse me, take a squat, in the same place. I never would've thought that people could endure so much... The interrogators had long lost all signs of humanity. Or maybe they were born beasts, not men."

"The interrogators weren't just Russians. There were Lithuanians interrogating people in Russian, too... Do you understand? Brother against brother – in Russian! Your father and I were both interrogated by a man named Čepliauskas – in Russian! You come to the interrogation room at night and the first question – do you have any objection if I interrogate you in Russian? Filth. He could do it in Lithuanian, too, but the translator's a *stribas* just like the rest of them, and he'll translate it any way he pleases. He'll write down whatever he wants and you'll have to sign under all of it, both what you did say and what you didn't. You say 'partisans,' they write 'bandits.' You say 'company,' they write 'gang.' You say 'men from the woods' and they write 'counter-revolutionary rebels.' That's how it was, son..."

"Did my father suffer much?"

Vaclovas looked up at Povilas. His dull eyes grew even darker. He swallowed and nodded slowly:

"Stasys never moaned or complained. He just prayed all the time and missed his family. He always only thought of you – whether you guys were alright, whether you had been left to fend for yourselves, whether you were going hungry, whether you had someone to hug... He said 'I would endure anything just to get to hug them again.' He also said 'they have my daughter somewhere in these walls. She's still a child... I hope they don't beat her or abuse her. They could hit me for both of us, just so they don't touch her...'"

Povilas' eyes glazed over with tears. He pulled his handkerchief from his pocket and threw it on his face, wiping away his sweat.

"Don't be ashamed of your tears, son," said Vacys, placing his hand on Povilas' shoulder.

"My father wasn't a partisan, he just knew them. Some men who came to visit us. I was just a child, I could only recognize a few on sight. They were from our village, our neighbours. Our sister talked to them too. That's why they took her and convicted her."

"I know... Stasys told me. He said 'my neighbours' boys came from the woods and asked for food. I fed them and promised not to tell anyone – and I didn't.'"

"So, as far as I know, he only gave them food once, and that's why he had to die – and why my mother was shot, and our home burned down, and my sister sent to a concentration camp... and the four of us were left orphaned... they came on Christmas, leaving us without a home or a family... And you, Vaclovas? How did you wind up there?"

"Much like him. My younger brother was in our woods. They tracked me down when I was headed to meet him. Those were terrible times, son. None of us knew how each day would end."

"Did they take you away for a long time?"

"Just like your father – ten years of concentration camps and five years of deportation. Except that I survived. I sometimes wonder – how much can a person endure? Ten years of hunger, cold and dirt, torn out of our nests and thrown into a hostile, foreign land..."

The men grew quiet and looked out the windows sadly at the receding Moscow suburbs.

"It's nice to travel by train when you can see the sky through the windows, instead of being boarded up on all sides like a coffin," Vaclovas smiled for the first time. "It's been seventeen years since I was last in Lithuania..."

"You didn't return after Siberia?"

"I only finished my sentence last year. After the concentration camp, I had five more years of deportation. Valytė and I met at the camp. She was much younger than I, a teacher. Beautiful and elegant. And what a voice! You could hear her singing in the barracks from afar, and even us men beyond the fence could hear it. I had already been an old bachelor in our village, and was reduced to an old man by the concentration camp, but Valytė liked me for some reason. We got married when we left. Had a kid, too. We really want to return to Lithuania."

"My sister is still in Balkhash. She also married a Lithuanian and is raising three children. I'm waiting for her to return to Lithuania. We've been scattered around the world..."

The men lost themselves in thought again. The unexpected encounter had awakened long-forgotten memories, sadness, pain, and hatred.

Vacys was the first to speak again:

"Life never stops. Even when it seems like all hope is lost, it never stops. However, that's when it becomes terrible and unjust and degrading. Suffering of the body is nothing compared to insults and mockery. We were all neat, honest people. But, like they say, you can't die before your time. You must carry your cross until the end. I'm returning to Lithuania after so many years. I don't know how my fatherland will receive me. If I manage to get settled, I'll bring my family over, too."

"How can I find you, Vacys?"

"Don't look for me. I don't know where I'll be. If God wills it, we'll meet somewhere in Lithuania."

Povilas quickly tore a page out of his notebook, wrote down his address on Čiurlionis Street, and gave it to Vaclovas:

"Write to me or visit if anything happens. I don't know how I could help you, but I'd like to meet you again. And thank you for what you've told me."

"Aren't you afraid?"

"Of what?"

"Don't you think someone will snitch on you if a Siberian exile comes to visit?"

"The times have changed, Vaclovas."

"The times are always the same. There are all sorts of people. You never know who's got something to hide."

"I'm not afraid of anything, Vacys..."

The men, leaning on the wall of the vestibule, looked off into the distance through the small train car door window. Their moist eyes saw summer fields drenched in rain, a darkening grey sky, and the sun setting far beyond. Somewhere, deep below Povilas' stirred-up thoughts, lay the now-hidden ecstasy of victory.

*

A heavy metal door crashed open and he hit a cold, wet wall, falling to the floor. Somebody grabbed him by the shoulder shook him hard and shouted "Vstat![62]" He wanted to raise his left arm so he could support himself on the slippery wall and stand up, but his powerless arm disobeyed him and hung there, as if it wasn't his. He extended his right arm, but it slid along the disgusting wet surface. "Vstatvai, svolach![63]"... Povilas jumped up from a powerful blow and opened his eyes. The train had jerked forward and was slowly rolling out of a stop he couldn't recognize. His left arm had grown completely numb on the train's hard cot – it felt like it wasn't his. He began to rub it vigorously with his right arm. "Good Lord, it was only a dream..." However, he still felt the cold, damp slime and hear the terrible shouting ringing in his ears. Povilas look out the window. The rising sun was illuminating a forest along the train tracks, beyond which he could see a field and a lone homestead in the distance. "We're probably

---

62　Rus. Stand up!
63　Rus. Stand up, you beast!

in Lithuania now," he thought, laying his heavy head down on the hard, public-use pillow. "I'll be home soon. I'll hug my Gita and Rasa soon."

When he got out of the train that early morning, Povilas couldn't find Vaclovas. There was much he still wanted to ask and learn. He had forgotten to ask where Vacys was from, where he had been taken, where he lived now, and what his surname was. He hoped to God that the fellow passenger had saved the address that Povilas had quickly jotted down and that he would find him. Or at least write to him…

*

22

It was probably the first time that the Lithuanian press focused more attention and praise on the Žalgiris four than the eight. By 2 July, almost every newspaper had something about the Great Moscow Regatta. "Sportas" and "Komsomol Truth" couldn't hide their surprise and praise for the members of the new four that had made it into the USSR team. Even "Truth"[64], which often portrayed the rowers in a poor light, published photos of the "rookies" at Trakai with a caption that read "We were especially happy about the victory of our Republic's second boat – the coxed four." Žalgiris Masters of Sports Celestinas Jucys, Povilas Liutkaitis, and brothers Eugenijus and Romas Levickas (coxed by Gerdas Morkus) defeated all of the country's strongest fours. This was the first victory of its kind."

Sovietskij Sport also expressed their surprise: "The first race of the men's finals brought the first upset as well. The Lithuanian four won a wonderful victory. The Moscow crew, stroked by D. Semionov, lost by 6 seconds."

For the four, this was like a second wind. They had finally been noticed, and they had finally showed that they are no less strong than their friends in the eight. But the men dared not celebrate. It was as if they were afraid of scaring away their unexpected good fortune. Besides, the perception of their crew as "second-rate" hadn't disappeared. The eight was still the most respected crew, and they were still considered a second, reserve crew.

However, the future looked bright – the path to the European Championships was all but theirs. All that was left was a grandiose sports event – the USSR Spartakiad of Nations – and the Lithuanian Spartakiad in Trakai. They only had a few days at home before hitting the road again.

*

---

64   Lit. "Tiesa" – A Lithuanian Soviet newspaper (separate from the "Komsomol Truth").

6 July, among much fanfare and parades, saw the opening of the 3rd Lithuanian Spartakiad. The celebrations on Gediminas Hill, with trumpets and tri-coloured – red, white and green – rockets, heralded the beginning of the major sports event in Vilnius. A column of almost two thousand athletes headed out from the youth stadium towards Žalgiris stadium, where the event would be opened. Youth at the head of the column, dressed in traditional Lithuanian clothing, carried the coat of arms of the Lithuanian SSR, and behind them marched athletes with LSSR, USSR and other nations' flags. They were followed by a parade of champions – USSR and European champions and medallists – wearing all their medals. The parade stopped briefly by Lenin Square so that Lithuania's best athletes could lay flowers down at the foot of the monument to Lenin that stood there and "express the nation's respect for the great leader of the proletariat and its gratitude to the Leninist Communist Party."

Gediminas Square was decorated with large displays featuring the athletes' photos. There were two large posters dedicated to the rowers. One of them displayed the women's quadruple scull, which was for some reason called a "four-seater kayak," and the other featured the Žalgiris men's eight, who were for some reason called the "world ex-champions." "Who's making these posters? They can't tell athletic boats from regular rowboats. And they're quite erudite, too, since they can't tell silver medallists and ex-champions apart" – both the athletes and journalists were upset.

The Vilnius residents who gathered in Žalgiris stadium were waiting for the upcoming parade, and the national party's leaders and invited guests were gathered together. Ieva Mizarienė stood out among them – a progressive American Lithuanian character. Of course, the spectators weren't looking forward to seeing them or hearing their speeches praising the Communist Party and the great motherland – they wanted to see Lithuania's best athletes. Spectators young and old could see them right here, marching by in the flesh – the athletes they had only read about in newspapers or listened to on the radio. There was Ričardas Tamulis, proudly carrying the Spartakiad flag, and Antanas Vaupšas, running with the Spartakiad torch. The children, in the mean time, revelled in the doves and colourful balloons rising up into the sky.

During the grand opening of the Spartakiad, the spectators didn't get to see the rowers. On that day, they were racing in Trakai.

The spectators who gathered on the shore of Lake Galvė sighed – they wouldn't get to see the famous Žalgiris eight, which was already headed to Lucerne.

However, the Spartakiad competition went smoothly and festively. Lithuania's strongest rowers gathered at the regatta to fight for their cities' honour.

At that competition, the Vilnius rowers couldn't be beat. Having calculated everything perfectly, the Moscow regatta champion four split up into other boats. Povilas and Romas joined a coxed four with Mikšys and Šarmaitis while Eugenijus and Celestinas raced in a coxed pair. In this way, they had no trouble in the finals and scored some easy points for their city. Right after that, Celestinas' four joined Vilnius' coxless four in the eight, beating the Kaunas rowers soundly by 13.6 seconds.

In the women's competition, the Vilnius rowers won in three events. Gita's sister Irena won the gold medal in the quadruple scull.

While the men were racing for the right to compete in the USSR Spartakiad of Nations, the women were racing just for medals. There was no women's rowing at the Spartakiad of Nations at the time. They would go to Moscow, but only to participate in the USSR championship.

For the first time, the organisers of the rowing competition presented the winners with more than just medals – they also received oak wreaths, which were a decoration at the third LSSR Spartakiad celebration.

Celestinas' four had become the media's new darlings – on Sunday, their photos were published in "Sportas" and the "Komsomol Truth", and both papers described them as the season's latest sensation.

*

Upon their return from Lucerne, the Žalgiris team brought home a confident victory, but a disappointment as well – they hadn't been able to face the Ratzeburg eight. The Germans simply didn't attend the Lucerne Regatta. There were all sorts of theories – that they had made financial demands of the event's organisers that the organisers refused to fulfil, or that they were afraid of the Žalgiris crew, whom they had recently lost against in Duisburg, and that they would only reveal their full strength at the European Championships, and so on… On both days, the Lithuanians won effortlessly against the GDR crew and the FRG's crew from Lübeck. In addition, the Žalgiris crew finished with an impressive time – 5.52 minutes. Of course, the weather had been in their favour, with a strong tailwind.

Upon his return from Switzerland, Ričardas presented the men with a new training schedule, which he had seen the German teams using. They called it the "German plan," and the Žalgiris team learned to read these words. They had never experienced such intense training before – 8-10 500-metre sprints, with only enough of a pause between them to turn the boat around, twice a day. They initially felt that their speed was growing, but after a few days of this training, they felt drained of energy. There were only two weeks left until the Spartakiad of Nations and the men's bodies, exhausted by the frequent races and impossible training work load, were begging for rest. However, they wouldn't dare complain – they believed in their coach and did what he told them to. What's more, the second half of July was unusually hot and dry. The sun was merciless. Daytime temperatures rose to 30 degrees with not a drop of rain.

On 26 July, the summer reached its record high of 34 degrees in the shade. That day was special for Povilas, and not just because of the heat – that was when his daughter celebrated her first birthday. It had been a year of long camps, training, competitions, and only the occasional brief moment spent at home with his family. He hadn't even been there to see Rasa take her first steps, say her first words, or begin to recognise people and objects. It always seemed like there would soon be more time to spend with her, but now that he was a member of the USSR team, everything was pushed back even further… The hastily purchased gifts from distant cities were a small consolation for Gita and all the sleepless nights and endless motherly tasks she faced.

*

23

Three days later, on Monday, the entire Lithuanian rowing team flew out to Moscow. After the exhausting heat in Lithuania, they looked forward to cooling off under Moscow's irritating but refreshing rain. In Moscow, however, they were greeted by even greater heat. As soon as they stepped out of the airplane, filled as it was with cigarette smoke, they wanted to tear their shirts off. The black asphalt gave off rolling waves of heat. As their bus rolled towards Khimki, the passengers tried to catch whatever gusts of air they could through the open windows. Fortunately, Khimki was a large open space, and they could enjoy a few gusts of wind here and there.

Competitors for the USSR Spartakiad of Nations and USSR champions' medals arrived at Khimki from a number of different republics. The Spartakiad would have only five events, and all of them were men's – the single scull, the double scull, the coxed pair, the coxed four, and the eight. Nobody could explain why they had decided to do this. It was also unclear why the women had been left out of the Spartakiad. It was the same distance, the same battle, the same suffering – but you'd receive either one medal or two. Spartakiad races also enjoyed more attention from journalists and spectators.

The participants found that Khimki had changed – to everyone's delight, the Albano system had been installed on the course[65]. The six lanes were marked with buoys to separate them. Steering would be much easier. There were only a few racing courses in the world that had this system, which had only been used for the first time three years ago at the Rome Olympic Games, but the upcoming European Women's Championships had insisted the organisers implement the system the international rowing federation's requirement to have six separate lanes had been fulfilled.

After the first day of the competition, Lithuania could boast of having seven boats in the final.

---

[65] The Albano system – this system uses buoys to mark rowing race courses. It was used for the first time in an international competition at the 1960 summer Olympic Games on Lake Albano in Italy.

The media lens once again focused on Celestinas' four. None had any doubt that they were the leaders in their boat class.

"For the final, put on white socks," Ričardas told the men in the four, "so we all look the same during the award ceremony."

However, the men felt that they weren't in the same shape that they had been in a month ago when they won the Great Moscow Regatta.

"I don't have any energy and my head hurts. Something's not right," Eugenijus complained to his teammates.

"We've over-trained," Povilas agreed. "It feels like I left everything behind in today's race and that I've got nothing left for tomorrow."

"It was definitely off," Celestinas agreed with concern. "My body feels like rubber. It won't listen to me."

"We have to go to bed earlier today. Maybe we'll all feel better after some rest," Povilas soothed them.

"But aren't we going to do some more training in the evening?" Romas asked.

"I don't think so, not today," his teammates responded in unison.

"You can go alone if you'd like," Povilas said, only half in jest. "I'm not getting into a boat again today."

Romas understood that their decision to rest for the day was final, so he stopped arguing. The next day would be another hot and exhausting one.

*

The next day, the heat still hung over Khimki. There wasn't a cloud in sight, it would be another hot day. It was the rowers' last day at the USSR Spartakiad of Nations.

The men envied the women, who would complete their USSR championship events by noon. The men would have to compete not just with their opponents, but with the blazing sun.

Though their race was only a few hours away, everyone gathered to watch the women's final.

The first Lithuanian crew to race was the women's quadruple scull, with Grucaitė, Tamašauskaitė, Lukošiūnaitė, and Juodytė, with Narvydaitė as the cox. Though they had performed unexpectedly well in the semi-final, the women were clearly nervous. The five finalists in the previous day's race had all been within 0.3 seconds of each other. They wanted to feel, at least once, the sweet taste of a USSR championship medal, but anything could happen. In an interview with journalists before the race, the women were modest: "We won't be taking home any prizes," said Sofija, the stroke.

It took less than four minutes for the women's quadruple scull to row a kilometre, so as soon as the green starting flare shot up into the air, the Lithuanian team rushed to the grandstands to root for their girls. They could see that they weren't giving up and, from the very start, kept up with the leaders. With only two hundred metres to go to the finish, they were ahead of the Moscow and Leningrad crews by almost half a length. The men in the grandstands shouted wildly, "Go! Go!"

"What a bunch of proper women!" they shouted and celebrated as the gong struck three times.

"Good work!"

"First!" the men celebrated the women's victory as they went down the stairs. "Time to prepare for our race."

The journalists rushed to take photos of the new sensations – the Lithuanian women's quadruple scull, the new USSR champions. The women smiled for the reporters, as they were surprised at the margin of their victory. However, the unexpectedly long silence of the announcer's loudspeaker started to make both the rowers and the fans in the grandstands uneasy. The women at the finish line looked at one another, waiting for the final results to be announced. The double sculls' final was approaching the finish line, and still the announcer hadn't invited the women to the award stand. It was only when the gong rang for the double sculls that the announcer announced that the Latvians had won the doubles race – before falling silent again. The women slowly moved towards the grandstand, hoping to hear the final results soon. They could see movement at the finish-line tower – next to the announcer stood the USSR women's team's senior coach and two finishing-line umpires, and the coach was waving his arms about. The women's eights had already covered half of their race, in which the Lithuanian women were fighting for a prize as well. Suddenly, the announcer's voice came to life.

"The results of the quadruple scull race. First place – Leningrad. Second place – Moscow. Third place – Lithuania…"

The grandstands roared, and the Russians stood up, whistled and shouted "Ura!"

The announcement wiped the smiles from the women's faces. It was the first time they had felt the taste of victory in the country's championships, and their first taste of lies and injustice. If someone had told them, that morning, that they would win bronze medals, they probably would have kissed them out of joy. But now, when they had so clearly crossed the finish line first – and all three of the coxes had seen this clearly – and they were only given third place, their anger and disappointment welled up in a flow of bitter tears. This had been their only opportunity to make it onto the team and participate in the European Championships. "Won't anyone fix this decisive mistake? Where is our coach? Can't he see what's happening?" It seemed like all they needed to do was to wake up for everything to fall back into place.

A couple of days later, a wall of the Moscow State Department Store was decorated by a large photo of the "new USSR champions " – the Lithuanian crew. Correspondents had hurried to send the photo to the printers without waiting for the final results.

*

"Dressed up" in their white socks, the men from the Žalgiris four pushed off of the dock with a strange unease in their hearts. They were now being carefully observed not just by Ričardas, but also by the USSR team's coaches. The playful atmosphere that they had enjoyed at the Great Moscow Regatta just a couple of months ago was now replaced by an uneasy feeling of responsibility and doubt. They saw the determined faces of the Moscow crew as they left for the starting line – they hoped to take back the first place that they had lost to the Lithuanians and return to the USSR team. And at the same time, the Lithuanians' exhausted bodies seemed to reject the boats. And there were the waves, too, whipping the reservoir into a sea. "This is the final race," "everything will be over in an hour," "only two hundred strokes" – each had a different way to calm his nerves as he chopped at the water with short, recovery-free strokes. The crew rowed away from the pontoon and from their coach, who stood on the end, shielding his eyes from the sun with his hand. The heat was baking their hands and their legs, sweat dripped down their foreheads and burned their eyes. Periodically, one rower or another would quickly grab some lukewarm water from the Khimki reservoir between strokes and splash it onto their uncovered heads. "We have to win, whatever happens..." Meanwhile, anxiety flowed into every muscle and cell in their bodies, freezing up the energy they needed for the race.

The shoreline receded, along with their friends, who were preparing for the eights race. Alfa waved from afar. He would be in the eight again, in the bow seat. For the Spartakiad, Suslin had returned to his Leningrad team, leaving the Lithuanians scrambling for someone to replace him. "Alfa won't do any worse, we'll be fine," Ričardas would say, encouraging himself and his team. And nobody doubted he was right. Though Alfa was smaller than everybody else, his age hadn't dulled his feeling for the team's rhythm, and the workloads of their training wasn't any different. It took only a few training sessions together for them to work as a crew again. The boat moved even better when Alfa was in the bow seat.

The four's thoughts returned to their boat, and they could already hear the "Внимание! Марш![66]" that was to come in half an hour's time. Their muscles grew tense. The men's bodies were overcome by a wave of adrenaline, their breathing grew faster, and their mouths were dry. God forbid their anxiety got the better of them and overcome them with weakness and apathy, when they didn't want anything more than to drop everything and hide. But this happened almost every time they left for the starting line – they would ask themselves – "what am I doing here and why?" And after the return from every finish, they felt a great burden lifted from their chests as they began to look forward to their next races.

*

"For Lithuania! One, two…," Gerdas yelled in a hoarse voice as they passed the lane numbers marking the thousand-metre mark overhead.

"The third five hundred," Povilas thought to himself as his eyes unwittingly darted to the sides. All he could see were the puddles left by their opponents' boats.

"Ten more!" Gerdas encouraged the men. "Let's take them on!"

The Russian boats were just barely growing closer, and they had more than 500 metres left to race.

"Let's work, don't let go!" shouted Gerdas, his body instinctively rocking forward as he tried to push the boat forward. "It's the last five hundred! And one, and two, and three!"

Long waves rolled in from the grandstand side, one after the other,

---

66   Rus. Attention! Go!

turning the racecourse into a chaotic mess. Their oars began to catch the water and they lost their clean finishing rhythm. Almost every other stroke had to be started anew.

"It's the finish!" they could hear their coach from the shore, though he was drowned out by the roar of the grandstands and the dull hissing in their deafened ears.

"Twenty more strokes! One, two, three!" shouted Gerdas, his defeated eyes still hoping for a miracle. "Let's go!"

It was too late. A moment later, the first gong struck. After two strokes, the second one, and after two more, the third. It was only after the fourth gong that Gerdas finally shouted, "Easy,…"

The men collapsed forwards – they couldn't believe what had happened. Fourth – they had lost to both of Moscow's teams, and were more than eight seconds behind the first. What had happened? What would happen now? Their crew was nothing like the one that had stunned everyone here with an impressive victory just a month ago.

The men had given it their all. They leaned back and forth in an attempt to catch their breath, poured water on their heads, and quietly swore to themselves. Gerdas's voice was filled with sadness and there were tears in his eyes. Pretending to wipe water from his face, he wiped the tears away with the back of his sleeve and grabbed the rudder wire again.

"Strokeside back, bowside forward."

Right up until they reached the pontoon, the men didn't exchange a single word. Each of them suppressed their pain, exacerbated by extraordinary fatigue and hopelessness. Behind their boat stood the medal pontoon, where the federation's officials stood with the fortunate prize-winners who had rowed up to them.

"That should've been us," Povilas thought to himself. "Instead, we were a total mess…"

"That should be us up there, not them," Celestinas thought.

"Why is it them, not us?" thought Eugenijus.

"I wanted that medal so badly! I hate them!" thought Gerdas, unable to cope with the loss.

The Spartakiad was over for the four. They didn't even want to look forward to any other races. All they could think of now was "what will happen now?" It seemed like the earth was slipping out from underneath them and that they had lost everything.

They were greeted at the pontoon by a crowd of Lithuanian team coaches and personnel, with eyes full of surprise and pity. Kikilas nodded – "Everything's alright, boys" – but everyone understood that it wasn't. It wasn't alright for the federation, for Lithuania, or for the coach. But it was the worst for the exhausted and crushed crew.

"What happened?" Ričardas asked anxiously, grabbing Povilas' oar and pulling it close.

The men were silent. They looked down as they untied their stretcher ties and loosened their gates. None of them knew what to say and none of them wanted to say anything. As strong as the men were, they were still fighting down the lumps in their throats that might erupt at the first word they say.

"Gerdas, what happened?" the coach repeated.

Gerdas shrugged and his chin trembled.

"Alright, I have to leave for the race. We'll talk when we get back," said Ričardas with tight lips as he turned to the shoreline and towards the eight waiting for him.

Kikilas consoled the four as they got out of the boat, shook their hands, and hurried off to watch the race.

After carrying the boat back and putting their oars away safely, the men sat down on the floor next to the brick boathouse and sat quietly for a while, trying to think of something to say.

"That was a mess," Povilas finally said.

"I don't know, I gave it everything I had," said Romas, with his elbows on his knees and his head in his hands. "Could it have been the sun?"

"Everyone had the same sun, but only we lost," said Eugenijus. "I think we over-trained."

"I think so, too," Celestinas agreed. "I rowed as hard as I could, but I never managed to hit thirty-eight strokes a minute."

"It's not your fault, Celestinas," said Povilas, reassuring his stroke. "We all over-exerted ourselves. What can you expect of us if getting into the boat made us nauseous? We clearly trained too much."

"Seriously, it was the same for me – I didn't even want to get into the boat," Eugenijus noted. "We had to rest a couple of days. Yesterday, I could already tell that there would be nothing left of me after the finish."

"Rychka pushed us too hard with his training, pushing us as hard as the eight," Povilas said angrily. "Why'd he give us so many five-hundred sprints before the race?"

"It's the German system..." Eugenijus said sadly.

"We could've been smarter ourselves and not have strained ourselves so badly."

In the grandstands, they could hear the announcer's elated voice, the orchestra playing a march, and the spectators clapping. Unfortunately, the applause wasn't for them. The men could feel their hopelessness and the hurt in their chests.

"Who won?" Celestinas asked.

"Bachurov[67] and Leningrad, I think. Sass[68] was second," Eugenijus had managed to see the results after the race.

"I can't believe it – we even lost to them, to Kuznetsov. Couldn't we at least catch up to them?" Povilas said angrily.

"I doubt it. I could even see their stern at the finish, they had about three or four seconds," said Eugenijus. From the bow seat, Eugenijus could best see which boats had passed them.

"One of Moscow's boats rowed non-competitively, right? Do we still get points for third place?" Romas reasoned.

"Who cares about the points when they got the medals?" Celestinas retorted.

"We trusted our tactical race too much. We had to go hard from the very beginning, and then see how things looked at the third five hundred," Eugenijus argued.

"But it feels like we did go hard," Celestinas responded with surprise.

"What would there have been left of us at the finish if we would have sprinted from the start?" Povilas asked doubtfully.

"Yeah, I gave it my all. I can't even remember finishing," Romas agreed.

"We won't change anything now, what's done is done," Celestinas said. He seemed the most dejected of them all.

Far off down the course, the coxed pairs were approaching. The Lithuanians, Vladas and Jonas, were sixth. It looked like they would finish that way as well.

---

67   Бачуров, Юрий Кузьмич (Yuri Bachurov) – the stroke for Leningrad's Trud coxed four.

68   Анатолий Фомич Сасс (Anatoly Sass) – the stroke for Moscow's Trud coxed four.

"The important thing is that all of our socks match," Povilas smiled.

They all looked down at their white socks and laughed for the first time. Uncomfortably, and with bitterness, but it still reduced the tension in their hearts.

"There goes Europe," Celestinas was the first to speak of what the rest of them feared.

The men all looked at the stroke.

"You think so?" Povilas still hoped that this was all a dream and that everything would return back to normal.

"Well, what do you think? There are two weeks until Europe and we can't hack it. If we'd have been at least second, then perhaps Rychka would do something. But now? Did you see how Samsonov looked when we returned?"

"And we don't have any excuses," Eugenijus agreed. "There weren't any waves, and nothing broke."

"Only we did," Romas nodded.

"What does Rychka think?" said Povilas, not losing hope. If their coach hadn't said anything bad about it, then perhaps not all hope was lost. He had fought so long and hard for a path to the USSR team – would it really all now be for naught?

"Rychka is on the water, they're about to race," Eugenijus reminded him.

"That's right," Povilas remembered, realizing that Rychka's silence didn't necessarily mean anything good at all.

"Well, what can you do? Certainly can't turn back time," Celestinas waved. "Where's Gerdas?"

"I'm here," they heard the boy's sad voice from behind them.

Povilas put his hand on the cox's shoulder:

"Everything's going to be alright. We'll win some medals yet."

Tears glistened in Gerdas' eyes.

"Let's go derig the boat. Bring the spanners," said Povilas, trying to help the boy forget his sadness. "And be a man, don't cry."

The rest of them, however, were devastated by such an unexpectedly poor performance.

Suddenly, the noise and fanfare of the Spartakiad, and everything about it, began to irritate them – the opponents and the fans, the medal winners, and the eight, posing with their oars after yet another victory and walking past them, looking at them like poor beggars. They wanted to leave Khimki, Moscow and the Spartakiad as soon as possible, curl up in a corner, and hide from the misfortune that had just befallen them.

*

"You derigged the boat?" asked Ričardas, looking around after hurrying over from the coaches' meeting. "Load it onto that trailer there," he ordered, waving towards the eight derigging their boat. "We leave for Jelgava tomorrow."

Povilas, Eugenijus and Celestinas looked at each other, stunned.

"That's right, what are you looking at? Everything's moving according to schedule – one week in Jelgava and then we return to Moscow from there. Where's Romas?"

"Romas, come!" Povilas shouted to Romas, who was tying up the oars. He couldn't contain his joy.

"Come here, I said!"

Leaving his work unfinished, Romas hurried over to his teammates.

"We're taking the boat to Jelgava," his brother told him impatiently.

The men could barely believe what they were hearing, but they were afraid of asking their coach anything, fearing that everything would change just as quickly.

"We're leaving for Copenhagen next Sunday. We will have five days of training in Jelgava. You guys have tomorrow off," their coach told them.

"So they're taking us?" Celestinas asked cautiously.

"Why not? You won that right during the Great Moscow. This was just a Spartakiad, not a qualifier," Ričardas explained.

"Really? Nobody said anything?" Povilas asked with surprise.

Ričardas smiled ironically:

"Oh boy, did they ever! All they ever do is look for reasons to send their own. Everybody wants to go abroad!"

"And? What did Samsonov say?"

"That their documents aren't in order. Good thing you guys won by so much during the Great Moscow. All they would've needed was to process your documents. Nobody thought another team would upset you guys. They won't manage now, there's no time."

The men looked at one another and finally smiled. When it had seemed like all was lost, they were served the trip to Denmark on a silver platter. Their bodies were overcome with joy and their unexpected good fortune.

"It's still too bad that we lost like that today," said Celestinas, trying to explain himself to his coach.

"Yeah. What happened?" Ričardas looked up.

"We were over-trained, we had no energy," Povilas was the first to admit it.

"It was very hard going. It seemed like we weren't moving no matter how hard we rowed," Eugenijus agreed.

"We were already exhausted when we got here, nothing like how we were a month ago. I tried to give it my all, but I just didn't have it in me," Celestinas explained.

"Maybe it was the heat? My legs felt like wood at the finish line, and my head still hurts," Romas agreed.

Ričardas carefully watched his young team. It was his creation and the result of his work. Mistakes had probably been made, but he couldn't admit to them. He had to put them back on track by the European Championships:

"We rest tomorrow, and we'll get back in shape in Jelgava slowly."

"Who'll be our cox?" Celestinas remembered that they had one more team member.

"Igor Rudakov."

"Alright."

Ričardas patted Celestinas on the shoulder and hurried off towards the trailer.

The men finally dared to look one another in the eye, and they were flooded with joy and a great sense of relief.

"You see how it goes? When I win, they don't take me. When I lose, I go," Celestinas noted.

"Well then, Celestinas, I suggest you keep losing if you want to keep competing," Povilas laughed.

"I really didn't think we'd be going," Romas added.

"Neither did I, though I did have a hope somewhere deep down. They said that the Great Moscow was the final qualifier, so that's what it had to be," Eugenijus reasoned.

"Yes, but when they beat us by this much, they could've changed everything."

"It's a good thing those documents take so long to clear."

"This time, it is," Povilas laughed, "It's the first time that went well for us."

The women's eight walked by them, chattering with delight. They would be staying in Moscow to prepare for the European Women's Championships. In addition, they had just become Masters of Sport!

After the Spartakiad, Gerdas would no longer return to the boat. The fifteen-year-old boy had a growth spurt and became too tall to cox. Though he bid farewell to the men and women of Žalgiris, he wasn't leaving sports for good. He had a victorious career in running to look forward to.

*

24

"That Ričardas of yours is a bold fellow," Povilas' father-in-law said, turning from his radio to Povilas just as the rower walked into the apartment.

"Why do you say so?" Povilas asked, dropping his bag with his athletic clothes and sitting down on a chair to listen.

"I was listening to the radio. There was a lot about the Spartakiad. That Ričardas of yours was talking, too," his father-in-law explained.

"And what did he talk about?"

"About the results, about medals, and about your four, and how you're going to the European Championships. But when the journalist asked him why the eight isn't all Lithuanian, why it has rowers from other republics, you know what he said?"

"No, I didn't hear the show, what did he say?"

"Well, he said 'what am I supposed to do if they don't let me?'" he said, surprised. "That's a bold fellow! He's not scared? Won't somebody want to have a word with him?"

Povilas shrugged:

"I don't know... he probably knows what he's doing."

"Povilas, you tell him to watch what he says so they don't take that eight away from him."

Povilas laughed:

"I will, I will," though he knew he'd do nothing of the sort. It would probably all be for the better if more people heard and understood what was happening on the USSR team.

"But boy, he's a bold one! He says the team management won't let him!"

"And that's true. They don't want the entire eight to be Lithuanian, they want to stick in as many Russians as they can. But it takes them so long to adjust and to learn to row the way Lithuanians row. I'm not saying they don't know how to row, but their technique is totally different. They're initially more of a hindrance than help."

"How about you, Povilas? Will you ever return to the eight?"

"I doubt it…"

"When are you leaving again?

"Right now, I'm packing my things for Jelgava."

"To Latvia? Vai tu runā latviešu valodu?" his father-in-law grinned devilishly. "Do you speak Latvian? I worked for some farmers in Latvia. That was when I returned from the war and got some land in Tauragnai. They give land to volunteers. Adele and I met in Latvia. She worked for the farmer too, so we got married. So Latvia, you say… When will you be back?"

"It's probably straight to Moscow from there, and then to Denmark… I'll be back at the end of summer…"

*

It was raining in Jelgava. It rained from the very first days of August. After the heat in Moscow, the rain was refreshing – but only for the first day of the camp. When their tracksuits stopped drying and their rooms filled with the smell of wet wool, the men began looking out the window more often, hoping for a ray of sunlight. But the rain wouldn't stop. Their clothes were always soaked after their marches from the hotel to the rowing centre and back again three times a day. Their raincoats didn't help them much, either. At least the hotel wasn't too far. It was just under a kilometre to the rowing centre – four or five minutes of running. Three of those were alongside the largest manor in the Baltics – the courtyard of the Agricultural Academy.

The wooden rowing centre building, along with its three boathouses right on the bank of the Lielupė, was one of the most important centres for the USSR team when preparing for competitions. Though rowing on a river was much different from rowing on still water, they didn't have much of a choice. There was a new hotel nearby, an excellent restaurant on the first floor with "the largest cutlets in the world" – what more could the rowers possibly want? There was even a bar nearby where they could spend their remaining food allowances on delicious milk shakes!

The only issue was the non-stop rain…

With ten days left until the first races in the European Championships, Ričardas finally let his rowers in Jelgava rest. The workload was much lower and the training sessions were shorter. All they had to do was pretend to be working hard whenever the team coach Samsonov showed up, and they occasionally hid from him as well.

Despite the endless rain, the four was in an excellent mood. It was the first time they would travel abroad with their team to the greater world that they had been dreaming of. The anxiety and uncertainty were finally over, and the hurts they had experienced were receding as well. Of course, they'd never be as important and necessary as the eight, and nobody would ever look at them the way they look at Zigmas, Antanas and the others, but the barbed-wire fence was finally melting away, opening a whole new world of international rowing to them. The desire to be as valuable as their teammates and to perform just as well unified their efforts and gave them discipline. Every word of advice and command from their coach was accepted without question – unless Ričardas were to actually ask the men for their opinion.

Receiving the team's new uniforms, with only a couple of days until the trip, was like receiving their medals all over again. The blue wool tracksuit bottoms had "CCCP" emblazoned on them in bright white letters, and the red sleeveless shirts had the USSR's coat of arms on them, but they were an acknowledgment of their achievements and their only opportunity to row on international waters.

After neatly folding and packing their uniforms into their suitcases, the men trained hard and awaited the journey they had been dreaming of.

"Don't forget to buy some booze. The stores might not be open in Moscow on Sunday," their friends advised the newcomers to the team.

"Really? You think we'll find someone who'll buy it?" Povilas had heard that everyone brought a little bit of something abroad to exchange for local money.

"We will. Everybody does it. What are you going to do there with twelve rubles?"

"Twelve rubles?"

"If not less. All you'll get is a bottle of soda and a pin. It ain't the Soviet Union, the prices are different."

"What else sells there?" Eugenijus asked.

"I don't know. Somebody said that they exchange rubles into krone on the black market."

"Rubles? Seriously?" Povilas said incredulously.

"Just don't tell anyone, they really keep tabs on everyone while you're there – who gets money and from where. Whoever can get dollars takes them. They don't take up room, just like rubles. But then you have to go to the bank secretly, because the KGB really loves to watch who goes to the bank."

"You're telling me they'll track every one of us like that?"

"Not every one of you but all of you together. They don't let you walk alone, you have to move as a group. God forbid you find yourself alone – you'll be in trouble then. They've sometimes got 'Uncle Vasyas' there too, one of your own who's been recruited to observe everyone and report who goes where and with whom. You have to watch every step," James explained.

"I've heard about 'Uncle Vasyas'… How can we recognize them?"

"You know, you're better off not looking for adventures. Then you won't get in trouble, either. Of course, the beautiful displays, the wonderful smells – you'll want it all. You have to be with trusted people, people you know. Any Russian can be an 'Uncle Vasya'. You have to be careful with them. They might be one of the coaches, too. The head of the team, of course, is definitely one of them. Just wait, there'll be training to teach you how to behave in capitalist states."

Indeed, on Friday, with two days left until the trip to Copenhagen, the entire team was called to a meeting. A stern-faced, middle-aged man, definitely a KGB man, delivered an instructional speech in Russian – one he had probably delivered hundreds of times before:

"The goal of the USSR's foreign policy is to ensure favourable international conditions for building communism… Soviet citizens must remember that strong moral-political virtues, an intense love for their Soviet Motherland, loyalty to the principles of proletarian internationalism, and constant vigilance when abroad will help achieve our goals and defend us from provocations and hostile intrigues. When abroad, citizens must promote the honour and dignity of USSR citizens in every field, and athletes must do so in their sport as well. They must also strictly follow the principles of the Moral Code of the Builder of Communism, loyally fulfil their tasks and responsibilities, remain well-behaved, unconditionally defend the political, economic and other interests of the USSR, and protect the state's secrets."

"What secrets?" somebody began to snigger with a whisper. "Will they share them with us?"

The athletes chuckled, but fell silent when they saw their coaches' angry glances.

"When abroad, it is important to be especially vigilant and to remember that capitalist states' intelligence agencies and their agents will try to get information they need from Soviet citizens, compromise Soviet people when this benefits them, and even coerce them into betraying their motherland. To this end, imperial states' intelligence agencies use modern technologies, surveillance techniques, and covert tracking and photography. They also use tricks, blackmail, fraud and threats. Capitalist intelligence agents often work as guides and translators, physicians, professors, tailors, cashiers, taxi drivers, waiters, barbers, and other service personnel. Capitalist countries' intelligence bodies seek to use individuals' weaknesses to their benefit – weaknesses like a fondness for alcoholic beverages, loose relationships with women, games of chance, the purchasing of various objects and the inability to live within one's means, carelessness, garrulousness, carelessness with one's personal documents..."

And on and on. They learned how they had to care for their Soviet citizens' passports, since everyone ostensibly wanted one. They learned that they had to report every contact with a foreigner to their team leader, to refuse any offers and gifts, to walk together everywhere, and to dress neatly. They learned how to behave in stores, cafeterias, streets and hotels, who to speak to and who not to at the rowing course... And they learned how they wouldn't be allowed to bring and resell vodka, food, or other products...

The veterans yawned throughout the lecture, which they had heard before, all while tallying in their heads how many krone they'd get for the rubles and vodka they'd sell.

Outside, they saw their first hot and sunny day without rain.

*

"Men, I'd like to tell you something," Romas told them in a subtly trembling voice at the dinner table.

Celestinas, Eugenijus and Povilas looked up from their plates, where they were hard at work on their huge Latvian cutlets:

"Yeah?"

Romas' eyes darted to the left and to the right, and in his plate stood an untouched cutlet.

"Come on, spit it out!" Povilas said impatiently. "What's got you so spooked?"

"I just wanted to tell you..." he started, but the words stuck in Romas' throat. He bent down, looking around to see if anyone else could hear them. However, the cafeteria was filled with the din of hungry rowers' plates, and none of them cared about what was happening at the four's table.

"Well?" Celestinas said, putting down his fork. "Do you want to tell us something or not?"

"I wanted to tell you that I'm going to be an 'Uncle Vasya' during our trip..." said Romas, his face growing red.

The men began to chuckle.

"Shhh, I'm serious," he quieted them.

"Are you kidding?" Eugenijus laughed.

Romas shrugged and looked around again:

"Keep it down. I'm not kidding."

"What are you trying to say?" Povilas said with doubt in his voice.

"Seriously."

"I don't understand...," Eugenijus, surprised, looked at his brother with fear and distrust in his eyes.

"They leaned on me. I could have refused, but I thought "better they pick me than anyone else." I'll find a way out of it," Romas offered an excuse.

"Now this is a surprise," Povilas said. "How did they get you?"

"You see, I'm a komsorg[69], so everybody thinks I was made for spying," Romas smiled. "That's how they found me. I resisted at first, but then thought that this would be better for everyone. I'll come home, tell them I didn't see anything and don't know anything, and nobody will follow us anymore."

"You're a clever one, Romas," Povilas nodded, unsure of whether to actually trust him. "Maybe you made the right choice. At least now we'll know who to avoid," he laughed.

"Definitely, I'd rather it be you than someone else," Celestinas agreed. "However, I probably wouldn't have agreed."

"Nobody would've asked you, Celestinas," Povilas laughed. "You've got to join the Komsomol, first!"

---

69   Someone responsible for organizing the Komsomol Youth.

"Will you tell the others?" Eugenijus asked, still stunned.

"Maybe I should tell the other Lithuanians. What do you think?" Romas asked doubtfully.

The men shrugged as they glanced at their teammates at the other tables.

"Who knows… What if they talk to the Russians?" Eugenijus seemed the most stunned by his brother's news.

"What of it? Let them know that they're being watched by vigilant eyes," Povilas laughed. "If they know there's an 'Uncle Vasya' among us, they'll think we're already being monitored and that they won't need to watch us."

"Right, you be careful, too. Don't get into any trouble because I'll have to report to them and won't know what to lie about," Romas laughed.

"You'll have to write a report?" Eugenijus was still uneasy.

"No, just report verbally. They didn't ask for a written report."

"So we'll have to watch out for you? Wonderful!" Povilas laughed.

"Well, what were you planning to do over there? Run away?" Romas asked.

"Relax, relax… Where could I run off to? I wanted to take some vodka to sell…"

"So will I. Everyone will," Romas assured him.

"An 'Uncle Vasya'…" Celestinas shook his head, smiling mischievously. "Think you're the only one?"

"I don't know, the Russians probably have their own 'Uncle Vasya'. I was only assigned to the Lithuanians."

"Where did they find you? Here or in Moscow?"

"No, back in Vilnius."

"So why didn't you say anything?"

"What do I have to boast about? The time came and I told you. What if we hadn't gone anywhere? Guys, I'm not about to go telling them anything. I'll tell them that everything was fine and that I didn't see anything, that I don't know anything."

"Alright, Romas. If you agreed, you agreed. Maybe it's better that way," Povilas said, ending the uncomfortable discussion. "That'll put our heads at ease."

The men finished their dinner and parted ways with new things to consider. You won't get far running from that barbed wire fence…

*

25

The USSR rowing team flew to Copenhagen on Monday morning. They flew from Moscow, where they spent the night in a hotel and heard one more instructional session. They also received the sport committee's inspiring words of encouragement and request to bring home some medals.

Dressed in elegant suits and white shirts with ties, the tall, strong men turned heads wherever they went.

"Who are those boys?" they heard women whispering in Russian behind them as they passed.

"They say they're athletes."

"Hey boys, what sort of athletes are you?" the emboldened young women addressed the Lithuanians.

"We're rowers."

"Where are you flying to?"

"To the European Championships, to Copenhagen."

"What's Copenhagen? What language are you speaking?"

"Lithuanian."

"Ah, good job, guys, we'll be rooting for you!" they giggled before running off.

The men shrugged and smiled forgivingly.

"Now I actually believe that I'm about to see a foreign country," Povilas turned and said to his friends as he climbed up towards the plane.

"Right. I don't think they'll pull us out now!" laughed Romas.

"It's just too bad that we couldn't come home before leaving. I've missed Gita and Rasa so much. She probably won't recognize me when I come home…"

"That's right, I've only seen Daina a few times since she was born. She's probably big now. I just take that one photo with me that I cut out of "Sportas"…"

Once he sat down in the plane, Povilas pressed his face against the glass and looked off to the distance. His heart skipped a beat as he thought: "Farewell, Moscow and your barbed wire fence!"

*

The men didn't know much about the country – all they could remember were their geography classes in school, when they were called to the board next to a large map and had to point to countries on the map as the teacher named them. Denmark, which seemed so close to Lithuania and yet so distant and inaccessible, was now just a few hours away by plane.

Overcome by joyous excitement, the men couldn't stop making small talk, cracking jokes, discussing past and future races, and guess at who would win what. They kept glancing through the foggy plane windows – were they close?

The insatiably hungry athletes devoured the airline meal that they always looked forward to in an instant and were impatient to cross the sea and finally land.

They passed somebody's old newspapers from hand to hand, reading articles on the Spartakiad of Nations that had just ended. The Russians read Sovietski Sport while the Lithuanians read their own press.

"Get that out of here, I don't feel like reading. I already know we lost," Povilas shook his head when Eugenijus slid the newspaper to him in between the seats from behind.

"This isn't "Sportas", it's the "Komsomol Truth". They wrote that we were third and had to make do with bronze medals."

"Does that make it easier for you?" Povilas laughed. "Did you get a medal because you read about it?"

The men chuckled.

"But he's right," said Celestinas, opening the newspaper after Eugenijus offered it to him. "They probably saw the spartakiad's general results and wrote us in."

"Don't remind me," Romas turned around. "I just hope it doesn't end the same way in Copenhagen."

The unpleasant memories from Moscow were fading, but their grief still wouldn't let them go.

"Whatever happens, happens. The important thing is we finally got to get out," Celestinas responded to his friends' anxiety calmly, as he always did. "We'll do what we can and that's it. And if we can't win, we won't."

"What are you guys up to?" asked Ričardas as he walked past them through the aisle. "Reading? How do you feel?"

"Great!" Povilas hurried to reply.

RIMA KARALIENE

"We're reading about the Spartakiad," Celestinas added.

"Forget the Spartakiad. That's behind us," their coach waved dismissively. "We have to think about our future races now. This is sport. You can be the champion and the loser on the same day. The next day, it all starts over again. You can't stop, or else someone will come along and take your place. That's how it is. And you can't ever celebrate or grieve for too long, either. I think you guys will do alright, though Samsonov doesn't expect much. But that's fine. When you can't meet their high expectations, everybody's disappointed. You have one mission – to make it to the final. Now the eight has to beat Ratzeburg, but you guys are new, so nobody has very high expectations for you."

The men listened to their coach with their eyes lowered, and their hearts were gripped by anxiety about the upcoming races.

The plane began to descend into the thick clouds. Their meeting with a new, free, alien world was approaching. There, they could look forward to new races and new opponents.

*

When the wheels touched down on the landing strip, the passengers began to shuffle about in impatient joy, of the sort that people usually only feel before important meetings. They wanted to stand up, run, and enjoy every moment of their brief trip abroad. Most of them were about to see a distant, foreign country for the first time in their lives, a place where people spoke and lived differently.

A gust of cool air flooded into the cabin, and the men, joyfully chattering amongst themselves, crowded into the narrow passenger aisle in between the seats.

Povilas took a deep breath as he descended from the plane. It seemed to him that the air in that free, foreign country smelled just as Lithuania had in his childhood. It seemed that he could take a deep breath of air here and that the air would heal the deep wounds in his heart. Suddenly, Lithuania seemed so hopelessly exhausted and unfortunate, so sad and oppressed, and so completely mired by fear, poverty and lies that it could never be saved again. Somewhere in that depressed homeland of his, his daughter Rasa was embracing her favourite foam rabbit toy, dressed in state-issued soviet clothing that Gita would rub into a washboard every night with her knuckles after hurrying home from work. Then, she'd dry the clothes, do the ironing and darning, boil some porridge for the little one in their steam-filled kitchen, feed her, bathe her, put her to sleep, and then rush off to work again in the morning. A lump of tears gathered in Povilas' throat and he took a deep sigh.

"What are you so sad about, Povilas?" asked James as he caught up to him and brought his thoughts back to his group of friends.

"Oh I'm happy, don't worry about me!" Povilas came to his senses. "I got lost in my thoughts."

"About the race?"

"Almost," Povilas smiled.

"The weather's no good. Maybe it'll get better until the race," James said, looking at the sky.

"There's nothing you can do about that. If it'll be bad, it'll be bad for everyone."

"I just hope there's no crosswind."

"I wonder what the lake's like."

"I don't know, none of us have ever been there before. We'll see when we get there."

The men, dressed in their raincoats, crowded into the arrivals hall.

The Copenhagen airport was larger than any they had seen before. It seemed like an endless street under a roof. It sparkled with storefront displays and smelled of coffee and cigarettes. Light-haired, smiling passengers in colourful clothing hurried to and fro, and workers weaved among them, dressed in elegant suits and riding unusual scooters. It seemed like they were wandering through another world – until they heard:

"Rebiata, siuda![70]"

∗

"We'll live right outside of the city, next to the course. It's about half an hour away," Ričardas said, the last to hop into the yellow bus that had come to greet the soviet team. "We'll put our stuff away and go check on the boats."

The men got comfortable in the bus seats. Those who had jumped in first were happy to have found window seats.

Though the route took them to the other end of Copenhagen, the driver,

---

70   Rus. Over here, guys!

seemingly intent on impressing his guests, took them through the centre of the city.

The red brick buildings and towers looked like postcard pictures. The neon signs on the walls and roofs reminded the rowers once again that they weren't in their own country anymore. Some of them had already heard of Coca-Cola and Philips, but they had yet to learn about other brands, like Nestle.

The streets, full of automobiles they'd never seen before, looked nothing like those of Vilnius, where one could only expect to see more than two cars at the same time in the city centre, not including the trolley buses. The most surprising thing for the new visitors, however, was the never-ending surge of cyclists. Young and old alike – city people in suits and skirts with babies or bundles of shopping, young children, and the elderly – all rode bicycles in various states of wear. Hundreds of bicycles waited for their owners next to shops, institutions, or simply on the sidewalk in special bicycle stands.

"How can they leave them like that?"

"Doesn't anyone steal them?" the men wondered in surprised.

"How do they pick out which one is whose?"

"Maybe they lock them up."

The city's yellow buses and trams seemed half-empty. There were no cheeks pressed up against foggy windows or purses and coats caught between the doors.

"I wonder, is that how they go to work, too?" Neither the Russians nor the Lithuanians could believe their eyes as they saw elegant men riding by with ties flapping behind them and briefcases on their handlebars.

"What do they do in the winter? Surely they don't still ride their bikes…"

"Why do we stop so often?" somebody asked from the back seats of the bus, and the men in the front looked out through the front window.

"He's letting people go. It's a crosswalk," one of them gestured.

"You don't say! A pedestrian crossing?"

"We're not in Lithuania anymore…"

"I couldn't imagine that happening at home…"

"And there isn't any honking."

"And that one's taking his time…"

The men were surprised by everything around them outside of the bus windows, and drank in every moment with their eyes.

However, what caught their eyes most were the shining shop display windows, each more beautiful than the last. They offered clothing, beverages, cakes, photo cameras, televisions, and more. Record store windows shone with Denmark's bright yellow pride – Grethe and Jørgen Ingmann, that year's Eurovision winners, and their Dansevise album cover. Restaurant waiters stood by doorways, inviting passers-by to pay them a visit, and city residents and tourists gathered by outdoor cafes for coffee. A solid-looking proprietor stood in the doorway of his bookstore, watching people walk by. In the window of a chocolate store, a young girl arranged chocolates that had apparently just been made… Meanwhile, their pockets held twelve rubles that had been exchanged into krone, and one question wracked their brains – "what can I get with these as a gift to bring home…" But that would be after everything – after the competition.

*

They left old Copenhagen's brickwork behind them, and the further they got from the centre, the lower the brick buildings got. However, the end of the city was nowhere in sight. The capital's suburbs were part of one big, smooth, flat metropolis.

Juozas was studying the map that he had borrowed in Lithuania.

"It should be close by somewhere."

"What is it called, exactly?" said Petras next to him as he glanced at the map.

"Bagsværd. It has some sort of weird letter, something between an 'e' and an 'a.'"

"Bagsværd, Bagsværd. I'll have to remember it somehow."

"Is the lake big? Do you know?" Povilas asked, turning around.

"It's hard to say, it's probably about two kilometres."

"It doesn't seem very big," Petras agreed. "Maybe a bit like Žydiškės."

At that moment, the bus turned off onto a narrower road and drove by a sign labelled "Gladsaxe."

"It's close but not here," said Juozas, looking up from the map.

The men fidgeted about the inside of the bus, straining their necks to see.

"We'll live here," Ričardas reassured them. "We have an hour to make ourselves comfortable, change and eat. Then we leave for the course."

The bus was driving down a suburban street surrounded by single-story buildings.

"Look at how these people live," Povilas observed. "A house for each of them, and not stacked on one another."

"Maybe this is a wealthy neighbourhood," Eugenijus guessed.

"Well then it's a country full of rich people, because these sorts of houses are all we've seen."

"Right," Eugenijus agreed. "And it's so neat. No fences, just trimmed bushes."

A light rain began to rattle the bus windows.

"Let's hope the rain doesn't pick up," said Ričardas as he bent down to look at the sky and search for a parting in the clouds.

The bus stopped by a building with a sign that read "Gladsaxe Skole."
*

"Did you see how short the beds are?" the rowers noted as they gathered in the school's lobby.

"They're probably kids' beds."

"This is a school, of course the beds are for kids."

"How are we supposed to fit? My feet hang down."

"How'd you manage to lie down so fast?"

"Forget the beds, we'll figure it out, but how are we supposed to sleep with twenty to a room, with someone rolling about, someone else snoring, and then someone else…"

"Cut it out," Ričardas silenced them. "You've grown used to this foreign country very quickly. How did you sleep before? In Kiev, Kavgolovo and Trakai?"

"We don't have any pillows. How about you?" Zigmas asked with surprise.

"I hadn't noticed. I haven't tried lying down yet," Povilas laughed.

"No pillows?" Ričardas repeated uneasily. "I'll ask them, there should be some."

"We don't have any either," said Romas, who had just entered the room.

"We'll figure it out after training. Right now, let's head to the course," said Ričardas, giving the men a headcount with his eyes. "Do you guys have everything? We'll only be returning in the evening. It shouldn't be very far."

When they walked out into the street, the men were surrounded by a crowd of children with notebooks and notepads. Apparently, they had been instructed by their teachers or parents to collect autographs from the athletes, whom they had never seen in their city. And they had such strange letters on their uniforms – "CCCP." This was something new and unexpected for them. The eight was experienced at giving out autographs, but the new rowers were surprised and stunned by the children's attention. They felt both important and uncomfortable. However, none of them even imagined passing the children by without paying them any attention. They earnestly tried to sign every single notebook, even trying to say a few words or simply pat their heads. The little Danes were just like children in Vilnius, except that their clothing was nicer.

*

26

When they left for the lake, the men were dressed in their blue tracksuits with the letters "CCCP" – their mandatory uniform every day until they head home. The sun broke through the thick clouds. Even had they not known the way, the steady flow of bicyclists would have shown them the way, along with the crews of rowers wearing their countries' uniforms heading for the lake and back again.

In the distance, between the trees and the bushes, they could see the boat racks, the boating area, and the usual hustle and bustle of a rowing competition.

The excitement to see the location and waters of a new competition always fuses with the first hints of pre-race anxiety. That's when the entire journey to the site of the regatta, in both a broader and literal sense, finally makes sense. As soon as you see the lake, course or river, you immediately realize how soon the competition is, and that you will soon have to strike forth with your oars and endure that which you have been fighting for weeks and months. You begin carefully watching the wind, the waves, and favourable and unfavourable areas – any hint that you might gain some sort of advantage over others, that you might have an easier time of it, or that your boat will move faster than others'.

Work on the training area, which had been calm up until now and had been home to just a single rowing club, had begun in the winter and had only been completed just before the championships. An attempt was made to cover up the work that hadn't been finished with posters, fences or advertisements. A thick layer of dark earth, dredged up from the lake, lay by the finishing line and the grandstands, haphazardly shoved into uneven piles. A scoreboard with Longines and Rivella ads stood on metal poles near the uneven mounds of dirt, which looked like a sand quarry. A number of trees had probably been cut down all along the large slope, because it looked like it had just been ploughed and then sewn back up with sidewalk tiles with wooden benches for spectators – the grandstands. At the top of the slope, above the grandstands, stood a tall structure covered in canvas – a tower for journalists and reporters. A hexagonal finish-line tower was built at the very centre of the grandstands, and that had a Longines ad as well. Behind that stood yet another structure – for a TV camera. The locals now called this place the Rostadion, or "rowing stadium."

The men from the eight felt like real veterans. They proudly greeted their opponents, and those who knew a word or two would greet them with a "hello" or "how are you?" They felt about a head taller than the "rookies" from the four, and they enjoyed this role. The men from the four, in the meantime, looked about sheepishly and waited for orders from their coach. Those who were attending such a competition for the first time had to keep track of English, French, and sometimes even Danish signs, labels and maps, and they didn't want to get lost among athletes who spoke another language, either. However, this also inspired a sense of joyful excitement that usually only came ahead of a great celebration. They were curious about everything – the foreigners' boats, their clothing, and their rowing techniques. Even simply being in the midst of that entire busy scene gave them an intoxicating sense of pride. Even the signs of incomplete construction and the hurriedly assembled fences couldn't ruin the mood.

Povilas removed the cover from his camera and began to snap shots –whenever he had a bit of spare time. He spared no film, taking shots of everything he could see – the race course, the grandstands, Ivanov's opponent Kozak from Czechoslovakia, the Norwegians, his own opponents – the Germans, his team colleagues – the Russians, and even the umpires. Everything seemed extraordinary and important. He didn't want to lose even a single moment from his memories of his first European Championships and his first encounter with the never-before-seen world of capitalism. He also wanted to show it all to his family when he returned.

The first thing they had to do was find their boats and ensure that they had completed the long journey successfully. Then, they would have to be lifted from the trailer and assembled. That was what most of the athletes were initially occupied with. Those who had hurried in and arrived the day before were carrying their boats to the water, or were even returning from their training. The men were surprised to see American, Japanese, and even United Arab Republic rowers. The open European Championships was looking more like a world championships. The Japanese team had brought only one eight, but it looked like they had a full team, as every step taken by the coaches, athletes and technical staff was accompanied by the clatter of journalists' cameras, which were filming the strongest teams from every angle. More were set up at the starting line, the finishing line, and on the shore. They were also interested in Ivanov, the Ratzeburg eight, and even the lesser-known teams of other countries.

"They probably want to prepare a team ahead of the Tokyo Olympics," the teammates gathered and wondered.

"I wonder how their eight will do."

"What I wouldn't do for a Nikon like that," thought Povilas, unable to take his eyes off of the Japanese equipment as he held his FED camera in his hands. "What wonderful devices! I'll buy myself one just like that some day..."

The men took to their work, impatient to get on the water and test out the waters of Bagsværd Lake. Their fingers, trembling with excitement, tightened bolts and wiped down slides while their eyes kept rising from their work to watch the rowing stars passing them by, the boats rowing down the course, and the uniformed international federation officials. It was so good to feel like part of such a large and important regatta that they didn't even mind the fickle weather and the intermittent rain.

*

Out of the seven USSR boats that had come to the European Championships, two were Lithuanian. Or almost all Lithuanian; the four was coxed by the Russian Rudakov, and three foreigners were placed on the eight crew – the Ukrainian Sterlik and the Russians Suslin and Lorentsson. Never before had so many Lithuanians come to a single international competition. Of course, they were referred to as Russians, as was everyone else on the USSR team. Even when they said "We're not Russian, we're Lithuanian," the other person would usually just smile kindly, soon probably forgetting the name. Or perhaps it was just easier that way. What's Lithuania? Some sort of part of Russia? A region? By the sea? By which sea? "But you speak Russian at home, right?" "No, not Russian, Lithuanian!" Holding a conversation was already difficult as is if they didn't know English or German very well, and explaining these sorts of things required a great deal of effort – they were things that only the listeners' fathers or grandparents might know. In any case, nobody cared much – everybody had come for the racing and everyone wanted to beat the Russians.

Out of seven crews, only two consisted of first-timers – both of the fours. Both the Lithuanians and Leningrad's coxless four were participating in the European Championships for the first time. Both of the fours burned with a desire to get to the starting line as quickly as possible and see what they were made of, even though their senior coach had referred to them as "second-rate."

Though everyone else had been to international regattas before, they also had people among them who could be considered novices in their boat classes. After losing the double scull qualifiers to Tyurin and Dubrovskiy, the legendary Yuri Tyukalov and his partner, Fiodorov, were to race at the championships in the coxed pair – a boat that had never been selected after the short but grand Jukna and Bagdonavičius "era." The new team surprised the foreign rowers and had them talking, although the previous year, the world champion, Yuri, had already raced in the coxed four. Everyone was used to seeing him in the double scull or the single. Moving from one boat to another was possible, but switching from a scull to a sweep, and to a boat as difficult as the coxed pair, was a job that would take more than a single season. Yet here they were – they had made it to Europe!

The sky above Bagsværd grew darker and darker. The wind began to blow from the south, whipping up waves on the lake. This was probably what FISA's organisers and leaders wanted least. The lake, surrounded by forests on all sides, was famous for always being calm. The wind usually blew from the east, from the sea, which would put it equally at everyone's backs. A southerly wind meant waves in the first half of the course.

*

"The lanes are very narrow," the Leningrad rowers from the coxless four complained returning from their first training session. "It's hard to steer. We nearly hit the buoys."

"If there's any crosswind, we'll have issues," Boreiko and Golovanov, the coxless pair rowers, agreed.

"It'll be hard work for the coxes as well, because the wind is really blowing us onto the buoys," Zigmas noted anxiously.

"This is like Trakai back home," Antanas observed. "Half of the course is like an ocean, and the other half is calm."

Ričardas turned his head to the side:

"The important thing is not to clash blades, because then that's it."

"Let's hope the wind turns before the race," Boreiko said hopefully.

The four returned from the water as well.

"We almost clashed blades with the Czechoslovakians," the cox, out of breath, complained. "The lanes are so narrow, and the wind really makes you drift. They had started to row into our lane. I turned around and saw that their bow was almost touching our stern."

"We have to be careful here," Ričardas warned them. "We're not used to such narrow lanes."

"That's what I'm telling you! What is this nonsense? It's just bubble buoys wherever you turn!"

"The lanes are more narrow. Not fifteen, but twelve metres."

"Am I right that there were only five lanes?"

"That's right, they probably can't fit anymore."

"There's not much space at the finish line, either, you have to brake immediately."

"Well, we weren't going too fast today. We will have to hold it up immediately after finishing so we don't hit the shore," Ričardas warned his eight cox.

"Right, that's what I said. We have to brake right away!" the cox said, jumping out of the boat and hurrying to pull his crew in with his oar blade. They had approached the dock from the downwind side, and the crosswind was pulling the boat back towards the lake.

"How is it, guys?"

"Everything's alright. Well, maybe not at the kilometre mark – there are big waves there," said Celestinas, removing his foot stretchers.

"If the wind doesn't change, we might take on water," Povilas said, throwing his soaked sneakers out of the boat. "Look at all the water that got in."

Ričardas watched the men's boat with concern. "It's a bit low. They might take on water," he thought.

"We'll have to raise the riggers if the wind doesn't die down."

*

On their first morning, the men woke up in the school classroom with aching necks. The hosts had been in no hurry to find such a large number of pillows and instead gave each of the men a pillowcase and an additional blanket to fold up, cover with the pillowcase, and use as a pillow. As they stretched their tired necks and rubbed them with their palms, the men were nonetheless more anxious about the nasty weather rather than their pillow necks. There was still time for them to stretch before the competition, but they couldn't stop the wind.

It was a half hour at a brisk pace by foot from the dormitory to the course. When it wasn't raining, the trip was an interesting one – they could watch the Danes' neat homes and inspect the strange automobiles and rackfuls of bicycles.

Today, they were drawing the lanes and would find out who was racing whom. They always hoped for the weakest opponents in their heat so that they wouldn't have to race flat out from the very beginning – so they could get a feel for their competition, have a good warm-up run, and avoid racing in the repechage.

In addition, that day was the day of the opening of the championships. It was an opportunity to see their competition from up close, perhaps to shake the hand of a famous rower, exchange pins, and of course, to eat, though nobody mentioned this out loud. The veterans proudly shared their advice with the novices on how to behave and what to do. They also explained their adventures from previous opening ceremonies and looked forward to meeting athletes they already knew.

∗

Unfortunately, the draw proved to be a worst-case scenario – six of the seven USSR crews would be facing the Germans – that is, the united German team consisting of crews from the GDR and FRG – in their preliminary races. Only the coxless four avoided facing these dangerous opponents in its first race. In any case, the Germans were currently dominant in all boat classes, especially in the sweep boats. Each team's leader wondered – how could everything have happened like this? However, fair is fair – the heats and lanes had been chosen randomly. They had to find some sort of advantage in their situation to inspire the athletes to fight rather than cower in fear. For example, after the first races, they would finally see their actual positions in terms of strength and what opportunities they had to win. They would then know how to distribute their efforts for other races – and there would be a much lower chance of meeting the Germans again in the semi-final. Indeed, many considered these initial races as important as the finals of the competition.

Before even departing from Moscow, the head of the team, Yevgeniy Kabanov, felt confident that the single sculler, Ivanov, and coxless pair, Boreiko and Golovanov, would win. If the eight or the Tyurin-Dubrovskiy double scull were to win just one more gold medal, the USSR team would win first place as a team. This would be a very important victory, though officially, team results weren't recorded. There were no high expectations for the four – all they had to do was make it into the final. Indeed, their situation was the best. Nobody knew them, nobody expected much of them, and there was none of the usual pressure and responsibility that can often make athletes fail.

The coxed fours always raced first. That was also good – they wouldn't have to endure the agony of waiting until the evening.

*

The morning of the competition, the men woke up earlier than they had wanted to. Although the school hosts had distributed pillows to everyone the night before and they no longer had to struggle with hard blankets under their heads, their pre-race anxiety was stronger than any alarm clock. Only the eight managed to sleep relatively calmly – their first race was not until the next day. The exception, of course, was Ričardas, who woke up with his athletes from the four and helped them prepare for their first race and their first performance at the European Championships.

A total of seventeen coxed fours were entered. If there were six lanes, three heats would be enough. Here in Bagsværd, however, there were only five. There would be four heats, and two boats from each would make it into the semi-finals. They had to come in second – or first...

The weather wasn't promising – they could see that the low clouds were on the verge of letting loose. The wind blew in gusts from the east. That meant they'd be racing with a tailwind and that there would be waves...

*

"Hello, my Lithuanian brothers," the men in the four heard a man's voice behind them speaking in Lithuanian as they carried their boat after they finished the race. But the accent was strange, not Lithuanian...

"Hello," they responded, glancing over their shoulders with surprise.

"I saw you guys come in second, right?"

"That's right, second. The Germans were first," Povilas answered joyfully as the men rested their boat on the slings.

"Alright, that means you're in the final, right?" the stranger asked, trying to continue the conversation.

"No, we're just in the semi-final for now," they responded, getting a good look at the man now that they had stored their boat.

He was about forty years old, not too tall, with an intelligent, light and open face. He didn't have the anxious wrinkles typical of soviet people, and he had a natural, inborn smile. He wore a neat suit, a watch that clearly wasn't soviet, a stylish coat, a hat, and a large, black umbrella in his hand. The rowers were impressed.

"How do you know Lithuanian?"

The man laughed out loud:

"How? Well, I'm Lithuanian. What, can't you see?"

"Do you live here?" Povilas asked.

"No, I live in London. I came to see the competition."

The rowers looked at each other. They had been taught to be careful when communicating with locals, so they didn't know how to behave.

"How many from Lithuania?"

"Besides our four, there's an eight," Povilas continued. He could see that his friends were careful about talking to the stranger – they had used the opportunity to turn back towards the pontoon.

"Jukna? Bagdonavičius?"

"Yeah. The Žalgiris eight. But there are two non-Lithuanians and a cox, too. Have you heard of them?"

" I saw them win at Lucerne. But everybody thought they were Russians!"

Povilas nodded, but didn't respond.

"I didn't see you there, though," he noted, looking at Povilas attentively.

"That's because I wasn't."

"Why not? Are the Russians better than you?"

Povilas could tell that the conversation was going in a strange direction and realised that it was unsafe for him to speak openly here.

"That's what the coaches decided," he responded curtly. "I was training for the four."

"Yeah, yeah…," the man continued. "How is Lithuania doing?"

"Well, it keeps on keeping on, not much else it can do. When were you last in Lithuania?"

"I visit it every night in my dreams," he sighed longingly.

"I'm going to go bring my oar back," Povilas politely ended the discussion.

"Ah, OK. We'll be here; there are more of us Lithuanians here. They'd all like to meet you."

"Alright, we'll be here as well," Povilas nodded, hurrying off to meet with his friends.

The men were on their way back from the boating area. Celestinas was carrying his and Povilas' oars.

"Povilas, don't start with them," Romas warned him. "You don't know what they want."

"Oh come on, they're Lithuanians for Christ's sake. What, I can't even talk to them?"

"What did he want?"

"Nothing, he just asked about rowing. He said there were more Lithuanians here and that they wanted to meet us."

"Meet for what?"

"I don't know, he didn't say."

"You have to be careful. There could be all sorts of temptations."

"You believe a whole lot of nonsense, Romas. Are you afraid I'll stay?" Povilas laughed. "I still have business in Lithuania!"

The man was still standing near the boat, a bit off to the side, and watched the returning four. He raised his hand and waved before walking off towards a nearby bar.

"Who was he?" Eugenijus asked.

"I don't know him," Povilas responded. "I didn't ask for his name."

"James calls them 'dipuks[71].' He said that wherever he goes, local Lithuanians always show up."

---

71 A Lithuanian term for Lithuanians who left Lithuania during and immediately after WWII. The term comes from the English term "displaced persons," or "DPs."

"And? Is talking to them forbidden? They're Lithuanians!"

"It's not forbidden, but…"

After polishing the boat and storing their oars, the men hurried off to the grandstands to continue watching the competition – until the rain picked up and drove everyone under the thick tree cover along the banks.

*

The first day of the competition didn't go quite the way the team's leaders had expected. In the pouring rain, Ivanov finished second in his heat, surpassed by Kozak from Czechoslovakia. The coxed pair, with Tyukalov and Fyodorov, only finished third. Meanwhile, the "second-rate" coxless four won their race. "Ivanov was probably too relaxed – all he needed was second, and things will go differently in the final. And he only lost by nine hundredths of a second," the team's leaders and coaches reassured themselves and others, but they nonetheless had an uneasy nagging feeling inside – Ivanov never let himself lose, not even in preliminary races…

*

The rain grew heavier by the day. Dry clothing became a luxury, and there were still three days until the end of the championships. For some, however, this was just the first day of the competition – the eight, the double scull, and the coxless fours would be competing in their first races that day. There were less entries, so they were starting with the semi-finals.

The strong gusts of wind in the first kilometre whipped the water up into waves that made the lake look like a sea. There wouldn't be any waves at the starting line because it was in a small inlet, but how would they get to it?

After pushing off of the pontoon, the men in the four looked towards the start line uneasily. The water in the inlet by the boating area seemed fine, but half a kilometre out from the peninsula, where there was a nearly kilometre-wide open area, the waves practically leapt into the boats. The boats' orientation, perpendicular to the waves, was the worst for these conditions. The riggers chopped the crest of each wave into a spray that drizzled the already-soaked rowers with each wave, and the boat, taking on water, would grow heavier and sit even lower on the water.

"What do we do, guys?" the cox asked with fear in his voice. The water was almost up to his waist.

"What do we do?" Celestinas repeated, turning to his team.

"We have to get out, we're not going to make it to the start," Povilas said, brushing water from his face.

"Steer us towards the shore, Igor," Celestinas translated for the cox. "We won't make it."

The nearest shore was ahead of them, a couple hundred metres from the start line. That bank, too, was being battered by waves. The men sped up their pace, and with every powerful stroke, about half a bucket of water poured into their boat along Igor's sides, and with each recovery, the same thing.

"Come on, guys, five more strokes. One, two," Igor encouraged them.

They were right by the shore now and could hear the reeds sliding along the hull. The waves were carrying the boat towards the rocks.

"Stop!" Igor shouted, yanking the rudder to the left. The bow turned in an arc and drew closer to the shore, while the waves hitting it in the side continued to push it towards the shore even harder. Suddenly, they heard a loud crack below the boat. The boat jerked to a stop, stuck on a submerged rock.

"Son of a bitch!" the cox cursed quietly, "What happened?"

"We ran aground, damn it," Povilas shouted.

"I think it cracked," said Romas, trying to examine the shell with his head between his knees.

"What, a hole?" terrified, Igor jumped out of the water and waded around the boat to inspect it. "Come on, quickly, lets pour the water out."

The men quickly hopped out, unloaded their oars, and slowly flipped the boat so it wouldn't break while they lifted it. What's more, lifting a boat full of water was no easy task. They poured out most of the water, lifted the boat over their heads, and rocked it back and forth from front to back, splashing out the last drops of water.

"Let's hurry up, boys, we start in ten minutes," Igor urged them onwards.

The men loaded their oars back in, pushed their boat into deeper waters, and got in, one after another. The Czech and Dutch boats rowed past them towards the start, and in the distance, the five crews from the first semi-final had covered the first 200 metres of their race, lost in a spray of white foam.

"God damn it," Romas cursed.

"What happened?" the cox stretched his neck.

"There's a hole, we're taking on water.

Indeed, the water in the bottom of the boat was already two fingers deep. At that rate, the boat would be half-full at the finish line.

"Can we plug it with something? Tape won't help, it won't stick...," Igor searched his pockets for a rag.

Just then, they heard the umpire calling the rowers to the starting line.

"Romas, take my jacket!" the cox shouted to Romas.

"It won't help. Keep it or you'll get cold."

Standing at the start, the men tried to bail the water out with their hands, and soak the water up with their tracksuit bottoms and then wring them into the lake. But there was no more time. There were two minutes until the start. Over the six minutes of the race, they could gain an additional ten to twenty kilograms of weight. This ballast would decide their fates. The wind had already made things difficult, and now they'd have to row with extra weight as well. And they had to be first. Only one boat would make it to the final. For the others, it would be a repechage race.

"Êtes-vous prêt? Partez!" the umpire shouted through his megaphone and the boats leapt away from their handlers.

Their only thought was to finish quickly so that they'd take on as little water as possible. The water sloshed back and forth along the bottom of the hull, faster and faster with every stroke. It had already reached their foot stretchers. Their lee from the wind would end in two hundred kilometres, and the waves grew larger with every passing metre. They had to dart through the first half of the distance as quickly as possible, but the water was coming in over the weighed-down boat's sides. "It should be calmer at the kilometre mark, as long as we don't sink." The men cursed to themselves as they tried to escape the weight of the water in their boat, but as their opponents' cries began to grew distant, their hope to win grew slimmer and slimmer.

"Ten more, guys, come on!" cried Igor, his body instinctively rocking back and forth to urge the boat forward. "It's the last five hundred! Let's finish!"

Unfortunately, the significantly weighed-down boat was being jerked back and forth from the water sloshing about within. It felt like one incident during a training session when they realised that they had been tugging a long tail of lake weeds caught on their rudder for about a kilometre. But this time, they were soaked to the bone and the oars were slipping from their hands. God forbid they slip away…

They finished not last, but third – they would race in the repechage the next day…

They had to make sure to fix the boat on time.

*

They were not the only ones to make it into the repechage race – the coxless four and both of the pairs would have to race again for the right to race in the final.

The eight, however, stunned everyone by beating the Ratzeburg team by a whole ten seconds. Their joy was mixed with concern – "what if they were saving their strength? Maybe they intentionally let Žalgiris shoot ahead, hesitant to reveal their true strength…" "It's hard to imagine that a stronger team would intentionally lose to a weaker one. Besides, in some places, the Germans' rate was 46 strokes a minute!" "It looks like they had a good reason for not going to Lucerne. After losing in Duisburg, they were afraid they'd lose again." "They say that before Copenhagen, they had a qualifier against the DRG and Berlin's Dynamo and barely won by two seconds at the finish. We beat them by six seconds, and their team had been strengthened. Looks like they just can't cut it anymore…" – the coaches, journalists, and the rowers themselves shared their various theories, opinions and conclusions. The clear advantage emboldened the Žalgiris rowers and gave them confidence, but the great battle would only come two days from then. They had to maintain a feel for their stroke and avoid burning out. And then, perhaps, everything would finally be fine…

*

The repechage races gave the Lithuanian four and the coxless pair with Boreiko and Golovanov a new sense of hope. Two boats were excluded from the final – the Leningrad coxless four and the famous pair with Tyukalov. The faces of the team's leaders grew grim – these loses did not bode well for the team. If it was all a coincidence – fine. They absolutely needed three gold medals, and two boats had already been eliminated. In the meantime, all seven of the German crews were in the finals. The primary fight against Germany wasn't over yet, but their forces were no longer equal. The finals were tomorrow, and tomorrow, Ivanov and the Žalgiris eight had to win!

*

The rain came down hard on the morning of the finals. It rained the entire day, every hour and every minute. The rain washed the soil from the grandstands at Bagsværd, and whatever wasn't washed down into the lake became slippery mud that the crowd of spectators, umpires, journalists and organisers trudged to and fro through. The spectators could hardly be seen under the mass of umbrellas. The cold water stiffened the rowers' muscles. The rowers waited in the changing rooms up until the last minute so they wouldn't grow cold outside.

Arriving at the course, Eugenijus, Romas, Celestinas and Povilas hurried straight to their boat to check if the crack in their boat caused by the rock the previous day had reappeared after the coach had quickly treated it with glue and sanded it down before the repechage race. Ričardas brushed the water off with his sleeve, pressed his cheek to the hull, and checked once again to see if he could find any uneven areas and whether the moisture had ruined his work.

"It'll be fine for now. When we return, we'll need to give it some serious work. Look, today, don't go rowing off anywhere," he warned them sternly. "There are no more repechage races."

"Who could've known that there were rocks there?" the men tried to defend their cox, though they knew well that it was his carelessness that had forced them to row an additional race.

"We'll leave for the start later so we don't freeze," Ričardas changed the subject. "Go to the massage therapist, he'll rub your legs with some lotion. You guys have an hour."

*

27

The rain kept coming and showed no sign of stopping. The wind turned from the east, so they were at least sure that they wouldn't be battered by perpendicular waves – although they didn't usually do well when rowing with a tailwind. Coxes and coaches hurried about on the shoreline. Despite the inclement weather, spectators were still gathering in the grandstands. Such competitions didn't happen here too often, and fans from throughout Denmark had come to see the action.

With their raincoats on their shoulders, the men looked at the Germans' warm, waterproof suits with envy. Their legs, however, were burning after being treated with a warming ointment that contained snake poison. Their final would be over first. After that, regardless of how their race went, they would be able to watch everybody else race.

"It's time," said Igor, nodding to the men as he hurried up with his tools in his hands.

The men turned to Ričardas.

"That's right, let's go," Ričardas looked at his watch and agreed.

And just then, the men felt a wave of lethargy and yawns brought on by the enormous anxiety that they had been hiding within themselves.

"It'll all be over in half an hour," Povilas reassured himself as he rubbed his hands together to keep warm. "Everything's going to be alright."

The five men kicked off of the dock. They were surrounded by the hiss of raindrops hitting the water, which drowned out the noise from the grandstands, the music, and the announcer's voice. Everything grew smaller in the distance – the trees, the people, the boats, their coach. All they wanted was for the end to come, to finish the race, come what may. The feeling that all of those people had come to watch you, that somebody was going to read your surname out loud – they couldn't decide if it was good or bad, but it raised a lump in their throats.

Their fingers were stiff with cold but their legs were still burning.

At least the waves were calmer and weren't spilling over the sides anymore.

"Despite everything, it's beautiful here," Povilas glanced back towards the shore in between strokes. "I wonder if anyone lives in that house. Back home, such homes were made into warehouses or cultural buildings ages ago... Damn this rain... What lilies! And how many! Celestinas' back is totally wet... We had to make it to the final and we did, so we can relax now... Why did they put on so much ointment? They should've wiped it off with a cloth or something. It's on my hands now, too... God damnit, what is it now?" His oar caught on the water, and then Romas did the same. The boat rocked from side to side.

"What happened?" Igor looked down one side and the other at the men sitting behind Celestinas.

"I can't row, the oars are slipping," Povilas responded, stopping.

"Me too," Romas and Eugenijus replied in unison.

The oars had been touching the men's legs and the ointment had gotten onto the handles, forming a layer of fat. Along with the rain, this made the oars impossible to hold. The men stopped and tried to wipe the ointment off, but it didn't help – the rain was falling and the fat wasn't coming off.

"Yeah, I have to squeeze it so I don't lose it. My hands are slipping, we can't row," Celestinas translated for the cox.

"We have to clean it off. I didn't take my rag..."

"It doesn't help. We have to roughen it up somehow," Povilas suggested, looking about for a sharp object. "Do we have a screwdriver?"

"I just have pliers," Igor offered.

"Give'em here."

"What are you going to do?" Celestinas asked, passing the tool to Povilas and watching over his shoulder.

"We have to do something, our oars will slip otherwise," Povilas said as he began to scratch down the length of his oar handles with the teeth of the pliers. He then grasped the handle, twirled it about and rubbed it a few times – it had worked!

"Give that here," Romas said, sliding up to him on his slide and extending his hand.

One after another, the men used the pliers to scratch grip lines into the wooden handles before testing them out – they'd manage. Proud of their inventiveness, they headed off towards the starting line.

The start line was at the end of the lake, right on the shoreline. Young children, oblivious to the foul weather, ran about on the shore. The five boat handlers in five waterproof raincoats were ready to release the five competing crews into their final race – the coxed fours. The winners would be the first champions and prizewinners of the 1963 European Rowing Championships.

"I guess it's time, right, boys? Our final battle!" Igor tried to encourage his crew as he turned the rudder towards the starting pontoon. "Bow, three – one stroke, fourth, back. Stop!"

The handler caught the stern of their boat. Under the hood, they couldn't even tell if it was a man or a woman.

"But these lanes are so narrow… Good thing we have a cox. He'll steer us." Even though it was their fourth race, Povilas was still surprised by the lanes. "We have to pass at least two. We probably won't pass the Germans." On the start line, all their opponents seemed threatening, though all of them had the same fear and were facing the same challenge.

The Germans were the last to make it onto the start. Unlike any other team on the water, they had been provided with waterproof suits. "They probably didn't need any ointment, either," the men thought, feeling their muscles grow stiff from the cold rain. In an effort to get at least a bit of warmth, they slid back and forth on their slides, slapped their thighs, and rubbed their hands. They opened their mouths to catch the rain and dry their lips, which were parched from pre-race anxiety.

"Let's undress," Celestinas turned around and reminded his team after the umpire announced that there were two minutes until the start.

The blue uniform with the white letters "CCCP" were replaced by red shirts with the coat of arms on the chest. The rain had soaked them through completely. At least the boat wasn't taking on water. The men used their tracksuits to rub the water from their oar handles one more time and prepared for the first stroke. With their legs bent and the red blades of their oars submerged in the water, they took a last deep breath and froze, their eyes staring straight at their crewmates' backs. The pre-race roll-call began – the umpire began naming the countries one after another and the coxes nodded, confirming that they were ready. The five boats in the final could no longer see each other – all they could see were their foot stretchers, their oar handles, and the backs of the crewmates sitting in front of them.

"Êtes-vous prêt? Partez!" with that, the boats' sterns slipped out of the handlers' cold hands.

The first starting strokes were powerful but careful – they had to let the boat straighten out and balance itself.

"One, and two…"

For the first five hundred metres, the boats went nose-to-nose, with the Germans ahead by a bit – only about a third of a length. The water ran down their faces and hands and over their eyes, forcing them shut. Their legs felt like giving up, but there was a kilometre and a half still ahead. The men knew that feeling well – it would soon disappear, replaced by a new burst of strength. Then, they'd have only a kilometre left – and then the third five hundred – and then the finish line.

"Keep that up!" Igor tried to encourage the men when he saw that the first two boats were falling behind. The men were being hounded by unavoidable muscle pain.

On their left side, the green lake shore shot past them, the course right near the bank. Rivulets of rainwater poured from the trees on the bank that erupted in spouts of foam as they hit the lake.

"One, two… twenty seven… not much left, just a bit," Povilas tried to encourage himself in his head. "For my father… for my mother… for Rasa…"

A buoy shot past the side of the boat. "Five hundred left…"

"Let's turn it up!"

"Damn it, that was only half," Povilas swore in his head, realizing that he had miscalculated and that there was a kilometre to the finish line. "Son of a… don't give up…"

As strange as it was, the third five hundred flew by more quickly than he had feared. He couldn't see the Germans or the Czechoslovakians, but they were third for now. "All we have to do is keep this up and that's it, we'll have our medals…"

"Come on, boys, one and two! The finish line is coming up! One!"

They could hear the roar of the grandstands, but the farther they got the worse things felt… Something was off. Somebody was messing up. It seemed like they could no longer row, that they were a different team from the one that left the start… One of them was late to match the rhythm and late pulling out of the water…

"The twenty last strokes, keep it up!" the cox roared, seeing that the medals were within reach. "Come on! One and two!"

Through clenched teeth, the men gave it all that they had. They couldn't feel their hands and their feet, but they rowed automatically, with darkness in their eyes. They focused on grasping their oars – God forbid they slip or catch a crab. That would end everything.

The announcer's voice melted into one indecipherable din that blended in with the sound of the falling rain. They didn't even hear the gong – only Igor's voice as he shouted "Stop!" The men collapsed onto their oar handles and breathed hard, trying to understand what had happened.

"Hold water!" Igor shouted, and the team immediately began braking with their oars straight in the water. There were only a few metres to the end of the lake.

"Bronze, hurrah!" the cox shouted out loud.

"Romas, what happened?" Povilas asked, turning to his teammate.

"I don't know. My eyes went dark. I felt that I wasn't keeping up, but I couldn't do anything about it…"

"One way or another, we wouldn't have caught up to them…"

"What is it?" Celestinas turned around.

"Nothing, it'll pass, let's go," Romas responded quietly as they all turned off towards the shore.

The umpires hung boards on the scoreboard one after the other – "Allemangne," "Tchécoslovaquie," "URSS," and the times next to each one – 6:29.60, 6:33.81, and 6:37.92. Over the loudspeaker, the announcer invited the winners to the medal pontoon. The rain was coming down hard, but the full grandstands stood and cheered from under their umbrellas for the first winners of the day. The "heads" of the team – Samsonov and Kabanov – waved from the shore as well. Next to them stood Ričardas, with a modest smile on his face. He was the coach of the new medalists.

The men could barely believe what had happened. They had heard so many times from the team's leaders and coaches that they expected nothing of them and that it would be great for them to make it into the final. Zigmas had even told the press that the four didn't have any experience, that they rowed unsteadily, and that they had poor odds. Deep in their hearts, however, the four yearned to prove that they were no worse than the eight – from which they had been thrown out numerous times for no reason. They had been considered second-rate rowers or benchwarmers – anything but champions.

"Bravo, Lithuania!" they could hear joyous shouts coming from the grandstands. The men saw a group of people waving to them with a yellow, green and red flag. At the head of the group stood the man with the hat who had addressed them on their first day at the competition. The men pretended not to see them, but out of the corners of their eyes, they watched the tri-colour flag, which they hadn't seen since their childhoods. Flying that flag in Lithuania would get any of them locked away in a basement prison cell for a long time, thrown out of university, or charged with betraying one's homeland.

"Who is that?" Igor looked at the shoreline and then back to the team. "What flag is that?"

"Let's go," Celestinas turned to the men and pretended not to have heard the cox.

"Bow, three, harder!"

The boat approached the medal podium in a gentle arc and docked. The new European champions, the Germans, were already getting out of their boat. The men's hearts were now pounding with pride and joy. They could no longer feel the rain or the cold – only an incredible weight that had been lifted from their shoulders.

*

The unexpectedly successful start to the final day gave the Soviet team great hopes. Though two crews hadn't made it into the finals, the first finalist – the Lithuanian four – was a good omen. The coaches and the team managers took a sigh of relief – the first final had brought their first medal. That meant that they had achieved their proper form just in time, and that they could expect medal placements from the remaining crews. Perhaps even better ones than were expected.

However, this didn't last for long. Fifteen minutes later, Boreiko and Golovanov steered off course into an opponent's lane and finished fourth. They couldn't manage to steer the pair along a narrower lane than they were used to. One oar got caught on one of the buoys separating the lanes and the boat turned at an angle. Straightening it out cost them precious seconds – not too many, but enough for them to lose... One of the main candidates for a medal was leaving empty-handed.

*

After putting the boat back on the rack and putting on dry clothes, the men ran to watch the rest of the competition.

"Look, what's happening to Ivanov?" Eugenijus gestured towards the racecourse.

Hurrying towards the grandstands, through the bushes growing along the shoreline, the young men tried to see the single scullers as they neared the finish line.

"It looks like his oars are getting caught. Did he get exhausted at the finish?" Romas wondered.

It was obvious that Ivanov was rowing entirely unlike himself. His famous technique was nowhere to be seen.

"It looks like his blades are sinking like rocks," Povilas agreed.

Unbelievably, the star of the USSR team, its unquestioned leader and champion, was trying to catch up to three single scullers with only 200 metres to the finish line.

"He's catching crabs on every stroke, something's wrong. You mean to tell me he's that tired?" a frightened Celestinas asked, shaking his head.

"It can't be... He's got to catch at least one of them!" Povilas commented, hurrying towards the grandstands at a half-run with his friends at his heels. "He looked so good yesterday!"

"Slava, davai!" came the shouts from the grandstands from men who probably didn't have any more finals that day. However, Ivanov had trouble lifting his oars out of the water and he finished fourth.

Kozak, the Czechoslovakian, won, with the Dutchman and German coming in behind him. And then, of course, Ivanov – almost ten seconds later...

"What happened?" the men asked as they ran to the dock and met with the Leningrad rowers from the coxless four.

"We don't know, something was probably wrong with his boat."

"That's what we thought, too."

"I can't believe it, Ivanov without a medal..."

Ivanov turned around after the finish and rowed off towards the pontoon, averting his face from the clapping public. His nervous motions betrayed the boiling grief and anger hiding within the champion.

Later, the men would hear that somebody had sabotaged his boat before the final by readjusting the angle of his oars. This determined the angle at which the blade entered the water and how it pushed during the stroke. The change didn't need much – pushing the metal plate under the oarlock back towards the stern a smidgeon would be enough to make the oars stick into the water like shovels. One wouldn't even have to bother to unscrew the nuts, as giving the plate a few whacks with a hammer or wrench would do just as well. It was no coincidence that he had seemed like his oars were sinking strangely. If the angle is at least the tiniest bit lower than it should be, the oar blades sink deep with every stroke, requiring significant effort to keep the spoons at water level. Under the strain, one's arms would never get a chance to relax and rest. But why would anyone do this? Who wanted their medal so badly that they resorted to foul play? Was it simply envy? Who was so against Ivanov's victory? The team's coaches, teammates, and Ivanov himself would repeat these questions over and over, but they couldn't turn back time, and they wouldn't be able to prove anything. What's more, every smile would appear two-faced and treacherous, and every consolation would seem malicious.

The Czechoslovakian Socialist Republic also won the double scull race. Tyurin and Dubrovskiy finished third, just like the Lithuanian four.

The hope to occupy first place as a team had been buried. However, it was still possible to win a gold medal. All predictions and calculations showed that Žalgiris' eight should win without much trouble. Even the men of the eight believed this themselves. That was, of course, if Ratzeburg didn't reveal some sort of secret weapon.

The entire team gathered on the grandstands to watch the final and most beautiful race in the rowing competition. The spectators rubbed their hands to keep warm and huddled under their umbrellas, but nobody left.

"Look, the wind turned. They'll be rowing into the wind," Eugenijus pointed at the flags, which were waving towards the east.

"That's right, it's changed completely," Romas agreed.

"They'll do better against the headwind."

"Look, the Germans are only leaving now. How much time is there until the race?" Povilas checked his watch, but it was so foggy from the rain that he could barely see its hands.

"Five minutes," Celestinas said with surprise. "They might not make it."

"They won't start without them, they'll wait. Our guys will just freeze while they wait."

"They'll be fine, they got that ointment, too. Just as long as they don't lose their oars."

"The Germans are well-dressed. They aren't afraid of the cold."

It was hard to see what was happening at the start line through the pouring rain – they could barely see the halfway mark. The German boat soon disappeared behind a curtain of rain.

"Hey, guys," the man with the hat turned around and greeted the men. He had apparently been sitting right there all along. Or could he have come after hearing the Lithuanians? "Good work! I saw how well you guys rowed."

"Thank you, thank you," Povilas smiled.

The man stood up and shook the men's hands.

"Are Jukna and Bagdonavičius going to row now?"

"Yeah, it's just the eight left."

"Will they win? What do you think?"

"They might. But those Germans are strong, they won't let us win easily. Maybe by just a second, but they can do it."

"Are you Levickas?"

"No, I'm Liutkaitis, Povilas Liutkaitis. These are the Levickas brothers," Povilas pointed to Eugenijus and Romas sitting next to him.

"Okay, sorry. My name's Kazimieras, or Kazys," the man introduced himself.

"This is Celestinas, our stroke," Povilas introduced his friend to the man.

The men politely nodded to one another and continued to wait for the signal for the start.

"Where are you staying?"

"Not far from here, at the school in Gladsaxe."

"At the school? But then where do you sleep?"

"We sleep in the classrooms."

"In the classrooms? On the ground?"

"No, they set beds up for us."

"Are they comfortable?"

"When we're not all snoring at the same time, they are," Povilas laughed. "There's a lot of us there, about twenty per classroom."

"Twenty?" Kazys was shocked. "Twenty to a room?"

"It's fine, we're used to it. More of us fit together in the main hall at Žalgiris. At our camps, we sleep in tents. When you get to bed after three sessions, you'll sleep like you're dead."

"Did you visit Copenhagen?"

"We just passed through it on the way from the airport. They said they'd take us after the competition. Maybe tomorrow."

"When do you fly home?"

"Wednesday, I believe."

The announcer's voice grew more animated, and all of the spectators looked off towards the right in unison – the race had just started. It was hard to understand the Danish announcer and learn what was happening off in the distance. The Danish eight hadn't made it to the final, but their fans nonetheless impatiently looked forward to seeing the finish of the blue riband race of the championship.

"It looks like the Germans are ahead," Celestinas announced the moment the boats became somewhat visible in the distance.

"Think they'll catch up? The Germans are rowing hard," Romas said, doubting his own words.

"Against the wind at such a rate!" Eugenijus noted with surprise. "Looks about forty-five!"

"Our guys are running at just about thirty-five," Romas added.

"Something's wrong there with our guys," Celestinas shook his head. "It looks like they're getting beat bad..."

"I think they grew cold while waiting for the Germans. They didn't do any warm-ups, nothing but that ointment on their legs. They rowed to the starting line and waited. The Germans were dressed up warm, at least. Our clothes aren't enough for weather like this," Povilas reasoned.

"They won't catch up," Celestinas nodded.

"Son of a bitch!" Povilas agreed.

"No good, guys?" Kazys interjected.

"No, it's not... But silver's good, too!" Povilas unclenched his fist and, for about the hundredth time and with a trembling heart, looked at his bronze medal, lying on blue velvet in a delicate grey box.

"They can't seem to make it out of second place, like they're cursed," Eugenijus shook his head.

"They can when the Germans aren't around," Celestinas smiled. "Like at the regatta in Lucerne."

"How did Ratzeburg get beat so badly that first day? It was about ten seconds...," Romas wondered.

"They probably didn't show their hand," Povilas nodded. "They tricked us a bit and our guys fell for it."

"Or our guys gave it their all too soon and left nothing for the final," Eugenijus considered.

The finishing gong sounded off, announcing a German victory. The second gong rang four seconds later – for Žalgiris.

"It's over, you can't change anything now," Celestinas wrapped his raincoat tighter around himself, though it no longer offered much protection from the rain.

"Silver and two bronze medals," Eugenijus summed up the final results.

"And one of them was ours!" Povilas thought to himself with joy.

"Samsonov won't be happy," they said together.

"He's probably already unhappy," Eugenijus noted, following the senior coach with his eyes as he walked away from the finish line.

With not a single gold medal, the team coach would once again have to sit for a gruelling session before the party committee and explain himself. He would once again have to prove himself, justify his actions, and make promises. After that, the athletes would once again have to listen to his reproaches and his orders, endure the inscrutable reshuffling of the teams, and undergo countless qualifications and test matches. What's more, there was only a year left until the Olympics.

"Let's go then, shall we?" Povilas was the first to stand up. "Let's go load our boat."

"I've gotten pretty cold," Romas shivered. "You don't feel it while you're sitting."

"We're soaked through, now," Celestinas agreed. "Not a single dry thread left."

"It was nice to see you guys!" Kazys extended his hand. "Will you still be here?"

"Not for long, probably. Just while we load our boat," Povilas nodded to the man, shook his hand, and followed his friends.

"Listen, Povilas…," Kazys stopped him after his teammates had walked off about a dozen metres.

Povilas turned around.

"I have a question," he said quietly.

"Yes?"

"Well, maybe more like a request…"

"What is it?" asked Povilas. The unexpected encounter prompted him to check if anyone was watching him.

Understanding that the men had been frightened, Kazys pointed towards the exit.

"Let's go over there, under the trees."

"I wonder what he wants," Povilas tried to understand the man's intentions as they walked through the crowd of spectators. "In any case, I'll be able to refuse if I don't like it," he reassured himself, but he marched along anyway, led on by his curiosity.

Next to the bar under the trees, Kazys stopped and looked Povilas in the eyes intently.

"I don't know why, but I feel like I can trust you."

Povilas laughed sincerely:

"And what, the others aren't trustworthy?" Povilas joked.

"I don't know, but every conversation I've tried to start with the others has ended in them running from me like I'm an enemy. It's unfortunate that Lithuanians have changed like this, that they fear one another. What have those communists done to Lithuania…"

"I don't run from people," Povilas laughed again, suppressing his anxiety.

"Beer?" Kazys asked, pulling out his wallet.

"How about some Rivella."

After taking an opened bottle each, the men moved off to the side.

"Here's the issue. I want to send a letter to Lithuania. To my relatives. I've been writing and writing but I don't think they're getting them. I think the KGB's taking them."

"Not a problem! Sure I can send it to them!" Povilas said. When he learned how simple the request was, he relaxed and flashed a broad smile.

"You're not afraid?"

"Why should I be? I write and send plenty of letters. That's in Lithuania, of course, or from my camps back to home."

"I don't want any trouble for you. It's better that nobody see that you're taking this from me. And that they wouldn't find it, because you might get into trouble because of me," said Kazys, seeming to adjust his hat as he inspected the people surrounding them.

"What's in there? How can you get me in trouble?"

"Nothing, it's just a letter. But the soviets don't like letters like these. And they don't like foreign Lithuanians. Not at all…"

Povilas looked around and, pretending to look at the boats rowing by in the distance, took the letter from Kazys' lowered hand.

"I'll send it," he promised. "I'll send it from Lithuania. I'll put it in a Lithuanian envelope and I'll send it."

Povilas carefully slid the letter into his bag, hiding it both from the rain and from the eyes of passersby.

"Thank you. The address is on the envelope. God help you!"

The men, who had begun to feel like conspirators, nodded imperceptibly to one another and parted ways.

"Who is Kazys? What's in the letter? No matter, I'll just send it and that's that. How hard can it be? If they don't let you write to relatives… Once, I had to wait so long for letters from Elzbieta… and they never came. Or when they did, they were in Russian, and I couldn't read them… Maybe my aunt didn't read it all back to me… But I still wrote and wrote… It's terrible when you can't communicate with your family..." Povilas' thoughts raced as he caught up to his friends and teammates gathered by the rack.

Their quiet, depressed and exhausted friends from the eight, soaked to the core, marched by them, carrying their boat on their shoulders.

"Everything's alright, guys, you're the best in our team," Eugenijus tried to encourage them. "You took the highest place!"

"They've probably been doping," said Zigmas, unable to control his anger as he laid the boat down on the slings. "How else could they shave off ten seconds in two days?"

"Alright, alright, stop complaining," Ričardas soothed him. "We rowed poorly, there's nothing else to say."

"We froze like little chickens! And they had such nice clothing!"

"They rowed out to the start line last. You were all there when they left," Romas interjected. "When you were leaving, they were just arriving."

"There you go! They rowed up last, saw that we were freezing, and then intentionally took their time getting onto the start pontoon, as if they couldn't line up. After that, they took their time taking off their clothing. Meanwhile, the rest of us were shivering! Four teams were waiting while they took their sweet old time!"

"Calm down. Everything's alright," Ričardas quieted them again. "We had to set out earlier to do a good warm-up. That's why your muscles stiffened."

"So whose fault is it that we left with less than ten minutes before the race?"

Ričardas grew quiet – he understood that much of the responsibility for their misfortune lay on his shoulders, as he was their coach. After five hundred metres, their chests felt like they were splitting apart, their arms grew stuff from the cold, the oars slipped from their hands, and they only stopped shivering at the midway point, which meant they had nothing left for their infamous "third five-hundred."

When the competition ended, the team was overcome by a truly dark mood. Everyone who had intended to win medals did worse than they had planned. Only the men from the four were happy. They were newcomers, so everyone's predictions for them had been conservative. They had been thrown from boat to boat and prevented from travelling anywhere outside of the USSR. Everyone, even their teammates, considered them to be benchwarmers with no serious prospects. Now, finally, on this rainy day in Denmark, on the muddy shore of Bagsværd, the tired and completely soaked rowers were happy. Even the pain of the Spartakiad had melted away.

*

The rowers were due to return home on Wednesday, 12 August, when Aeroflot's plane returned from Moscow to Copenhagen.

Immediately after the competition, they were transferred from the Gladsaxe School to the luxurious Egmont hotel in the centre of the city. That evening, after changing out of their competition clothing into evening suits, ties, and shined shoes, they walked to Copenhagen town hall, where the competition's closing ceremony was to be held.

The rowers stood in a group to listen to the short formal proceedings, glancing shyly at the rowing stars and foreign rowers who had attended. When the banquet began, however, and after they had downed one or two mugs of beer each, their words began to flow freely – even the handful of German and English words they had picked up in one place or another. They even started to make friends. This was, of course, only after they completed three revolutions around a table laden with food that the perpetually hungry rowers could only have dreamed of.

The guests were invited from City Hall to the nearby Tivoli Park to enjoy the amusement park's rides and watch some fireworks that had been organised for the closing ceremony.

Before their journey home, they had enough time to see the city, think about their families, "get rid of" the products they had brought, and exchange them for beautiful gifts for their beloved women and children. The men walked through Copenhagen's fairytale streets and their shimmering and fragrant shops to gather gifts and souvenirs. Their eyes nearly popped out of their sockets at the sight of something they had never seen before – magazines with completely naked women on their covers. The only problem was that they were followed around everywhere by the team's "chaperones." In addition, they all had to stay together. They were followed everywhere by the vigilant eyes of the KGB's officers, who were impossible to miss. Anyone who brought rubles or dollars they had scrounged from one place or another to exchange for krone in the hotel lobby had to help one another draw the officers' attention, because bringing currency was one of the greatest offences they could possibly commit.

The weather didn't get much better, but the rain wasn't as torrential as it had been on the day of the finals. The mornings were covered in a thick fog, much like autumn.

*

28

The rowers encountered rain upon their return to Lithuania as well. It seemed like they would never see the sun again. However, after a long and exhausting journey, they were finally home.

Povilas' home on Čiurlionis Street was prepared for his arrival as though it was a great holiday. On Sunday, when they had learned of Povilas' medal from the sports managers who had been maintaining a vigil by the phones, the entire household prepared to welcome him home in kind.

"Rasa is walking!" Povilas said as he stepped in through the door and saw Gita holding her little daughter's hand. He crouched down and opened his arms: "Hello, Rasa! Come here!"

The child, however, faced by an unfamiliar man, buried her face in Gita's arms and clung to her leg.

"This is your father. Say hello," Gita soothed her, but Rasa, with her arms thrown around her mother's neck, looked at the man with fear in her eyes.

Povilas approached and hugged them both:

"I've missed you so much…"

"She's forgotten you… But no matter, she'll get used to you…"

Povilas stroked his daughter's head as tears gathered in his eyes: "I hope I don't miss how she grows up," he thought.

"Look at the gifts I brought you," he said, picking up his suitcase and carrying it into the family room. Gita, with Rasa in her arms, followed him. Povilas opened his tightly packed suitcase and took a bag from the top that was filled with his still-damp kit, carefully placed a separate bag with rolls of film onto the shelf, and revealed an array of clothing the likes of which had never been seen in Lithuania before – skirts, shoes, elegant dresses for his beloved wife, and gifts for his parents-in-law and others at home.

"I missed you so much…," Povilas said as he sat on the edge of the bed and watched Gita's smile as she happily unwrapped the gifts. In his hand, he held the European Championships bronze medal he had taken out of its box.

"How did you guys get on here without me?" Povilas asked, as if to himself, after resting from his endless journeys. "Here, Rasa let me show you something," he said, extending his clenched fist.

Wary but curious, Rasa glanced at her father's hand. The gesture was a familiar one – this was usually how her grandpa hid candy or lumps of sugar in his palm. She already knew what she had to do. With step by careful, trembling step, she approached Povilas, shyly touched his fingers, and began to pry them open.

"What have you got there," Gita turned around as she sorted the gifts into neat piles.

Povilas smiled and let his daughter pry open his fingers, hardened with endless calluses, one after another. The medal, glimmering in Povilas palm, slipped from Rasa's hands and clattered down to the floor. Povilas picked it up and set it back in his frightened daughter's palm.

"Look at my little champion here! Give me your hand, let's go show grandpa," he said, taking Rasa by the hand and leading her through the door to the kitchen. The hard, sharp calluses felt sharp on her little palm, but it was a feeling that the little girl would never forget and that she would always recognize. Those were the hands of a Father, and they were her Father's hands.

*

They had collected almost every newspaper that had written anything about Copenhagen on the kitchen table. The heap had a letter on top addressed "Повиласу Люткайтису[72]," with "Балхаш[73]" as a return address. After seating Rasa on his lap, he tore open the letter and, rocking Rasa back and forth, immediately read the letter.

"Hello, Povilas. How are you doing? How are Gita and your little Rasa?... My husband, Vytas, will be traveling to Lithuania in September. If you can, please take him in for a night. He should show up on the 25 or 26 September. He will travel from Vilnius to Radviliškis to his family. He will spend a week there... Give my regards to our aunt and uncle. I hope we will see each other soon as well! Kisses, your sister Eliza, Balkhash, 12 July, 1963."

"The letter took that long to get here?" Povilas flipped the envelope over

---

72   Rus. Povilas Liutkaitis
73   Rus. Balkhash

and inspected the postage stamp, which had been stamped 12 September. "Vytas, my brother-in-law. I've never seen him, except in photos… Good thing he is visiting… Good thing the letter came in time. How much time do I have left? Two weeks? Three? I'll have to prepare everyone."

After placing the letter back in the envelope, he picked up his daughter under her arms and lifted her up high: "Rasa's flying!" With the medal clenched tightly in her little fingers, the baby extended her arms and began to giggle. "My champion is flying!"

The little girl's bright laughter brought the rest of the surprised family into the kitchen – only now did they realize that their Great Rower had come home.

*

The next day, the rain ended and gave way to an unusually hot end to August.

The press was ablaze with red headlines – "Vilnius' Žalgiris eight wins silver and the four wins bronze," "Back from Copenhagen with medals," "Žalgiris' rowers – European championship finalists." However, these headlines hid a disappointment in the team's results. "This annual competition was unusually unsuccessful for our athletes, who didn't win a single gold medal," "Sportas" wrote. The "Komsomol Truth" also pulled no punches: "Over all, the Soviet Union's team had a poor showing at the championships. Not a single gold medal was secured." The "Truth" paper joked that "the final races at the European Rowing Championships were more like a submarine race… Bagsværd Lake near Copenhagen seemed like a giant aquarium," "Our country's rowers took their several European championship gold medals to Bagsværd Lake and recast them into one silver and two bronze medals. The races were unsuccessful."

The silver medal was just another defeat for the eight.

The four's victory was the only one that everyone discussed and wrote about with joy – "Bronze medals are a great prize for their first race at the European Championships!" "In their debut at the European Championships and fight for gold medals, our men – Eugenijus and Romas Levickas, Povilas Liutkaitis, and Celestinas Jucys – rowed well and didn't lose by much to their experienced opponents." "Truth" published the following headline – "Participating for the first time in such a large international competition, THE ROWERS FROM VILNIUS DID

FAIRLY WELL, WINNING THIRD PLACE AND A BRONZE MEDAL AT THE EUROPEAN CHAMPIONSHIPS," – in block letters and placed a photo next to the article featuring the four in centre stage, with a smaller inset featuring the Žalgiris eight.

"Being a novice is not so not bad," Povilas smiled to himself, "but that probably only happens once, the first time… Now, everyone will want more and more from us…"

*

29

The world of Lithuanian sports was still living off of their fond recollections of the Spartakiad. News of it could still be found in the pages of "Sportas". The Spartakiad displays still stood in the streets of Vilnius, but they had been so soaked by rain that neither the athletes nor the prints were visible.

Meanwhile, Moscow was preparing for the European Women's Rowing Championships. The Žalgiris women were also preparing for their first European Championships, together with coach Eugenijus Vaitkevičius. For everyone else, all that was left was the Lithuania-Poland match and the University championship.

This was the first time that Žalgiris' four would watch the students' competition from the shore, because the autumn also brought some fateful new changes with it – their carefree days as students were over. They would now have to train in the evenings, after work, and they'd have to run early in the morning somewhere closer to home. As a freshly-minted economist, Povilas was to receive his first real job on 2 September,, the day after the race in Trakai against the Polish rowing team – he would work as an accountant at the Vitenberg fur coat factory for a 90-ruble wage.

Now, he would truly no longer have time for anything except for work and training, with only whatever time was left over for home… Now, his photos would only ever receive one or two hours of attention. He could forget things like concerts, the theatre, or films for the time being. For the rowers, a seaside vacation at the beach was but a dream. And that was the summer when they say the Amber Museum opened up in Palanga…

*

The unseasonably hot beginning of that September was made even hotter by the first news from Khimki. At the European Championship that had begun on 6 September, the women's eight had serious competition to look forward to. Though they had been second in the Spartakiad, they were new to the international scene. It was a good thing that the championship was happening on what could be considered their home waters – the Khimki Reservoir they had rowed so many times before.

Ričardas also flew to Moscow to support his brother and the Lithuanian team.

Sports experts and journalists were still asking the question – why was the eight selected not the first-place Moscow women, but the Žalgiris women who had taken second place? Their anger was quelled by USSR rowing federation chairman Konstantin Morari: "This year, the Moscow women significantly updated their team roster. An experienced rower, Goncharova, left the team. This changing the team's competitive level. The crew could only sprint short distances quickly, but they need to learn to distribute their strength over an entire kilometre. In this respect, the Žalgiris crew was the best one available..." Of course, he didn't tell journalists about the qualifying races they held almost every day and the many exhausting sessions they had done to prove themselves worthy of being the USSR's first crew. Or perhaps this was a consolation to Lithuania for the quadruple scull that had been unfairly eliminated... In any case, without Eugenijus' stern words, everything could have ended much differently for the Lithuanian women. And there wasn't even a single attempt to "strengthen" the team by replacing any one of the nine women with a Russian rower.

Five eights– the USSR, Germany, Romania, Poland and Czechoslovakia – would qualify direct for the final, so evaluating their strength was incredibly difficult. Almost all of the teams had undergone changes since the previous year, so there weren't really any ways to compare them. They would simply have to line up at the starting line and do their best.

There was good news from Moscow and the soviet team camp – the four and the quad had already won gold medals. There were three final races, two of which included Baltic teams. The Latvian women Pumpura and Melenberga were to race in the double scull.

*

Tuesday's newspapers once again flashed out in red – "We congratulate the women's golden eight!" "The women of Vilnius' Žalgiris – European champions!," and "Great job, Žalgiris rowers!" Eugenijus' girls had achieved a strong first-place win, leading ahead of the Germans by more than a length. All of Lithuania celebrated. The Soviet Union celebrated too, because all five of its crews had won gold at the championship. The men of Žalgiris also celebrated, although they also felt a returning sense of sadness because of the heights of the European Championship that they had failed to reach. It had all seemed so easy for the women...

The stranger Kazys's letter was placed in an envelope with a picture of the cinema in Druskininkai and a red, 4-kopeck postage stamp. It was addressed in Russian and sent from a mailbox on Lenin Avenue to Kaunas.

*

30

What followed was a warm and peaceful September and a break from training and camps. Whoever wasn't chained to their work or their families flew out to relax in Sochi. The Sports Committee handed out tickets to Sochi every year to its best athletes.

Lithuania was still reverberating with shouts of congratulations for the European champion women. They were invited to meetings with the leaders of the Supreme Council, the Sports Committee, editorial staffs, schools, and labour collectives. They, just like the men of Žalgiris a year before them, received a grand reception at Žalgiris football stadium during the half-time . They, just like the men the previous year, ran a victory lap – with bouquets in their hands, oak wreaths on their necks, and with their eyes lowered modestly – before a crowd that gave them a standing ovation. Almost every day, the newspapers published photographs of Ala Perevoruchova, Irena Bačiulytė, Aldona Margenytė, Stasė Bubulytė, Leokadija Semaško, Rita Tamašauskaitė, Gita Strigaitė, Sofija Korkutytė, and, of course, Eugenijus Vaitkevičius – all smiling. In "Sportas", Eugenijus thanked the Communist Party and the Government for the attention they had paid to his crew.

The men's silver and bronze medals were soon forgotten by all.

However, despite all of the honour and praise that the women received, only the men looked forward to the last remaining years before the Olympic Games. The Olympic programme did not yet include women's rowing, and the next international race for the Žalgiris women was only in 1964 at the European Championships in Amsterdam. The Žalgiris men's eight and four were written into the list of candidates for the USSR Olympic team, but that meant a long and exhausting battle for a spot in the Olympic team. However, that battle would only begin after the New Year. Now, it was time for a holiday. Their training in Lithuania would only begin in October.

Only Romas failed to make it into the team's list of candidates. He had hoped that Samsonov might not have noticed his painful finish during the race in Bagsværd, but it was not to be. "Your Romas can't keep up with the others," he briefly informed Ričardas of his decision to replace Romas. Soon, Romas received his draft for military service, which athletes were usually sent to when they had to be separated from the team – as if "by coincidence." As if it was just an inconvenient occurrence – "you have to fulfil your duty to the motherland..." After basic training, however, it was usually too late to return. It wasn't yet clear who had thrown him into basic training, either. It could've been the KGB agent for whom Romas had refused to write a report upon his return from Copenhagen. "There was nothing suspicious there, I didn't see anything," Romas answered curtly. "Write!" the agent commanded. "I'm not going to write anything, that's not what we agreed upon. I didn't see anything and I don't have anything to write!" And that was the end of their short conversation – nobody from those governmental bodies ever spoke to him anymore. They probably understood that they had made the wrong choice... Or perhaps they discovered that, in Copenhagen, Romas had secretly done an interview with the BBC about the relationship between the Russians and Lithuanians on the team. Maybe he was taken for "re-education," but who knows...

*

"You know, Povilas, I think it's time for Audra and I to get married as well...," James said one day as he visited Povilas to pick up some photos. He shyly awaited his friend's approval.

"Oh, why not? Do it as soon as you can! How long can we go without a good party?" Povilas rejoiced.

"That's what I'm saying," James smiled.

"So what's the problem? Have you proposed to her yet?"

"We've discussed it..."

"Autumn is the time for weddings. The camps will begin later. Don't delay!"

"There's one problem... We don't know what we should do..."

"What is it?" Povilas studied James carefully.

"You see, Audra's father lives in Canada..."

"You want to invite him to your wedding?" Povilas asked, surprised.

"No... I'm afraid that when we get married, they won't let me out into the West anymore..."

"That's right... you'll probably be nevyezdnoj...," Povilas agreed, laughing. "So find someone else! Some communist gal..."

"Man, your sense of humour some times..."

"Jokes aside, you either marry the one you love or the one that's convenient."

"But what should I do? We want to have a family and live together, but I want to row, too..."

"So don't get married!"

"So how should we live together? As partners? We'll be denounced by the Komsomol... they'd never give a libertine like me a recommendation," James smiled sadly.

"Then get married in a church and live your lives! You'll be honest before God, and that's that!"

"Yeah, right! So they'd tighten my restrictions even more? There is no God, Povilas!"

"I don't know, James, I don't know..."

"We keep looking for a way out and can't think of one."

"Have you proposed to her yet?"

"I guess so..."

"Congratulations, then!"

"What if..."

"What if you throw a party and just tell everyone that you guys signed a civil union?" Povilas interrupted him.

"That's what I just thought of!" James remarked with surprise.

"Right? Everyone will know you guys are together and you can live your lives. If they check your documents – no connection with the rest of the world!" Povilas explained, happy to have found a solution for his friend.

"I had been thinking about that, too. We'll go to the church, but not to the civil registration office. We'll just have a party instead," James seemed much happier.

The men liked their unexpected brilliant plan and began to prepare for it. They enjoyed secret affairs like these.

"Povilas, I need trusted witnesses who won't say a thing," James said as his face grew serious. "Since you're already entangled in this mess..."

"There's no question about it, James! Nobody's going to hear a peep out of me!"

"I knew I could trust you... You'll need a woman as well. Could Gita do it?"

"Probably not. Every moment she can spend with her daughter is dear to her..."

"Who out of our own people could I ask about this..."

"Irena?"

"Hmmm, she might agree. We won't tell her much. Audra will tell her something, since they are friends..."

"There you go."

"Would you take pictures?"

"Of course!"

*

Now that he had the occasional free weekend, Povilas had a good opportunity to visit Prienai, where he hadn't been for so long, to see his uncle, his aunt, and his sister Ona. He showed them Rasa, who had grown. He would also help them dig up potatoes, collect the apples and pears in the orchard he had planted, and help them stack their firewood. Sometimes, he visited his Mother's grave or his relatives in Strielčiai, or invited them to his aunt's home. His hands had missed the earth, even though he had once thought that he would never want to weed another garden patch or chop another piece of firewood for as long as he lived. "I'll have to tell them that Vytautas is coming and that Elzbieta may return soon with her children. I'll tell my uncle about Copenhagen and about the race. He finds everything interesting. I can't forget to bring some photos. This autumn feels more like a summer – I will be able to go swimming in the Nemunas as well.

*

31

Everything settled into a routine on Čiurlionis Street after the summer. Finally, everybody was home. Mother would leave to clean university auditoriums when it was still dark out, while Father would sweep leaves off of the Čiurlionis Street sidewalks. When they woke up, everyone at home would find the table already set with steaming tea. Kazlauskas the naturalist's birds would chirp on the other side of the wall. Soon after, they'd hear childish chattering and the pitter-patter of bare feet on the floor. Developed photos were hung up to dry on a rope next to the laundry in the bathroom, and piles of photos labelled "Sportas," "Copenhagen," "My photos," and "Rasa" came and went from the living room table. Everyone would hurry to the trolley-bus station whenever they heard the slam of their neighbour's door.

During the weekends, things worked a bit differently. There were family walks through Vingis Park, guests, meetings with sisters, general household tasks, and long conversations in the evenings. Everyone was happy and there was enough room for everyone. When they heard that Elzbieta's unknown husband would be arriving from Balkhash, there were no questions about where he would be given room to sleep or how he would be fed. They prepared as though they were receiving a very special guest. For his arrival, they even saved up a bit of white bread loaf, which was only ever sold to families with young children.

Vytautas arrived on 26 September, as promised, from the train station. Povilas, who was on his way out to work, recognized the tall, strong man with thick hair looking around the gate from the photos Elzbieta had sent him.

"Might you be Vytas?" Povilas approached him boldly to greet the surprised guest.

"I am. Hello, Povilas," he extended his hand to his brother-in-law, whom he too had only seen in photos.

"Hello! How was your trip?"

"It was long... Balkhash is pretty far away, apparently... I hoped to arrive yesterday, but I was late to board the train in Moscow."

"No problem. Elzbieta said you'd arrive yesterday or today. Let's go inside. I'll introduce you to my in-laws and you can have something to eat."

"Is this where you live?" Vytautas asked, looking around the university courtyards.

"Yeah, here with my in-laws. They moved here from Tauragnai after the war."

"It's beautiful here. When I lived in Vilnius, we'd visit Vingis Park."

"You lived in Vilnius? I had no idea."

"Yes, my previous home was in Vilnius. After that, I no longer lived in Lithuania..."

"Let's go inside. I have to hurry off to work. You can rest and have a walk. In the evening, we'll have a lot to talk about."

"I hope I'm not a burden..."

"Nonsense! I've been really looking forward to meeting you. The only issue is that it's mid-week, so I have to go to work. I'll try to get them to let me leave early."

"I'll just put my things down and head out into the city. I'd like to see Vilnius. I haven't been here in so long..."

The men turned towards the low door that led to the long corridor, at the end, the smell of food wafted through the open door. They heard the clatter of metal dishes and the chirping of birds.

"Birds?" Povilas' guest asked in surprise.

Povilas cracked a broad grin:

"That's the apartment of a naturalist named Kazlauskas. Sometimes, his grass snake gets out, too. His home is full of life!"

Vytautas smiled. It Povilas wasn't convinced that he had believed him.

"Come in," Povilas opened the door. "Vytautas is here!" he shouted to his mother-in-law working in the kitchen and his father-in-law, who was listening to the radio. "I'm heading out. I'll try to be home by four. Farewell, Vytas!"

There was so much he'd have to ask Vytautas... He was the closest person to his sister Elzbieta. The sister that the war had separated from him so cruelly seventeen years ago, when he was only eight years old and he hardly knew her. She was a grown-up high-school student at the time, while he and Juozas had both been just little boys who cared about nothing more than racing toy boats, running around in the fields with their neighbours' children, and skating on the frozen creek... As he thought of the creek, a hard lump of tears rose in Povilas' throat. That had been the last day he had seen Elzbieta. Only a few hours later, their home was engulfed in flames, their mother lay on the ground in a pool of her own blood, and his father and Elzbieta were taken from him to God knows where... He, still a child, kept hoping that he would soon see them – that his father would soon come home and that his sister would come wash his hands and sit him down at the table, pour them some soup, give them a slice of bread, and stroke their heads the way she usually did when helping their mother. Then, she would fix her braids, seat little Ona on her lap, and start telling stories about the high schoolers' adventures with her and Kazys... Povilas' unbearable longing and hopelessness returned, as did the feeling of guilt he had that he hadn't done anything to rescue and save his family. Throughout his childhood, he would look with envy at any of his peers who still had at least one of their parents, let alone both of them. Such children seemed like the luckiest people on earth to him. They had someone to hug, someone to share their fear and pain with, and they always knew that they wouldn't go hungry or barefoot because their parents would always give them their last morsel of food. They would never have to look for a way to earn a coin or two for a notebook or shoes.

*

"Who took the photos?" Povilas asked as he flipped through the photos with the eyes of a professional.

"A man named Vasilijus, a neighbour," said Vytautas. "Vasia."

"My sister's beautiful. She looks like our mother. And your children are beautiful. How old is the little girl now?"

"She'll be two on 20 January."

"She's older by Rasa by half a year. Do her brothers love her?"

"Do they ever!" Vytautas broke into a broad grin.

The two men remained alone by the kitchen table. The rest of the family had already eaten and chatted. Gita had left to put Rasa to bed and Povilas' in-laws had left to get some rest. The pavement outside the window emptied out and the streetlights lit up. They couldn't see the sky through the trees, but it was supposed to be a starry night. Vytautas pulled a bottle of cognac out of his suitcase, uncorked it, and filled their glasses.

"How did you and Elzbieta meet?"

"She never told you?"

"She just mentioned that both of you wound up in Balkhash."

"Yes, a strange coincidence. Over ten years, our paths always crossed as they transferred us from concentration camp to concentration camp, but we couldn't see one another because of the high walls. We only figured it out later. We began in Ukhta and ended in Balkhash."

"Ukhta? Did Elzbieta tell you that our father was there as well?"

"She didn't need to. If not for him, I might not have met her. He slept right next to me on the lower bunk, just through the doorway."

"My father? Stasys?" Povilas' heart began to race in his chest.

"Yes, Stasys... He told me about you, as well. He said, 'if you make it out of here alive, help my children with at least a word of advice or a bite of bread.' As it happened, they released us from the Balkhash concentration camp in '56 – fifteen men and two women, Elzbieta among them. We talked to each other and shared our experiences. That's how we came together."

"I see... I never understood what she meant by 'father's friend...' So you're probably the only person who knows how things truly ended for him, right?"

"I might not be the only one, but I don't know who else survived there or where they wound up..."

"My father died in Ukhta..."

"Right, you could say he died in my arms... I visited him on his last day in the hospital. The next day, he was gone... the morning of Christmas Eve..."

"Christmas Eve? You mean 24 December?"

"Yes, yes..."

"My mother on Christmas Day, my father on Christmas Eve... He only lasted a year. Mother probably called him back to her..."

"He didn't want to live anymore. He no longer saw any purpose. He didn't believe he would be able to escape that place. He starved... many starved there... He was desperate to be with you. He said, 'I'll protect them from there, up high,'" Vytautas pointed towards the sky.

Povilas' lip began to tremble. He rubbed his eyes with his hands so he wouldn't burst into tears.

"Let's have a drink, Povilas," he extended a glass to his brother-in-law.

The men lifted their glasses and, without hitting them together, empty them, nodding... After some silence, Vytautas continued:

"Stasys told me a lot about you guys. I knew Elzbieta well by the time I met her. I also knew about you and your brother, and about Kazys and Ona. In the evenings, after work, we would lie on our bunks and have long conversations. He said that he had been a Lithuanian military volunteer and that he had received land because of it. I'll never forget how he talked about nature – about the beautiful pine groves by the bends in the Nemunas, about Bagrėnas Hill, about the nightingales' concerts... Every time I listened to him, I found myself in Lithuania. It was as if I could smell the fields and the forests... He told me about how he had worked as a forest ranger. About how he had logged the forests, how he planted trees, how he'd go foraging for mushrooms with his sons and sing songs..."

Povilas nodded, but he couldn't say a word. He bit his lip and swallowed the lump that had risen in his throat. He felt as though he would break down in tears if he uttered a single word. Vytautas poured them another glass each. The men raised their glasses, took a deep sigh, and emptied them. Povilas looked the photos over in his hands, nodding as he wiped away the rogue tear that had fallen onto a photo.

"Did my father say why he wound up there?" Povilas looked up after he calmed down a bit. "Did he tell you what happened to us that Christmas?"

"He did...," Vytas said, falling silent. He watched Povilas, wondering whether or not he should continue. He waited a moment, , "We told each other everything. He always tortured himself with the question 'Why?' He always beat himself up about what had happened. He thought that your mother didn't have to die. If she had said something while climbing the ladder. Out of fear, he had been unable to say a word. That's why the men in the attic shot their guns through the lamp, when they saw someone's head and a light appear. They threw a grenade into the porch... He said that there was a big firefight and that it took them three wagonloads to cart away all of the *stribai* afterward..."

The memories of that fateful night came to life in Povilas' mind once again, and again he was overcome with hopelessness and a sense of guilt. He could still feel his childish scream inside of him, hear his crying brothers, and how little Onute said, "my feet are cold, Uncle..."

"He really agonized over all of you. He'd say, "If I knew what has become of them, it would be easier to die"... He always waited for news from home, but he never received any. He said he had received one message in the summer, while still in Marijampolė... but out there, there's no telling when your post will come, or whether it will come at all, or whether someone hasn't intercepted or stolen it... Sometimes, someone would be walking by with their post and the jackals would come and take it away."

"You know, we were still kids... We saw everything differently. We had a beautiful dog named Murza, so I cried a lot for him... I didn't understand that I would never have parents again... Everything happened so fast..."

"Your father tormented himself over you guys... He kept on talking about each and every one of you..."

"How did he die?"

Vytautas leaned back, took a deep breath, clapped his hands down on his knees and looked up at the ceiling, working to keep his own emotions down as well:

"He was very exhausted. And then he decided to starve himself as well... He died in the hospital... There was a medical assistant there named Edvardas. He told me that my countryman had asked me to visit, that he was doing poorly and that it was unclear how much longer he had left to live. I went and I could barely recognize Stasys – he was lying in bed with a yellow and sunken face, and only his eyes moved when he blinked. He didn't even have the strength to speak. He had eaten nothing but water and government bread for a month and had decided to end his life on his own terms. He had no more hope that anything good would come from the Russian system..."

"Why did he decide to leave us? Why didn't he try to survive for us?" Povilas looked up. "We were still little children, orphans who had lost our mother... he was the only one left for us..."

"I don't know... I can't answer that... Everything was too hard over there... He had already become very exhausted on the way there. He probably never recovered from the interrogations: they had us in those train cars for about a month... He didn't believe he'd ever be free of the camps. He knew that his loved ones or friends would have to sacrifice something that could have gone to you so they could send him something. Maybe he didn't want to be a burden... Those places filled you with hopelessness. It seemed like you'd have to live in those barracks for ages, without food or warmth and constantly being kicked and insulted... He probably believed that he could do more for you from heaven than from the concentration camp. I remember that final evening when I visited him. I left the hospital and saw the beautiful northern lights outside... After that, I understood that that was how Stasys left our world. His tired heart found its way back to you and Lithuania along that shimmering path..."

The men grew silent again. Lost in thought, their tears welling up, they looked at their reflections in the window and at the amber-coloured glasses.

This time, Povilas raised his glass first and gestured towards Vytautas with his eyes. The clock struck one.

"What did you do there?"

"There was a forest in Ukhta. Chopping, sawing, and taking it all away."

"My father knew that work well..."

"He did. But everyone had to work like slaves there, hungry and cold. Wading through the snow in the dark. On both sides, you'd have guards on skis with dogs. All day, all you do is chop and saw. After work, you're in the dark again, but now you have to bring home wood to burn. Eat your slice of bread. As soon as you grew warm and fell asleep, they would wake you again with the sound of iron on iron. And again, march off into the forest in the dark..."

"This went on for ten years?"

"Some places had forests and others had construction. They took people from concentration camp to concentration camp in stages. It was hot in Balkhash and the work was even worse. Mines and construction... when you look back on it – ten worthless years. How do you think those cities were built? On bones, corpses and tears. How can slaves work? Every centimetre of that land is cursed, every brick...," tears began to well up in Vytautas' eyes as well. "I was also exiled when I was still almost just a child. I was seventeen when they arrested me. I had joined the Žalgiris football team in Vilnius. I weighed 98 kilograms, but a year later, I could almost reach around my waist with my fingers. My legs wobbled and I fell to my knees often on my way to work..."

The men grew silent again and looked out the window at the tree leaves blowing about in the streetlamp light. They sighed.

"There hasn't been a single day when I didn't think of them... How did Elzbieta survive all of that? Did she tell you?" Povilas asked quietly.

"We told each other so much. We both went through the same things and we could both understand one another... It was hard for her, as a girl, but she was young and strong, so she endured. In Marijampolė, an executioner named Raslanas interrogated her, and she still breaks down into sobs whenever she remembers it...we never talk about those times. I want her to forget as soon as she can..." Vytautas explained, pulling a handkerchief from his pocket. " You can't imagine what it was like. Torn away from your family and your home, somewhere in a foreign land with foreign people and brutal overseers... She said that the saddest part was when her friends in the barracks got letters from their mothers, while she no longer had a mother... Her mother died before her eyes because of her... She felt a great responsibility for her mother's death. She said 'it all happened because of me. I invited them. My parents didn't like it, they were afraid someone might see them and find out...' And you could say she didn't have a father, either... She didn't know he was somewhere nearby in Ukhta, so close to her. She received mail, but it didn't have letters from her mother or her mother's love. There was none of the warmth that a girl at that age needs so much... There was nobody awaiting for her back at home. You were all that was left for her. Her relatives had their own troubles, and comforting her was not high on their list. She wrote to cousins and friends, but few wrote back... Maybe they were afraid, or maybe the letters never reached her as she moved between camps... Maybe nobody wanted to reveal that they had known Liziukas..."

"Liziukas?" Povilas looked up.

"That was her codename. Didn't you know? The partisans gave it to her."

"How would I have known it... Nobody told us anything. We'd hear someone talking quietly, but Juozas and I didn't know anything. We were kids and only cared about running through the fields... I thought that that had been the only time she invited the forest men into our home..."

"That wasn't the only reason they arrested her. She was a liaison – she gathered food and medicine for the partisans... And she carried the Freedom Scout. Do you know the Freedom Scout?"

"No," Povilas shook his head, looking at his brother-in-law with a questioning glance.

"It was a newspaper published in the Tauras partisans' district. In your region. I'd never seen it, I only heard of it from Elzbieta."

"Perhaps I did see something at home on the table, but I didn't understand it then. I just remember the Lithuanian flag and a long text written using a typewriter. My sister always quickly hid it, so I thought they were her love letters..."

Vytautas smiled sadly:

"She said that she wasn't the only one arrested for those "love letters" of hers. She heard that the teacher from the high school and some of the other high school students were arrested.

"What did they take you away for?"

"Just like everyone else... for anti-soviet activities," he uttered quietly, assuring himself that they were alone.

"Don't worry, everything's peaceful here," Povilas reassured him.

Vytautas continued, nearly at a whisper.

"I worked at an industrial bank as an accountant. There was an underground group in Vilnius called the Mortals. Partisan liaisons. A man named Noreika from the Lithuanian People's Council gathered them together. I wound up in the group through the Šileikaitė sisters. We were all young – some were eighteen or nineteen, and I was seventeen. We were university students, pedagogical institute students, and a few of us from the Spindulys printing presses. Everyone came from their own villages and knew the partisans there – from the Panevėžys, Trakai, Alytus, and Žemaitija legions. There were liaisons between the partisans and the Council. We collected medicine, paper, pencils, and ammunition, and we distributed the 'Bell of Freedom[74]'. Those who worked at the printing press brought us typographic fonts. I brought paper from the bank. At the bank, while inspecting the premises for repairs, I found cartridges – Russian and German ones. But they tracked us down. We were the first to be arrested – about seven of us on 22 March. Then they got the others, too. I had just returned from a work trip to Radviliškis and had been able to meet with my family. They interrogated us until the middle of August and then there was a tribunal. They tried nineteen of us all at once; half of them were girls. Most of us got ten years with five more years of exile. Some got a bit less. The interrogations were terrible. One-on-one at first, and then in groups. They'd repeat the same questions over and over. They wouldn't let you sleep. They'd take you away at night and keep you on a stool until morning with a lamp in your eyes. If you grew weak and fell off of the stool, you'd wake up quickly from the jackboots kicking your head and stomach... When we met during the trial, we could barely recognize one another – that's how tortured and bruised we were, how much weight we had lost. They took almost all of us to Ukhta."

---

74   Lit. Laisvės Varpas, a newspaper published by Lithuanian partisans.

"They interrogated you in Vilnius?"

"Yes, in Vilnius, in the basement of the NKVD building."

"But you're not from Vilnius?"

"No, I'm from Radviliškis. I just worked here for some time. I was born in Gudžiūnai in the Kėdainiai region. I'm going to go to Radviliškis now as well. I have to see if I can return and bring my family home. We don't want to live there anymore. We want to come home."

"How is your mother? Is she still alive?"

"She is... I'll see her tomorrow. You know, Povilas, I'm afraid. I gave her so much pain... My father, in the mean time, didn't make it... He left us at 53..."

"Don't worry, Vytautas. Trust me, your loved ones don't care why you were sent away. The most important thing is to see you and hug you."

Vytautas nodded his lowered head and, for the first time, seemed to be at a loss. With his head in his hands, he tried to fight back his tears.

"Maybe you're right. Tomorrow, we'll see..."

"I can't wait for you guys to return. I haven't seen my sister in seventeen years... I can't wait to see her! I always used to think that she's about to show up at the gate. When I was little, I would never leave the window... I was waiting for my mother and my father... Juozas and I didn't see each other every day, because he was with another aunt in Strielčiai. We were twins: as children we were inseparable... Kazys was always nearby, but it was hard for him to be a father to us. He was only fifteen. He needed a father, too. You know that feeling when you're torn away from your loved ones... It seems like everything has been cut off... It's like all you need is to hold them close, hug them, and all of your troubles will go away. People can't live alone after all, we so need someone to be close to..."

"Yeah, yeah, I know that feeling well... I lived with that feeling for ten years... Povilas, did you have any trouble travelling abroad when your sister was a political prisoner?"

"I did, of course... They didn't want to let me go for a while and pulled me out of the eight. Then they put me in and pulled me out again when they had to go abroad... I was pushed around for two years."

"What did you do to finally get to leave?"

"What could I do? I rowed and I rowed until I broke through the barbed wire fence...," Povilas smiled.

*

In the morning, Vytautas left for his parents' home to Radviliškis, promising to visit again on his way to Balkhash to pick up gifts and letters for his family.

That same day, 27 September, the home on Čiurlionis Street received another stroke of good fortune – Gita's sister Genutė gave birth to a son. Vida had a new brother, Gita's parents had a new grandson, the sisters had a nephew, and Rasa and Audrius had a cousin.

"Life never stops," Povilas told himself, hugging his daughter and beloved wife close. After taking a deep breath of the refreshing autumn air, he smiled at the maple trees, which were sprinkling Čiurlionis Street with their leaves, and immersed himself into the whirlwind of a new day. The stories he had heard the previous night would long yet torment his heart and leave new, painful scars there, and still he could not spill his heart out to anyone or seek comfort. Those thoughts would always be with him and always remain close. Both Christmas Day and Christmas Eve would now be a holiday of grief, with visions of death returning every year...

Yesterday's warm, summery day had given way to one that truly smelled of autumn. Small clouds gradually covered the clear sky, bringing with them showers of mist.

*

32

The year was coming to a close, and there were more and more hints circulating about the approaching Olympic Games in Innsbruck and Tokyo. Aldona Margenytė from the Žalgiris women's eight smiled out at shoppers from the covers of the latest issues of 'Soviet Woman' magazine lined up in press kiosk windows.

Yet another free-time activity appeared on Lenin Avenue in Vilnius – the Vilnius cinema. Visitors could go see an old British movie – The Life and Adventures of Nicholas Nickleby. Gediminas Jokubonis received the Lenin award for his sculpture, the Mother of Pirčupiai. Women hurried to bookstores to buy the newly published 'Hostess' Almanac', and those who were lucky also bought Stendhal's 'The Charterhouse of Parma'. They bought their children 'The Swan Will Rule Alone' for Christmas.

The large new National Library was completed and opened in Vilnius near the Youth Stadium.

The first woman astronaut, Valentina Tereškova, married astronaut Andriyan Nikolayev.

The world was swept by a wave of Beetlemania, but in Lithuania, the only news of them came from the hearsay accounts of those who had managed to go abroad or to "catch" foreign radio waves.

In the beginning of October, Hurricane Flora killed 7,000 people in Cuba and Haiti, and on 22 November, America lost its president, John F. Kennedy.

The world also discovered the next Olympic city – the 1968 Olympic Games were to be held in Mexico City.

125 Lithuanian athletes received Sports Master badges, and the number of physical culture advocates swelled to 400,000.

For the first time since 1960, the rowers didn't make it into the top-ten list of the LSSR's best athletes. The women's Žalgiris eight was named the best team, while the men's eight was left in fourth place. They were surpassed by the Atletas handball team and the national gliding team. This was a painful injustice for the rowers – someone considered their European silver a lesser achievement than glider pilot Jaruševičius' USSR champion title and the handballers' victory in the national championships. It seemed as though the sports world had grown accustomed to Žalgiris' victories and that a change of face would be more interesting.

James danced at his wedding. A huge group of rowers, coaches and friends gathered. It seemed as though everything had gone smoothly according to his and Povilas' plan. However, a couple of days later, he was called by the KGB to explain himself and his deception. Povilas was invited as well...

∗

Though he had just begun working at the fur factory, Povilas soon had to knock on his manager's door to request permission to leave for training camp. Of course, nobody would be paying him any sort of wages for the time spent at the camp, but his family still had to eat.

"Get signatures from the Sports Committee," Ričardas suggested as soon as October training began. "Starting after the New Year, we'll have to prepare for the qualifiers and the Olympics at full speed. We won't spend much time in Lithuania."

Of course, the factory had never had such a famous athlete before. It was a new and interesting experience for everyone. The management and his colleagues supported him and didn't resist, allowing their young specialist to leave for eleven months. Luckily, the Committee had paid a 120-ruble stipend for the European medal. Together with his wages, that was almost what a professor would get, but what could he do – he had to choose.

∗

Next came 1964 – the Olympic year, a celebration that happened only once every four years. Almost half of all news stories concerned developments from Innsbruck and Tokyo. Whether they were good or bad wasn't as important – the important thing was that there was finally something to read. People thirsty for a life of freedom devoured news about the free world.

The world began to count the days left until the year's largest sporting event. The Winter Olympics were to begin on 29 January in Innsbruck, and nine months later, the Olympic flame would travel to Tokyo.

The boat builders in Kaunas received a large order and began to make oars for the Olympic team and paddles for canoes and kayaks.

The rowers began preparing for the Olympics immediately after the New Year by skiing and with a general physical fitness competition in Zvenigorod. The eight and the four were joined at the camp by Jonas Motiejūnas and Vladas Milieška. There were rumours that Jonas would replace Romas in the four. After his basic military training, he had lost his form.

After returning home for just a few days, they flew out again for Bakuriani, to the familiar mountains of Georgia and to the wonderfully clear sky and pine-scented air. There, they could get half undressed and walk along mountain paths, climb up to 2,400 metres, ski among the incredibly tall fir trees, bathe in snow, and enjoy slalom competitions and other fun activities on their off days. In the evenings, they gathered at the lobby of their cottage to play chess, wait for news from Innsbruck, read, write letters back home, study, or just chat. Each morning at six, the medical staff would burst into their rooms, connect their equipment, take cardiograms, poke them with their fingers, and rattle their test tubes. Scientists would lay the athletes on specially constructed beds with dynamometres to measure the strength of their legs and arms and write dissertations. Once a week, the athletes would race on the ski courses and compete in the sports gyms while their coaches sketched charts, filled in numbers, pushed names around, crossed things out, drew arrows and added exclamation and question marks.

Only Celestinas didn't leave for Bakuriani. As soon as he returned from Zvenigorod, he was drafted into the military and left for a month of basic training. A month would leave a huge hole in his exercise regimen that he would have to make up for at other camps if he didn't want to be left overboard. The rowers could only guess at who had made an effort to get Celestinas stuck in basic training and why, but nobody dared name their suspicions out loud. Once – in '61 – Celestinas became the USSR champion when Zaikauskas was removed from the eight for basic training that made him fall behind.

In the first days of March, the entire rowing team descended from the hills and travelled 460 kilometres east – to Mingachevir in Azerbaijan, a still-young city built by German prisoners in 1948. It was built with a dam on the emerald-coloured river Kura, which flowed from Georgia. There, they were awaited by their boats, which had grown lightly dusty over the winter. The area had a newly built three-door brick boathouse – the first structure built for the upcoming Olympic rowing centre. Though it didn't look very new – the brickwork wasn't very neat and it wasn't very straight – its construction had been a significant event nonetheless.

Celestinas also flew in from Vilnius from the camp after being released from basic training.

Nobody was surprised when Jonas Motiejūnas was invited onto the four crew and Romas was placed in the pair with Vladas Milieška. From now on, however, the four would be different – it would be coxless. Only a few coaches knew who had decided to put Žalgiris in a coxless four and why. "It'll be better this way," Ričardas responded briefly. "You'll just have to learn to steer. Eugenijus is a naturally born cox, so he can do it." Probably... Rowing at full strength at the highest stroke rate and remembering to turn one's right leg to one direction or the other to turn the rudder, which was attached to the foot stretcher with a cable, was no small feat. However, it could determine the success of a competition. Last year's European Championships had been an excellent lesson for those who couldn't control their rudders...

That was the beginning of a long training regimen on the water. They sometimes rowed 30 kilometres in a session. It was 17 kilometres downstream, or 15 if you took the shortcut. The return trip was all the same, but against the current. The current flowed much more quickly in narrower parts of the river. After their first training session, the blisters on their hands began to bleed. The iodine bandages they used every evening dried out their wounds but didn't heal them. Towards the middle of the camp, the skin on their fingers became hard and calloused, remaining this way until the end of the season.

Qualifying races in pairs and fours became an everyday occurrence. The team tried to find the best crew lineup by switching rowers from boat to boat in various combinations. However, this seat-racing exhausted the rowers – mentally and physically. There was almost no time for the work planned by their coaches – the work and the athletes' strength were overcome by the constant races.

*

On the horizon, the emerald waters gave way to an emerald sky. They were pierced by a knife-sharp ray of sunlight from the rising sun, incredibly bright, yet refreshing. The water was as smooth as glass. Standing on the green slope, all you would want to do is open your arms and fly. Suddenly, he felt a hand on his shoulder. He turned around and saw his mother's face in the sunlight. She was dressed in a long, red dress, and she was smiling, but she didn't say anything, only stroking his head and growing distant along the green grass fields. "Why did they tell me my mother was dead? Mum, wait!" He wanted to shout out and follow her, but his voice wouldn't follow his commands and his legs wouldn't obey him, no matter how hard he tried...

Povilas opened his eyes when he heard a knocking on the door. "Get up!" the coach's voice echoed down the hallway in Russian. He closed his eyes again and tried to return to his dream, but the images were fading from his mind, leaving only the feeling of well-being that his mother's hand and smile had left him with. "What a dream...," he thought, burying his face in his hands and enjoying the fading feeling before his teammates started waking up from their sleep.

"Padjom!" Povilas shouted, running past his friends with a towel and a toothbrush as he pulled off his friends' covers.

"Now hold on, I'll get you," Eugenijus hopped into his shoes in an attempt to threaten his friend, but the door had already slammed shut.

Though that day was a free day, the morning regimen was the same as always. They would exercise, eat breakfast, and then do whatever they wanted to.

In addition to their morning food, breakfast had an additional benefit. Whenever Murad, the letter-boy, appeared in the doorway, everyone in the cafeteria who was expecting a letter would drop their forks and run to the "post table." Though few read while they ate, a long-awaited letter sitting by one's coffee made it taste that much better.

"Did you get anything, Povilas?" Celestinas , pouring him a cup of tea as he returned to the table.

"Yeah, I did," Povilas' face lit up. He was one of the most frequent recipients of letters, given that he wrote them nearly every day as well. He placed it next to him and patted it – it was from Gita.

"You're lucky. People just keep writing to you."

After depositing his breakfast plates, Povilas ducked through the door and tore open the airmail envelope, which was marked around the edges with red and blue stripes.

The envelope contained two cuttings from "Sportas". One, with a red headline, read "Boats for the USSR's Olympians." It was about the boats made by Dzintars in Riga. He set it aside to read later. The other headline, from March 7, was entitled "The Champions' Stories." It was about the Žalgiris women's eight. He would read that one later as well. The letter was brief, because that was how Gita wrote. The sheet of grid paper had been neatly cut from a notebook. "Everything here is fine. Thank you for the 8 March postcard. The flowers are very beautiful... I have sent you a few newspaper articles about rowing. Perhaps you'd like to read them... At home, it's the same old story. It's not spring outside yet, but the snow is melting. It was very cold on Women's Day. Rasa was sick and had a cough, but she got better quickly. I think she might have a brother or sister one day..."

A wave of warmth washed over Povilas' body. "A brother or sister..." – his eyes began to blink rapidly and a few hot tears began to roll down his cheeks. He turned to the window so that the men walking by wouldn't see him. It didn't matter that they were great tears of joy – the idea that "men don't cry" had been hammered into him from his early childhood... "There's what my mother wanted to tell me in my dream... How does she know everything?" Povilas raised his eyes up towards the sky and towards the clear, blue morning sky and the sunlit, budding trees. Nature was waking up from its slumber. A new and beautiful spring was beginning.

*

By the end of the camp, they had formed the crews that would challenge for a place in the main Olympic team, right up to October. The only rowers that raised no doubts for the team's coaches were single rower Ivanov, double scullers Tyurin and Dubrovskiy, and the Žalgiris eight. There were many competitions still ahead of them. Convinced that the best basis for preparing for the Olympics was simply increasing the workload, the team's coaches had no doubt that they could only achieve the results they had planned for by squeezing every last drop of energy out of the athletes. Their plan was to have gold medals for the single, the double scull and the eight, silver medals for the coxless pair and four, and bronze medals for the coxed pair and four. And, of course, first place in the team standings.

*

33

When Žalgiris' rowers returned to Lithuania in the mid-April, they found that their waters had already thawed. The women, who had returned earlier from their camp in Poti, were already rowing on the Neris. The men's boats, however, went straight to Trakai. The Neris was swollen with meltwater, and the river carried debris and sticks that it had swept up from its banks. However, this didn't stop anyone from rowing. On 1 May, someone hung a photo of a rowing oar cut out from a newspaper and a poem underneath it up on the wooden wall of the boathouse:

"A BALLAD FOR SPRING
The ice on the river has left,
The ground's getting dressed all in green,
You know you could never forget
Your oars and your fond thoughts of spring...

The races will colour the waters,
And the boats that slept through winter's night
Your sleepless nights will grow longer,
When the cherries in the garden grow white."

The anonymous poem was soon passed around by word of mouth, especially among the women, and when the students' spring vacation began, it became a song that would often be accompanied by guitars during the warm sunsets at the Trakai boathouses.

*

The men and women of Žalgiris had missed the still waters and were impatient to begin training on Galvė Lake. Though it was often windy there, they would finally get to experience some true competitive rowing and gauge their actual speed. There was just a month until the first selection race, and every day had become a valuable one. It was a good thing that the USSR team's coaches would no longer be around. Their methods had raised doubts not just among the rowers, but among their coaches as well. The rowers often had to hide from them to ensure that they avoided over-training.

The Žalgiris centre's wooden building had not yet warmed up after the winter months and it wasn't yet a very cozy place, it was downright cold during the nights. Those who had the option returned home at the end of the day and could at least train in dry clothing the next day. Others tried to light the ovens to dry out the walls and the moist air in the rooms. The fickle May temperatures varied from 10 to 20 degrees during the day and sometimes fell to 2 or 3 degrees at night. The women shivered from the cold when they gathered on the pontoon in the morning with their toothbrushes, and that was all the men needed – to tease the women by splashing them with the icy water of Galvė Lake.

In the men's room, the rowers enjoying their afternoon recovery hour. The wind and the rain raged outside. Those who had "endured" the morning session read in their beds, slept, or focused on studying their notes. Their sports kit had been hung up to dry above their heads, but it was doubtful that they'd dry before their next session in just a couple of hours.

"James – you're lying there and looking at the ceiling. Why aren't you doing anything?" Celestinas, lying on the next spring mattress bed over, asked his friend.

"So what. And what are you so busy with, Celestinas?" James lazily turned his head to Celestinas, who was lying in bed just like he was.

"I'm very busy, actually. I'm serving in the Soviet army!" Celestinas retorted.

"Ah, that's right! I forgot! Serious work, that... 'The soldier sleeps but his service never stops!'" James laughed.

"What are you guys joking about?" Povilas opened his eyes.

"Celestinas and I are arguing about which of us is doing more important work."

The door opened and Ričardas walked in.

"On 25 May, we're going to Kavgolovo," he announced. "The Moscow-Leningrad match will be our first selection competition. We have to win. Take care of all of your affairs tomorrow and the day after so that we can train at full capacity. Every session is important. Are we clear?"

"Yes," the rowers responded in unison. Their coach's words were more than just an order. An order had to be fulfilled whether you wanted to or not. They, however, unconditionally trusted their coach's word. None dared to contradict him, except for Zigmas, who occasionally expressed his opinions. He had that right, but even he wasn't often allowed to speak by the coach. There was a time when he would simply send home anyone who complained or was lazy and replace them. After that, it was very difficult to return to the team.

"When we return, the Baltic championship will be on 7 June," Ričardas continued. "We probably won't make it in time for the national championships, because it'll be in the mid- week, on a Wednesday. If our boats do make it back in time, we'll row in that as well – another race can't hurt. Today, we'll do some sprints. Get ready."

The men began to stretch on their creaking beds. There was still more than an hour until their training session.

"Povilas, can I take a look at your book?" Jonas reached towards Povilas' cupboard.

"Sure, it's boring," Povilas yawned.

"What's this photo?" Jonas bent down to pick up some newspaper clippings that had dropped out of the book.

"Hey, now I won't be able to find my spot. I'm going to have to start all over," Povilas teased his friend.

"I'm sorry... I'll find it. Here, I think you were here," Jonas flipped to a yellowed page. "What team is this?"

"This is our eight, back when Celestinas and I were still on it."

"Why aren't you in it now? I never understood the change, after all... Didn't you guys row with them?"

"Well, we were 'nevyezdnoj' back then, so they pulled us out," Povilas cut straight to the point.

"Why?" Jonas was surprised.

"'Vrag naroda!'" Povilas smiled. "They didn't like my family's history."

Jonas stopped his questioning and pressed his lips tightly. A wave of unease and doubt swept over his body. In the spring of '51, KGB officials came to his home in Kyburiai in the middle of the night where his family lived and took his father... Nobody knew or understood why, what for, or where – where they locked him up, where they took him, or how much time he got – even his wife, Jonas' mother, couldn't find out... As the years passed by in total uncertainty, fear and pain, a letter came from the concentration camp in Ukhta – "Gruodis lent me 25 rubles. When I come back, I'll return them." That was all the message said, but it had to be read correctly – he had received 25 years in the camps because Gruodis, the district party secretary, had said something about him... Jonas had been ten at the time... He would only see his father when he turned 35... But at least he knew he was alive. Four years later, the "thaw" began. His father's case was reviewed and, in the absence of evidence for his collusion with the partisans, he was set free. Without any deportation or restriction on his freedom... "If anyone digs it up, they might not release me, either"- Jonas thought to himself. And he too had begun to dream of going to the Olympics...

*

34

The weather in Kavgolovo during the last weekend of May seemed much like a real summer. The thermometre stayed at 21-22 degrees. If not for the wind, one could even go tanning. On the day of the competition, a crosswind picked up, the waves from the far shore picked up speed, and the course began to feel much like the one at Khimki. The official name of the competition – the Moscow-Leningrad Match – had long since stopped representing its size and purpose. All of the country's strongest crews gathered here. This year's match was especially important – this was where the candidates for the Olympic team would begin to be tested and where their strengths and weaknesses would be tallied. Whoever gathered the most "pluses" or victories during the season would go to Tokyo.

For the women, this competition also represented a team selection process, just not to the Olympic team. The most important race of the year for them was at the European Championships in Amsterdam.

Celestinas' four entered a competition for the first time with its new crew – with Jonas in the two seat.

After returning home, Povilas hurried off to the "Truth" editorial office with the report he had promised.

"ŽALGIRIS' VICTORIES ON HEPOYARVI LAKE." The Žalgiris men's eight once again won with a confident lead. The Žalgiris coxless four however had a harder time of it (as Povilas said of his own crew). Two other strong crews that were also candidates for the Olympic team raced against Lithuania – Leningrad's Trud and the rowers from Dynamo. Once again, everything was determined at the finish line. With long and harmonious strokes, the Žalgiris crew broke out into a lead and won by a second over Dynamo, who took second place. With a victory in this race, Žalgiris coxless four member Jonas Motiejūnas completed his Sports Master requirement for the first time... Ukraine's women rowers put up a tough fight for the Žalgiris women's eight, who only defeated the Ukrainians right before the finish line – by 0.4 seconds.

Spirits were high on the Lithuanian team. After such a successful showing, three boats would be heading to international races. Though they had all won their first "plus," there were more selection races ahead of them. Only the men's eight could feel relaxed. It was unlikely that anyone would catch up to them. Miracles like that didn't happen in rowing.

*

Upon their return to Lithuania, they had an even warmer summer to look forward to. Daytime temperatures reached 27 degrees. Everything was blooming and fragrant.

After their victories in Kavgolovo, Lithuania's strongest rowers managed to compete in the national championship as well, which was to be held on Wednesday in Trakai. There were no teams fit to rival them there, but participating in the Lithuanian championships was a matter of honour for them, so none of the crews had any doubt whether they'd race. Beating their opponents was easy, but beating themselves wasn't. They had to keep on trying to stretch their abilities and put forth the best times they could manage.

It was the same situation at the Baltic Championships, which was held that same weekend. Two of Moscow's Spartak women's fours also came to test their strength, though they had no serious competitors. They were there to "select themselves" for the regatta in Grunau.

Both fans and large television teams descended upon Trakai to see Lithuania's best rowers and possible future Olympic medalists. The cameramen filmed from the shore, from the umpires' boats, and from the start pontoon. They filmed the impressive finishes, the oak wreaths and lilac branches the winners received, the coxes as they swam, and the happy athletes' faces. The spectators filled the grandstands and bobbed about in rowboats crowded up next to the race course.

The most impressive lead at the finish probably belonged to Celestinas' four, which finished 28 seconds ahead of the Estonians. The women's eight left the competition standing finishing 19 seconds ahead. The men's eight finished with a healthy lead over the Estonians as well, and with a very good time – 5:53.4. The new coxed pair – Romas Levickas and Vladas Milieška – also did well, finishing 9 seconds ahead of the second-place competitor. There was finally a streak of good fortune for the men's double scull from Klaipėda who had finished third in their event in Kavgolov, but here, at the Baltic Championships, they won. The single sculler from Kaunas won as well.

The Lithuanian team welcomed the summer with a broad grins after their confident victories over their neighbours, Latvia and Estonia. The results suggested that the season of '64 would be a good one.

On Monday morning, Povilas once again hurried to "Truth"'s editors with photos he had developed overnight and a new article that would be published on Tuesday, 9 June, with the title "The rowers' victorious races." The "Truth" editors were overjoyed to have finally found someone who could recount the rowers' achievements first-hand, who could do so in beautiful Lithuanian, who could provide such beautiful photos, and who could do so quickly!

*

June passed by in the blink of an eye. There was no time for anything between training, but food and sleep. Sometimes, after their sleep, it became impossible to make it out of bed for their afternoon training – that is how deeply their dreams called to them. Their bodies were so exhausted that even their mouths seemed to be melting. It was only after the first few kilometres that their eyes brightened and their muscles finally felt up to the task. However, nobody complained. Everyone knew why they were working so hard. Žalgiris' eights were the clear leaders in their own boat class and looked forward to a trip to England to the Henley Royal Regatta. Meanwhile, the four absolutely had to repeat its win at the Great Moscow Regatta. All of the coach's attention was focussed on achieving this victory.

"We do nothing but prepare for qualifiers," Ričardas complained to his colleagues. "We should be improving our form for the Olympics, but instead, we're improving it for the qualifiers. At this rate, we'll be totally exhausted by autumn."

He was right – maintaining such a pace for the entire season was incredibly difficult. The USSR team's coaches, however, did not agree.

Both Žalgiris and all of their primary opponents focused all of their attention on the qualifiers. Everybody was preparing for just one thing – to win the Moscow Regatta.

*

The Great Moscow Regatta presented the Žalgiris men's four with an Olympic set back. They lost to their primary opponents – Leningrad's Dynamo – by just 1.4 seconds. They had to start from zero again. There was just one consolation for the Žalgiris rowers – they had already won a trip to the regatta in Lucerne. If they were to race well there, they would get to go to the European Championships in Amsterdam as well.

"We have to see how they race abroad," head coach Samsonov decided. "We'll bring both crews to Lucerne."

This meant another selection competition and another psychological and physical battle. There was no more time for additional preparation, and there was no point in changing the training regimen, either – the competition was in ten days, and they were flying out in five. They would simply have to race and win. There would be nobody to consult with, either – Ričardas was on his way to England with the eight. This was a constant process – constant replacements, second teams, eight reserves...

In Moscow, before the flight to Lucerne, Jonas was called to meet with the KGB. He was the only rower who had not yet received the KGB's approval. His friends were afraid for him, as these weren't Vilnius' security officials – this was Moscow. There was no knowing what they were like. The KGB officials had found his father's case and questioned him at length about it. Fortunately, Jonas could now confidently tell them that his father had returned to Lithuania and was working at a kolkhoz. That was enough for them to allow him to leave.

*

A week later, Ričardas' eight brought the Grand Challenge Cup – the grand prize from the Henley Royal Regatta – back from England. This was the oldest and most important prize at the regatta, and it went to the best eight team in the competition. In addition to the prize, the Žalgiris crew entered a new number into the history of the regatta, hitting a new all-time record in the semi-final – 6 minutes and 23 seconds. In the final race, they beat the University of London eight by seven lengths, becoming the new stars of they regatta – the "Amazing Russians." Though the competition was at the club level, and the difficult-to-pronounce name "Club Žalgiris Vilnius, USSR" had been written into the competition roster, the team managers ordered the rowers to race in red shirts with the USSR coat of arms on the chest. Their oars had red blades as well.

With the impressively large and beautiful 125-year-old cup they brought home, the Žalgiris men were to once again march a victory lap around Žalgiris stadium and receive a standing ovation from the crowd of football fans gathered there.

*

35

When the eight returned home, the four had already flown out to Lucerne.

"Look at the mountains, Celestinas," Povilas admired the green Swiss landscape through the porthole as their plane descended towards Zurich's airport.

"Yeah, they look completely different from up here."

The men were stuck to the windows. James and others had told them so much about Switzerland that it seemed like they were landing in a real fairytale kingdom.

After an hour-long trip by bus, the team found itself in Lucerne in a hotel at the very centre of the city – the Bernerhof. It was just a few steps from the Lucerne Theatre and the historic bridge that they had seen in the postcards their friends returned home. The not entirely new but cozy little hotel had a friendly host, its own restaurant, and balconies from which they could see the river flowing by. Most importantly, however, Lucerne's town centre and its many shops were within arm's reach. The hotel would serve as the rowing team's home for a week. The unbelievably beautiful buildings, castles and bridges, the sky-blue lake surrounded by mountains, the cleanliness, and the order depressed the soviet rowers. As soon as they got out of the bus, they found themselves in the busy heart of an enchanting town, which practically smelled of cleanliness, refreshing water, chocolate and coffee.

Being together with their greatest opponents – the Leningrad four – proved to be no problem at all. Though both of the teams wanted to win, friendship among the team's members was a fact of everyday life.

It was two kilometres from the hotel to Rotsee lake, where the regatta would be held. Immediately after putting their things away and changing, everyone hurried off to see the race course. As they walked across that famous bridge for the first time ever, the men couldn't take their eyes off of the old frescoes, perfectly carved wood, and carefully crafted details. The bridge and the surrounding areas were always filled with tourists taking photos. Walking across this bridge would soon become an everyday occurrence, though, to shorten their trip, they often chose the straighter and shorter bridge a little way off. In addition, it provided them with a more impressive view of the old bridge.

Though the Rotsee wasn't much different from other rowing courses they had visited, it was still special – it had a neat, rectangular shape and was surrounded by green nature and the mountains. Cows with bells on their necks grazed at its shores, and a train occasionally huffed and chugged past the shoreline as well.

The grounds of the rowing club, which was surrounded by a residential neighbourhood, was neatly trimmed and enclosed with a wooden fence. The colourful Rivela sales tables and umbrellas next to the boats were a temptation for the rowers.

A photo in a black frame hanging on the wall of the centre caught their eyes – a photo of the men's fours that had died in an accident on their way to the 1958 Lucerne Regatta. They had represented Switzerland's Olympic dreams, and some of the men had only been eighteen years old. They might have become Olympic champions in Rome.

The mood of the approaching race could be felt at the rowing centre. The athletes carefully lifted their elegant wooden boats from the frames on the structures located on the top of the buses and put in their oars and riggers. One or two women could be seen among the men hurrying back and forth, but they were primarily medical personnel or local rowers' wives with their children. This regatta was just for men.

With a few polite glances, the men began to prepare their boat for the competition. There was no coach present, so they had to do everything themselves. However, their rituals had been repeated so many times that they didn't need to encourage each other and were soon dipping their oars in the waters of Rotsee.

"Hello, men!" they heard a Lithuanian greeting as they pushed off of the dock.

The men were startled – no Lithuanian rowers had come here besides them. They looked around and saw Kazys approaching from the dock – the same man they had met in Bagsværd.

"Who is he?" Jonas asked, surprised.

"That's a guy named Kazys. He was in Copenhagen last year," Povilas explained.

"A Lithuanian? A local?"

"A Lithuanian. He said he lives in London."

"He must be rich if he can travel this much."

"Looks like it," Povilas agreed.

"Do you think he came here just for the competition?" Eugenijus asked.

"Who knows. Maybe he misses Lithuanians," Povilas shrugged. The four rowed off towards the starting line.

*

The qualifying races went off without any surprises. Both of the USSR fours easily made it into the final, though the Lithuanians' time was a good five seconds faster than that of the Leningrad crew – 6:33.0 and 6:38.4. Both of the crews wanted to win, though the regatta wasn't as important to them as beating one another. The primary selection process for the Olympics would only be in the second half of August during the USSR championship, but an additional victory up until that point would mean an additional plus.

Like every year, Povilas brought his camera with him everywhere he went and took pictures of everything – his friends, rowing stars, his opponents, the races, the city, the shop displays, and the signs. It seemed like every step brought something new and unexpected - something he'd want to look at again many times once he returned home. He wanted to savor the feeling of wonder he felt in Switzerland over and over.

"Taking pictures?" Povilas heard a familiar voice from behind as he did his best to zoom in on the coxless pairs' rowing through the reeds.

"Yes, good day, - Povilas spun around and shook Kazys' hand.

"How's it going? There aren't many of you here, are there?"

"There's four of us this time, the four. The eight is at Henley."

"Yes, I saw, I was there. They had a beautiful victory. But why were they wearing those red uniforms? The programme said 'Žalgiris,' but they had a Russian uniform! That's all anybody said - 'the amazing Russians.' I kept trying to explain that they were Lithuanians, but you can't explain anything to a crowd like that. They're Russians, period."

"What can you do? If they tell them to race in red, they have to. If we could, we'd always race with "Lithuania," but they won't even let us wear our uniforms in the street – it's CCCP only. The programme here says Russland, not even USSR."

"By the way, Povilas, thank you so much!"

"For what?" he asked, surprised.

"For the letter you sent. They received it."

"Ah, I had forgotten," Povilas laughed. "Good thing they did. I didn't even add a return address."

"I know. That's why they couldn't find you."

"What did they want me for?"

"They wanted to send me some information. But it's alright," Kazys waved dismissively.

"I didn't think of that..."

"Listen, Povilas. Could I give you a letter this time as well? Would you send it?"

"Sure. It's not hard," Povilas smiled. "But why don't you mail them yourself, though? Do they not make it through?"

"Sort of. They do make it, but not all of them, and the ones that do are crossed out. They censor what they think is unfitting, or they just tear off half of the letter. All of their letters from abroad go through the KGB."

"Really?"

"Will you help me?"

"Of course, in a heartbeat! Bring it to me. However, I won't be in Lithuania for another two-three weeks. What if I send it from Moscow?"

"That might be even better. Less suspicion."

"Alright then, give it to me."

Thank you, Povilas. You'll be a great help to me," Kazys bowed, shaking Povilas' hand. "When are you going to race?"

"The final is tomorrow. We have to win against Leningrad, and I hope to God that we win the competition, too."

*

On the start line, the Žalgiris crew looked around to find their primary competitors – the Leningrad crew – but they couldn't see them. It was unusual for them to be late. The umpire, after finding the sixth boat absent, began his pre-race survey. Leningrad still hadn't shown up. Though it would have been much more pleasant to win in a true battle, the tension in the Žalgiris boat was reduced considerably when they saw that the Russians hadn't made it to the starting line. Now, all they had to do was row a proper race and be done with it.

After shooting out from the starting line, the Italians tried to break away with the lead, but the Lithuanians never let them get too far. The two crews raced neck-and-neck for almost half a kilometre. It was only with 500 metres left to the finish line that the Italians began to break away bit by bit. And that was how they finished – with the Italians first and the Lithuanians – or the USSR – second.

Just like in Copenhagen, crowds of Lithuanian expatriates chanted "Lithuania!" from the shoreline as they waved yellow, green and red flags in their hands.

When they returned after the award ceremony, they found the Leningrad rowers on the shore, sadly inspecting the broken stern of their boat. They had collided with the Dutch pair near the starting line.

"We'll repair it and send it straight to Amsterdam," Samsonov declared curtly. "Whoever makes it into the European Championships will race with it. Take the riggers with you on the plane. Don't load them on the trailer."

*

Their short journey was coming to an end. Hidden from the coaches and their political minders, they sold the caviar they had brought from Moscow in the restaurant next door and made their rounds through the local souvenir and chocolate stores. Upon returning to the hotel, they were greeted by a surprise from the hotel owner, Fulz. The good-hearted Swissman had unlocked the heavy wooden doors to his wine cellar and invited the rowers in to drink their fill, or even more. At night, they evaded their watchful minders and snuck out to enjoy Lucerne the nightlife. The dazzling signs, advertisements and shining shop displays were even more beautiful in the dark.

"Hold on, I've got to go get my camera," Povilas left his friends in the street and bounded up the hotel stairs, returning a minute later, switching in a new roll of film as he walked.

"You think the shots will come out ok?" Eugenijus wondered.

"There's no knowing if you don't try," Povilas winked. "Who knows if we'll ever return here again. Maybe it will work. I don't want to just leave this beauty behind as-is."

"You'll make it happen. You always manage something," Eugenijus smiled as the four teammates headed down the street for yet another breath of air in the free world.

*

36

The rowers were once again the centre of the press' attention, and not just their national press. In July, Ogoniok, a Union-wide magazine, published an issue with photos of both of the Žalgiris eights – the men's and the women's – on the cover, along with an article that took up three magazine pages.

When the team returned from Lucerne to Moscow and met with Žalgiris' eight, there were only two weeks left until their departure for the European Rowing Championships, so the team managers didn't let them return to Lithuania. As a result, they also had to miss the third Amber Oars regatta in Trakai, which had been moved to the middle of July that year.

The USSR team's training camp began at the Voskresensk tourism centre near Moscow. Only one boat hadn't been "selected" yet – the coxless four. They still had qualifying matches to look forward to. Once again, they didn't have any time to prepare for the championship in peace, having instead to focus all of their attention on the most important race ahead of them – the qualification race.

Near Voskresensk, the Moscow River was rather straight, and for at least two kilometres, they could row just as easily as on a rowing course. Of course, the current did have an impact – whoever caught the faster current would win, and whoever stayed closer to the shore would have a harder time of it. Both crews wanted to take advantage of this.

The coaches umpiring during the qualification race had a hard time keeping both of the boats straight in the swift river. One boat or the other was always being pushed half a length or more ahead. Even their motorboat almost drifted onto the teams prepared for the race a few times. When the race finally started, the straightaway on the river had grown about 100 metres shorter. After drifting off-course because of the current, the stern of the Leningrad boat shot out sideways at the start, cutting off the Lithuanians. After being warned three times by megaphone, the Dynamo crew just about managed to correct their course, but this left them in the middle of the river. The Žalgiris crew, forced to the edge of the river, was three boat-lengths behind the Russians. However, they started to catch up, growing closer stroke by stroke. On their Kazan motorboat, both of the teams' coaches and Samsonov followed every stroke and every crew member's effort and technique. In their hearts, they each hoped their team would win. With about 300 metres left, and Leningrad just one length ahead, the Leningrad crew again "drifted" towards the Lithuanians, sending dirty water down to their opponents and finishing ahead by half a length.

"It's not fair, Rychka!" the men argued after the race. "You saw what they were doing with your own eyes. From the very beginning, we weren't able to row consistently or put down any power!"

Their coach, also upset, spread his arms and shrugged:

"I saw it all, boys, but they said whoever wins gets to go."

Ričardas' reserved attitude and hesitance to challenge his superiors often worked to his team's detriment. The much bolder and more audacious Russian coaches often managed to influence Samsonov and win favourable decisions for their athletes – decisions that were sometimes dishonest.

"You go talk to him, Eugenijus," Povilas turned to Eugenijus. "He likes you. Maybe you'll come to an agreement."

Indeed, Yevgeniy Borisovich Samsonov did like Eugenijus – many thought that it was because they shared the same name. After telling him what to say, the men sent their teammate off to his negotiations and waited by the boat.

"Everything's alright, we'll have a rematch this evening!" Eugenijus announced happily when he returned.

"How did you convince him?"

"He said 'I saw it all with my own eyes. The race didn't prove any true superiority. I agree that we should hold a rematch.'"

Ričardas' face lit up – he had stayed behind to await the results of the negotiations. However, he felt uncomfortable for not having fought for his team.

"Good job, men. Go take a break. Eat well. You know what you need to do – get out of the start first. I'll try to make sure they don't start you until the boats are straight."

With their spirits raised and a new, more combative spirit, the men hurried off to the tourist centre to await their evening race.

"He's supporting the Lithuanians," Leningrad's coaches complained behind them. "A win is a win. We won."

However, the decision had been made and the rematch would be rowed.

That evening, everything went differently. There was a strong headwind, and even though the boats were headed downstream, they stood in place without drifting down. Since they knew that this was their last chance, the Žalgiris crew shot out of the start like wild animals. Their first strokes already gave them a lead of two to three metres. With every stroke, they added more and more to their lead, finishing three lengths ahead of Dynamo. This was the nail in the coffin in their tense battle of nerves.

*

After flying into Amsterdam on 1 August, and with less than a week until the beginning of the European Championships, the men's team managed to gett to the finals of the Women's European Championships. What they wanted to see most, of course, were "their girls" – the Žalgiris eight – fight for the gold. The women had also fought for this right until the very last moment. The countless selection and qualifying races eventually fell in the Lithuanians' favour. The purely Lithuanian team was represented by their coach Eugenijus, who knew who to talk to and when to talk to them.

"Your boat isn't here yet," a worried Ričardas told the four, "but Samsonov went to talk to the locals to rent something for you."

"It didn't arrive?" Povilas asked, still scanning the trailer for their four.

"They haven't finished repairing it. They promise to bring it by the time racing starts. We'll train today after the women's races," Ričardas explained, rushing off towards the boathouse when he heard Samsonov calling his name. "I'll be right back, wait here! Get your blades ready in the meanwhile."

The Bosbaan was full of athletes, coaches and journalists. The entire course, down to the very start, could be seen from the boathouse. At the end of the perfectly straight lanes, the women were nearing the finish line. There was always a crowd of men gathered by the water to watch the races or to feed breadcrumbs to the fish swimming in the water. The enormous grandstands were full of people gathered to watch a double rowing championships. A large truck with grandstands installed on the back decorated with Rivella posters drove back and forth along the bike path on the other side of the course. The spectators on the truck were ready to watch the races from start to finish. The scoreboard near the finish line, with its Longines and Rivella ads, could be seen almost as far as the starting line. Men and women rowers and their coaches rested on woven recliners in a large white tent, waiting for their races.

"Alright, you have a boat. Go to the boathouse, they'll show you. You'll just have to rig it," Ričardas waved to the men and hurried off to the eight.

They found a shiny, near-new four boat labelled "JASON" in the boathouse.

"It's beautiful," Eugenijus said, running his fingers along the hull.

"Let's pick it up," Celestinas told his friends.

The men carefully lifted the boat off of the trailer, turned it to the side so it wouldn't hit the boathouse doors, and carried it outside.

"It's so light!" Povilas noted with surprise.

"Yeah, nothing like ours," Eugenijus agreed. "It doesn't have its riggers on yet but you can still tell."

"Here, put it on the slings," Celestinas instructed them, and the men slowly lowered the boat.

"It's so well-maintained! It looks new," Povilas exclaimed happily. "I just might need to readjust the stretchers and that's it."

"I think so too, they seem too close," said Jonas, looking for his pliers.

"Who has the spanners? Let's rig it now and see about the heights on the water, there's no sense in changing them now," Celestinas suggested.

"We might be fine with the height. Let's just adjust the stretchers and go watch the final," Povilas said, finding a spanner and bending down over "Jason."

"I'll adjust mine, too," Celestinas bent down to adjust his stretchers. "Eugenijus, check the rudder."

Suddenly, the announcer's voice grew excited, and the men looked up.

"The double? Are the Latvians winning?" Eugenijus tried to spot some red shirts.

"Let's run and see!" Povilas grabbed his camera.

"Let's go, we'll finish when we get back," Jonas put his pliers down on his seat and all four of the men hurried off towards the grandstands to watch the Latvians, Maja Kaufmane and Daina Melenberga, become European champions for the second time.

Upon returning to the boat, the men found the women's Žalgiris eight preparing for their race. After exchanging a few words, they understood that now was not the time to tell jokes or try to distract the women, who seemed like tightly coiled springs. Instead, they got back to work on "Jason." The eight and the pair's coach polished their own boats alongside them.

"We're going to the hotel. The bus arrives in twenty minutes," Ričardas announced out loud. "The competition finishes at six and then we'll go on the water."

"We can't watch the eight?" James asked, surprised.

"We don't have time. If we do, we'll have to spend a long time waiting for the bus, and you guys need to eat. You'll find out the results. There's no sense in sitting here, you guys need to rest."

*

The women finished in second place, losing to the Germans by three seconds. The USSR team's good fortune from the previous year, when the women won all of their races, was not to be repeated. This time, single rower Konstantinova, the Latvian double, and the Moscow Spartak four won gold. The quad, like the eight, came in second.

By the time the men rested and returned to Bosbaan, the number of boats was considerably smaller – the girls had finished taking derigging and loading their boats onto the trailers, and were neatly packing their riggers, seats and oars. The winners proudly walked about with their medals around their necks while others watched them, jealously. However, all of them were now relaxed, chatting happily, joking and laughing. Their championships were over, but the men's championships were about to begin.

*

"How's the boat?" Ričardas asked after training as he approached the four.

"Excellent!" the men responded in unison. "It glides really smoothly, it's comfortable, it's a pleasure to row."

"Just be careful with it, make sure nothing happens."

"What could possibly happen? We'll be safe."

"You can see that there's not much room to warm up. Be sure to follow the rules in training so you don't veer into another lane. The lanes here are good, but you should still be careful."

"Of course! If everyone else follows the rules as well, nothing will happen."

"Exactly! We can't answer for others. Keep an eye out!" Ričardas warned the men once more before returning to the eight, whose rowers were chatting with their opponents from Ratzeburg.

"It would be great to race with 'Jason' here," said Povilas, stroking the Swiss boat.

"Maybe they won't bring ours. We could win with this one," Celestinas said hopefully.

"It's a pleasure to row with her," Eugenijus agreed. "And it's so easy to steer!"

"Should we ask Ričardas for this boat for the competition?" Povilas shared a thought that had just occurred to him.

"Hold on, maybe the other boat won't arrive at all," Celestinas reassured him. "Maybe we'll stay with this one anyway."

*

With a day left until the beginning of the championship, Leningrad's four boat finally rolled into the Bosbaan on its trailer. The bow of the boat didn't seem too bad for having been glued on, but such a large scar couldn't help but impact the boat's handling. After bidding farewell to "Jason" and returning him to the boathouse, the men lifted "their" boat from the trailer and began to prepare it for the competition. The old Leningrad four was nothing like "Jason," which was a strong and elegant boat. Their's was well-worn and patched, and was not only heavier than the Swiss boat, but heavier than their old German boat at home as well.

"Shit, this boat's no good," Povilas swore as soon as they paddled off on their practice run.

"Yeah, it seems heavy," Celestinas, who was sitting in front of him, agreed. "The other one was so good!"

"Maybe we just have to get used to it," Jonas suggested.

"We don't have time to get used to it, we race tomorrow," Povilas said, searching for a more comfortable sitting position. "Something's wrong. Can we try adjusting the slides?"

"Are you leaning on something?" Celestinas turned around.

"It's breaking my legs. I have no idea how they rowed with this."

"We'll adjust it when we get back. Let's deal with it for now."

The session was dominated by the effort to control the heavy, uncomfortable boat. Their starts and bursts were nothing like those of the previous day. The boat rolled from side to side and the oars hit the rowers' knees, even though the water was calm.

"What should we do?" the men couldn't hide their disappointment when they got off onto the dock after their session. "Maybe we should ask them to rent 'Jason' for us again."

"Let's go talk to Ričardas, maybe he can take care of it for us," Povilas suggested, taking a determined step towards the group of coaches standing nearby and nodding for his friends to follow him.

"How did it go?" their coach greeted the rowers.

"Not well. We can't row with that boat. It's no good for us. It doesn't sit level and it's heavy," the men heaped their complaints one on top of another at their coach's feet.

"Could we race with the Swiss boat?" Povilas worked up the courage to ask what the whole crew was thinking.

"I don't know, we should ask."

"It went so well yesterday. It was like a dream! We could win with it. This one's like a bath, though."

Ričardas scratched the back of his head and, after looking around to see whether any of the team's managers could hear him, said, "I'll try to ask, but I don't know."

"We really need it, Rychka, nothing good will come of the other one."

"Alright, we'll try. Go wash up so we can go home," the coach nodded and turned towards the boathouse.

The men watched their coach walk off with doubt in their eyes.

"Let's wait to see what he says," Povilas couldn't let it go. "It'll be easier when we know how we'll have to race tomorrow."

"If he can find anyone there," Eugenijus said doubtfully.

"If he wants to, he'll find someone. If not at the boathouse, then elsewhere. We have nothing to lose. Either we get "Jason" or we lose to everyone. Nobody's going to offer it to us if we don't ask."

"You're right, Povilas, we have to stand up for ourselves next time, as much as we can. Whether it's giving up your oar or your spot...," the pain of Celestinas' past came rushing up to the surface. "If they don't manage to sort this out, perhaps that means they don't want to..."

"He's coming," Jonas quietly warned his friends.

"I doubt he's got good news," Eugenijus said, trying to read the coach's face.

"It's no good, boys," Ričardas announced, with his face turned away. "The boat has already been rented to someone."

"Is there another similar one? Any of the boats here would be better than Leningrad's!"

"I can't do anything, your boat is gone."

"Maybe you could talk to Kabanov. Maybe he can make a deal..."

"That's who I was talking to. He said 'I can't help you.'"

"Someone simply doesn't want to help us," Povilas retorted sadly, turning around to leave. The men turned their heads down and followed him.

"What can you do? The Dutch probably fear us. They don't want competitors like us," Eugenijus considered.

"Or, somebody in our management doesn't want us to have a good race, so they could say 'the Lithuanians are falling off ahead of the Olympics,'" said Celestinas, who still couldn't believe that the boat was taken.

"It could be anything," Povilas agreed.

"We can't change a thing now. We have to prepare for the second scenario now and try to row as well as we can," said Eugenijus, trying to regain his faith in himself.

"We'll row it, but who knows if we'll do as well as we can?" Povilas said doubtfully. "Let's go at least try to look at the rigging. I don't understand what's wrong with it."

"Me neither," Jonas agreed. "It's not too high and it doesn't wash out."

"Same for me, and the rudder is loose as well," Eugenijus agreed uneasily.

The men spent almost two hours by their boat, which they would need to learn to use over the next three days.

*

The four had bad luck in the draw for the qualifying heat – they would have to race the Italians again. After their loss in Lucerne, the Lithuanians felt uneasy around the Italians. The tail wind wasn't very favourable. The heavy boat had a hard time gliding forward. The Lithuanians remained level with the Italians and broke away from them at the finish line, but the Dutch rowers, who had a better lane, finished even more quickly. Second place meant a repechage race, an additional race they would have to row. Meanwhile, "Jason" rested quietly in the shadow of the boathouse.

"I knew nobody would be rowing it," Povilas said with disappointment.

"They did it on purpose," Celestinas agreed. "They could see the boat was doing well and didn't want us to win. We'll qualify during our repechage, and then what?"

"We'll see, we can't decide on anything now."

"At least we beat the Italians," Eugenijus tried to cheer them up.

"Yeah, that was good. It's a draw for now," Povilas smiled, wiping his brow.

"Perhaps we won't be put in a race with them anymore."

"Are you afraid of them? You think it was fluke?"

"Who knows? It didn't seem like they were holding back."

"Oh, if only we had 'Jason' again! I can still feel how that boat glided under us..."

"Who qualified in the first race?"

"Probably the Germans. Who else could it be?"

"They should've brought the boat later. We would have got into the final with 'Jason' and wouldn't need the repechage."

"Can't turn back time."

"Let's go have a drink, my mouth is dry."

The men marched off towards the Rivella umbrella together, keeping their eyes on the course. The eights were supposed to start soon.

"So what happened, warriors? Lost your edge?" Kabanov commented in Russian as they walked past. "You'll make it through the repechage."

"We know, but we could've made it through today if they'd have given us that boat," Povilas revealed.

"What boat?"

"The Swiss one we trained with."

"What's the problem?"

"We don't know. They said it's taken, but we can see it lying there."

"Really? I hadn't heard. Who said that?"

"Rychka. He already asked, but he said they won't give it to us."

"I'll ask around. I just don't know if it's worth it now. Nobody changes horses mid-stream..."

＊

It was six kilometres from the course to the hotel. A bus that travelled to and from eastern Amsterdam every hour took the athletes to their training sessions and races. The rowers' home was the large and modern eleven-story Casa Hotel, which had been opened just two years ago and was primarily for students. It was located just a few blocks from the Amstel river crossing. Some of the windows looked out on Frankendael Park, the narrow canal that surrounded it, and the Amsterdam summerhouse area. Other windows looked out on an Amsterdam suburb with a real mouthful of a name – Oosterparkbuurt – and the port behind it, which bristled with cranes. The double rooms had beds that were much too short for the rowers, but they had showers, bathrooms, radios and telephones. The large windows, which took up almost the entire wall, made the small rooms feel larger. But how much space did they really need? Only enough to stretch out their legs and set down their two brown pieces of luggage – one for each rower. The restaurant on the first floor was the rowers' meeting place. They discussed their most pressing matters while they ate.

"Put in another session in the evening. A few laps. You've got a race tomorrow at 10:30," Ričardas quickly briefed the four as he walked up to their table. "There should be an even stronger tailwind tomorrow, but everything should be fine."

"That boat is heavy. We might be ok against the wind, but with a tailwind, everybody will leave us behind," Povilas once again tried to appeal to his coach.

"Everything will be fine. I watched from the sidelines and there's no difference. Eugenijus, lengthen your catch a bit, it's not quite in time with Povilas'. Have you guys eaten? Go rest."

Without saying anything else to their coach, the men finished eating and left for their rooms. In the hallway, they met their friends from the eight. They were in a jovial and carefree mood, having won their heat by a huge margin. There were only seven eights, so it hadn't even occurred to anyone to fear not making it into the final.

*

The repechage wasn't difficult, but the four weren't happy with their rowing. They couldn't seem to master the boat.. "Jason" remained in the boathouse, untouched.

"We could go rent the boat ourselves, but where could we get the money?" Eugenijus wondered, still hoping for a miracle.

"I brought a camera to sell," Povilas smiled.

The men looked at him, unsure of whether he was serious:

"Are you kidding?"

"Why not?" Povilas smiled. "I could sacrifice it for a medal. You'd chip in to pay me back afterward, right?"

"Stop joking around," Eugenijus said, having believed that Povilas might have been telling the truth. "You'd be better off buying something for your kids."

"Kids?" Jonas looked surprised.

"Povilas is going to have a second one soon," Celestinas explained.

"Is that right? Then definitely make sure you save your camera. You'll have two kids to photograph so you'll need two cameras," Jonas joked.

The men all laughed, but they all longed for a grain of hope and good luck.

*

On the day of the finals, the wind calmed down and turned to blow from the side. The water was almost as smooth as glass. The beautiful, sunny day attracted thousands of well-dressed spectators to Bosbaan.. The sky occasionally became overcast before clearing up again, but it was nothing like the previous year's championship in Copenhagen.

The first of the finals were, as usual, the coxed fours. The united Burevestnik and military naval crew scored a confident first-place victory and, at least initially, raised the team coaches' and managers' spirits.

"If you can catch up the Italians, you'll be fine. The Germans and Danes are very strong right now. They're probably in good shape," Ričardas was direct. "When you pass the kilometre mark, pick it up. Povilas, help Celestinas get into the rhythm."

"With the other boat, we'd be alongside the Germans, too," Povilas nodded towards the boathouse.

"That's enough, forget the other boat. You won't get it. You have to row well with this one."

"We know, but when everyone's racing with good boats and we have to chase after them in a pig trough, it's no fun. We had the opportunity to race with a good one but they took it away from us."

Ričardas looked up at his team:

"Who took it away?"

"We don't know, we can only guess."

"How about carrying your oars instead of guessing," Ričardas no longer knew what to say. "Everything will be fine, just hold on to them, don't let them break away. Keep up there right from the start. You've got lane two. The Germans, Danes and Italians will be on your left, but don't look around. Pick up the pace on the third five-hundred, as always," Ričardas looked at his clock, "It's time. Go."

*

All of the boats left the start line together. Only the Danes managed a small lead after the first three hundred metres. The Lithuanian – or, as their competitors knew them, Russian – crew was rowing in the traditional configuration with alternate bowside and strokeside rigging. The other five boats had adopted what was known as the Italian system – right-left-left-right. Scientists were still fiercely debating whether or not this configuration actually gave them any sort of an advantage at all. The new "trend" was another way to try to get the boat to glide even more smoothly and quickly.

The Lithuanians, Germans and Italians remained bowball-to-bowball until the middle of the race. The half-way mark was the hardest part of the race, when the rowers felt like their strength was spent and that they had no air left in their lungs. However, Ričardas had chosen that moment in each race to be their greatest sprint. The "third five hundred" had been their secret weapon so many times that it had even begun to hurt less than usual. After breaking into third place, the Žalgiris crew carefully watched their opponents to the left out of the corners of their eyes. The Italians had noticed the Lithuanians' sprint and picked up their pace as well. The heavy boat was resisting their efforts to accelerate, rolling from side to side. Povilas hissed through clenched teeth – "They're gaining on us!" – and sharpened his catches to drive the stroke onwards. This time, however, something was wrong. The rate increased but the boat didn't move any faster. Instead of increasing their speed, their rowing became a convulsive racket, where the only thing left of their rowing technique was the tempo. Žalgiris finished at forty strokes per minute but still finished fourth. All they needed was a quarter of a length – and some luck and some strength...

The Danes, who had started so well, caught two large crabs in the last few metres of the race, finishing second to the Germans...

*

There is probably nothing more disappointing in sports than fourth place. Just a step away from a medal, just a few strokes, and just a bit more suffering at the edge of losing consciousness – that would've done it. Unless, of course, you expected to finish sixth, in which case fourth is two whole places better. However, this is rarely the case. If you've made it to the final, you want to win a medal – even though that might sometimes take a miracle.

Of course, second place is almost as painful as fourth if you are convinced you will win or if your margin of defeat is microscopic – like a 0.02-second loss: impossible to see with the naked eye and requires a photo-finish to decide. That's when you understand that even a stronger portion of a single stroke might have been enough. Second place also hurts when it follows you around like a curse, and when everyone looks forward to your gold because your silvers have become boring. This is what happened to the Žalgiris – or USSR – eight. The curse of second place. The four envied the eight's silver medals, but the eight was overcome with grief and shame.

Only Ivanov and the Tyurin-Dubrovskiy double scull managed to overcome their opponents. The coxed pair with Rakovschik and Safronov also came in second.

*

The colourful spectators at Bosbaan seemed playful and carefree. They took pictures with their cameras, smiled, waved "Hi!" to each other as they passed one another, and generally improved the unpleasant atmosphere of the final day. They could no longer change a thing, so there was no sense in exhausting themselves with questions of "why" things had gone as they did. Their former opponents became their friends, and the photos they took with the Danes and the Italians would remind them of yet another journey to a beautiful and free country. Perhaps they would meet each other soon at the Olympics for an opportunity to get back at them. For now, however, they had to enjoy the time they had left abroad and see a bit of the Netherlands. The spectators in the grandstands were still humming the songs they had heard during the Beatles concert they had attended in the beginning of June, and posters in the streets invited people to the very first Rolling Stones concert in the Netherlands, which would be happening that same day.

"Do you speak English?" a man about the same age or a bit older than the Lithuanians addressed them as they browsed souvenirs at a tent.

"Yes," Povilas turned around. He had received a 5^{75} in English at school, the highest grade possible.

"How did the race go?"

"Not very well. We were fourth."

"Good job! Congratulations!"

"Thank you," Povilas smiled sadly.

"You wanted medals?"

"Yes. We were third last year in Copenhagen."

"Fourth place is good, too!"

Povilas shrugged, remembering how poorly the final had gone.

"What is life like in Russia?"

"We're not from Russia."

"But it says CCCP here, right?" he pointed to the letters embroidered on the front of Povilas' sweatshirt.

"We're Lithuanians."

"Do you speak Russian at home?"

"No no no, we speak Lithuanian," Povilas shook his head.

"How do you say 'Hello' in Lithuanian?"

"Labas. La-bas."

"Lyabas," the man smiled. "What's your name?"

"Povilas. It's Paul in English."

"I'm Richard," he extended his right hand to Povilas. "That's a nice photo camera," he said, noting the FED in Povilas' right hand.

Povilas lifted the camera up and inspected it.

"I have two of these," he smiled. "I'm selling one."

"Is it new?"

"Yeah."

"How much?"

Povilas shrugged:

75

"A hundred," he hadn't been ready for such a quick deal.

"Deal, I'll take it," the man said, pulling his wallet out of his pocket.

Glad to have been able to quickly get rid of something he had brought to sell, Povilas continued to talk to the stranger named Richard – about photography, about competitions, about Lithuania, about his family and his home...

"Do you know Kazys?" Richard asked out of the blue.

"Kazys?" the unexpected question surprised Povilas.

"Yes, Kazys, from London. He was at Lucerne, too. Do you remember him?"

Povilas instinctively looked around to make sure he didn't know anyone nearby before shyly nodding his head:

"Yes, I remember. You know him?"

"He asked me to give you this letter."

Everything seemed very strange. "How could this Richard person have recognized me? How did he find me? How does he know Kazys? Who is Kazys? Why are there so many coincidences? Someone who knows Kazys suddenly needed my camera and has a letter from him... it seems like everything was planned ahead of time."

"A letter? For me? From Kazys?"

He pulled a brown envelope that had been folded in half from his inner coat pocket and gave it to him.

Povilas felt like he was in a detective film. Now, all he needed was one or two people in grey raincoats to turn the corner and start following him. However, all he could see was the rush of the colourful crowd. Even his teammates had gone off somewhere – probably to the trailer.

"Here's my card," said Richard, extending a business card to Povilas. "If you need any help, you can call me. Here's my number and address."

Povilas placed the envelope in his backpack, brushed his sweaty palms on the sides of his tracksuit, and scratched the back of his head. He still had no idea how to respond to the stranger appropriately.

"It's a nice camera!" the man waved, holding his new FED in his hand as he gradually disappeared into the crowd of spectators who had left the grandstands.

*

Povilas brought home an entire roll of film from the Amsterdam old town filled with photos of bridges, canals, bicycles and bicyclists, homes, store displays, automobiles – everything that was different from his life in Lithuania. He spent the hundred guilders he had received for the camera on a suitcase full of gifts for the women he loved.

The men were still looking for opportunities to "shake" the KGB officials monitoring them and to have some free time in the free world, speaking Lithuanian out loud intentionally so nobody would confuse them with Russians.

One of the 'Uncle Vasyaes' on the team would write the following about Povilas in his report: "Conspiratory separation from delegation."

＊

37

There were exactly two months left until the beginning of the Tokyo Olympics and exactly two weeks until the USSR championship – with less than two weeks to prepare for the final qualifiers for the Olympic team. In reality they had less than two weeks because the trip from Amsterdam through Moscow back to Vilnius would take almost a week, with long waits and transfers – and all to eventually fly back from Vilnius to Moscow again.

The USSR championship in Khimki was supposed to be the final say, so any mistakes or surprises there could decide their fate. There was no room for error – whoever won would be going to Tokyo.

Sample kit and dress uniforms had already been sewn for the Olympians. This was the first time that the athletes' kit would feature four colours – red, blue, turquoise and white. The men's recreational shirts and women's skirts were decorated with Vologda "Sniezhinky" lace. A red hammer and sickle shone out from the white background of the Olympic team's pins, along with the year "1964" and golden Olympic rings.

Japan published its first series of five postage stamps that featured the Olympic flame and the country's primary athletic arenas. The most passionate philatelists waited in front of post offices in Tokyo overnight, buying two million postage stamps in just a few hours.

Practice for the Olympic opening ceremony began in the national stadium in Tokyo.

*

Khimki had intense battles to look forward to. In the early morning, hundreds of spectators began to gather to watch the future Olympians.

The weather was excellent – it wasn't too hot. However, Khimki's waves had nothing to do with the weather. Boats continued to criss-cross the waters as they always did, carrying cargo, passengers, and tourists having fun.

"You understand that you have to win," Ričardas repeated. "The most important thing is to get ahead from the very start so you can control the situation. If you win, you go. If you lose, you stay. Leningrad looks mediocre. You shouldn't have any problems with them."

The men, diligently polishing their boat, listened to their coach quietly. In their state of mind, they didn't feel like speaking or listening to anyone. Anxiety was taking over their bodies, and some feared that it might turn into panic. Everything began to annoy them – the loud music, the stupid jokes, the terrible questions before the start of the race from people who had long since left their rowing days behind them or had never rowed to begin with – "so, are you going to win a medal?" or "How are you feeling? Lighten up!" They wanted to get to the starting line as soon as possible and let it all out.

The semi-final was not expected to be difficult. The main fight would be the next day. However, they would still have to get through it – and avoid any mistakes. Precise and manageable rowing had to become a habit. Winning in the semi-final against Leningrad's Dynamo, with their stroke, Polkovskiy, would be a great psychological victory in itself.

Both boats flew out of the start together, leaving the other competitors behind. The Leningrad crew kept up bowball-to-bowball for the first 500 metres, but as the halfway point crept closer, they started to gradually fall behind. To avoid wasting their strength, Žalgiris lengthened out to a lower rate, monitoring their opponents in lane six out of the corners of their eyes so they wouldn't be passed. They had to maintain their lead up to the grandstands, because the waves of Khimki were still capable of their usual mischief. As they approached the thousand-metre mark, they heard a loud buzzing in their ears. Even through their ears, deafened by the pressure, they could hear it louder than even the grandstands – like a car's engine. Then, they heard a loud crash and swearing. The shock stopped all of the crews mid-stroke – a motorboat with four passengers bobbing up and down on the lake had crashed into the Leningrad boat. "Are you drunk or something!?" they heard angry cries and swears in Russian. The umpires' boat hurried over, waving a red flag, and pulled the wet Leningrad rowers out of their boat. The red flag meant the race had been cancelled, so nobody was in a hurry to finish. All of the remaining boats slowly rowed off to the dock.

*

"There will be a re-row tomorrow morning," Kikilas, the team manager, announced, after hurrying back from the umpires' meeting.

The men looked around for their coach, but Ričardas had already left for the start line with his eight.

"Is everyone redoing it?"

"No, just you."

"That's ridiculous! Why just us? Trud and Bachurov are just going to get to rest? Hmm?" Povilas was the first to boil over.

"That's what the umpire decided," Kikilas deflected.

"I'm just curious what the umpires were looking at. Couldn't they see that someone was coming onto the course?" Eugenijus asked angrily.

"I don't know. They were drunk. We don't know where they came from. Their boat is totally ruined, but they have another."

"They could've killed them," Povilas agreed. "Like they needed more space... kicking up waves and running people over!"

"Somebody could sit out there on a motorboat and regulate traffic," Jonas added.

"When is the race tomorrow?" Celestinas had the most reserved reaction to the accident.

"9:30."

"I see, we'll have to go to sleep early, then."

"Let's go home. No reason to wait for the finish. We'll stretch our legs," Povilas suggested.

"Sure, no reason for us to sit here, everything's clear as it is," Eugenijus agreed, and the men left for the locker rooms.

*

"Third place is good enough," Ričardas gathered his four after an early breakfast. "Don't go too hard. The final is in less than three hours. Save your strength. How do you feel?"

The men shrugged: "We're alright."

Everything went to plan during the race as well. Celestinas, Povilas, Jonas and Eugenijus gave their opponents the lead and finished in a safe second – without wasting their energy. There were two and a half hours left until the final. They were somewhat concerned by the Trud crew, who had been resting since the previous day and would now be racing completely refreshed.

"It's alright, because you guys have had a warm-up instead," Ričardas reassured his rowers. "It'll be easier to know what to expect from the final. You're in lane six, on the edge, so you won't get waves from the grandstands."

Athletes and spectators began to gather in the water stadium to watch the final race. They were sprinkled by occasional light August rain, but this didn't bother anyone. That Sunday had a jovial atmosphere – everyone was impatiently waiting for the race between the best rowers in the country.

The men waited for the start quietly, hidden from other athletes, coaches, and prying eyes in general. Every single one of them counted the minutes they had left until the race that would determine everything. The massive responsibility they felt to themselves and those around them tormented them and drained their energy. Though they had wanted this and striven for it, the race placed enormous pressure on them and felt like a burden – one that would change their lives as soon as they got rid of it. The coxed fours, one after another, began to move towards the starting line, followed by the pairs and the singles.

"Shall we?" Povilas stood up first. He was always the most upbeat. "Let's warm up."

"How much time do we have?" Celestinas asked.

"It's twenty past."

"Let's go before everyone else lines up so we don't have to wait," Eugenijus had caught Povilas' impatience as well.

The USSR team managers and coaches were gathering by the pontoons. As the rowers approached with their oars, they tried to talk to them, as if they could help: "How are you guys feeling?," "Five minutes short of being Olympians!," and "Not five, seven!" – They laughed at their own jokes.

"Jonas will be following our race," Kikilas reassured the rowers. "Just in case..."

"How can he help us?" Povilas asked.

Kikilas shrugged:

"Who knows, at least you'll have another person out there."

Celestinas cracked half a smile and waved dismissively before following his friends towards the boat.

*

The six boats lined up on the start line bobbing up and down on the waves kicked up by passing steamboats. The rowers glanced at each other and looked towards the finish line nervously, straightening their boats. Ever since the Albano system had been introduced to Khimki last year, steering had become much easier. The cox no longer had to look around, as he could steer using the long line of buoys.

"Vnimanie, marsh!" the start umpire's voice echoed through his deafening megaphone as a green flare shot up into the sky. With short, sudden strokes, the six crews tried to get their boats moving as quickly as possible and grab a lead, which would be very important along the distance yet to come.

Lanes one and six immediately shot ahead from the starting line – Leningrad's Dynamo and Vilnius' Žalgiris, as expected. Up to 500 metres, both crews remained level, leaving their much weaker competitors behind. After passing the buoys marked "500," however, the Leningrad crew began to fall behind. In the third lane, the umpires' boat followed the Trud boat, which had fallen further behind.

"We're doing well!" Povilas encouraged Celestinas quietly from behind. "Keep it up!"

The men had never before rowed so harmoniously. The boat simply flew ahead, seemingly without any significant effort. Without having to look to the right, they could see the Leningrad four fall behind in the distance. At the midpoint of the racecourse, Povilas gave one of his strokes a strong finish – the signal for Celestinas, the stroke, to pick up the pace. The first and second then picked up the rhythm, and all four of them finally felt that this was their day. In the third five hundred, the men increased their lead to a length and began to believe in their own victory. There was only a quarter of the race left before they would become Olympians!

The grandstands were bursting with cheers and applause. There was no understanding who was cheering for whom. Everyone was simply enjoying the extraordinary battle and potential new sensation unfolding before them.

Their deafened ears could not hear what their coaches were trying to tell them from the shore, though they were shouting themselves hoarse. Their bodies were screaming with pain and only one thought consumed them – "Where's the finish line?" There were only a hundred metres left, and there was no way Leningrad would catch them now! Only ten more strokes and that would be it!

"Ten!" Povilas hissed through his clenched teeth as he began counting in his head "one, two..." Everything was going so well that they didn't even need any great effort to win. And then they heard a tremendous thud – Eugenijus' oar had hit a barrel-sized side buoy, followed by Povilas' oar, and then a second and a third buoy – "boom, boom, boom." The men felt like their bodies had been struck by lightning. They were in such shock, they couldn't respond fast enough. The boat had stopped and had turned perpendicular to their lane. The noise from the grandstands died down for a split second before coming back even stronger. In the first lane, the Leningrad crew flew by the standing Žalgiris crew... Setting the boat back on course and getting it moving took time – time that the Lithuanians didn't have. Dynamo won by 1.9 seconds...

A silent scream began to grow within the rower. They wanted to shout and cry and turn back time. From the finish line, they could clearly see the irregularities in the lanes. Right at the end of the course, the line of buoys was bent in towards the lane, all of its terrible barrel-sized buoys. Yes, Eugenijus could see them when he turned around, but who would've thought to look for them at the very end of the race, and on an Albano racecourse?

There was no sense in complaining or blaming anyone. Everything was clear. The men hung their heads low and remained silent for a while. Their lives ran through their heads, all of their victories and misfortunes, all of their hopes and dreams. All they wanted to do, over and over again, was to shout "Stop! Turn back time! Let's try it again!" It seemed like all of this had happened before, just that it was more painful now... This time, all they had lacked was a bit of luck, or some caution. Or perhaps someone had given them this lane on purpose, or perhaps... But they couldn't change anything. Whoever wins goes. There had been heart-breaking losses before, but this one felt incredibly unjust and painful. Even these strong men, who had learned so much in their lives, felt tears rising in their throats.

All they wanted was to hide in a corner and scream. Not at each other, but at their bad luck. Everyone understood that all Eugenijus had to do was turn around once for everything to end differently, which is why the idea of arguing with and blaming a teammate who was already drowning in guilt never even crossed their minds. They had to keep silent and hope that time would heal all.

"Come on guys, how could you?" "You couldn't see the buoys?" "We have to submit a protest, the lane wasn't even!" and "Don't let it get you down, Boreiko and Golovanov were third!" – some of the people who surrounded the men tried to reassure them while others simply nit-picked.

"It can't be that that's the end of it. Samsonov clearly saw that we had a strong lead, he has to consider that..." – Eugenijus blamed only himself.

"There will be a coaches' meeting after the race," Kikilas tried to fill the athletes with hope. "That's where they'll decide on the final list."

The announcer's unrelenting voice continued to ring out through the stadium. The competition would continue. The eight was to start soon, but they didn't want to watch. The eight had been where Celestinas and Povilas got their start. Everything could have turned out differently. They could have been in that crew now and winning confidently with the rest of them...

There was an hour until the coaches' council meeting. They wanted to fall asleep and wake up after it was all over.

"What happened? Did you steer off-course?" Ričardas hurried to the four after claiming his gold medal in the eight.

The men remained silent and looked at the ground. Eugenijus' eyes shimmered:

"I didn't see the buoys..."

"We had a strong lead..." Povilas added.

"I saw, they were way behind," Ričardas nodded.

"We steered off-course, but the lane was off, too, it was bent," Celestinas added.

"No good, guys... I don't know what they will decide. I'll go to the meeting," their coach had no reassuring words for them. "It was them yesterday and you today, though it wasn't their fault..."

"It wasn't ours, either. How are we supposed to steer if the course is crooked? Then what are the lanes for?" Povilas was angry.

"I'll tell them, maybe they'll consider it. What time is it?"

"1:15"

"I'm going. Keep your fingers crossed," Ričardas said, leaving for the meeting hall.

There had never been a longer two hours in their lives. Perhaps only when Povilas and his brother Juozas embraced each other at the *stribai* headquarters in Prienai as they waited for their father and their sister Elzytė to return. "There are worse things in life," Povilas thought, trying to heal the pain. "I'd give up all of my medals and Olympics to go back in time and save my mother and father." His thoughts flew to his childhood, and to the cosy family home in Rūdupis. He didn't even know that a sport like rowing existed at the time. He and his brothers would row their rowboat along the Nemunas, but it was usually just Kazys rowing. They would only get to row sometimes, because the strong current of the Nemunas would usually carry them towards Birštonas. "If my parents see me now, they have to understand how tough this is... they've got to help me..." Povilas thought, looking up. The sky was filled with white clouds. A flock of sparrows flew by, and he could see the white contrail left behind by a passing airplane.

*

Khimki had begun to empty out. The marches died down, the grandstands emptied out into the metro, the trailers filled with boats headed off in their separate directions, and the athletes dispersed. The only ones who remained waiting were two fours, a few coaches, and a few federation representatives. The coaches' meeting was taking longer than it ever had before.

Eugenijus, Povilas, Jonas and Celestinas were silent as they sat in the concrete grandstands, lost in thought. The accursed Khimki reservoir had once again punished them, destroying their dreams and crushing their confidence.

When it seemed like their wait would never end, they heard voices approaching. The heads of the coaches appeared as they left their building – they had red, flushed cheeks and were waving their arms as they laughed and cursed at one another.

The men looked up, looking for Rychka among them. First, they saw Kikilas, waving a stack of papers. Behind him came Ričardas. The men rose from their bench and stood, rooted to the spot. This was their last minute of hope, which they would savour before hearing the verdict. Upon seeing his rowers, Ričardas raised his hand and bounded up the stairs in twos to reach them.

"Everything's alright, men, you're going! The council voted for you!"

The words echoed in their heads like a dream. For a moment, they remained silent, unable to believe what they had heard. Povilas buried his face in his hands and rubbed his face, trying to wake himself. Eugenijus dropped down onto the bench, and Celestinas and Jonas looked each other in the eyes. Suddenly, the tension brakes out into convulsive laughter.

"Seriously?" they couldn't believe their good luck.

"Seriously. Samsonov saw it, they all saw it. You're definitely stronger than them. There were other complaints about the racecourse. It was seven to three in your favour."

Suddenly, their bodies were overcome with exhaustion. The same chain of events all over again seemed impossible. This was exactly how they had left for Copenhagen the previous year after their loss, and now, they were headed for Tokyo. It seemed like every loss opened doors for them.

"So we're going to the Olympics?" Povilas still couldn't believe it.

"Yes, there won't be any more selection races. Our camp is in Sakhalin, and we will acclimatize there. We have to put our papers in order by 1 September, get measured for our uniforms, kiss our wives goodbye, and that's it, we fly out for the whole deal. We'll only return in the second half of October. We have a week."

"Great news, Rychka! Thanks!"

"I had nothing to do with it, you guys won this."

"We'd lost hope..."

"They've got some smart people there, too. Samsonov supported you. Of course, under one condition... that the crew line up might change."

The men looked at their coach. Could it be that even they would not be allowed to have a fully Lithuanian crew?

"Sass will be joining us."

"Why? We have never rowed with Sass! He's a single sculler, what is he going to do in a sweep boat?" Povilas disagreed.

"That's why they're taking him, because he can row on either side."

"They think they can turn a sculler into a sweep rower in a month?"

"I guess they think they can."

"They won't let us prepare in peace. They can't do without their experiments."

＊

38

Lithuania's sports fans were ecstatic. "Two head to Tokyo!" the red headline on the first page of "Sportas" shouted. The adventures of the four were described in detail, but, as always, the lion's share of the praise went to the eight.

The team began to prepare for its long journey. The rowers were invited to get measured for their parade uniforms. They had to take the athletes' exact athletic uniform measurements, shoe sizes, heights and weights. Celestinas was ordered to join the Komsomol. Povilas was almost too old for Komsomol membership, so he wasn't asked. Many questionnaires had already been filled out in the summer, but they also had to fill out documents and write their biographies. These weren't just for the KGB, they were for the press as well – so that the journalists would have something to write about the Olympians.

The men enjoyed a festive mood for the entire week. Their wives, accustomed to spending long periods away from their husbands, felt their usual pangs of longing, but also great pride in their husbands.

"I hope the baby will wait for me," Povilas sighed. There was a bit more than a month left until the baby was due to arrive.

*

A crowd of people gathered at Vilnius' airport to see the Lithuanian rowers off to Moscow on 1 September, including representatives from the Sports Committee, the Sports Federation, and the Central Committee. After bidding farewell to their wives and children, the men ascended the ramps into the airplane that would begin their extraordinary adventure. One after another, waving to the crowd from the door of the airplane, they vanished inside and pressed their faces against the small portholes. In the refreshing sunlight of that first day of September, they watched the women's scarves flutter and the men in suits wave their hands. After half a day in Moscow, they had a long flight to look forward to from

Moscow to Yuzhno-Sakhalinsk airport, with a transfer to another aircraft in Krasnoyarsk and an additional landing in Khabarovsk.

*

The members of the USSR rowing team gathered in Sheremetyev Airport were happier than they had ever been. Now that the torturous selection process was over, they could finally all be friends. They chatted happily, told jokes, and discussed what they'd do for the rest of the long flight. Those who had been to America recounted what they remembered from their trip and shared their advice.

The flight to Krasnoyarsk in an IL 18 took almost seven hours, and with the four-hour time difference, they were to arrive in Krasnoyarsk at eight in the morning – if the plane didn't get held up. After sitting in the Yemelyanov Airport lobby for a couple of hours, they headed out once again to Khabarovsk, losing another three hours of their day. Khabarovsk would be the "last stop" for the Olympians. The entire city was proud to see the Olympians – and possible future Olympic champions. The athletes would head from there to Tokyo non-stop – but they still had their acclimatization in Yuzhno-Sakhalinsk to look forward to.

The Khabarovsk regional government waited for the first Olympians with pride, sending an entire delegation to the airport to greet the rowing team.

"No, you won't fly to Yuzhno-Sakhalinsk on a regular route," the head of the regional committee declared. "We'll get you a charter flight. You'll rest, have dinner, and the airplane will be ready."

This gesture surprised the Olympic delegation, but the team managers agreed. They were exhausted from the long flight, so they also wanted to rest and have a proper meal. And then there were the athletes, who couldn't stretch their legs out or sleep in the cramped IL 18s. The cigarette smoke on-board burned their eyes and their throats. It was a good thing that their baggage was packed separately, making it easier to get their luggage out.

A restaurant was quickly provided for them and the rowers had an excellent dinner – and the airplane left for Yuzhno-Sakhalinsk without them.

While waiting for the promised airplane, the coaches began to doubt whether they had made the right decision, because their wait grew much longer than expected. Fortunately, their bodies were still on Moscow time, and when the airplane was finally prepared at 3:00 in the morning, it was 2:00 in the afternoon in Moscow.

"They'll treat you right when you get there," The city government representative told them, shaking the hands of everyone on the team as they entered the chartered airplane.

*

The first dawn twilight was just beginning to appear. From the sky, Sakhalin Island looked like a long, humped sea creature. The entire stretch of dark green land was surrounded by the sea. "That's Japan over there," the stewardess pointed through a porthole on the right. In the morning light, it was hard to see the country where, a month from now, they would experience the greatest sporting event in the world, but it was right there.

After landing in Khormutov Airport early in the morning on 3 September, the men looked out to see the Yuzhno-Sakhalinsk delegation that was supposed to come greet the Olympians. The rowing team was the only Olympic team to prepare for the event here in Sakhalin. However, the empty airport runway had only one thin young man standing outside. The greeting they had been promised was nowhere to be found. This wasn't an issue for them but it still seemed strange.

Exhausted from their long journey, the men hurried to leave the airplane and find their way to their beds. The young man who came to the ramp politely introduced himself and showed them the way towards the exit, where a bus was waiting for them. After gathering their luggage, the rowers pushed past one another to get on the bus. Only Jonas, who felt like a newcomer to the team, waited until the team's veterans took their seats before getting on last. The only spot left was in the front, next to the young man who had greeted them.

"Good morning," Jonas greeted the young man.

"Welcome. How was your flight?"

"Alright, but very long."

"Yeah, we're a long way from Moscow. However, you could shake hands with Japan from here if you wanted to. Sorry, I haven't introduced myself. I'm Viktor, the secretary of the Komsomol in Yuzhno-Sakhalinsk."

"Nice to meet you. I'm Jonas, from the four."

"This is the first time we'll have rowers training here. They built a centre just for you."

"For us?" Jonas asked, surprised.

"Yes, and they connected two lakes as well, to make you a race course."

"Interesting," Jonas smiled. "Why are you so sad, Viktor? Had a bad night?"

"Yes, actually," Viktoras grew quiet, looked around behind him, and then quietly whispered to Jonas, as if he was afraid and yet unable to contain the terrible thoughts on his mind: "there was a terrible accident here."

Jonas grew curious:

"What happened?"

Viktor bent lower, looking around again:

"An aircraft crashed yesterday. Not far from Yuzhno-Sakhalinsk, near the village of Pereval. It was flying from Khabarovsk and never made it. It crashed and almost everybody died. 87 people and the crew. They took six to the hospital, but I don't know how they're doing."

"When?"

"At about 9:00 in the evening."

"Were they flying from Moscow?"

"Yes, they were. They landed in Khabarovsk. I don't know the details. Everything was so terrible... They ordered me not to talk, but it's all too terrible!" the young man began to tremble.

"Relax, you can't change anything," Jonas tried to soothe Viktor, but he was overcome with such terror himself that he could barely control his thoughts or words.

"Don't tell anyone, it's a state secret," Viktor said, realizing he had said too much.

"If what you're saying is true... we were supposed to fly on that plane... they switched our plane in Khabarovsk..."

Viktoras suddenly looked up:

"You were supposed to be greeted by people from the city council, but they have problems to deal with now. You understand... They sent me. All they told me was that they changed your route."

Jonas shivered. The terrible bit of news seemed unreal. Some local Khabarovsk leader, likely a glory hound, had surprised them by changing their flight, and this had been the difference between life and death for them, between the life and death of the entire Olympic rowing team... "We're sitting here in a bus, tired and cranky, lost in our own concerns and problems, and almost one hundred people who flew together with us are no longer alive... And only their loved ones will learn of their deaths. The government will hide them from everyone else..." Jonas crossed himself in his mind, sighed deeply, and closed his eyes. His face and body were overcome by a wave of heat.

"What is it, Jonas? Are you feeling sick?" Povilas asked. He was sitting behind him across the central aisle, and he thought Jonas was nauseous.

"No, everything's fine, I'll tell you later," Jonas wiped his sweaty brow. "I'll tell you later..."

*

39

The last stage of the long journey was forty kilometres by bus to the east to the town of Okhotskoe on the coast of the Okhotsk Sea. Then, there were five more kilometres to the forested tourism centre on the shores of Tunaycha Lake, which had once been called Tonnai-ko. In a remote corner of the earth surrounded by beautiful nature, they had built a three-story centre just for the rowers. The windows opened onto the narrow lake of Chervyachnoe[76], which had apparently been named after its worm-like shape. A course had been dug between it and Tunaycha Lake just for the rowers, and a reinforced concrete bridge was built across the top. The tourism centre was decorated by a large seagull. That was what they called the tourism centre – "Chaika," or "seagull." The earth around the centre had clearly only been levelled out recently, as not a single weed or blade of grass had taken root yet. Boards had been laid across the dirt to walk on so the rowers could reach the sandy shore where they would embark and disembark from their boats. The lake had two lanes in it marked with buoys, but because the lake was too short – at just one and a half kilometres – they would have to row into the larger lake Tunaycha by crossing under the bridge.

The building, which still smelled of paint and lime, had everything that the athletes could need – twin bedrooms with showers and balconies facing the south-west, new furniture, a gym, a recreational room, a cafeteria, physicians' offices, and massage rooms. Outside, they enjoyed the pure and refreshing air of the forested region. There were just three kilometres from the sea, so only the hills and the thick forests protected them from the strong winds.

When they arrived, the rowers found breakfast had been prepared for them. The men couldn't believe their eyes. At first, they thought that the leaders of the town had prepared a celebratory feast for their honoured guests, so the men ate as much as they could. On that first day, however,

---

76   Rus. Червячное – worm-like

they had no idea that the big bowls of red and black caviar they had enjoyed would be available every day for breakfast, lunch and dinner.

The cool morning began to warm quickly from the hot rays of the rising sun, promising a beautiful summer day – one that the rowers would primarily sleep through, as they had not yet adjusted to the time zone.

*

The exhaustion from the trip and the seven hours' time difference led to disorder in the team's schedule. After sleeping through the day, some of the team began to wake up at 2:00 or 3:00 in the morning, turning on their desk lights, opening the doors to their rooms, and looking out their balconies.

"Good thing there's still a month to the Olympics," James said in the next balcony over as he leaned on a post and gazed up at the starlit sky.

"Damn you, James! You scared me! You can't sleep either?" Povilas, startled, jumped up in the dark.

"Ah, Povilas, is that you? I didn't recognize you in the dark. Thought you were Celestinas."

"Yeah, it's me. Who else? My eyes are open, my sides are sore, and my stomach is growling like a truck. How long did we sleep?"

"I'm not sure. What's the time difference here?"

"Seven hours. It's 7:30 in Lithuania right now."

"So we'd be going to bed soon, but we're just waking up here. I always feel so strange in my first night in a new place. I wake up with no idea where I am."

"Look how beautiful it is here, James! Look at the stars reflected in the water!"

"You're such a romantic, Povilas!" James laughed.

"I grew up in nature. I love the forests, the fields, and the water most of all. But they've got strange trees here. I've never seen such crooked trees. I wonder why. Could it be the wind?"

"Yeah, and they have such thick foliage. What are they, cottonwood? I couldn't see yesterday."

"I'll have to check in the morning," said Povilas, crossing his arms and rubbing his shoulders. "It's chilly. The nights aren't warm anymore. I'm going back under my blanket. There's nothing to do here in the dark, anyway."

"You're right, we need to get as much sleep as we can," James agreed, turning towards his room.

Above them, someone on the third floor opened the door to the balcony, leaned on the railing, and yawned loudly.

*

Finally having slept, everyone was impatient to get out on the water. It had been more than a week since they had sat in any boats. Their hands had missed their oars and their bodies had missed their work. Immediately after breakfast, everyone gathered in a special field only thirty metres away next to a newly built basketball court. On that court stood their boats, which had been brought across the entire Soviet Union – seven thousand kilometres. They first wanted to make sure they had arrived safely and then unload and rig them as quickly as possible to try out the waters of Sakhalin.

"Anatoly Sass will row with you today," Ričardas told the four. "Jonas, you're rowing a single."

"But I've never rowed a single," Jonas shrugged, surprised.

"That's fine, you'll learn. Here, rig this boat. Don't go far, just in case you fall out or something."

The men knew that they would try to put Sass into the four, they just didn't know who he would replace. They weren't very enthusiastic about learning to row with a new member, but they had no other options.

*

The last stage of their preparations for the Olympics had begun. The team's coaches, believing that the rowers were not yet in their best possible shape, and that their best shape could only be achieved through the most intense training regimen possible, unveiled an unprecedented training regimen for the camp. Such a plan might have seemed normal in the beginning of the season, but now, in September, after so many selection races, their bodies felt on the brink of failure and the work loads seemed impossible to handle. Only Ivanov and the double refused to follow the plan. Nobody else had the courage to oppose the coaches, and they simply didn't have any other choice.

The stylized rowing course at Chervyachnoe grew rough from the constant sprints and races – between the pairs and fours and the fours and the eight. The lanes, narrower than usual, exacted a toll on their oars. Celestinas was the first to crack his oar. The number of cracked oars glued together and drying in the sun only grew from there. Jonas was the only one who didn't have to race anyone. He rowed his single, calmly so he wouldn't capsize, and sadly watched the four pass him by.

"Rychka, it's bad. We can't row with Sass. We can't sit the boat – it tips from side to side.. If we have no balance, how can we even consider sprinting?" the men couldn't take it any more after two weeks of training. "We need Jonas back! We can fix our rowing while we still have time. It'll be too late after that."

"I can see that something's off with you guys. I don't know, I'll try to talk to Samsonov," Ričardas said. This was the last thing he needed right now.

"If anyone cares about the outcome, they have to see that we can't row like this! How much more of these experiments can we take? There's no time left for normal training."

"I understand, guys, relax, I'll talk to him," Ričardas reassured them. "Here he comes right now."

"How are things, guys? Why the long faces?"

"Yevgeniy Borisovich," Eugenijus was the first to speak, "we can't row with Anatoly. We don't have anything against him, he's a good person, but we can't row together. The boat tips onto the left side with every stroke. We need Jonas."

Yevgeniy Borisovich pressed his lips tightly, frowned, and nodded.

"I understand. After lunch, you'll row with your old line-up and we'll see. I'll tell Anatoly."

"Thank you, Yevgeniy Borisovich! We won't fail you!" Ričardas shook the senior coach's hand.

The men started high-fiving each other with joy.

"Let's go find Jonas," Povilas waved to his friends.

"There he is, returning with the single," Celestinas was the first to see him.

"Thank God, maybe we'll start rowing properly."

"Thank Jonas, not God," Eugenijus laughed as the three of them practically ran to greet their teammate.

*

With Jonas, they began rowing the way they should have been all along. However, they did regret losing two weeks of proper work, and it took more than a day for the team's spirits to return. The abundance of good food and the care of the medics and physios helped them recover their strength but didn't ease their psychological stress. The only bad thing was the weather. The constant wind, rain and cold fatigued them. One after another, the rowers began to cough and sneeze. The men were counting the days until their trip to Tokyo and began to grow uneasy. The letters they wrote home and that they received from Lithuania, calmed, supported inspired and comforted them. Their families back home also sent them Lithuanian newspapers, full of Olympic spirit. From the newspapers, they discovered that the Žalgiris women's eight had once again become the champions of the USSR, and that Tamulis the Lithuanian boxer and five track and field Lithuanian athletes – K. Orentas, J. Aleksiejūnas, A. Vaupšas, A. Varanauskas and B. Kalėdienė – would also be heading to the Tokyo Olympics.

Whenever they gathered in the recreational room to relax, the men played chess, listened to the radio, read, and chatted.

On Sundays, after lunch, when they didn't have any training, there was a cultural programme planned for the rowers – basketball games with the locals, meetings with the military naval sailors in Korsakov, rides on torpedo boats in the sea, outdoor fishing and picnic excursions, and a reception at the Yuzhno-Sakhalinsk garrison soldiers' homes. They also attended sports camp in Yuzhno-Sakhalinsk, where a special memorial, entitled "Friendship," had been built to honour the Olympic Games.

*

The Olympic uniforms arrived at the "Chaika" about halfway through September. The muscular rowers wore the light brown parade uniforms well on their shoulders, although many of the jackets were a bit too narrow. Along with the uniforms, they received Olympic team badges, embroidered casual clothing, brown and multi-coloured flannel shirts, training and racing kit, regular and sports shoes, and Olympic kit bags. They began to feel the Olympic spirit more and more, and became proud to call themselves Olympians.

With five days left until their journey, the carefully de-rigged and wrapped boats were loaded onto their trailers to be taken to the port in

Korsakov. There, they'd be taken to the port of Nakhodka near Vladivostok, where they would "meet" with the kayaks and canoes, the weights and platforms for the weightlifters' practices, the boxing gloves, and the 14 beautiful horses that would all travel on a ship called the Mayakovsky to the Olympics in Tokyo.

After a couple of days, a grand farewell ceremony was organized. The rowers were outnumbered by government representatives wanting to wish the rowers good luck.

Dressed up in their Olympic uniforms, the rowers lined up by the centre to pose for photos together – as teams and all together as Lithuanians.

"Will your camera survive so many rolls of film?" his friends joked when they saw Povilas shooting with no regard for saving film.

"It will; it has no choice. I'd like to buy a new one, though. In Lucerne, I saw someone with a Japanese Nikon, and it made me drool. I want one so bad!"

"Maybe they'll have them in Japan. If the Japanese make them, maybe they won't be expensive."

"Maybe. But how many rubles are they going to exchange for us? It certainly won't be enough for a camera… I'll have to bring something again."

"Of course, we'll all take something. It's not like we'll be walking around there like beggars. They say they have all kinds of radio devices there."

"I want that camera the most, though… Oh, the pictures I'd take!"

"But Povilas, your photos are beautiful as they are! None of us can take photos like yours…"

"But they'll be even better," Povilas smiled, wiping the side of the FED lens with his sleeve.

Povilas' suitcase had a separate corner for rolls of film and the camera's accessories. Sakhalin had enchanted him with its beauty and the events they saw, but he had to save film. Every step they took was bound to be interesting in Japan, and film might be expensive there.

25 September finally came – the day of their trip to Tokyo. With the service they received, the bowls of caviar, and the natural peace, "Chaika" had become a second home for the rowers, but they had been separated from the rest of the world and missed the bustle of city life. Unfortunately, they weren't exactly overflowing with energy and strength, either. Their

bodies felt exhausted from the incredibly long season. After all, the first selection matches had begun in March, and it was now the end of September. Seven months of constant races, sprints, and trials.

"We'll be flying to Khabarovsk. The others from Moscow will be there. From Khabarovsk, everybody will fly straight to Tokyo," the delegation's managers explained at a meeting. "We will fly for three hours from Khabarovsk to Tokyo. Wear your parade uniform."

*

"I miss home so much!" Povilas said, as if to himself, while sitting with his friends on the shore of the lake on their last evening before flying out towards Tokyo.

"Yeah, definitely," James agreed. "Since we left, we've missed most of the Lithuanian summer."

"It could be that there'll be four of us when I return…"

"I hope to make it in time. Ours should be born in November."

"It's too bad that I won't be home again. But maybe the baby will wait… Why hurry?" Povilas smiled.

"There's no scheduling that, and it's not just a headache that you can get over," James laughed.

"You know, before going, I submitted a request for an apartment. Eugenijus said I should. It might get tight for the four of us in just one room."

"If we race well, they should give you one. Just like they did for us after America."

"I hope to God we have a good race. But it's hard now… They ran us ragged here. We're too tired… I don't know what it's like for you guys in the eight, but we don't like getting into our boat anymore. We need a few days of rest."

"You want rest? Just keep rowing… Everyone is exhausted in the eight, too. I just hope nobody collapses. Petras is complaining that he's having trouble… Antanas can barely touch his back…"

"I wonder how the coxless pair will race. Their selection isn't even confirmed yet… It's nonsense. Can't they just decide?"

"I've been watching them and I don't envy them. Boreiko and Golovanov could just relax and prepare, but no, they keep setting those young rowers on them like dogs."

"I heard they'll have their final trials in Japan."

"Yeah, they told me..."

"Have you realised that we're all the way on the other side of the earth?"

"You're right... If you dug a hole all the way down, you'd come out in Lithuania," James smiled.

"I never thought I'd ever travel this far," Povilas spread his palms on the ground and leaned back, letting his head hang back. "And yet everything here's the same... the sky, the sun, the water. Even the people are the same..."

"We'll be in Japan tomorrow..."

"We're in Japan now, too, James. But they have a different name for it, and the locals are all gone for some reason..."

"What are you saying? Quiet!" James cowered down.

"What? Am I wrong? This is just like Lithuania! What do you call Lithuania? Lithuania or Russia?"

"Quiet, Povilas, you'll get in trouble," James quieted him.

"Yeah, yeah, it's easy to get in trouble... just open your mouth and you're in trouble," Povilas laughed.

"It's better to keep your tongue behind your teeth."

"Anyway... I read in "Sportas" that the Olympic village was built in a former American military base and that we'll be living in a former barracks, or soldiers' dormitories," Povilas changed the subject.

"It'll be interesting to see if they look anything like ours."

"Have you ever been to basic training?"

"No, but I've heard stories."

"Celestinas is a soldier, we should ask him"

"Ask me what?" Celestinas had heard his name.

"What it's like in basic training, in the army," Povilas responded. "They say that, in Tokyo, we'll live in barracks, so we're curious whether they'll be different from ours or not."

"Ah... We'll see," Celestinas said. "But why barracks?"

"They said that when the Americans left, they had a lot of buildings left there, so they were adapted for athletes."

"So how many of us will fit in each barracks?"

"I don't think they'll be barracks, they said there'll be houses or something."

"How do you know?" Celestinas asked in disbelief.

""Sportas" said so. They sent it to me from home. I can show you later."

"I believe you," Celestinas laughed.

"I read that the women's zone there will be separate from the men's," Eugenijus jumped in. "They'll even have policewomen making sure men don't get in."

"Yeah, they wrote that, too," Povilas nodded. "I don't mind, but what are you old bachelors going to do there!?" he laughed at his friends.

"But women will be able to enter the men's zone. We'll just wait until the bolder ones come by, we won't need any parties," Eugenijus laughed.

"We'll see how it all is tomorrow," James said as he looked off to the south.

"They also wrote that the Japanese will use jets to paint the Olympic rings in the sky during the opening ceremony," Povilas continued.

"Too bad we won't be there. Maybe we'll see it on TV."

"Maybe we'll be able to see it from the village. I'd like to at least take some pictures…"

*

On Thursday, 24 September the rowers bid farewell to the centre by the two lakes that had become their home and to its welcoming workers and managers. They took a bus toward Yuzhno-Sakhalinsk airport, where a crowd of schoolchildren waited to see them off with bouquets of wildflowers in their hands.

The short flight away from Japan towards Khabarovsk was happy and fun. The men were gradually overcome by the spirit of a new adventure. When they arrived in Khabarovsk from the quiet island of Sakhalin, the Olympics were within reach. Here, the largest airliner in the world – the TU-114 – awaited them for their flight, complete with slightly happier-looking stewardesses and proud pilots. However, they had to spend one more night in Centralnaya, a large, newly built hotel where the rest of the Lithuanian Olympians had been staying for several days already. They had a grand farewell celebration to look forward to with long speeches and a generous feast.

*

40

On 25 September, after an unexpected snowfall had blanketed Khabarovsk in white, after southern Japan was flooded by a typhoon that sank a British cargo ship on its shores, and when Soviet radios, hissing with static, caught hints of radio signals from America carrying a song by an unheard-of fellow named Orbison called "Oh, Pretty Woman," the USSR Olympic team, dressed in its new Olympic uniforms, departed for the airport.

After their final photos on the airplane's ramp, more than two hundred Olympic team members, accompanied by cameramen, video cameras and reporters, left the Soviet Union.

*

"Look, our little Sakhalin looks like a shark from above," Povilas heard someone on his team behind him say in Russian.

"Sure, our Sakhalin[77]..." – Povilas mocked them to himself while he flipped through the photo album given to him as a gift by the schoolchildren of that island. The photos featured sights from the city and Japanese architectural elements. "Lithuania and Japan, they're all yours..."

After two hours airborne over the sea, the TU-114 began to descend towards Japan. Excited by their extraordinary journey and the experiences that awaited them, the plane's passengers chatted, joked and laughed merrily the entire way there. Only the party representatives' faces remained ice-cold and serious, swollen with fat and a constant internal anger. They had a long month of monitoring, following and controlling the athletic delegation ahead of them. Though all of the athletes had been debriefed many times at various meetings, when they actually went abroad, they would once again need to have the Soviet citizen's code of conduct explained to them.

The TU-114 continued to descend, but all they could see below them was water.

---

77   Rus. Our Sakhalin.

"Where are we supposed to be landing? The sea?" the passengers grew anxious.

"Where's the airport?

The aircraft's wheels seemed about to touch the water when a strong jolt notified them that the airliner had finally touched down on solid earth. The massive "miracle" of Soviet engineering hurtled along the runway at a breakneck speed, and all the passengers could see through their portholes was the water of Tokyo bay growing closer and closer.

"Whoa whoa whoa, are we going down?" some of the men began to grow seriously worried, while the women in the front began screaming.

With a powerful shudder and some vertical shaking, the aircraft finally came to a stop at the very end of the runway. The grass was only a few metres way, and the open water stood half a kilometre away. A wave of expletives and groans passed down the passenger cabin. Some scratched their sides, and those who had already undone their seatbelts were rubbing their heads after they had hit them on the ceiling shelves. It was the first time that Haneda airport, which was surrounded by water on all sides, had received an airliner so large and its landing strips were too short for it.

"Citizen passengers, our aircraft has landed in Tokyo city airport," the stewardess' relieved voice said over the intercom.

Outside the portholes, they could see a modern airport building with the words "TOKYO INTERNATIONAL AIRPORT" on the roof and an Olympic poster with a red circle on a white background, the Olympic rings, and the words "TOKYO 1964" on the bottom. Next to the building, they could see crowds of people, cameramen, and photographers, as well as men and women in beautiful matching uniforms carrying luggage.

"Everyone's gathering there," somebody noted from behind.

"I wonder where those people with the blue jackets are from."

"Could they be Americans?"

"Everyone please stay in your seats!" the stewardess cried, seeing that the athletes were impatient to get out of the still-moving aircraft.

"Comrade athletes, when you get out of the plane, please stay together until I say so," said Mashin, the head of the delegation, as he stood up from the first row and turned around to the rest of the cabin. "We will be greeted by comrade Vinogradov, the USSR ambassador in Japan."

The Aeroflot TU-114 slowly approached the SAS, PANAM and Japan Airlines aircraft and stopped to wait until a ramp would be brought to its doors. Here, the aircraft looked like an overgrown child. There were no other airliners of its size anywhere in sight. A ramp soon approached the doors, but the stewardess wouldn't let anyone leave. The impatient passengers looked through the portholes as journalists and uniformed officials gathered outside. The airliner's engines had long since powered down, but they still weren't being let out.

"Why are they delaying us?" the heads of the delegation began to complain impatiently.

"The ramp can't reach us, it's too short," the stewardess explained in a hushed tone.

"Will we have to jump? Ladies, unwrap your skirts, we need parachutes!" someone laughed at the front of the aircraft.

"Only the USSR has aircraft like this. They don't have any this large. That's why their ramps are too small," the dark-haired stewardess tried to explain, though it was clear that she was also lost in the situation.

The men, their faces pressed against the portholes, watched the comical situation unfold. Indeed, the ramp's platform was about a metre lower than the door of the TU-114. Three airport workers stood at the top of the ramp, inspecting the plan and shrugging at one another.

"What happened?" one of the track and field athletes asked impatiently.

"The ramp is too short. It doesn't reach the door," James replied. "They say we'll have to jump down."

"We've enjoyed our giant aircraft, and now we can fly home," Antanas laughed.

The pilots showed up in the cabin and began lifting something together with the stewardesses, raising a clatter. After a few minutes, they lowered a set of steps to the ramp platform.

"Be careful," they warned each passenger, holding their arms so they wouldn't fall down the long set of stairs on the ramp.

"Let me through, Eugenjus, I want to hop out first and take photos of us as we get out," Povilas held his camera firmly in his hand, and his pointer finger rested on the trigger.

"Go ahead, but you're never going to make it into any photos, the way you keep taking pictures of us."

"That's fine, I'll have my chance," Povilas smiled as he forged ahead through his teammates. As always, his proposition convinced them all to move out of his way.

The airliner was already surrounded by members of different organisations and journalists who were there to welcome and greet each team. Everything necessary for a brief press conference was prepared.

*

41

There was a festive atmosphere at Tokyo's Haneda airport. The arrival hall was covered in flags, posters and advertisements and was full of smiling officials and reporters. Though they were tired from their trip, the sight couldn't help but bring a smile to the travellers' faces as they waited in line to have their passports checked. This process went unexpectedly quickly and smoothly. From their very first steps in Japan, the team was provided with guides in beautiful suits who were tasked with accompanying the team throughout the entire Olympic Games. Representatives of the organisational committee didn't wear suits, but they had special armbands on their left hands.

The square at the other end of the building was filled up by a neat row of buses that were prepared to take their teams to the Olympic village.

"Hey, Povilas, can't find the door?" Antanas caught up to Povilas, who was standing by the buses and looking around. "It's like England here, the traffic is on the other side of the road."

"Hah, I thought I'd have to climb on the roof to ride in it, too. I thought I was going nuts."

"When we were in England, the same thing happened. I almost got run over several times. You have to look to the right first and then the left when you're there, it's all backwards."

At the airport, the Lithuanian rowers and track and field athletes parted ways. The rowers were headed right to the Olympic village while the track and field athletes had one final practice left at the resort city of Nikko.

During the half-hour long trip north from the airport towards the Olympic village located in the central neighbourhood of Yoyogi, the bus was escorted by police motorcycles. The never-before-seen vehicles, strange buildings, three-story streets and bridges, countless Japanese neon signs, Olympic flags on every lamp post, tangled nests of electrical wires above the streets, and the mass of dark-haired locals hurrying to and fro stunned the rowers, plunging them into a whirlwind of new, exotic experiences. They wanted to hop from one window to the other. Those without photo cameras had to make do with their eyes to remember the strange sights of Tokyo.

Passing by busy streets, tall buildings covered in Japanese characters, taxis weaving in and out of traffic, modern world-class buildings, and even the new Olympic arenas, with their unusual architectural shapes, the bus finally rolled into the Olympic village – a green oasis of peace surrounded by a three-metre wire fence. It was hard to believe that this place, the most important gathering place for the athletes, was just about at the centre of the massive city of Tokyo. The collection of cottages and houses, which were referred to as "Washington Hills," had been US military barracks and homes from 1946 until the Olympics, when they were re-purposed for the Olympians. The old base was now beautiful and green, and there were no freshly bulldozed patches of earth that turned into dust under the athletes' feet or pools of mud when it rained – a welcome surprise for Olympic veterans who had spent time in newly-built Olympic villages. The carefully mowed grass, flowerbeds, and plants, trimmed in the Japanese style, provided an atmosphere of peace. At every turn, their eyes and their souls were soothed by cleanliness and precise order.

The buses stopped at the edge of the village, next to the new four-story buildings with open stairwells at the end of each building. Several of the identical buildings were surrounded by the same three-metre wire fencing that surrounded the rest of the village.

"Is that the women's zone?" James asked jokingly after remembering their conversation in Sakhalin.

When she noticed the men's curious glances, their small guide explained in her broken Russian:

"That's the women's zone. It's secure, and men can't get in there. There will be police at the gates."

The men looked at one another and burst out laughing:

"What are they being protected from?" they shrugged and asked each other in Lithuanian in wonder.

"From you! Who else?" Ričardas explained, laughing.

"Can they visit us, though?" one of the Russian men asked the guide.

"Yes, they can, but you can't visit them."

"How secure!" Antanas laughed.

Other members of their team who had arrived in another bus were already gathering next to the building marked with the number nine. The entire area was filled with bicycles provided for the residents of the village.

"The USSR team will live here," Mashin announced proudly. "The men. The women will live behind the fence. On Tuesday, we'll gather for a ceremonial USSR flag raising. At 12:00, please gather at the flag square in your parade uniforms, as you are right now. Coaches, please manage this process."

"When will we go to the course?" Zigmas asked Ričardas.

"Tomorrow. The boats aren't here yet. Today, we get settled and rest. We'll go tomorrow morning."

*

There were exactly two weeks left until the Olympic opening ceremony.

After sleeping in the new triple rooms, the rowers gathered at the Olympic village canteen.

"I woke up to find that my bed was moving," Antanas recounted an incident in the night. "I asked, 'where are you dragging me to.' I couldn't see in the dark and though they'd decided to play a prank on me. I turned on the light and they were pretending to be asleep. I shook them so hard that Zigmas jumped out of bed. He was about to start hitting me!"

"That's because you frightened me, Antanas!" Zigmas explained. "He said 'where are you taking me!?' We weren't taking him anywhere."

"How was I supposed to know? I ran out into the corridor and the orderly was gesturing 'relax, relax.' He said something in Japanese and shook himself, and I took it to mean there had been an earthquake. They might be used to it, but I didn't like it at all."

"I was surprised, too. In the morning, my bed was by the other wall. I thought that perhaps I had gotten something confused," Jonas commented when he heard their conversation. "It was a strange feeling."

"My bed moved, too. I thought it was on wheels. When I turned on my side, it moved," Povilas added. "When I got out, however, I realised that it was bucking. I jumped back in and pulled the covers to my eyes so I wouldn't see it," he laughed.

"I wonder, does that happen often here?" Celestinas asked.

"Who knows…," Antanas shrugged.

"Let's go see what they eat around here," Povilas waved, and they all headed off towards the large cafeteria together.

The last few training sessions would be held on a real Olympic course. It was thirty kilometres from the Olympic village to the Toda Rowing Course. In Tokyo's traffic jams, the trip could take up to an hour.

A long line of buses stood next to the block of new buildings to take athletes to the main competition arenas throughout the city. Twice a day, a bus would go to Toda and back with a police motorcycle escort and a car with a megaphone to chase Tokyo residents' vehicles out of the way. The trips consumed up to four hours per day, so the bus seats and their beds were all they had as far as rest was concerned. After the first day, it was decided not to return to the village for lunch. Instead, they would rest and wait for their second session at the course in rooms with cardboard walls prepared for the athletes above the boathouse. They had lunch in the cafeteria on-site.

There were already rowers gathering at the course, taking care of their boats, cleaning off the thick layer of salt that had been deposited on them after a storm, carrying them to the water, and taking a few initial test strokes.

The course, which had been dug for the 1940 Olympic Games, remained unused for its initial purpose right up until 1958, when it became clear that the 1964 Olympic Games would be held in Tokyo. The course was rebuilt again and refurbished according to the latest requirements, but the lanes remained 12.5 metres wide, and the steep sides meant that any waves would bounce back, much like in Khimki. They had to hope that there wouldn't be any strong winds during the competition, but the latest weather forecasts were worrisome – the typhoon battering the nearby coasts of Japan was due to reach Tokyo as well.

Through the thick fog, they could barely see the end of the course, making it seem endless. Occasionally, boats came streaming out of the white wall of fog.

Much like at the Olympic village, everything had been very neatly arranged and organised at Toda. Everything worked like a good Japanese watch. There was no sense of stress or hurry. It seemed like the Japanese managed to solve any problem calmly and with a smile.

The boats had arrived and everyone got to work. They still had many intense sessions ahead of them.

White chrysanthemums began to decorate the fence of the women's "compound," and in the evenings, couples could be seen chatting on both sides of the fence. Nobody ever thought of climbing the tall, spiky fence, and the policewomen who had initially busied themselves picking the flowers out of the fence eventually left them alone, having decided that there was nothing immoral in this gesture.

When it made its way to Tokyo, the typhoon tore off the roofs of several buildings in the Olympic village, broke some windows, and tore up a few trees. That was the extent of the damage, however. Soon, the army appeared at the Olympic village and got to work repairing the buildings.

The unpredictable weather changed training plans and the preparations for the Olympic opening ceremony. The sudden rains sometimes lasted a full day.

On Sunday and Monday, two more aircraft full of USSR athletes arrived. The last ones were to arrive on Friday, 2 October.

On Tuesday, 29 September, the Soviet athletic parade lined up outside of building number 9. The men wore white embroidered shirts and the women wore white embroidered dresses. The Soviet Union flag was raised ceremoniously near the Soviet athletes' buildings, with speeches and applause from their managers. With that, the entire column headed out towards the flag square, where an orchestra played a march to welcome the delegations. The only flags flying there when they arrived were those of Germany, Great Britain, South Korea, and Japan. This was a sign that the majority of the USSR team had established itself at the Olympic village.

*

"What are you writing, Povilas? A letter home?" James addressed his friend, who was bent over a notebook.

"I promised "Sportas" I'd write a letter, so I'm hurrying to make sure I can bring it to the post office on time. There's a plane leaving for Moscow tonight, so I hope the letter makes it in. I took my film to have it developed, so I'll put in a few photos from Sakhalin and from here."

"You're fast! Where are they developing your photos?"

"There's a lab here in the village. I took my bike there. They work fast."

"Show me! Please?"

"Just don't mix them up, they've been set aside to send."

"Is this us flying out of Yuzhno-Sakhalinsk? There we are… Antanas, Zigmas, Sterlik… And still in Sakhalin… Did you take this photo of the eight from the bridge? Good work, Povilas… we look good in those suits… Good thing you lined everybody up. We'll have some photos to enjoy now. Did you write anything interesting for them?"

"A few details. About the flag raising, the course and the living conditions. You know it all, no sense in my explaining it."

"Did you see the pairs' qualifier?"

"I did, and I wrote about it, too. It went exactly as it was supposed to. Boreiko and Golovanov had to win. It's a shame for those youngsters, of course, but they've still got their whole careers ahead of them."

"I just hope their health holds out for the races…"

"I can't imagine… Samsonov's going to run us all ragged before the competition begins…"

"Alright, let me get out of your hair, keep writing. Have you heard from home?"

"I got a letter in Sakhalin. I doubt anything will get here quickly…"

*

There was less than a week left until the Olympic opening ceremony. Training twice a day had become a regular routine and the Olympic village had become their home.

The Soviet rowers, and especially the eight and the single, were constantly followed by the watchful stares of their competitors, as well as curious Japanese photo and video cameras.

The Toda course was still covered in thick fog, and the lane buoys were rocked by large waves that the steep banks of course did nothing to help quell. The waves were made even worse by the umpires' motorboat. Though he understood that it was probably too late to do anything, Thomas Keller, the president of FISA, listened to the teams' complaints and apparently mentioned something to the organisers about the significant problem. The rowers could see him pacing back and forth along the side of the course with the organising committee. The next morning, the athletes were stunned to find a tight, horse-hair fabric net hanging along the banks of nearly the entire course. It was a "water curtain" that the Japanese said should protect them from smaller waves. Several hundred men worked all night on the "wall." Unfortunately, when a headwind blew from lane six, nothing could stop the waves.

The life that always unfolds on a rowing course is like nothing else in the world. At the Olympics, this unique experience was also interwoven with a feeling of importance and significance. If you were there, that meant you were the best in your country and among the best in the world. New friendships began to form. Despite the fierce battles they had ahead, the men were glad to make friends with the Danes, Germans, Canadians and Italians. The Žalgiris four quickly became friends with the Australians, while the eight enjoyed the company of the Ratzeburg eight. Ričardas and Karl Adam shared their coaching experiences – as far as they could understand each other and without revealing their secrets. There was no romance at the rowing competition, which was restricted to men. All they could do was speak to the women through the fence at the Olympic village.

*

42

"I feel broken. I've had such strange dreams," Povilas said. He had stayed in bed for longer than usual.

"It's probably from the wind. I can still hear it whistling in my ears," Eugenijus stretched himself.

Outside their windows, they could see the sun shining through the clouds.

"At least it's not raining today…," Celestinas said as he leaned on the windowsill and looked off into the distance. "You guys hungry?"

"Celestinas, would you bring us breakfast in bed?" Povilas asked, pulling his blanket up to his forehead.

"Should I bring the boat to your bed, too?" Celestinas laughed.

"Sure, that'd be nice…," Povilas trailed off wistfully. "I can't recover from all the dreams I had… I wonder if I can find any fortune-tellers around here. Maybe they'd tell me what my dreams mean," he laughed.

"There's a church, so you can go confess," Eugenijus laughed as well.

"A Japanese church? But I don't know how to pray in Japanese yet!"

"We have the same God, he'll understand Lithuanian."

"Hold on, I've got to return from my dreamland and we can go," Povilas stretched with a loud yawn and rolled out of bed.

They heard a knock on the door.

"Who is it?" Celestinas asked, heading for the door.

"Open up, guys," they heard a solid and familiar voice say in Russian on the other side of the door.

"Yes, one moment."

With a single bound, Celestinas hopped to the door and opened it. In marched Mashin, the head of the delegation. The men hopped from their beds as if they had been zapped.

"Good morning. Which of you is Liutkaitis?"

A wave of dread shot through Povilas' body from his head to his toes.

"I'm Liutkaitis," he said, stepping forward with trembling legs and quickly putting on his blue tracksuit with the letters "CCCP" on it.

"You've received a telegram," he said, extending a bluish envelope with the words "INTERNATIONAL TELEGRAM" on it and a clear window in it, behind which he could read a printed address: "LT LIUTKAITIS POVILAS DELEGATION SOVIET UNION OLIMPIC VILLAGE TOKYO."

Povilas took the envelope:

"What is this?"

"A telegram. Won't you open it?" Mashin smiled.

Povilas looked at it with frightened eyes and his lips began to tremble. With his hands shaking, he carefully opened the neat envelope and pulled out a telegram of the same blue colour with a red stamp on it – "3 October, YOYOGI VILLAGE." "CONGRATULATIONS IT'S A GIRL KOSTAS." Tears welled up in Povilas' eyes as his frightened friends tried to guess what the news was.

"I have a daughter!…," he finally announced with a trembling voice as the tears he had been holding back began to stream down his face. "I have a daughter!" he repeated in Russian.

"Congratulations!" Mashin held out his hand. "The first Soviet baby in the Olympic team! I wish you all the best!" he said, patting Povilas on the shoulder and heading for the door. Of course, he already knew what the news was on his way over. All letters and telegrams were carefully inspected by the KGB before going through. Perhaps that's why he decided to present the telegram himself – everyone enjoyed bringing good news.

"Thank you!" Povilas managed to say before his friends hugged him.

"Congratulations, Povilas, congratulations!"

After seeing the head of the delegation depart, Povilas' other teammates began to gather out of curiosity.

"Povilas has a daughter!" Eugenijus shouted as he stuck his head out into the hallway. He was answered by shouts in Lithuanian and Russian from down the hall – "valio!" and "ura!" The doors down the hallway opened and, for about ten minutes, the whole block of buildings hummed with the good news.

"Just take a look at that telegram! Everything's packaged so nicely! It's nothing like our paper, with the roses and the telegram band," one after another, the men inspected the telegram, patting Povilas on the shoulder. Povilas' thoughts, however, were far away, in another part of the world…

"A second daughter! You probably wanted a son, though, didn't you?" Juozas winked.

"I don't care, as long as there are more and more! Daughters are great, and ten would be even better!" Povilas finally came to his senses and, after putting the telegram into the new Olympic book he had received just the day before, he dove into his extraordinary Olympic Sunday. The first thing on his agenda was to run to the post office to send a telegram and a letter home.

*

43

The final week before the Olympics was even more intense, and the training workload grew even greater.

The men's eight began to feel uneasy. Antanas kept complaining about his back and all of them were exhausted. There were only four days left until the Olympic opening ceremony.

"Yevgeniy Borisovich," Antanas addressed the national head coach directly, "I need a day off. I'm at my limit."

"What is it?" Yevgeniy Borisovich turned towards Antanas while impatiently checking his timer.

"I need to rest. At least a day."

"I don't think so. Your numbers are all normal, they don't indicate any fatigue."

"I feel that if I don't get some rest, I won't be able to race properly."

Samsonov finally looked up, pressed his lips tightly, scrutinized Antanas, and, after a long pause, said:

"Alright, just one short session. The start and some finishes, and then that's it, we put the boat away."

Antanas took a deep sigh – "I'll try my best..." His body was begging for a break. He didn't want to get into the boat, and he shuddered at the thought of having to do a finishing sprint.

"Warm up before the start. Five strokes out of the start, then five and five, then five and ten twice. Got it?"

The cox nodded. Ričardas also nodded, and together, they all pushed off of the pontoon, soon rowing off into the distance, followed by curious Japanese onlookers. Reporters armed with cameras and other devices stood along the bank of the course, presumably collecting material for the next day's newspapers. Indeed, one of their sleeves had an armband with the words "Tokyo PRESS" with the words "Asahi Shimbun" on the breast of the jacket. During Games time, this newspaper was published twice a day – 4 million issues in the morning and 2 million in the evening. There were plenty of them in the Olympic village as well. Unfortunately, they were all in Japanese, so all the athletes could understand were the photos.

After completing their warm-up lap, the Žalgiris eight emerged from the fog.

"Go back nice and slow, and do a max piece off a standing start. One hundred percent!" Samsonov shouted from the bank.

"Come again, Yevgeniy Borisovich!?" Yuriy, the cox, held his hand to his ear and waited for a response.

"Two kilometres, top speed! From the start! Got it?" he shouted again, mounting his bicycle and pedalling off towards the starting line.

"Got it!"

"Rychka, why is he doing this?" the men couldn't believe what they were hearing.

"Are we really going to do this? Top speed? Why?" a wave of discontent rippled through the crew.

"Did you hear? Samsonov's orders. We're doing it!"

"Rychka, this is madness! We can barely walk as it is. We have no strength left… Petras has a fever."

"He's the boss here, we have to listen," Ričardas cut him off.

Nobody dared challenge Samsonov. His experiments were suspect for many, but with only a few days left until the Olympics, they had to believe in something or someone.

"I don't know, my back's not giving me any peace," Antanas quietly complained. "I hope it doesn't get any worse."

The four had returned to the bank and the men listened, surprised at what was happening.

"Why are they doing this?" Celestinas asked incredulously.

"They say it's Samsonov's orders," Povilas shrugged.

"If we had to do that, it'd probably be our final practice," Eugenijus shook his head. "Right before the competition! They'll need time to recover!"

"Maybe they won't row at top speed and they'll save their strength…," Povilas thought out loud. "That would be the smartest thing to do. What's the point of doing this?"

After bringing their boat back, drying it, and storing their oars, the men hurried back to the finish line to see what would happen.

The rumours about the incredibly strong and powerful Soviet eight had enticed rowers from many other teams to come along and watch. Unfamiliar language from behind – neither French nor German – intrigued

Lithuanians and they turned to see who it was so enthusiastically chatting away. Young rowers with blue letters NEDERLAND on their orange tracksuits seemed to be discussing the Žalgiris eight. Povilas smiled and nodded to them.

"Hi!" a tall blue-eyed guy lifted his hand.

"Hi!" Povilas answered back.

"Are you from the Soviet team too?"

"Yes, our friends row in that eight"

"Russian eight? From Vilnius?"

"Yes, from Vilnius. Žalgiris eight. Not Russian though, Lithuanian. Vilnius is the capital of Lithuania."

"I see." The guy smiled distrustfully, "I'm Bob. What's your name?"

"Povilas. Paul in English."

"Hello Povilas. Nice to meet you!"

"Nice to meet you too!" Povilas shook Bob's hand.

"What does it mean CCCP on your shirt?"

"It's in Russian – soyuz sovietskih socyalystitcheskyh respublik. P in Cyrillic is R, and C is S."

"I see. See see see peee." Bob smiled. "What boat do you row Paul?"

"The coxless four."

"I'm in a coxed four, so we won't race each other."

"Did you race last year in Copenhagen?"

"No no, last year I had just started rowing!" Bob shook his head.

"Really? And straight to the Olympics?" Povilas could not believe.

"It was a good year for me." Bob smiled shyly.

"Good luck then." Povilas nodded still greatly surprised. "Good luck Bob!"

"You too, Povilas, have a good race!" Bob shook Povilas hand and the Dutch crew turned to walk back along the course towards the boathouse.

"Who are they?" asked Celestinas.

"The coxed four from Holland. You know, that tall boy started rowing just one year ago!"

"Hard to believe." Celestinas raised his brows.

The silhouette of the Žalgiris eight started to appear in the thick mist of Toda.

"Write down the time, I'll count their stroke rate," Eugenijus asked Povilas.

Povilas checked his watched:

"Hup!… Hup!…"

"Forty-forty two…"

"It's like they're in the finals…"

"Why aren't they saving their energy? Why do they have to show what they're capable of?" Jonas said with surprise.

Samsonov rode up and jumped off of his bike with his timer in his hand.

"Good work, boys, five fifty-four!" he announced Žalgiris' finish time, serious as always, but clearly happy with their result. He rubbed his hands with joy.

The men fought to catch their breath and rocked back and forth in the boat in an effort to recover. The Japanese reporters' cameras snapped furiously.

"I can't get out of the boat," Antanas said through clenched teeth as the boat approached the dock. He was clearly in great pain. "My back…

"What happened?" Ričardas asked, jumping out of the boat and running to Antanas.

"My back… I can't move…"

"Guys, help him get out!" Ričardas, terrified, threw Antanas' arm over his neck and carefully lifted him from the boat. "This is all we needed…"

"What happened?" Samsonov shouted from a distance.

"His back…"

"Where's Tatyana? Get him to a doctor, quickly!"

"I told him I needed rest, and he said 'just a start and a sprint, and then we put the boat away...,'" Antanas said through clenched teeth at the massage room. "I can't move. It's over…"

Rumours of the stunning "Russian" eight's result spread quickly. The Japanese press predicted they'd win gold and their opponents began to worry. The rowers themselves, however, felt hopeless – their strength was gone and their health had deteriorated… Turning back time was impossible…

∗

The next morning, Petras Karla didn't get out of bed - he had a fever of 39.6 degrees Celsius. Antanas was bedridden with terrible back pain and muscle spasms that wouldn't even let him turn onto his side. Reserve rowers – A. Shevelyov and I. Kuprin – took their places for the training sessions. The rowing in the eight suffered. The new crewmembers failed to adjust. This wasn't their fault – they had simply been coached differently and were students of different schools of thought. It became clear that they wouldn't be able to race with their current roster, and that they had to do everything they could to rescue their original rowers – Antanas and Petras. They managed to suppress Antanas' pain with massive doses of drugs, but the drugs suppressed more than just the pain in his back – they suppressed most of his strength. Petras had less than four days to get better – or simply to get rid of his fever. Everyone doubted whether anything could restore the strength he lost to his illness...

The mood in the Lithuanian camp grew darker and darker. They hated the uncertainty about their friends' health. They hated the endless wind and rain that blew across the race course and clearly making the lanes unfair. The speed of the headwinds between lanes on and six differed by a whole three metres per second. They hated that nobody responded to any of the teams' complaints, that the organisers made barely any effort to solve these problems, and that FISA was moving so slowly. They hated that the beginning of the Olympics would come down to luck...

*

There was only one day left until the Olympic opening ceremony and two days until the first race. The atmosphere on the rowers' floor was filled with anxiety over the approaching races.

Ričardas had his two crews sit together in the lobby every evening to review their practice schedules and the next day's plans. He was a rower, too, so not only did he have to inspire his men, he also had to come to terms with his own fears about the race better than any of them could.

"I have two bits of news today," Ričardas began mysteriously, clearly having difficulties mastering his anxiety. "One's good, and the other is... how should I put this... Which one do you want first?"

"Give us the bad news first," Zigmas was the first to respond.

"Alright, then... they told us our lanes for the qualifying races... The eight will be fine. They've got France, the United Arab Republic, and South Korea. The four, on the other hand... You've got the Germans. Might be a tough race... you've got lane two and they're in three. The conditions will be nearly identical, or perhaps a bit in their favour, depending on the weather."

Povilas pressed his lips together tightly, and Celestinas scratched his forehead. Racing the Germans or the Italians was the last thing they wanted.

"I doubt anybody's going to have an easy time of it," Eugenijus nodded.

"If you don't win, you should make it through in the repechage. The other races are much easier. Yours is the hardest. That's just the luck of the draw...," Ričardas said, trying not to crush his athletes' spirits. However, fair was fair, and they couldn't change the outcome of the draw.

It seemed that, during this season, fortune was off wandering somewhere far away and playing tricks on the Lithuanians.

"Would you like to hear the other news?"

The men looked up curiously at their coach.

Ričardas raised a blue telegram in his hand – just like the one Povilas had received a few days ago.

"A telegram?" Povilas noted inquisitively.

"It says LIUTKAITIS VILLAGE USSR OLIMPIE TOKYO."

Povilas smiled broadly and took the blue envelope.

"Another daughter? I already got the news...," he took the blue telegram, scanned it, and laughed out loud, reading, "'The rowing federation congratulates Liutkaitis and Briedis the birth of their daughters. Raudonius[78].'"

James' face grew white for a moment, and the rest of the men looked at him with surprised faces.

"James, you have a daughter!"

Stunned by the surprise, James tried to understand what had happened. Meanwhile, the lobby was flooded with the sound of men cracking jokes and congratulating the new father. The two friends and new fathers, linked by fate, looked at one another with tears in their eyes.

"You guys must have had a great new year's celebration!" somebody joked.

"But it's early, she's not due for another month," James still couldn't believe it. "Perhaps it's a mistake..."

"Nobody jokes about these things. If it's written, that means you've got a daughter!"

---

78   The president of the Lithuanian Rowing Federation.

"I don't believe it, it's just eight months!"

"Who can say, sometimes babies arrive early!" his friends reassured him. Some seemed happier at the news than James was, who was more stunned than anything.

"I've got to know. I'm afraid of celebrating too early…"

"What will her name be, James? How about Olympia?"

"If we win, that's what I'll call her!" James joked. He had finally come to his senses.

"What's this whole celebration about?" Vitaliy Kurdchenko from the four stuck his head out of his room. Above his appeared Yevseyev's head as well.

"A daughter!"

"Another one?"

"Yes, James is the father."

"Excellent! Congratulations! You guys are something else. Two daughters! Who's next?" he laughed, disappearing back into his room.

"You guys will have a heck of a celebration after the competition!" Antanas patted James on the back.

"We will, won't we, James?" Povilas carefully folded the telegram and placed it back into the envelope. "Want to keep it?"

"You watch it for me, Povilas. You've got everything put away so neatly, you definitely won't lose it…"

"Alright, I will… You see, they missed the word 'on.' The federation probably wanted to save money," Povilas laughed. He had grown accustomed to having a daughter.

"I can't believe it! I thought I'd definitely make it home in time… Hold on, I have to go see if this is real. Maybe there was a mistake…"

"Are you serious? Do you really think there was a mistake? That Raudonius would've have written it?"

"I hope everything's alright… How do I find out what day she was born on? A daughter… I need to send a telegram home."

"We can go to the post office if you like."

"Could we? Is it still open?"

"What a party, James! What a party! Olympic daughters!"

*

44

On 10 October, the day of the Olympic opening ceremony, it seemed like someone had changed Tokyo with the flick of a magic wand – after many long and rainy weeks, the city finally saw a clear and sunny day. From the early morning, the Australians, dressed in everyday clothing, practised their parade in the square by their building. They had a signal for taking their hats off to the right, and they wore broad smiles, marching in step like soldiers. The Japanese, dressed all the same in red tracksuits, marched along the street with their white hats pressed to their chests.

In the afternoon, the Olympic village began to grow more and more colourful. For the ceremonial parade, the teams all dressed in their parade uniforms – from elegant dresses, suits and jackets to the traditional outfits of the African continent, which looked like colourful sheets thrown over the shoulders. The elegant athletes from Great Britain, Australia and America were particularly eye-catching. The women wore elegant dresses, suits, hats, and white gloves, though they were about to engage in rather masculine athletic battles. Most of the Olympians, however, were dressed in red jackets and white pants – the delegation of the host country, Japan.

The rowers did not participate in the opening ceremony parade, but even they managed a brief visit to the nearby National Stadium to watch the colourful Olympic column assemble and march into the stadium, to watch the Olympic flame be carried into the stadium and light the fire, and to see the jets draw the Olympic rings in the sky. They wanted to feel the Olympic spirit and to be a part of the celebration. They could hear salvos being fired outside of the stadium and saw thousands of balloons with the colours of the Olympic rings rising into the sky. When the Olympic fire was lit, a huge flock of doves was set loose as well. Fortunately, someone had advised them to bring newspapers, which protected them when all of the birds decided to take a shit all at once.

The action from the stadium could also be seen on TV – and on colour TV! The USSR did not yet have such TVs. The rings being drawn by the jets in the sky could be seen throughout the city. For the first time, the

Olympic Games were broadcast around the world. There were televisions located throughout the Olympic village, which was protected by a tall wire fence and policemen. In addition, the Soviet athletes were watched over by KGB officers, who enforced much stricter rules and limits on movement. On the other hand, the athletes hadn't even thought of walking around much and wasting their energy before the races. Only the doubles and eights wouldn't be racing the next day, but they also wanted to save their energy for the upcoming races.

Watching the Olympic opening ceremony for the first time, albeit on a TV screen, was extraordinarily fascinating. Until then, they had only seen photos from other Olympic Games or read other athletes' memoirs. The parade of participants, the raising of the flag, and especially the lighting of the Olympic flame – all of these things stirred pride and other emotions in the athletes. The occasional chill ran down their spines as they thought of the competition that would begin the next day.

"I wonder if it was always like this, that the rowing competition comes right after the opening ceremony," Povilas turned to his friends.

"It was the same in Rome," Antanas nodded.

"Seriously? So rowers will never get to walk in the opening ceremony?" Eugenijus wondered.

"Other countries will at least stay until the end of the Olympics. They'll fly us out as soon as we're done," Povilas smiled sadly.

"Yeah, no opening and no closing, either," Eugenijus agreed.

*

The first day of the Olympics and of the rowing competition, 11 October, was a beautiful and sunny day. Thousands of spectators gathered at the Toda Rowing Course filling up the grandstands and the shoreline. Vehicles with video cameras and cameramen constantly drove back and forth along the banks of the course, broadcasting directly to reporters' screens.

Japanese newspapers boasted about how local boatbuilders had successfully repaired Ivanov's new English single boat after it had been punctured in two places on a Soviet ship during its journey from London to Yokohama.

Though watching their team's rowers' first races at the Olympics would have been incredibly interesting, Celestinas' four would be heading to the course later to save their energy. Luckily, the TVs at the Olympic village would broadcast all of the action.

"Everyone drew great heats except for us. Just our luck, as always," Eugenijus couldn't hide his disappointment.

"Definitely…," Povilas agreed. "It sometimes feels like you'd turn back time if only you could…"

"Which race is Yevseyev[79] in" Jonas looked up from his book.

"The third, I think. 10:40," Povilas flipped through a brochure.

"Who're they racing? Do you have the schedule?" Jonas closed his book and watched the TV, which was now showing shots of the Toda course.

"The French, Poles, Finns and Danes."

"They should make it through. Unless the French beat them," Eugenijus predicted.

"Did you see, Povilas? It says 'reserve' by your name, and that Sass has your position," Celestinas noted with surprise.

"I did… That makes no difference to me, but it is strange, since it's long been clear that Sass isn't racing… Want to see how your last name looks in Japanese?" Povilas turned to Celestinas. "It's just three characters. Mine has six! They've got an interesting way of writing. Some last names have the first letter of their name next to them, but Jonas' is all characters."

"How can they understand those characters of theirs? Learning to write them looks hard! One stroke straight, two diagonally…," Celestinas shook his head.

"The numbers are normal. Don't they have their own numerals?"

"Look, they have the times here from previous Olympics. You know how much coxless fours' times have changed? By more than half a minute! It was 7:08.8 at Melbourne and 6:26.26 in Rome."

"They said they had a strong tailwind in Rome, and that's why the time was so good. I doubt we'll see anything like that here," Celestinas said doubtfully.

"When are we leaving?" Jonas asked anxiously.

"We should head out at 2:00," Celestinas turned around.

"Won't that be too early? The race is at twenty to 5:00," Eugenijus furrowed his eyebrows.

---

79   The coxed quad scull: V. Yevseyev, A. Tkachiuk, B. Kuzmin, V. Kurdchenko, cox A. Luzgin.

"No, it's not too early," Celestinas opined. "Who knows, what if we get stuck somewhere or something…"

"What time is it now?"

"Ten to 10:00."

"We'll still manage to get two meals in," Povilas smiled.

"I can't stomach anything today," Eugenijus grabbed his stomach.

The TV screen switched back and forth between track and field, swimming, boxing, volleyball and rowing.

"They're second…"

"They're doing well, a kilometre left…"

"Looking good, they're going to win…"

"They're going to win, 'atta boys!"

"They got pretty lucky there."

The first victory raised their spirits. Everything should only get better. The coxless pair and Ivanov's single didn't expect any significant opposition, either. Only the coxed pair and, of course, their four, might have a harder time of it. Their greatest misfortune was the unfavourable lane draw. The double and the eight would be racing the next day. The press was already predicting that the eight would take the gold.

Unfortunately, everything began to fall apart on the second race of the first day. Boreiko and Golovanov finished fourth – or last, since the Finns didn't finish at all. Ivanov lost to an American. Not because he was weaker, but because he missed the beginning of his sprint. Once he saw that he wouldn't catch up to the American, he completely stopped rowing, slowing down to conserve his energy. The coxed pair – Rakovschik, Safronov and Rudakov – lost by a hundredth of a second to the French, missing a place in the final.

The last race on the first day – the third heat for the coxless fours – started at 4:40, when the sun was already setting in the west and shining into the rowers' eyes. The French and British fours, who had already won the right to race in the final and had never been serious competitors for the Lithuanians, celebrated on the banks.

"Êtes-vous prêt, partez!" the start umpire's voice echoed through the megaphone and the French, USSR, German and Austrian fours headed out into their first Olympic battle.

At the very start of the race, the red oars hit the waters of the Toda Rowing Course at a rate of 44 strokes a minute. The Lithuanians racing in lane two refused to let the Germans in the three get ahead by so much as a hair. Their despair about the draw and their anxiety overflowed through their clenched teeth in true athletic rage. For five hundred metres, they remained perfectly even with the Germans, with the men pulling in every stroke like it was their last. There would be only one spot in the final and only one winner.

"For my daughter..." – Povilas repeated to himself in his mind. – "For my daughter." "Halfway... Gotta pick it up... let's go... for my daughter...," he thought, as the thousand-metre buoy flew by. When they each saw the half-way marker out of the corner of their eyes, they began strengthening their finishes in unison. Somewhere, as though from the bottom of a lake, they could hear the roar of the grandstands. Their deafened ears could only hear their own thoughts, which had nearly melted away. When it seemed like they couldn't go on, when their eyes began to grow dark, their bodies continued to perform the movements that they had practised hundreds of thousands of times before, and their thirst for victory wrung strength from beyond a dangerous boundary in their bodies. They heard the echo of a muffled gong – "boom, boom..."

Second... second... second... two seconds. Only two seconds.

The outcome wasn't exactly unexpected – not for Ričardas, not for Samsonov, and not for anyone else on the team. They lost to the European champions by only two seconds. However, they were overcome by disappointment when they saw all of the fours' times. The Danes had made it into the finals with 6:51.78, the Brits had made it through with 6:47.07, and the Lithuanians had missed the mark with 6:40.12.

"If only we'd made it to the next race!" the men couldn't believe it. "Just our luck!"

"Look, all of the best times are in our race! Only the Brits would've made it in, too...," Jonas pointed to a sheet of paper stapled to the wall.

"What happened to the Italians? Only fifth place? Their time is worse than ours by half a minute!" Povilas wondered.

"Lane five...," Jonas noted. "They began to fall behind at the 500 mark."

"You'll rest tomorrow and the repechage is the day after. You'll make it through," Ričardas reassured his men.

"What's the ambulance doing here?" Povilas turned around when he saw doctors rushing to the dock.

"One of the Germans can't seem to recover. He vomited over half of the pontoon."

"From our race?"

"Yeah, yeah. They won but they broke themselves. They can't move."

"They could've taken it easy, as far as we're concerned…"

"They probably overloaded themselves. You guys gave them a fright. Look, they're sticking him into the ambulance."

The ambulance turned on its emergency lights and raced out through the gate to the course.

"And so what? We can't seem to avoid repechage races this year, we can never just make it straight into the final," Eugenijus shook his head.

"I wonder how the lane draw will go for the repechage as well."

"Go home and rest. Yevgeniy Borisovich will let you know about the lanes in the evening. You weren't the only ones not to make it. Only Yevseyev's four made it. Neither the pair nor Ivanov made it straight through."

"We heard, but that doesn't make things any easier for us."

The spectators began to leave the course, and, one after the other, the water filled with crews practising for the next day's races.

"Don't worry, guys, you'll get through the repechage," James reassured them.

"You lost?" Antanas asked as he passed by with an oar on his should. "There's no shame in that, the Germans are good."

"We know. We would've won without doubt in any of the other races," Povilas complained.

"Really?"

"By seven seconds at least."

"Really? That much of a difference?"

"Yeah. The Danes' time was a whole ten second worse, and they're in the final now!" Eugenijus added.

"How's your back? Can you row?" Povilas asked, remembering Antanas' injury.

"It's not good… They drugged me so the pain's gone, but I'm afraid I might fall apart after the start."

"Seriously?"

"I told Samsonov to give me a day off, but no, he needed starts and sprints. And then another two kilometres…"

"You guys looked good, but…"

"And so what, if now I can't row?"

"Yeah… so what…"

Antanas waved and turned towards the dock.

Their race was the next day.

*

45

The second day of the competition began well. The entire team gathered at the Toda Rowing Course in the morning and applauded Tyurin and Dubrovskiy, who had made it into the final with an easy victory over the Dutch, Japanese and Mexican crews. The Žalgiris eight would be racing at 11:40. There were four boats in their race, but they needed to be first.

From 10:00 in the morning, the athletes who didn't have races that day gathered in the grandstands to enjoy the Olympic regatta. The water was unusually calm. The sun was shining, albeit through a light fog. It seemed as though the irritating Tokyo rain had finally ended. The Danish coxless four, seated nearby, beckoned to the Lithuanians to come take a photo together. They knew them from Amsterdam. "You didn't make it into the final? Don't worry, the Germans are strong. It's alright, you'll make it in the repechage tomorrow. We'll meet in the final! We were surprised at how easily we got through. Good luck tomorrow!"

The Lithuanians and the Russians waited uneasily for the eights' race. Just a week ago, everyone had been full of confidence about this race, but now, after the unexpected injuries and illnesses, nobody was sure the Žalgiris crew would have as easy a victory as they had hoped for.

"Look what's happening in the first race! All of the strongest crews, just like in ours!" Povilas noted as he flipped open the race schedule. "Italy, America, Australia, Yugoslavia, Germany…"

"Povilas, let me see, I left mine at home," Jonas asked.

"Take it, I'll go take some pictures," Povilas gave him the pamphlet and stood up.

"They're going! Look at the Germans and the Americans fight!" Eugenijus stood with a stooped back so he wouldn't block anyone else.

The grandstands erupted into cheers. The crowd on the other side of the course also began roaring and waving, taking photos of the rowers while the camera vehicles matched the boats' speed. At opposite sides of the course, in the lanes one and five, the German and American boats flew by, each refusing to let the other go. Behind them, further back but racing neck-and-neck, came the Italians and the Yugoslavians, but, with only 100 metres left, they no longer stood any chance.

"It'll probably be a photo finish," Eugenijus decided.

"Who won?" Celestinas looked at the scoreboard, which hadn't yet shown the outcome of the race.

"Looks like the Germans."

"Are our guys racing now?" Celestinas asked Jonas, absorbed by the schedule flier.

"Not yet, they're after this race."

"They got a good draw," Celestinas nodded.

"Yeah. The Americans are probably just as angry now as we were yesterday," Jonas nodded sadly.

"How's Petras' health? Have you heard?"

"I think he's doing alright. We talked by the TV yesterday and he said everything's fine."

"Look, Povilas, our guys are boating!" Eugenijus waved to the right. Povilas pointed his lens towards Žalgiris' eight, which was rowing out to its first ever Olympic race. They were focused and serious, and only Zigmas had a smile on his face. All of them except Zigmas were dressed in warm jackets, which they had missed so dearly in Copenhagen. Only Zigmas was wearing short sleeves. James glanced at the grandstands one more time after hearing "Go! Go!" being shouted in Lithuanian. With a few long strokes, the boat glided off towards the starting line. The clock showed 11:15.

*

For the first 500 metres, the French crew kept up with the USSR eight, but, stroke-by-stroke, Ričardas' team began to leave them behind. At the kilometre mark, the scoreboard showed a three-second lead.

"They'll win, everything's fine!" Eugenijus leaned back when they entered the final fourth of the race.

"It looks like the times were better in the first heat," Povilas noted.

"I don't remember, I didn't see the half-race times," Eugenijus responded. "What were they?"

"At the kilometre, I think it was 2:53 in the first heat and about 2:57 in the second one."

"Ah, theirs is almost three, less a hundredth. They don't have very strong competition. Think they're saving themselves?" Eugenijus reasoned.

"Could be," Povilas agreed.

"Yeah, with a time like that' they'd have been fifth in the first heat,"

Eugenijus noted after the race. "They wouldn't have made it in the second one, either."

"Good thing we got this race. 6:06, nothing like their qualifying, record-breaking training piece…"

"The Germans have probably broken that record already."

"When's the next race with our guys?"

"Boreiko and Golovanov at 3:00 on the dot, and Ivanov at 4:40. There'll be a break now until 2:00."

"Let's go have lunch."

"How about we go home? Want to eat at the village?"

Eating at the Olympic village was one of their favourite daily "activities." The Fuji and Sakura cafeterias on the men's side could house 1,000 people at once. The men weren't allowed into the women's zone, but there was a separate cafeteria there with seating for 230. The tickets they had been allotted for breakfast, lunch and dinner at the cafeterias were supposed to ensure a daily ration of 6,000 calories, and the self-serve system let them sample various dishes. There were salads, cold and hot dishes, fruit, juice, coffee and tea at the self-serve buffet, with milk, ice cream, water, Coca-Cola, and other beverages located in various refrigerators. The variety of food available stunned the Soviet rowers, who wanted to try everything. Of course, after the first few days, a sign appeared in Russian that read "Please do not take the fruit out with you. Leave enough for others." Someone had noticed the Leningrad rowers filling their backpacks with apples.

Not all of the teams ate there. The Italian, German and Hungarian teams brought their own chefs to Tokyo. The Indian team brought two chefs while the French team brought three. The Polish team had brought their own nuitritionist.

The USSR team was assigned to the first hall at the Sakura cafeteria, which they shared with athletes from Czechoslovakia, Bulgaria and Mongolia. They could watch the Olympic athletes in the other halls eat through the glass walls of the hall.

At the Fuji cafeteria, and in the gardens next to it, they could always hear the very Japanese acoustic music of Kuniharu Akiyama. Special stone megaphones had been installed just for this purpose. This filled the area with a friendly, festive and very positive atmosphere.

In the evenings, everyone would hurry out of the cafeterias to have some fun on Melbourne Street, where the International Club was located. This was the noisiest part of the Olympic village, and it was always filled with music and laughter, even though the only things served there were milkshakes and chocolate milk. It was a fun place to have a party, but whenever the athletes had a race the next day, that was the last thing on their minds…

*

Boreiko and Golovanov never recovered after their loss the previous day, finishing fourth in the repechage. They were almost 14 seconds behind the Finns, who finished first. They were out of both the grand final and the small final. Ivanov, however, had gotten "back on his horse," rowing the best time of the day and leaving the Australian rower three lengths behind. Once again, after comparing the results from the three races, the Australian and Czech men cursed their predicament and wrung their hands. Their chances at the final were gone on account of their poor draws.

*

"You race tomorrow at 11:20, lane three," Ričardas had returned from Toda with the next day's race schedules. "You're racing Canada, Argentina and Italy…"

"Italy?" Celestinas grabbed his head and sighed. "As if it couldn't get any worse…"

"How come they're in this with us?" Jonas wondered.

"You were second and they were fifth in their race. That's how it goes. The strongest get the weakest."

"The weakest? I doubt they're as weak as their result would suggest," Eugenijus said doubtfully.

"We're tied with them this year, one-all… we have to win tomorrow, there's no other way…," Povilas added.

"That's right, you've got to win," Ričardas encouraged them. "Your time from yesterday was better."

"Much better!" Eugenijus corrected him. "But we were fighting all the way. How about them?"

"Nobody knows how they felt out there…"

The men grew quiet as the happy and noisy eight walked past. The anxiety they had been fighting for so long began to gather as a dark cloud on the horizon. Their bodies dreaded just the thought of the next day's race.

"Son of a bitch, this I did not expect…," Povilas swore.

"How did this happen?" Celestinas unconsciously wrung the newspaper he had been flipping through in his hands.

"We got our greatest fear…," Eugenijus sighed deeply.

"Celestinas, don't panic. You'll burn out and we'll all be worse off," Povilas reassured their stroke. "They aren't unbeatable."

"I know, but what if we don't win?" Celestinas' voice was filled with self-doubt.

"We will! Let's stop guessing. We're better off thinking about how we're going to crush them," Povilas tried to cheer his friends up.

"Which lane are they in?" Jonas looked up.

"We didn't ask… what difference does it make?" Eugenijus shrugged. "That won't change things one way or another. Will we feel better if we know?"

"You know, you always want to find some sort of silver lining," Povilas smiled. "This evening, let's go drink a bunch of milkshakes so we sleep well. Everything will be alright."

"Since when were you such an optimist, Povilas?" Jonas turned to him.

"Because I've had such a beautiful life," Povilas laughed. "Until now…"

Of course, all of them were worried. They wanted their chain of troubles to end. Some might say – "Troubles? They were sent to Tokyo after losing, and last year, they went to Europe after losing… Sounds like a great big pile of good luck!" However, they had hoped that, after so many painful defeats, unfortunate steering errors, and un-earned capsizes, something had to change… But it hadn't…

"I have a daughter!" Povilas thought to himself. "That's a stroke of good luck!" However, his thoughts kept returning to the next day's race, filling his body with dread. "Others can't even dream of seeing the Olympics, and yet here we are – and in Japan, no less. At the Olympics, the most important thing is participating!" His thoughts spun round in circles, filling him with dread and fear. "Tomorrow – 13 October – my daughter will be exactly ten days old. I need to give her a win in the finals as a gift…"

*

RIMA KARALIENE

46

"The 13th day is only unlucky for the superstitious," Antanas encouraged the four as they ate their breakfast in the early morning.

"So I guess everyone who loses today is superstitious," Povilas ventured a response to the joke as he tried to swallow his breakfast.

"There's a strong wind today," James joined the conversation. "Which lane do you have?"

"Three."

"And the Italians?"

"I think they're in four."

"Then it should be about the same."

"Celestinas, where are you hurrying off to?" Povilas stopped Celestinas, who had jumped up from his chair.

"I don't want to eat. I'm going home."

"Hold on, we'll all go together! Are you going to the course?" Povilas turned back to James.

"We will. We all need to do a bit of shouting. After all, our race only comes the day after tomorrow."

"I might stay behind, with my back the way it is."

"You guys are nervous," James could see that his friends couldn't relax.

"How should I put this…," Povilas' thoughts were elsewhere. After quickly finishing his tea, he jumped up from his chair as well. "We're off." He waved his right hand, took his tray, and hurried off after his friends.

James and Antanas followed the four with their eyes.

"When it rains, it pours," Antanas shook his head.

"Who's it raining for?" Juozas heard the men talking and sat next to them on one of the chairs that had freed up.

"Not for us, but for them," he gestured towards Celestinas, Jonas and Povilas as they left. "That's the second time their draw ruined everything for them."

"How?"

"They're racing the Italians. If they lose, that's it…"

"But look at what's happening! There are stars getting knocked out of the finals!"

"You know, I thought we were doomed yesterday, too. We kept rowing and that French crew never let go!"

"Yeah…"

*

The trip to the course, escorted by police and their sirens as it usually was, seemed to take an eternity. They stared out of the windows, missing the beautiful sunrise that graced Tokyo that morning, the giant buildings and advertisements, the billowing Olympic flags, or the Japanese people waving at them. In their eyes, all they could see was the water of Toda, their oar handles, their friends' red backs, and the lane buoys. It was probably the first time that their hands had shook so much, and their ears could no longer hear any of their coaches' advice…

The wind was once again blowing across the course, but the best lanes – five and six – were usually empty. Repechage races usually only had four, or sometimes five, boats.

All of the team's staff had already gathered at the canal. Tatyana, their trusted doctor, marched briskly at the head of the pack with her black suitcase in her hand. She was wearing a colourful brown Olympic shirt and a black skirt with white sandals, and puffed on a cigarette as she walked. Other countries' rowers always took curious glances at her little suitcase, soon spreading rumours that she used it to carry drugs for doping the USSR's rowers.

"Any problems, guys?" Tatyana hurried over to the four after seeing Celestinas' face more worried than she had ever seen in her life. "Does something hurt?"

"No, it doesn't…," Celestinas shook his head.

"Are you having an anxiety attack?"

Celestinas swallowed hard.

"I'll give you guys a pill each so you don't feel so nervous," she said, opening her suitcase and drawing out a brown glass bottle. "Take this pill an hour before your race and you'll feel fine!"

"What is this?" Ričardas appeared behind his athletes when he saw the doctor with them.

"They need to relax, so I'm giving them a pill each to make everything better," she explained.

"Alright, what is it?" Ričardas took the bottle and put it in his pocket. "Aspirin…"

There were almost two hours left until the race. "The quicker we start, the quicker it'll all be over…" The men stretched out in the recreational room to spend the final minutes before preparing for their race. Through the windows, they watched the coxed pairs finish and saw the victorious cox, Rudakov, raise his hand.

"Don't overdo it, guys," Ričardas reassured them. "You can't row like that. You've got to jump out at the start like always and keep it up until you finish. Today's your most important Olympic race. The weather's not with you, but it's no better for anybody else. I want you to boat at 9:50."

*

The grandstands were full of spectators. The Japanese applauded both those finishing and those leaving for the starting line. The commentator spoke ceaselessly in his machine-gun-fast Japanese. On the left side waved a row of twenty white Olympic flags, like weather vanes that showed the relentless and almost unchanging wind from the northeast that was whipping up the water.

"I don't know, Celestinas, my body feels like rubber," Povilas complained quietly to Celestinas' back. "Something's off."

"Me too. I feel like I'm about to fall asleep. What was in those pills that Ričardas gave us?"

"He said it was aspirin so we don't feel anxious…"

"I doubt aspirin makes you this sleepy… They're probably some sort of depressants… They said they'd relax us, but my legs are shaking…"

"It probably wasn't aspirin… How do you guys feel? Is everything fine?" Povilas turned back to Jonas between strokes.

"Why?"

"No reason…"

The American four quickly shot past. Their race was the first one, so there were only ten minutes left.

*

There are days that you want to erase from your memory as quickly as possible and bury in the dust of time, if turning back time isn't an option…

13 October was a great day of defeat for the Žalgiris four. They

completed the first 500 metres in the lead, after which, stroke by stroke, they fell behind the Italians. The countless months of exhaustion got the better of them. The things they had achieved in countless qualifying races could not be reproduced in that fateful race. Their exhausted bodies had reached their limits, and perhaps even stepped beyond them. And then there was the anxiety that had robbed them of their strength before even leaving for the starting line… In the last 500 metres, the men won back a hard-earned second, but it wasn't enough… They were three seconds short of the final and sixteen seconds ahead of the Canadians they left behind. Had they won the first race…

The Italians won. So did the Americans and the Dutch.

Soviet and Lithuanian journalists, coaches and teammates were all more infuriated by the injustice of their situation than the rowers themselves. They didn't need to make any excuses – it was clear to everyone that fortune had turned her back on the Lithuanians and that their circumstances had stolen the final from them. However, they were not the only victims of unlucky draws. Many strong and medal-worthy teams were side-lined because they received "bad" lanes. The greatest shame of all was that this had happened at the Olympics. The next opportunity would be four years later… The entire season had plunged them into a whirlwind of misfortunes, and the fear of new defeats kept tripping them up…

There were rumours and anger that the Italian team that had started the Olympics off so poorly couldn't possibly have "put their backs into it" to such an extent without doping. However, these remained guesses – there was nobody to confirm these suspicions.

The Olympics didn't end that day. When the situation changes, so do one's goals. Now, they had to take the highest position among those who remained – to be the fastest rowers in the small final. "Seventh place is still placing in the Olympics," their teammates reassured them. The heads of the delegation, however, only wanted medals. Gold medals!

The small final would be the following afternoon.

However, the Soviet delegation did have something to boast of to the entire Olympic village. That evening, the USSR Olympians were called to the flag square to hear about a "great feat of the Soviet people," another "victory for USSR science and technology" – they had sent the first spacecraft with three astronauts into space. "The first time in the world!" TASS soon found a poorly organized photo of the eight crew smiling and laughing that had been taken back in Sakhalin and quickly sent it to Lithuania, where it appeared in the 14 October issue of "Truth" with the caption "Tokyo Olympic Games. Žalgiris eight rowers V. Briedis, P. Karla, V. Sterlik, R. Vaitkevičius, A. Bagdonavičius and J. Jagelavičius listen to TASS' message about the Soviet spacecraft's flight." It also told the Soviet people about how everyone at the Tokyo Olympics was still discussing Nikita Khruschev's letter to the Olympians.

*

The Russians Boreiko and Golovanov, who were watching the races from the side-lines for the second day in a row, were among the first to comfort the Lithuanians:

"What can you do, guys? That's sport. One day you're the champion, the next you're nothing. Don't let it get you down. You still have an opportunity to prove you are not last. Look at us – we're out until next Olympics."

"Thanks," Eugenijus smiled and hung his head. "How are you guys holding up?"

"We're fine now, we've come to terms with it. But we can't forgive them for all of this. They took our Olympic medals away from us!" they nodded towards the USSR team coaches chatting by the boathouse. "Trials every week, and a selection race three days before the Olympics! We had proven a hundred times that we were stronger, but they kept going up to the last moment... Our nerves could barely take it, not to mention our bodies... We were speechless..."

"Yup," Povilas nodded.

"Look, Slava and Tyurin trained according to their own plan, and they're showing some results! Meanwhile, they drove us like dogs... And during the selection race, we breathed plenty of smoke from that factory over there," they gestured towards the chemical factory spewing smoke at the kilometre mark. "We were coughing all night."

As they looked at the rowing veterans and Olympic champions who had lost what was perhaps their last opportunity to win Olympic medals, their own misfortunes no longer seemed so great. But, just like everyone else, the loss made the hurt from the entire season come rushing back.

*

47

There was always some sort of meeting or another held every single evening next to the 9th building area in the village. The government would congratulate its medal winners, wish others luck in their preparations, hand out telegrams, and so on.

This evening, however, was different. After a general team meeting, all of the Lithuanian rowers were told to gather at the recreational room. "Participation is mandatory for everyone!" Ričardas warned them. Nobody ever tried to avoid the meetings, though they knew well that these were usually held to lecture and scold them rather than praise them. "We're gathering in the lobby on the first floor at 7:00. Don't be late. We'll be having guests." There were rumours abound that a Russian sailor had escaped from a Soviet ship that had come to bring tourists and was requesting asylum. The KGB had been put on alert and the athletes were now being watched twice as carefully.

"I don't want to listen to their lectures anymore," Povilas, stretched out on his bed, flipped through Japanese postcards.

"Yeah," Celestinas agreed. "We already know everything they tell us."

"I miss home... I want to see my daughter soon... both of them," Povilas sighed.

Celestinas smiled:

"Have you thought of a name?"

"I haven't had time. We'll think it over when I get home. I have to see who she looks like first. If she looks like Gita, she'll be Brigita, and if she looks like me, she'll be Paulina," Povilas laughed.

"It's ten to seven, we'll have to go soon," Eugenijus rose from his seat.

"One more day and we can celebrate," Povilas sat up.

"Sure, you and James have something to celebrate about. The rest of us will celebrate the small final, right, Celestinas?"

"There's nothing to celebrate. We'll see how everything goes tomorrow," Celestinas was doubtful.

"What do you mean? How do you think it's going to go?" Povilas was surprised.

"Everyone's been saying that the Austrians are really strong and that we won't beat them."

"Weren't they just third in the repechage?"

"They were leading and should've been in the final, but their rudder broke, or something like that…"

"Don't listen to them, Celestinas! We have nothing to lose anymore. It's our last race, and there's nothing else to save ourselves for. As for the Austrians – nonsense! Did you see them row? They're nothing to worry about," Povilas wanted to dispel his friends' doubts.

"Alright, let's go," Eugenijus roused them again and the three of them left the room together.

Ričardas and Zigmas were already waiting in the first-floor lobby. Other voices could be heard down the corridor.

"Hey, guys," they were greeted by a man they felt they had seen somewhere before. He was probably from the Sports Committee. "How are you guys holding up?"

"Not very well," Celestinas answered quietly, lowering his head. "We lost today…"

"Don't worry," he reassured them, "We'll raise your spirits soon enough! Where is the eight?"

"They're coming, they'll be here soon," Ričardas paced about impatiently. It seemed like even he wasn't sure what the "government" had called them here for.

James, Petras, Juozas and Antanas were having a loud conversation when they entered, but when they saw government men from Lithuania, they greeted them and grew quiet. They understood that a long conversation would surely follow.

"Dear Olympians, I'm not going to do much talking today. The fact that you're here at all is a great accomplishment for Soviet Lithuania. Never before in our history have we had so many Olympians from Lithuania – sixteen in total, with ten rowers. Everyone understands full well that these results wouldn't be possible without difficult work and sacrifice, so everyone is very proud of you and sends their warmest regards from Lithuania. We haven't arrived empty-handed. We've brought you some gifts as well."

The men looked up and, curious, bent forward, as if that would give them a better look. The man placed a stack of letters on the table:

"This is for you. Your loved ones have sent you all of their love and their best wishes. I'll hand these out in a moment, but that's not all."

The man walked to the table and pushed a button on the record player standing there. After a few seconds of static, they could suddenly hear Irena's voice: "Hello, Zigmas. Congratulations on successfully making it to Japan. Artūras and I send you our best regards from Vilnius and your favourite song..." With that, a melody began to play. Out of surprise and wonder, the men laughed and then grew silent as they were overcome by incredible longing and emotion. They hid their feelings by burying their faces in their hands, behind their friends' backs, and behind Japanese newspapers. The voice from home seemed like an impossibly distant crumb of warmth and cosiness. Separated from their families and homes, the men were turning into fearless battle machines. The Lithuanian song, however, reawakened their emotions, their gentleness and their longing. When the song ended, the men, in an effort to control themselves, began to clap.

To Celestinas' great surprise, he received a congratulatory message from his uncle Adolfas, an academic who hadn't supported his athletic career much. His uncle's warm voice and encouraging words, however, inspired him.

One after another, their loved ones sent their regards to all of the Lithuanian rowers present.

"Dear Povilas," – everyone there recognized Gita's voice and looked at Povilas with mischievous but supportive glances. – "Rasa and I are very proud of you. Everyone at home misses you very much and sends you their regards. I hope that, wherever you are, you never forget your home and Lithuania. I send you my kisses and await your return... I'm sending you this song." As the first chords played, they could hear Daunoras[80]' voice:

"I sing you the most beautiful words that I know,
Oh, Motherland.
I see you wherever in the world I go,
Oh, Motherland.
Every thing I find here is dear,
The mornings are so beautiful and clear,
Oh, Motherland.

---

80   Vaclovas Daunoras, a famous Lithuanian opera singer.

I'll love you until the end of time,
Oh, Motherland.
With the dear ancestors and parents of mine,
Oh, Motherland.
The land that sung me softly to sleep,
Where I had a name for each grain of sand and each creek,
Oh, Motherland.

Each fiery battle you saw me through,
Oh, Motherland.
The joy of sweet love I learned from you,
Oh, Motherland.
I'll live in this part of the world I love best,
Until I'm finally laid to rest,
Oh, Motherland.

Everyone grew quiet, overcome by deeply suppressed emotions, and remained that way for a long minute. The word "motherland" contained everything – their homes, the women they loved, their parents, their children, the streets of Vilnius, the homesteads of their childhoods, the bends of the Neris, the autumn rain... that was Lithuania. Not the broad country, but the Lithuania that they had all been born in and that they could no longer discuss out loud... It was the tears and the hopes of their loved ones who had returned from Siberia and of those who never would....

"Can we play that one more time?..." Ričardas stood up unexpectedly and asked in a voice muffled by emotion. "Men, it is for that motherland that we will all line up at our final decisive starting lines. For Lithuania..." Povilas stood up as well, and they were joined by the rest of the men, who stood and hummed to the second playing of Daunoras' song. They were drawn together by an indescribable unity and the constant hidden pain they felt for their homeland. Now, they had an opportunity to express it through song. They feared nothing, not even the KGB officials whose ears were pressed to the walls. It was easy to explain what the song was about, and without even lying – "it's a song about our motherland!"

*

48

It was raining again on the morning of 14 October, but the Olympic village was as lively as always. The residents rushed to and fro under large, colourful Japanese umbrellas, which were available in every building. They headed to the cafeterias, buses, post offices, shops, or call centre. Those who'd managed to grab a bike headed to the cafeteria on two wheels. Ethiopian marathon runner Abebe Bekila, a champion from the Olympics in Rome, ran by with his friends. There weren't any journalists yet, however, as their visiting hours at the Olympic village were limited.

On that day, the regatta was only set to begin at 14:00, so nobody was in any hurry. Only those who'd be racing in the next day's final headed to the course to practise. The small finals were the only races to be held that day. The men from the four gathered in one room together to spend the last hours before their last race – the small final for places seven through twelve. "No, it's only for 7th place! No anxiety, no aspirin, no fear! All of this nonsense has to end today!"

"We have the lane one again, as luck would have it," Povilas shook his head, as he grew curious about who was responsible for handing out lanes.

"The wind, of course, will be a headwind from the lane six," Celestinas frowned as he looked out of the wet window.

"Look at the flag, it's the same as yesterday, the same direction…," he gestured at a red flag waving in the yard.

"When it rains, it pours. Think it'll die down?"

"Doubt it… I just hope it doesn't pick up…"

"We have to take our coats," Eugenijus added. "It's cold."

"Will we need our white socks?" Povilas laughed.

"Why white?" Jonas asked, missing the joke.

"Oh, well last year, during the spartakiad… they told us in the four to put on white socks so we'd look good when receiving our medals, but we finished fourth… We don't wear matching socks anymore. We've become superstitious," Povilas chuckled.

"But they gave us all matching socks, so what are we supposed to do?" Jonas still couldn't tell whether or not Povilas was kidding.

"Put on any socks you like, as long as we don't agree on making them all match. Whatever happens happens."

After packing their racing kit, coats and towels into their identical Olympic bags with red hammers and sickles, the men lay down to rest. As they stared at the ceiling, each of them gathered their strength in their own way. When there were only a few hours left until their race, they weren't very talkative – their mouths had grown dry, their words came slowly, and every piece of advice or encouragement only served to irritate them.

*

"The Austrians might give you trouble. They'll be next to you in lane two. Don't give them an inch," Ričardas have them his final advice before the race. "The Romanians in the lane three are strong, too. But the wind's not in your favour today. Anything can happen. It'll be easier near the finish, but you'll have to endure it for the first thousand. Warm up with your coats on and only take them off before you start so your muscles don't grow cold. Eugenijus, the most important thing for you is to watch your steering. Don't forget to turn around occasionally."

When the men left the recreational room, the clock showed 2:30. There was less than an hour until their last Olympic race. They went through the usual procedures – they greased their oars, and Ričardas tightened the nuts and bolts, checking whether anyone had made any holes overnight. "We ready?" "Ready!" Each of the rowers took their oars and marched towards the dock, before any lines had formed.

Some of their opponents – the French and the Austrians – were already stretching on the dock. The Canadians jogged by as well.

Instead of his usual advice, Ričardas, wrapped in a raincoat, shouted from the dock: "For Lithuania, guys!" He waved and watching them row off before heading to the grandstands.

The wind blew in their faces, and their oars were like sails, getting blown back whenever they lifted them. "We'll really have to dig in against this wind," the men quietly thought to themselves. Eugenijus was anxious about his steering – "with wind like this, I hope I don't veer off course."

The coxed pairs were already out on the race course. At 500 metres, the Germans were already ahead by two lengths. The next race would be theirs – the coxless fours. From the very beginning of the heats, all of the races were 20 minutes apart – probably in an effort to avoid collisions during warm up due to the lack of space in the course. The clock showed 3:05. They had fifteen minutes until their race.

The starting line looked like a sea, and the nets didn't help one bit. The steep banks made things even worse, and the waves were at their most intense near the lane one. Lanes five and six, which were in a lee, were nearly calm.

"It's not the Olympics, it's a lottery," Eugenijus complained after turning his right foot with the rudder cable all the way back.

"Eugenijus, you just make sure it doesn't take us into the bank," Povilas said, also reminding him of a rule they all knew well: "If you see you can't steer us in, tell us who needs to slow down. We'd rather have a couple of weak strokes than hit a wall."

"That's right," Jonas agreed.

The start umpire turned on his megaphone and began to call out the names of the four crews. There were five minutes until the start of the race.

The long season ran through their minds – the mountains, the skis, the foggy windows of the gyms that reeked of sweat, the waves in Khimki, the victory gongs, the starting flares, hitting the buoys, the bridges in Lucerne, the river Kura near Mingechaur, the red newspaper titles, the endless sprints, starts and finishes... "This is the Olympics, this is our final Olympic race..." – Povilas tried to focus. "I've dreamed about this for so long! And now I can't get excited about it... I have to remember every moment." He took a deep breath, looked around, and smiled broadly at the course and the clock above the starting line. "I'll have a story to tell my daughter... when she grows a bit... not everyone gets to be born during the Olympics... maybe she'll be a rower... or maybe not... it's too hard... but how do women manage it at all?... My final race, I have to enjoy it and do what I can... as long as Celestinas keeps the rate up... he will, I'll help him... the Austrians are afraid... how much time is left? Ten minutes and that's it..."

The umpire's call came – two minutes. The men took their jackets off, under which they wore red, short-sleeved shirts with the USSR coat of arms on their chests. "I'm ashamed to take these jackets off... I wonder how the athletes feel who are proud of their clothing and who race for their homelands..." – Povilas felt the absurdity of his red uniform, which turned him into a Russian and a communist, a faceless and subjugated soldier who was just following the orders of a country hostile to the world. He was locked behind a barbed wire fence and punished for his opinions, for his desire to be free, and for his desire to love his homeland… He would never carry the red flag and wave it with pride the way the Americans, French, Italians, Australians, and all the rest did. He would never cheer "USSR" – only "Lithuania!..." "Oh, Motherland."

*

"Êtes-vous prêt, partez!!"

The oars squeezed the choppy waters of the Toda course. Half, two-thirds, three-quarters, a full stroke, and one, and two, and three… the start was successful! The Japanese immediately fell behind, as did the Canadians. The Austrians were keeping up, stroke for stroke. Occasionally, one oar or another would trip up over the waves, the headwind seeming to tear them from the rowers' hands. After 500 metres, the Romanians fell behind by half a length, with the French and Canadians behind by two. However, the Austrians weren't breaking. The water was splashing in over the sides, but their experiences in Khimki helped them avoid crabs or rocking the boat. Their legs burned with fatigue and they started to gasp for air, their bodies wracked with pain… but this was nothing new. All was as it should be. It would pass… One, two, three… for the Motherland… for Lithuania… for Lithuania… The Austrians were on their heels, behind by just a few metres. They needed to finish them off… the third 500 was approaching… Almost… Ten more strokes… One… Two… Three… At the kilometre mark, everyone knew – "the third 500." Their finishes grew stronger with each stroke, their rate slowly rising and rising. They were moving… one… two… three… They heard Lithuanian cheers from the bank – "Go! Go!" The men had found their stride and were rowing at a rate of 40 per minute, leaving the Austrians a length behind them. 500 more… "Hold it!" Povilas roared in his mind. "Hold it!" – the crewmembers all understood one another. The Austrians glanced to the left in their attempts to respond to the "Russian" attack, but there wasn't much left until the finish line. "The last twenty!" somebody shouted from the grandstands, but the wind carried their voice off. The rate was 42 strokes per minute, and the Austrians were hitting 44, but their strokes were shorter. "Don't let go," the men told themselves in their heads. "Don't let go..." The roar of the grandstands muffled the gong, and it was only the yellow finish line board that told them as it shot by – that's it! It was over… At least one victory… a victory at the Olympics!

It was over… Their times lit up on the scoreboard: 1 URS 6:22.03, 2 AUT 6:24.15. The Romanians finished three seconds later, the French were behind by 14, and the Canadians trailed by 21. The hosts, the Japanese crew, finished 27 seconds behind, but they received the loudest cheers of the day.

Samsonov waved from the shore – "row to the award pontoon!" "What is he saying?" – the men didn't understand – "the award pontoon?" They couldn't hear what the announcer was saying over the noise in the grandstands. Ričardas waved from the bank. "Should we row?" – the men looked at one another. Then, the umpires' motorboat approached them – they were being invited to receive their awards.

The men, surprised, turned their boat around and rowed to the award pontoon, which was decorated with flowers. For first place in the small final, they received elegant boxes covered in red and gold fabric. Inside, they found tiepins made of real pearl and attached to white velvet. After admiring the beautiful gifts, the men waved to the audience that was clapping for them and returned to their boat. The enormous sense of responsibility and tension that had burdened their hearts and their shoulders slipped away, shattering into a million invisible little pieces…

When they came to the pontoon, they met the French rowers there as well. They were the first to congratulate the winners and invite them to take a photo together. Just that moment, Anatoly, their reserve rower, ran by with Povilas' camera…

"Good thing that we all have the same socks after all," Povilas laughed. "Not black or white, but the same. The photos will be nice."

The men looked down at their socks and laughed. Their exhaustion had left them, and it seemed like their strength had returned twofold.

"If only we had felt this good yesterday!" Povilas still had a speck of grief left in him.

"Yeah, today was totally different," Eugenijus agreed. "I felt like my body was all off yesterday."

"Look, we beat the Olympic record!" Jonas pointed to the scoreboard.

"Really?" Celestinas said incredulously.

"We got six twenty two, and it was six twenty six in Rome."

"We beat it for a day… There's still the final…"

"Another reason to celebrate!" Povilas said happily. "Today, while we're still record holders."

"Let's go get some milkshakes," Celestinas laughed.

*

The Olympic Games were over for the four, so they could finally enjoy what was happening around them – to take walks through the Olympic village, sleep in, and perhaps, with a KGB escort, go out into the city beyond the village to see some shops. The next day's finals were to start at 1:30, so that night, they'd be able to spend some more time at the village bar – of course, with the KGB's permission.

*

49

On 15 October, a local English-language newspaper, The Japan Times, had an intriguing headline on its front page. The Soviet athletes who understood English grabbed copies to read and translate for their friends. "W. Germany Won't Grant Asylum To Soviet Sailor." The brief article stated that the West German minister of foreign affairs in Bonn had said that Germany could not provide the Soviet sailor with asylum because this would violate international law... Had the sailor made it into Germany directly from the Soviet Union or if he would have faced danger while in Japan, he could submit an application for political asylum. In this case, the 28-year-old Soviet citizen would have to ask Japan for political asylum...

It seemed like the man was in a tight spot... and the KGB officials who had come to Japan were in a tight spot because they had failed at their jobs. The KGB officials in the Olympic village wore gloomy faces as well.

The poor weather was the cherry on top of the bad news. There was rain and a strong wind from the north-east – another diagonal headwind.

From the moment they woke up, eight were fidgety. They had an unpredictable final ahead of them. Only one of them felt lucky, and that was Volodia Sterlik. It was his 24th birthday, and he hoped to give himself an Olympic medal for his birthday.

All of the final participants – the coxed four, the double scull and pair, and Ivanov the single – spent the entire morning looking out their windows uneasily and hoping for a miracle.

In the meantime, Celestinas' four was able to enjoy a looser schedule, leaving to walk through the city together. Tokyo was even more colourful and diverse than they had seen through the bus windows. Narrow, winding streets branched off from the wide avenues of tall, shining buildings, and they were full of shops with products hung or laid out outside. The retractable cloth awnings practically met at the centre of the streets, which were covered in incomprehensible signs, Olympic flags, and incredibly polite and happy Tokyo residents, among whom the men felt like giants. There were also strange spots of disorder, and sad and exhausted people dragging their daily burdens behind them in carts full of trash. They were surprised by the fact that the streets didn't even have names – or if they did, they were names that foreigners wouldn't understand... They were afraid of wandering far and not finding their way home. On the other hand, there were more good people interested in helping the Olympians than they could have possibly needed,

Their eyes were drawn by the electronics shops, filled with new devices – from regular TVs to portable TVs the size of women's purses.

"Look, they've got rowing on!" Povilas began to take photos of what he saw in one TV screen.

"What races are these? Today's races haven't begun yet," Eugenijus squinted at the small screen.

"I think this is the Japanese eight. They're probably talking about their athletes."

"It's probably just a news report," Eugenijus smiled. "But look at those TVs! You can go wherever you want with a TV like that. It's like a briefcase."

"I wonder how many years until TVs like these show up in Lithuania. We don't even have regular ones yet..."

The used electronics stores were filled with items that, while well-used, were still much newer than those in the Soviet Union; TVs, radios, and kitchen appliances that Soviet housewives might have only dreamed of, like cocktail shakers, juicers, and others. Their eyes glittered with the amount and quality of the products on offer. Sony, Toshiba, Sharp and Mitsubishi advertisements competed amongst themselves on the fronts of the building.

The men walked along the street and browsed the colourful wares until they realised that there were only three of them – they had lost Povilas.

"Where did Povilas go?" Eugenijus asked, gazing past the throng of dark-haired Japanese heads. He didn't even need to stand on his toes.

"Should we go back? I have his backpack," Jonas suggested.

"Let's wait, he'll come by in a moment. Maybe he ducked into one of these stores."

After waiting for another minute, the men began to slowly walk back. A short way off, they found Povilas, his eyes glued to a store display.

"What did you find, Povilas? We were waiting for you!" Eugenijus was happy to have found his lost friend.

"Look at that Nikon!" Povilas was enraptured and couldn't take his eyes off of the cameras in the store's display window.

"Which one? This one?"

"Yeah… I've been dreaming about a camera like that…," Povilas' eyes were shining.

"It's a hundred and twenty dollars… It ain't cheap," Eugenijus shook his head.

"I think that if I sell everything, it should be enough…"

"You're going to buy it?"

"What did you find?" Jonas approached them.

"A Nikon camera… I'm drooling over it…"

"Ah, I see. You know more about these matters than I do. It seems too expensive for me…"

Povilas sighed, glanced at his old FED, and followed his friends away. He looked back once more at the storefront of his dreams before walking down the street.

*

It stopped raining and the sky grew clear and sunny just before the race.

Everyone that had finished racing tried to find the best seats available. The men with the word "NIPPON" on their chests were also eager to see the final, although none of their rowers would be racing – the entire Japanese rowing team had failed to make the cut.

Five USSR crews focused on preparing for the races while the remaining two grappled with the heartbreaking thought that they should've been racing here today as well.

The relentless north-eastern wind whipped up the water in the lanes closest to the grandstands, while lanes five and six were calm. Those who had been drawn in the far lanes rejoiced before the race had even begun.

People began making predictions – about who would win and who would lose to whom and by how much. Toda had its own plans, however.

The coxed fours' race had already shown that the finals would be decided by luck rather than each crew's strength. From the middle of the course, the advantage in lanes five and six was clear. At the finish line, the boats finished in the same order, according to their lanes – sixth, fifth, fourth, third, second and first... In this simple system, the Soviet four – that year's European champions – finished in fifth place. The Germans won.

"What can I say. If this is how Olympic medals are decided, then...," Celestinas shook his head in disappointment.

"Bob won bronze!" Povilas said joyfully.

"Who?" asked Celestinas.

"Dutch four. Remember that tall youngster Bob, who just started rowing? In the bow seat."

Eugenijus opened the page with the start list for the coxed fours:

"Three Graafs in one boat!"

"What are you talking about?" Povilas.

"Three men in their boat with the surname 'Graaf'. Are they all brothers?"

"I have no idea." Povilas shrugged.

"Good for them. So young and already medallists." Celestinas scratched his head.

"If we could race for Lithuania we would have gone to Olympics after just a year or two as well..." Povilas said with disappointment.

"It would be funny if it weren't so sad..." Nodded Celestinas.

"Let's see how the coxless pairs do," Eugenijus scanned the programme. "The Germans are in the lane one."

"Who's in six?"

"Canada."

"Wait. The Dutch beat them in Europe, right? The Germans were second?" Povilas turned around.

"I think so... I don't remember. All I know is that our guys were fourth, just like us," Eugenijus looked up from the schedule. "Jonas, who won the coxless pair in Europe?"

"The Dutch, I think."

"They're in lane four," Eugenijus continued inspecting the race lineups. "That's better than the Germans in the lane one."

"I think the wind's growing stronger," Celestinas looked up at the Olympic flags waving on the other side of the course.

The Olympic finals were held every half an hour so that there would be time for the medal ceremonies between the races. While the champions received their medals and listened to their national anthem as their flags were raised, the second- and third-place winners waited patiently in their boats for their chance to receive their Olympic medals. The orchestra played Beethoven's Ode to Joy to honour the united German team.

The flame in the torch that stood across from the award pontoon in the grandstands flickered to the side, almost down to the spectators' heads, just like the flags, which were blown taught at an angle, barely even waving.

The coxless pairs' race ended with a great surprise. Or rather, not a surprise, but a repeat confirmation of the rule du jour – the Canadians in the lane six were the champions.

"They're a totally new crew. They're reserve rowers for the eight," Povilas pointed at the Canadians. "Their first race together was in their heat."

"How do you know?" Jonas wondered.

"I was talking to a rower from Canada's eight yesterday. He said that one of their crew dropped out due to an illness a few months ago. The bow, I think. So they put two reserves into the pair right before the Olympics, and here you go! I'm gonna run and take a picture."

The two tall men stood on the award pontoon, barely able to believe what had just happened. Not only had they not expected to win – nobody else had, either. Not their coaches, not their delegation managers, and not the Canadian press, which hadn't sent a single journalist to the course that day. They couldn't have known that this would be Canada's only gold medal in the entire Tokyo Olympics, either.

"It looks like they're going to postpone the remaining races," Povilas told his friends when he returned.

"Who told you?" Jonas asked.

"Nobody. I heard the journalists over there talking, though," Povilas pointed at the press grandstands. "They should probably announce it."

"Look, nobody's going out onto the water," Celestinas nodded towards the boathouse.

"They're calling a break?" Jonas looked around, as if expecting to see a confirmation.

"But the singles are supposed to start now," Eugenijus noted.

Indeed, just a few minutes later, the announcer indicated that the competition would be postponed by an hour. The grandstands didn't disperse though; instead the crowds watched the award ceremony and waited for the continuation of the finals.

There was no let up in the wind and the finals were postponed again - to 16:30. In addition to the poor conditions, the rowers had another obstacle to contend with – their growing psychological tension. When an athlete is focused and ready for a final, its postponement can knock them off kilter and put all of their body's systems out of sync. They are filled with doubts and apathy. They become reliant not on their own physical and psychological status, but on surrounding circumstances. The winner becomes whoever manages to cope best with these chaotic circumstances. The men, all from different countries, lay on mats spread out in the recreational room, trying to master the emotions racing through them. Celestinas, Povilas, Jonas and Eugenijus didn't even try to approach the men from the eight. When facing such anxiety, there was no helping them – any attempt would make things worse. Any word of advice could fill them with unnecessary passion.

The singles race finally started at 16:05. Ivanov was lucky with his lane. There was almost no wind on the fifth lane. The German in the lane one who tried to oppose him – Hill – finished almost four seconds behind.

The coxed pairs raced at 16:30. The clear leaders – the US crew – managed to overcome the waves in lane two to finish first, with everyone else following the rule of the lanes. Safronov and Rakovschik in the lane one were fourth, finishing three and a half seconds behind first place and only a second and a half off third.

"I wonder how everything will go for the fours," Eugenijus wondered impatiently as the American anthem played.

"I wonder where we'd be…," Povilas smiled half-heartedly.

"Which lane are the Germans in?"

"They're in five and the Dutch are in six," Eugenijus checked the schedule.

"How about the Danes?"

"Two."

The sun had moved off towards the west, and to save time, the fours were released ten minutes earlier – at 16:49.

Theirs was probably the first race to overcome the "curse" of the lanes. That, or it showed that one had to be head and shoulders above the rest to break the mould. In the middle of the race, it was clear that the primary battle was between lanes two and four – between the Danish and British fours.

"Where are our Germans?'" Povilas looked towards the distant lane five, shielding his eyes from the sun with his hand.

"They're getting trounced. They're fifth or sixth, I think," Eugenijus stood up.

"They could've taken it easier on the first day, now they can't row at all…"

"Look, the Danes are in the lead!" Jonas interrupted his friends.

"You're right! I didn't think they could win. And in the second lane, too," Povilas was surprised.

"They're strong," Celestinas shook his head. "And I thought they had simply blundered into the finals…"

The Danes won, beating the Brits by a second and the Americans by two. The Germans finished the race sixth, almost at the same time as the Italians – 11 seconds behind the champions.

"Six fifty-nine for first place!" Celestinas raised his eyebrows. "Wasn't our time yesterday six twenty two?"

"Yeah," Jonas nodded. "Is the wind really that strong? We rowed against the wind yesterday, and in the lane one, too."

"Maybe it was more of a crosswind yesterday."

"Sure, but we had the worst lane with the biggest waves."

"Alright then, our record stands!" Povilas laughed. "We can celebrate."

Because it was clearly growing dark, another hurried race followed immediately after the fours finished – the double sculls. Tyurin and Dubrovskiy were lucky – they had the lane six. With that came Olympic gold medals as well. However, this wasn't the only thing that had determined their victory. Those without medals all discussed how Samsonov's "hard" training schedule had ruined their chances. Only those who had dared refuse the schedule won Olympic gold medals. All that was left was the eight in tricky lane two.

It was quickly growing dark. The grandstands could no longer see the start line nor the middle of the course. The mood grew tense. It began to seem that, by postponing the races twice, FISA and the organisers had created more problems than they had solved. It was clear from the announcer's voice that the race had started. As usual, two or three vehicles with cameras drove along the sides of the course, but it was unclear whether they could see anything in the growing darkness. After a few minutes, the course was illuminated by red military flares that were shot up into the sky, finally revealing the six eights. Identifying who was in the lead was impossible.

"I've never seen anything like this," Eugenijus wondered.

"We've finished a race at dusk in Kiev during the Union championships, but it definitely wasn't this dark," Povilas agreed.

"If only there was some sort of lighting," Jonas said. He, a physicist, would have come up with a solution quickly. "Why didn't they think of this?"

"I can't see anything," Celestinas shook his head. "What is the announcer saying?"

"As far as I understand, the Americans, Germans and our guys are tied," Povilas listened attentively as he translated the English announcer.

"How are they going to tell who finished when in the dark?"

At that moment, a number of vehicles and firetrucks drove up to the bank and directed their lights at the finish line area, but they only illuminated half of the course. The lights didn't reach the other bank.

"That's an idea," Jonas commented.

"Our guys are fourth," Povilas repeated the announcer's voice a minute later. "America's first, the Germans are second, and the Dutch are third."

"Maybe they'll come back during the third five hundred," Eugenijus added.

"Maybe," Celestinas was doubtful.

The spectators were growing restless. Not only could they no longer see the course, the spectators' silhouettes were growing faint as well. Only the Olympic torch illuminated the faces of those sitting near it with bright orange light.

"How much is left?"

"About five hundred."

Signal flares shot up into the sky again, but they descended very slowly this time, casting their red light on only the last five hundred metres of the course – and the eights fighting for the Olympic gold.

"They're descending with parachutes!" the spectators pointed up at the slowly descending red dots of intense light.

In those few seconds, they could clearly see the US eight in the furthest lane, which had a comfortable lead, and the Žalgiris eight far behind them… The grandstands erupted with cheers, with spectators and journalists jumping out of their seats. The red flares lit up the Olympic event's final rowing champions as they crossed the finish line.

"There it is… What happened to our guys?" Povilas stood up. "Let's go."

"Aren't you going to take photos of the award ceremony?" Eugenijus asked.

"I won't get a good shot in the dark," Povilas raised his FED and shrugged. "I'd need a tripod, but even then, I wouldn't see much."

"Maybe we should go after all. It'll be packed afterwards…"

"Don't want to get lost?" Povilas laughed, and they all headed for the returning eight. At the boathouse, they could hear the American anthem being played as the slowly descending flares finally went out.

*

Everything that happened afterwards was familiar to any athlete in the world who's ever experienced a serious setback in their life – the desire to cower and hide, to fall asleep and wake up only once they'd forgotten everything and when the pain inside has grown dull, when they could finally convince themselves it had all just been a bad dream. Instead, however, they were bombarded by questions – what happened, why it happened, how they felt… It's a good thing that human pain has boundaries, because otherwise, athletes might never recover from losses like this one. It took two days for everything to collapse. From Olympic gold to Olympic nothing… Nobody dared to say that fifth place was good, too – that would've been a mortal insult…

*

50

Mornings don't always bring fresh starts. There are mornings when you don't want to wake up and return to reality. When one can experience both a physical and emotional "hangover." Depressed by their brutal defeat, the Žalgiris eight didn't want to speak to anyone. In their minds, they probably couldn't stop replaying the events that led to their defeat, trying to understand what had happened and find an explanation or an excuse. They were ashamed to return home empty-handed.

Everyone was in shock – the rowers, coaches, team managers, heads of the delegation, and journalists. Seven crews and only two with medals. They walked around the Olympic village with their heads hung low. The rowers had to recover their strength and their spirits to get back to their training, while the coaches and managers risked being kicked out of their positions, or at least having to explain themselves to their seniors.

However, the rowers' job routine wasn't quite over – they still had to disassemble their boats and load them up, which meant another trip back to the now-hated Toda Rowing Course.

Like a cruel mockery, the morning was a beautiful one – the sun shone clearly and there was little, if any, wind.

"I told Samsonov that winning in the lane two was impossible, and that it would be better to take a safe second or third position," Antanas took his time mixing the sugar in his tea. "But he said "нет, только золото![81]" There you have it… How did we look from the grandstands? Terrible?"

"We couldn't see a thing," Povilas shrugged. "It was so dark that we could barely see each other. We could only see at the finish when the flares and the scoreboard lit you up."

The Sakura cafeteria slowly filled up with rowers, their eyes scanning the tables for their crewmembers.

"We thought the wind might die down, but it only got worse," Antanas

---

81   Rus. No, only gold.

continued. "But the wind wasn't everything… Something in our boat was off. We were floundering like novices."

James approached the Lithuanian table with his tray.

"Why'd you take so little?" Povilas looked up.

"No appetite…"

"It'll come back while you eat," Povilas laughed in an attempt to lift his friends' spirits.

"Did I interrupt something?" James looked at the other rowers.

"No, no!" Povilas reassured him. "Antanas was just talking about your race."

"What is there to say?" Antanas continued mixing his tea. "They trained us to exhaustion. I can still feel my back, and Petras barely recovered…"

"I think so, too. We didn't have anything left in us after the five hundred, no matter what we did," James agreed. "Nothing like how we looked a week ago!"

"They ran everyone into the ground. Everyone who didn't listen to Samsonov has medals now!" Povilas nodded toward Tyurin and Dubrovskiy, who were sitting by the window.

"You could've been in the final," James nodded, "if not for your draw."

"We could have… but at least we made the Germans pay. They were sixth yesterday," Povilas laughed.

"It wasn't an Olympics, it was a lottery," James smiled sadly.

"There's nothing you can do… Celestinas, come sit with us!" Povilas noticed Celestinas looking around. "What are you looking for?"

"Jonas said he'd come, but I don't see him."

"If he comes, we'll invite him here. Sit down. Where were you so long?"

"I watched the news on TV. They showed Brezhnev and Khrushchev, but in Japanese, so I didn't know what they were saying."

Eventually, Jonas, with a newspaper under his arm and a tray in his hands, showed up as well.

"Are you learning Japanese?" Povilas grabbed the newspaper from Jonas. "Do you understand anything in here?"

"I look at the photos. Thought I'd find one of us," Jonas said, sitting down for breakfast.

"Look, it's Ivanov. I didn't realise how big the waves were. Is this Anatoly? I don't recognize him," Povilas pointed.

"The Japanese work quickly!" James noted.

"Yeah. The race was yesterday, and the photos are in the paper already," Antanas agreed.

"I wonder what it says," Povilas looked around. "Think anyone here could translate it?"

A young waiter passed them by. Povilas waved to him, pointing to the headline and asking: "Do you speak English? Could you please translate this?"

The men looked at the men with the letters "CCCP" embroidered on their shirts, looked at the newspaper, back at the men, and then said, with a strong Japanese accent:

"'Soviet athletes celebrate the toppling of the government...'"

He handed back the newspaper, bowed, and returned to his work.

"What government?"

"What do you mean? What kind of news is that? What happened over there?"

"I told you, they were showing Khrushchev and Brezhnev on the news!" Celestinas reminded them. "Maybe Brezhnev's has taken over from Khrushchev now…"

"You're kidding! No wonder the KGB guys looked so sour yesterday! I thought it was because of that sailor, but look at what's going on!" James exclaimed.

"Is it really a real takeover?" James looked up.

"You think anything will change because of it?" Povilas smiled. "We'll continue living the way we did before. It can't get much worse. As long as they don't start shooting us…"

"What a day!" Antanas smiled sadly. "They could've postponed the competition until today… no wind and not a cloud in sight."

*

51

The Olympics were almost halfway. The newly crowned Olympic champions began celebrating in the village more and more often, while those who had lost did their best to hide their grief. Some were still preparing for their races while others were enjoying their free time walking through the city, in movie theatres and souvenir shops and going to various events. The women were interested in tea-drinking ceremonies, flower arrangement classes, and other Japanese national "activities."

The American anthem was played much more often in Tokyo than any other countries' were, which infuriated the Soviet propagandists. They were counting their own medals and watching with anger as the bourgeois press focused on the gold medal count rather than the total count. The efforts of the massive propaganda machine were instead aimed towards convincing the Japanese of the advantages of a Soviet state. The Soviet athletes met with the Japanese public several times a day. At a pier on the coast of the harbour, the USSR's embassy held concerts featuring the artistic volunteer group on board the ship "Uritsky". However, their competitions were the most important thing for the Olympians – that was what they had come for – not a single one went to the mass meeting between the Soxö socialist party and the Japan-USSR Association. The women didn't participate in the meeting at the USSR embassy organized by the Japanese women's democratic movement because they wanted to watch the track and field high jump competition instead. The KGB officials were distracted, unable to control their Olympians. "They demand gold and then want us to spend our free time at boring meetings!" the athletes complained amongst themselves.

*

"Povilas, we're the only ones who've got something to celebrate," James smiled mischievously as they walked along Melbourne Street.

"I was waiting to hear these words from you, James," Povilas laughed. "My daughter turns two weeks old tomorrow."

"Mine will be a week old…"

"Want to go have a look?" Povilas nodded towards the International Club.

"Hello Paul!" men heard a call behind them. They turned around and saw Bob, Dutch guy, happily smiling. A wide ribbon of the Olympic medal was seen under his tracksuit. Even though the final races had finished yesterday, most of athletes still wore their medals with pride.

"Hi Bob! Congratulations! Show us your medal!" Povilas asked enthusiastically.

"Sure!" Bob took his bronze medal out of the track suit. Povilas touched the beautiful heavy medal – the trophy and dream of every athlete in this village – an intangible treasure. He was filled with anger for a fleeting moment. "It could have been ours if not for that stupid Soviet regime and that misfortune that had followed us from the first race. Four more years separate us from another chance for an Olympic medal," Povilas thought to himself.

"Nice, congratulations Bob!" Povilas patted Bob's shoulder. "We saw your race."

"That Russian four failed. Nice guys. I'm sorry for them."

"It was a kind of lottery."

"Yes, the conditions were not fair." Bob nodded and noticed that Lithuanians were heading to the International Club. "Let's go for a drink?"

The men looked at one another, glanced about to see if there were any KGB men about, and then headed towards the door, which read "International Club."

The Soviet athletes were drawn to the busy noise inside. There, they could be like everybody else – melt away in the crowd of free and noisy people and let themselves feel like "foreigners."

The men from the Australian and Canadian eights were at the bar, laughing loudly.

"Look at that! They didn't win a thing but they're celebrating like champions nonetheless! We need to learn from them," Povilas pointed at the Australians.

"I think they're a bit warmed up. They're probably drinking something that they brought," James shyly approached the bar.

"Hi!" a dark-haired Australian shouted. "Join us!"

Povilas raised his hand: "Hi!"

"Do you know them?" James turned to Povilas.

"We've spoken a few times. They're nice guys! Let's go…"

The joyful Australians patted the Lithuanians on their backs, shook their hands, and introduced themselves – it was impossible to remember all of them. They gave the Lithuanians a glass each of some sort of drink. With a loud clink of their glasses, the Australians emptied their glasses. Povilas and James looked at one another and smiled – "to your health!"

After the first glass of whiskey, the English came easier to them.

"Are you from the four? And you? You're from the eight, right?" the Australians began to ask. "How did you guys do? The weather was terrible! The lane draws were terrible! Only the Canadians got lucky," they said, pointing to the Canadians next to them. "Reserve rowers who won gold! But where are the rest of you guys? Why aren't they celebrating?"

"They have nothing to celebrate," Povilas smiled.

"How about you?"

"We do!…"

"Oh?…," the dark-haired man's eyebrows shot up inquisitively.

"My daughter was born two weeks ago…"

Before he even finished, the Australians began to clap loudly – "Congratulations!" Povilas smiled and waited impatiently for them to quiet down.

"And his daughter was born a week ago," he pointed at James.

"What? Really? Two daughters on one team! No way!" and again they began clapping and shouting – "Cheers!"

"We need to drink to your daughters!" a man named David pulled a bottle out from under the bar and poured them another glass each.

"To our daughters, Povilas!" James turned to Povilas as they raised their glasses. "Maybe it's a good thing we didn't win. We won't have to call our daughters "Olympia," he laughed, finally able to relax.

"By the way, he turned twenty four yesterday!" David pointed to the dark-haired man sitting next to him. "Happy birthday, Martin!"

"Happy birthday!" the Lithuanians raised their glasses.

"Sterlik turned twenty four yesterday, too!" James noted in Lithuanian. "They were born on the same day!"

"How do you say "cheers" in Russian?" Martin asked.

"We're not Russians…"

"Really?"

"We're Lithuanians!"

"Lithuanians? Really? I know Lithuania! You guys were occupied by the Soviets, just like us…"

Povilas and James drew back, afraid to say anything.

"I'm Hungarian," Martin continued. "My family and I escaped Hungary in 1956, during the revolution… I was sixteen at the time."

"We haven't heard much about your revolution… Our press doesn't write about everything…," Povilas explained.

"It was a real war… Especially when the Russians came…," Martin's lips tightened and nodded before shaking the thoughts from his mind. A spark returned to his eyes: "How do you say "cheers" in Lithuanian?"

"Į sveikatą."

"I svakata!" Martin tried to say in Lithuanian.

"Į svei-ka-tą."

"I svei-ka-ta," he made his best effort to pronounce it correctly.

James gave him a thumbs-up. They raised their glasses and the festivities continued. As they tried to shout over the music and one another, the Australians asked the Lithuanians strange questions, cracked jokes, and told their own stories. The club was nearly packed full.

"Listen, guys, you want to go back to our place? We have more whiskey!" David rose from his seat.

The men looked at each other and shrugged:

"Let's go… But we have to run back home for just a moment," Povilas said, turning to James. "We have to pop in, right?"

"Alright, let's go. On the way, I'll show you where we live. Are you in those new dormitories?"

"Yes, the ninth building."

The entire group went out the door and the refreshing evening air hit their faces. The sky was shimmering with thousands of stars. The chattering group of men walked past smaller and larger houses flying the flags of different countries towards the one flying the Australian flag.

"Here we are. We'll be looking forward to you guys! Don't get lost!"

"Alright, we'll be right back!" Povilas and James waved before heading off towards the ninth building and the red flag that flew over it.

On the wall next to the door, there were fresh newspaper clippings with the "great feats" of the "Voschod" astronauts, and the table had unfinished cakes that were presented there every day for the prizewinners by the delegation's senior master of ceremonies, Mikhail.

"I'd rather they give us some liquor. These cakes are nonsense. They treat us like children!" the two young fathers laughed as they passed.

"Should we go change?" Povilas asked as he headed up the stairs. "I don't want to walk around with the CCCP anymore today. See-see-see-pee, that's what they all called it. Did you hear them?"

"Yeah… See-see-see-pee… let's go, we need to say hi."

They were joking, but Povilas and James had a difficult task ahead of them – making it so that, at least for a little while, nobody would miss them.

*

Having successfully "covered their tracks" by ensuring that the KGB officials had seen them there, the men changed into identical team sweatshirts without the "CCCP" embroidery, tucked a bottle each of vodka they hadn't sold yet under their belts, covered the necks with their sweaters, and sneaked back out into the dark.

They could hear the music and noise of the Australians' home from a distance. When they entered, the hosts greeted them like they were close friends.

"Here you are! Good thing you came!" they said. The small room was full of both Australians and Canadians. "Sit down wherever you can find room. Oooh, Russian vodka? I've never had any! Thanks!"

"Oh, the Russians are here! Hi!" the ecstatic rowers cheered.

"They're not Russians!" Martin tried to shout out over his friends. "They're Lithuanians!"

"What's the difference?"

"Lithuanians live in Lithuania! They were occupied by the Soviets, just like Hungary, where I'm from! Don't confuse them with Russians!"

"OK, got it…! How do you say 'thank you' in Lithuanian?"

"Ačiū!" Povilas and James said in unison.

"A-choo? Like when you sneeze? A-choo!" everyone began to pretend they were sneezing.

"Yes, yes, that's it!" the Lithuanians laughed.

"To the Lithuanians!" the Australians lifted glasses of beer and Coca-Cola. "For Lithuania!"

"How are things in Lithuania?" Martin turned to Povilas, and he had shed his broad smile.

Povilas shrugged:

"We make do…"

"If not for the revolution, I'd be living in Hungary right now and competing in the Olympics for my homeland… But in Australia, they were very kind to war refugees. They gave us citizenship quickly… Living there is nice."

Povilas nodded, smiling half-heartedly:

"I'd also like to row for my homeland, but I have to compete for the country that killed my parents…"

"What do you mean?"

"After the war, in 1946… Everyone who fought for Lithuania was either sent to Siberia or shot," Povilas said, realizing he had said too much. "Don't tell anyone. Even he doesn't know," he gestured towards James. "They could throw me out of the team for what I'm saying right now… and put me in jail, too… I barely got in as it is. For a long time, they wouldn't let me go abroad because of my parents…"

Martin frowned and leaned back:

"Bastards…"

"It's fine, forget about it… We came to celebrate!"

"That's right, Paul. To your daughter! Hey, everybody!" he turned to his noisy companions, "to their Olympic daughters! To their future rowers!"

"Cheers!"

The evening was only getting more and more festive. Women from the women's zone appeared in the doorway.

"Hey boys! Are we going out into the city?"

"Dawn! Come here! Try this!" David gave her a glass of vodka.

"Are we going?" she took the glass and smelled it. "What is this?"

"Guess! If you drink it, we'll go!"

The woman shook her head:

"OK…," and emptied the glass in one go.

"Who's going to the city!?" somebody shouted.

"You guys going?" Martin turned to the Lithuanians.

"Where are you going?" Povilas asked.

"We'll see Tokyo at night, go to the Australian house, have a good time, and come back. Let's go!" he urged them on.

Povilas and James looked to one another:

"Should we go?"

"Yeah, why not. When will we ever again get to see Tokyo at night!?"

"OK," they nodded to one another. Their eyes were on fire.

"Let's go!" Martin shouted to everyone one more time.

After grabbing their half-finished bottles and their jackets and sweaters, everyone headed out the door.

"The car's over there!"

A few steps away stood a blue Toyota Tiara. About ten men crowded in one after another. Whoever couldn't fit into the cab sat backwards in the luggage compartment, raising the back end door like a roof while hanging their legs out the back.

"The others can take the other car. Let's go! Hey, Lithuanians, what are you worried about?"

"You know, there is a soviet supervisor at the gate checking which athletes are trying to leave the village…" James worried.

"Oh! Really? You think they can recognize you?" Martin asked.

"Oh yes. They are real hawks!" Povilas laughed sarcastically.

"Guys, we have to hide these Lithuanians somehow!" Bob started searching around the room.

"Easy! We'll give them our tracksuits." David took off his jacket with its blatant AUSTRALIA printed across the back and gave it to James. "Martin, get one more jacket for Paul and a couple of caps!"

The Toyota, nearly scraping the ground, crawled out the gate of the Olympic village into a shimmering night in the largest city in the world. The Australians found it easy to drive in Tokyo, as cars there drove on the left side of the road, just like in Australia. The masses of bright shining advertisements, the store windows, and the cars in the streets made the streets seem bright as day. Colourful lights ran, flowed and flashed across the tall buildings. Orbs and rings of light spun round, making the entire city seem like a dancing mosaic of colour. Povilas and James had never seen anything like it. They felt like they were on an extraordinary adventure.

The overflowing Toyota, with feet poking out from the luggage compartment, was soon noticed by the police. The host city was forgiving to the Olympians, however – the moment they identified them as athletes, they let them go, wishing them a pleasant journey. The car rolled through busy city blocks and narrow streets to a neighbourhood with single-story buildings.

"Where are we?" Povilas and James looked around, but they couldn't see anything over their fellow passengers' heads.

"We're here!" one of the Canadians shouted. "Let's go!"

The entire group practically rolled out onto the sidewalk.

"These are our friends. Let's pay them a visit! They're expecting us!"

"Where are the rest?" Martin looked down the street they came from. "Where are the girls?"

"They probably went straight there. We'll just pay them a short visit, say hello to our friends, and continue on," one of the Canadians explained.

The Lithuanians couldn't understand everything the Canadians were saying, and the Australians were even harder to understand.

"Are we going somewhere else?" James wondered. "What are they saying?"

"I think so... let's go, there's no way we're getting home without them anyway."

Inside, Canadian tourists, or perhaps people close to the athletes themselves, were watching footage from the races on TV. Upon seeing the crowd of Olympians, they stood up joyfully and began to applaud.

"Welcome! There's so many of you! Sit down, we've got wine and local sweets."

"We're only here for a bit, we'll be continuing on," the first Canadian from the eight, a few drinks in, took a bold step forward. "Pour on!"

Povilas and James stood by the door, shy.

"Come on, Paul, James, come in!" they were handed a glass of wine each. "These are Lithuanians from the Soviet team. They're rowers."

"Oh! What happened to Khrushchev over there, huh?"

"We don't know. They say he retired...," Povilas explained.

"Our newspapers say he was toppled. Here, look, it's on the news now," he pointed at the TV.

"We don't know," Povilas shrugged.

"Cheers! To all of you!"

After a half hour, they all happily bid each other farewell and hopped back into their car.

"I'm going in the back, my feet are numb from sitting here," James sat in the open luggage compartment with two other men. Their feet nearly reached the asphalt.

"Wow, I'll have to watch my shoes so I don't lose them," he laughed.

"You can kick the ground so we go faster," Povilas laughed as he turned to his friend.

The Toyota once again rolled off into the night-time Tokyo streets, leaning from side to side with the athletes horsing about inside. Suddenly, they heard sirens and saw a police motorcycle quickly coming after them.

"Again, damnit," one of the passengers cursed. "Stop..."

After inspecting the cab, the police officer nodded and let them go.

"Being an Olympian isn't too bad, is it? You'd never get to take a ride like this in Australia!"

Ten or fifteen minutes later, the Toyota entered a well-lit street and stopped next to a two-story house flying the Australian flag on the front.

"Here we are! Welcome!"

They could hear people talking and music playing through the open windows.

"They're probably already here," David guessed once he saw a red car parked out front.

Indeed, the spacious home's living room was already full of the women and a few men that they had seen at the Olympic village, and they were having a party together with a few other people. The table was covered in glasses, bottles, and snacks. Two couples were dancing, and another was speaking privately on the couch.

"Alright, then, the party has started!" a Canadian hopped onto a chair and shouted. The Lithuanians could never remember his name.

"Dawn, to your medal!" the Australians raised their glasses.

Everyone raised their glasses and they all clinked together. "To gold!"

"What does your name mean, Dawn?" James asked the woman who people said was a swimmer.

"Dawn is when the sun rises," the woman explained, illustrating with a hand gesture.

"Ah, like Aušra, I see. Did you hear? Her name means 'Aušra,'" James explained to Povilas.

"That's a good name," Povilas smiled. "Are you looking for a name for your daughter? Besides Olympia."

A wild night had begun. The record player blared out the Beatles, the girls danced, strange drinks came one after another, and toasts were made – to rowing, to Lithuania, to Australia, to Canada, and so on. Their tongues grew loose, and they discussed sports, politics and life. The images came one after another, like a movie. They wanted to be free, to go wild, to party and not to have to fear for anything.

"Ah, James. Whatever happens, at least we will have seen what real life looks like, even for a little while," the men encouraged one another occasionally after their eyes strayed to their watches or their thoughts strayed to the Olympic village. From there, the Soviet building seemed dark and stifled. So what if they had cakes and applause? They didn't have life, they didn't have authenticity, they didn't have emotion. Everything was full of contrived enthusiasm and fear of saying the wrong thing at the wrong time, or of not winning a gold medal. They could only say what they were told to say and only to people they were allowed to speak to. They had to celebrate their victories or drink away their defeats in their own rooms with vodka they had brought, which they had to use here as a currency, since the money they had brought was only enough to buy a cup of tea a day. There, they were taught every day that they lived in the best country in the world, even though they could see that the rest of the world was beautiful, colourful, free – and out of their reach...

"If not for my family, I'd probably give them the finger and stay here...," Povilas muttered. "Maybe not in Japan. Maybe in Switzerland... You know, when we were in Amsterdam, they offered me political asylum..."

"Seriously?" James was surprised.

"Yeah... Seriously. If I didn't have a family, I'd stay... There's not much else tying me to Lithuania... My brothers and sisters are all over the place, my mother's in her grave, and I've only got photos of my father... James, you won't tell anyone, will you?" Povilas came to his senses.

"What are you talking about, Povilas? I live in the same filth as you..."

"I know... Look at how they celebrate. They're fearless!" Povilas nodded towards the Australians. "They know that they won't face any consequences tomorrow for this..."

"Yup..."

The party was in full swing. It was already over for one athlete, who had fallen asleep in a corner, but the girls were twirling their skirts over their heads, the Beatles record was playing for about the tenth time, and a chorus of muscular men sang along together with drunken voices.

The clock showed six o'clock. They were starting to feel tired, and the occasional tremor ran down their bodies.

James went to the door for a breath of fresh air and jumped back – a policeman was standing right in front of him, maybe ten steps away.

"What is he doing here?" he asked, running to Martin.

"Who?"

"The police officer in the yard!"

"Police? Where?"

"He's standing right there!"

Martin looked out the window past James' shoulder.

"Ah, it's nothing. Someone probably called him because of the noise, but you can see they don't do anything. They just stand outside, they won't come in."

"What is it, James?" Povilas saw his friend's frightened face.

"The police are in the yard!"

"Really? What are they doing here?" he turned to Martin and asked in English, "What are the police doing here?"

"Nothing, just standing and observing. They aren't coming in for now."

"For now? What if they come in?"

"Worst case scenario? They take us to the police precinct, write us a ticket, and let us go! Relax!"

"To the police precinct? We can't go to the police! Things will be terrible for us if we get caught...," Povilas shook his head.

"It would be best for us to return to the village," James agreed, trying to overcome his anxiety. "If they see that we're missing, they'll never let us go anywhere ever again..."

"I understand, guys. If you have to, then go. I can get you a cab. I can see our driver can't drive you anywhere right now..."

"That'd be great, but we didn't take our money," once again, they felt like beggars... they wanted to bite their tongues out of shame.

"Here, take this," Martin reached into his pockets and pulled out forty yen coins. "This should be enough. I'll call a taxi."

The shocked rowers shyly took the money, but all they wanted to do now was to leave this difficult situation as quickly as possible.

"We'll pay you back tomorrow..."

"Forget it! The taxi will be here in five minutes. Don't go out the door. Come to the kitchen," Martin opened the window and James and

Povilas ran through the back yard. "Go along through the cemetery to the corner, take a right, and the taxi should be there. Good luck!"

The refreshing early morning air came with a dark realization – they had to return to their ninth building and hope that nobody had noticed anything...

*

There were various legends about Tokyo's taxi drivers. The locals called them "kamikazes" because of how they sped down busy streets. This time, that was an advantage – Povilas and James made it to the central Olympic village gate in just ten minutes. Glad to have escaped the police, and safely home at the village, the men happily shared their experiences from their unforeseen adventure.

There was about half a kilometre to the ninth building. The sight that greeted them was promising – while the village still slept, it was full of bicycles, which were hard to get during the day. They grabbed a bicycle each and, energized by the refreshing and moist morning air and shaking from their sleepless night, the men pedalled home as quickly as they could on their shaky legs. They wanted to slip into their warm room as quickly as possible and draw the blankets up to their eyes. It's unclear whether the path was uneven or whether their eyes fooled them, but at their first turn, their front wheels got stuck and they both fell to the asphalt.

"God damnit!" Povilas cursed as he inspected his scraped palm.

"Good thing you didn't land on your nose," James laughed, hopelessly trying to disentangle their bicycles and rubbing the elbow he had hurt in the fall.

"It seems that I did..." Povilas could hardly touch his injured face. "When it rains, it pours... Did you break anything?"

"No, I just hurt my hand... The chain came off..."

After disentangling their bicycles and putting them back in working order, the men continued on, laughing at their misfortune.

"Son of a bitch...," Povilas swore. He had looked up and seen exactly what he had least wanted to see. Next to the ninth building, next to the red flag with the hammer and sickle, stood a completely pale Ričardas and an entire brigade of KGB officers with their arms crossed across their chests...

"God damnit..." James swore too, tossing his bicycle and hiding behind a corner. Hiding was futile, however – they had definitely been seen... There was no hope of getting in without being seen...

"G... g... guys," Ričardas could barely say a word. His lips and his hands were trembling. "Wh...where were you?"

"We were in the city...," James didn't know what to say.

"They're back," they heard someone say in Russian.

"We're back, Rychka. Did we do something wrong?" Povilas defended himself.

"Do... do you know how much they were looking for you here? They thought you had run away!" the colour in Ričardas' face gradually recovered, but he did his best to remain stern. "Povilas, you were nevyezdnoj once. Would you like to be again?"

"Where are we going to run, Rychka?" Povilas smiled. "We want to see our daughters!" he joked, trying to lighten the mood.

"I don't know what's going to happen to us now... But it's a good thing you showed up," their coach took a deep sigh, clearly relieved. "Go to your rooms."

They had less than two hours left to sleep. The night's sights played like a video reel in their minds, their beds spun, and when they closed their eyes, everything became a colourful and shimmering mosaic full of laughter, music, freedom, and adventures – mixed in with brown uniforms, icy stares, angry questions, and red flags.

*

52

On 17 October, the front page of The Japan Times had an article with portraits of Brezhnev and Kosygin. In the Olympic village, other athletes asked the Soviet Olympians about the situation, but they just shrugged – they didn't know what to say because the "government" was still lost and still hadn't sent instructions on what to say.

In addition, the newspapers also flashed with headlines like "Bald Beauty, Where Are You?," "'Mystery Girl' Clips Her Curls," and "There's a bald-headed beauty who speaks Russian roaming the Olympic Village today." They were writing about USSR javelin thrower and Rome Olympic champion, Elvira Ozolina, who had shaved her head as though she had lost a bet. The team managers had to produce a wig and pretend that it wasn't a Soviet athlete who had done this, to convince the world that this was the truth.

The two newly "guilty" rowers only added on to the long list of new and as of yet unsolved issues that faced the Soviet team. When called upon to explain themselves, they had to listen to a lecture on how their actions hurt the prestige of Soviet athletes and the Soviet state. Their friends also had questions, but of a different sort. "You could've told us, we would've covered for you!" their friends complained to them after they saw their teammates get in trouble. – "We just kept on lying until we didn't even know what to say..."

As for the guilty rowers – through their headaches, they could barely hear the questions, complaints and threats. All they wanted was to sleep.

In the morning, the members of the four were loaded put on a bus and taken to an equestrian competition in Karuizawa – a town 150km from Tokyo. The unusual punishment – holding horses for the Soviet riders – didn't go down well with Povilas. Standing around for half a day under the bright sunlight, sleepless and without water, seemed harder than rowing an Olympic race. Later, looking their friends in the eyes was difficult as well, although none of them complained. They even expressed their sympathy.

"Please don't be mad. We wanted to celebrate our daughters…"

"We're not angry, we don't mind," Celestinas smiled warmly. "Look, we got to ride around and see Japan."

"But dragging these horses around…"

"We'll get to see an equestrian competition for free!" Jonas smiled.

"When we saw those pale political types upon our return, we thought that was the end for us…"

"I think they're just pretending to be mad. Really, they're happy you've returned. They were shitting themselves. Imagine… you've got the defector sailor, and then followed by two athletes!" Celestinas reassured them. "If this is the only punishment, then they just want to teach you a lesson."

"I think so, too. Unless they write a minus into your ratings for next season," Jonas agreed.

"They've got enough on their plate with Khrushchev. Two athletes gone in the night are small fry!" Eugenijus laughed.

"The Australians invited us tomorrow. Are we going?" Povilas suggested.

"Recovering quickly, Povilas?" Celestinas wondered, and everybody laughed.

"What if I am? They were great guys. They'll take us there and send us back by taxi."

"Are there any girls there?"

"The girls are great, too. You'll like them!" Povilas winked.

*

The last few days in Olympic Tokyo went far quicker than the rowers wanted, but the call for home was growing stronger. Athletes from across the globe were still enjoying the festival, whilst the Soviets were packing to leave the village. Those who had finished their competition were not allowed to stay for the closing ceremony and had to return to the Soviet Union.

"Hi Povilas! Going already?" Povilas heard Bob's voice on the way to cafeteria.

"Bob! Hi! How are you? How did you finish that party?"

"What's wrong with your face Paul?" Bob was greatly anxious to see lots of bruises on Povilas face.

"I fell off the bike…"

"Did they beat you?"

"Who?"

"The KGB?"

"Bob, I fell off the bike, it's the truth!"

"They thought you were going to run away?"

"Probably yes. But we came back!"

"And they beat you?"

"No, they didn't! Honestly! James and I both fell off the bikes, but James managed to avoid injuries."

Bob shook his head disbelievingly and smiled.

"You know, and I cannot remember how I got back to the village…"

"I hope at least you didn't lose your medal?" Povilas laughed.

"Oh no, it is safe! I'm so pleased that we've finished and can enjoy the Olympics. Others haven't even started yet."

"Yes, right… But we have to leave, so no more celebrations."

"See you next year Paul?"

"Certainly!"

"Have a good trip home! Lucky you, you'll be home soon and will hug your baby!"

"Yes… Bye Bob! It was really nice to meet you!"

"By Paul! Po-vi-las! Let's keep in touch!"

*

The Soviet delegation continued to frantically tally its medals in an effort to surpass America at any cost. The athletes joked that neither Khrushchev's letter to the Olympians nor the flight of the "Voschod" had helped, because the Soviet Olympians only took first place after Khrushchev was toppled.

Having gathered its Olympians by the ninth building, the delegation management finally explained what was happening in the USSR: "This is an ordinary procedure when the head of state retires due to advanced age. Rest assured that there hasn't been a revolution. You'll return without being able to tell that anything has changed. The CPSU Central Committee sent its leader off for his well-earned rest, and the party will now be led by Leonid Brezhnev. The party will not be changing its political course and this will make no difference for you, our Olympians. When speaking to foreign athletes and journalists, please hold to the standardized answer we've provided you with now."

The Olympics had ended for the rowers, and it was time for them to pack their bags. Their suitcases were too small for the Olympic souvenirs, books, brochures, and the gifts they had bought by selling their vodka, so they had to buy new ones. The Nikon camera Povilas had been dreaming of remained in its shop display. The "illegal" 120 dollars he had managed to scrap together bought a new suitcase filled with women's and children's dresses, jeans, shoes, and infant's clothing and toys.

On the morning of Tuesday, 20 October, the first "wave" of USSR Olympians left the Olympic village and departed for the airport. The weather was once again overcast and cool – just like the rowers' moods. The blame for the "catastrophic" display at the Olympics fell more on the shoulders of the athletes rather than of the national coaches who had brought them to their defeats. The most important athletic competition of their lives had ended, and they were returning empty-handed. The next attempt would be in four years – if there was to be a "next time" for them at all…

During those three weeks, an "extension" was found for the airport ramp to seat the Soviet athletes into their TU-114 – a set of steel steps. Next to the ramp was a table, where officials checked tickets and stamped passports. At 11:00 in the morning, the aircraft lifted off from the Haneda runway. A few second later, Tokyo disappeared behind them, wreathed in thick fog.

After having sent the Olympians off to Japan four weeks ago among much fanfare, the city of Khabarovsk greeted them with bread and salt. After refuelling, the TU-114 flew straight to Moscow. The Lithuanians left the colourful and happy world of the free behind them, flying over the Siberian expanses towards their poor and subjugated homeland. "My Father was left here somewhere," Povilas thought as he gazed through the porthole at the endless forests, crossing himself instinctively. "His soul wanders here somewhere, and no one will ever visit his grave… We've been ordered to call this land our motherland… What have they done to Lithuania…" A ball of tears gathered in his throat, and in his ears, he could still hear, "…I'll love you until the end of time, oh, Motherland…"

*

53

When they landed in Moscow on Monday afternoon, the Lithuanian athletes received allowances for food and a few rubles for train tickets. Nobody wanted to go through the trouble of travelling by train at night, so they pooled their money and bought tickets to the next flight home. They wanted to return as quickly as possible.

The men could only guess who had told Lithuania they were coming, and when and how, but when they landed the Vilnius airport tarmac was full of people who had missed them – wives, children, parents and friends. Lithuania awaited its Olympians as victors. Their homeland loved them. For Lithuania, seventh place in the Olympics was a great achievement. It was only the Soviet system that considered everything but gold to be a defeat.

They began to receive invitations to meetings, TV shows, and schools. The newspaper and magazines wrote about them right up until the New Year, publishing photos taken by Povilas.

*

Not all sport stories have happy endings. Especially when the athletes live behind a barbed wire fence…

Povilas' international rowing career ended in the summer of 1965, immediately after the Lucerne Regatta, when he was "spotted" in Zurich meeting with Kazys Makūnas, a Lithuanian living in England whom the Soviets suspected of having ties with English intelligence services. Together with a CSK VMF rower, they almost missed their flight home. From that day, all roads to international competitions were closed for Povilas, and there was no room left for him in the boat. He could only guess at who had informed on him…

From that day on, he always felt himself being followed by strange men. New and curious "well-wishers" began to appear in his circles of acquaintances. After Povilas was noticed with his camera next to a "restricted military object" that was part of a military unit being relocated to the Far East, on 30 October 1969, the KGB registered an operative investigation case and gave him a nickname – "Skitalec," or "wanderer." The reason for the investigation was "betrayal of the motherland by spying." All of his acquaintances were investigated, all of his communication with the rest of the world, and even his relationships with the rowers and soldiers from the military naval club – the people he had gone to rowing camps and formed friendships with. Povilas' life was examined under a microscope, thread by thread. He was drafted for a brief period of military service and had a KGB special operations agent "assigned" as his leader. His nickname was Avots, and his task was to identify whether Povilas was gathering secret information from the soldiers. Another agent, code name Dneprov, was hired at his workplace in the Vitenberg fur factory. An agent named Jezhy investigated his connections with officers from the Vilnius garrison. Andreev, the agent from the KGB's 3rd administrative unit who had informed on Povilas for his "anti-Soviet claims" and for meeting with Lithuanians living abroad, was from that same USSR rowing team. The progress of the case was managed by KGB 1st division 2nd administrative unit head Major Yevgeniy Gecman. KGB agents followed him on his work trips, to international exhibitions in Moscow, pretended to be his friends to extract information from him, and followed his family when they went on vacation. In May 1973, the agency's operations and surveillance became especially active ahead of the Zapad-73 military training event. Towards the end of 1975, after failing to find proof of spying, the operative case was closed and archived.

In the summer of 1965, after losing confidence in itself, the famous Žalgiris eight crumbled. Good, strong, accomplished rowers who loved their sport very much were left without a boat to row.

In 1968, after a great number of qualifying races and difficult battles, the eight once again raced at the Mexico Olympics. Unfortunately, there were only four Lithuanians left – Vytautas Briedis (James), Antanas Bagdonavičius, Zigmas Jukna, and Juozas Jagelavičius. After an eight-year break, the Žalgiris eight earned themselves the bronze medal.

Having endured the Soviet system's repression and discrimination and the pressure of communist propaganda, the Žalgiris rowers from the 1960s laid permanent foundations for the sport of rowing in Lithuania and inspired a great deal of youth to follow in their footsteps.

* * *

Table of Contents

Table of Contents

About the story

For too long was the word "Motherland" taken away from us – the land of our ancestors was reduced no more than our "place of birth." However, this only made the post-war generation, which suffered occupation, deportation and painful losses, love their Motherland even more fiercely.

Almost every family has its own long-hidden stories about loved ones who went into the woods, supported the partisans, were deported to Siberia, or were tortured in prisons.

My father's sister, Elzbieta, had just turned seventeen when her classmates and teacher from the high school in Prienai left for the forests to join the armed resistance against the occupation.

As a partisan liaison, she was soon targeted by armed occupiers, and so was the rest of her entire family – the parents and five children.

On Christmas Eve in 1945, the occupants and partisans encountered each other at their family's home in Rūdupis. After that, all that remained of their beautiful family life together was a burned-down home, their mother's grave, Elzbieta and her father's prison cells, and four orphans.

As if that wasn't enough, the children, when grown, were labeled and persecuted as "enemies of the nation."

The barbed wire fence was more than just the gulag where the main character Povilas' father died of hunger and where his sister suffered through ten years of imprisonment and five of exile. That fence was also all of the persecution and indignities that they suffered in everyday life – simply because their family believed that Lithuania could defeat its terrible foe.

There are many post-war dramas like this one.

While writing this book, I spoke at length with the characters in this book and was shocked to learn how many of our rowing families had suffered various tragedies and losses. They were forced to live in fear and keep silent.

About the story

Suffering through these injustices also marked them as lesser citizens, forbidding them from leaving the country to participate in international competitions.

This book is about them – about an entire team of rowers who were considered enemies of the nation. They were thrown overboard but they did not break – because they believed in themselves and in Lithuania.

This story reflects a great desire to live and to survive. It reflects determination, true friendship, faith, and a thirst for freedom. And, of course, it is full of the wonderful sport of rowing.

This story features real young people in real places living through real events.

Many of these rowers lived long, happy lives and are still among us today. Others look down upon us from up above.

Each of them would warrant an additional book all to themselves, if only to explain to today's youth just how wonderful it is to see athletes at today's sports competitions flying the Lithuanian tri-color flag instead of the blood-red flag of their former occupiers.

Rima Karalienė

About me

I was born to a family of rowers when my Father was preparing for his first race at the Tokyo Olympics.

I am a rower, a rowers' daughter, a rower's wife, and a rowers' mother. Rowing became my way of life, and researching stories in rowing has become my greatest passion.

I began my rowing "career" when I was thirteen. Four years later, I became a USSR Master of Sports, and a year later, I also became a USSR senior championship prize-winner. Further progress was difficult due to USSR sports policies and clear discrimination against Baltic rowers.

I wasn't known for my athletic fury, but I tried to leave everything out on the water during practices. I loved the everyday routines of rowers the most – the exhausting practices, the rush of the water below the gliding boat, the trail of puddles left by my oars, the constant time spent outdoors, the camps, the trips, the traditions, and the colleagues.

I never considered rowing to be a sport unsuitable for women. I was proud of my height, my athletic shoes, the calluses on my hands, and the wrenches and pliers rattling about in my purse. During physical education classes, I tried to do less push-ups than I knew I could so I wouldn't hurt the feelings of the boys in the class.

I've always enjoyed the support and blessing of my parents' rowing crewmates, who have gone on to become coaches. To this day, these wonderful people are very special friends of mine. They inspire me, honestly support me, and help me disentangle the knots of history and travel back to a time when there wasn't yet even a thought of my existence.

Rowing came into my life the day I was born and has been by my side every day since. In the interest of spending as much time as possible with this passion of mine, I left my native Vilnius for the Trakai of my childhood and exchanged my regular job for a business – a private rowing club and a rowing museum.

Rima Karalienė

Made in the USA
Middletown, DE
24 November 2020